Advance Praise for

hope
=== *and* ===
hard time

In *Hope and Hard Times*, Ted Bernard tempers his optimism
in the power of collaborative conservation with a down-to-earth
account of nine communities and how their restoration efforts have
fared since the 1990s. Despite the adversities he details, Bernard
inspires passion for grassroots initiatives. And he tells us where
to find hope: Off the beaten path in the company of those
who have shed ego for community and dedicated
themselves to making their worlds sustainable.

— JANE BRAXTON LITTLE, author of national magazine articles
exploring natural resources, the scientists who study them
and the people who manage them.

Updating true stories of communities collaborating
for self-regeneration, Ted Bernard's gracefully written
Hope and Hard Times is an essential read for anyone serious
about organizing for eco-social resilience. A wise,
richly informative and inspiring book.

— STEPHANIE MILLS, author of *Tough Little Beauties*

Intuition might tell us that ecological resilience requires
community resilience, and vice versa. In this collection of
updated case studies, some disturbing, most uplifting, Ted Bernard
shows how and why this is true. In the process, he shows how
the struggle for sustainability is never easy and never ends.

— THOMAS PRINCEN, Associate Professor of Natural Resource
and Environmental Policy, University of Michigan, and
author of *Treading Softly: Paths to Ecological Order*

hope
=== *and* ===
hard times

COMMUNITIES, COLLABORATION
AND SUSTAINABILITY

TED BERNARD

NEW SOCIETY PUBLISHERS

307.1097
Per

Cataloging in Publication Data:
A catalog record for this publication is available from the National Library of
Canada.

Cover design and digital composite by Diane McIntosh.
Cover photos: Background © iStock/Sascha Burkard; inset © iStock/Vinko Murko.

Printed in Canada by Friesens.
First printing January 2010.

Paperback ISBN: 978-0-86571-654-4

Inquiries regarding requests to reprint all or part of *Hope and Hard Times* should
be addressed to New Society Publishers at the address below.

To order directly from the publishers, please call toll-free (North America)
1-800-567-6772, or order online at www.newsociety.com

Any other inquiries can be directed by mail to:
New Society Publishers
P.O. Box 189, Gabriola Island, BC V0R 1X0, Canada
(250) 247-9737

New Society Publishers' mission is to publish books that contribute in fundamental ways to building an ecologically sustainable and just society, and to do so
with the least possible impact on the environment, in a manner that models this
vision. We are committed to doing this not just through education, but through
action. This book is one step toward ending global deforestation and climate
change. It is printed on Forest Stewardship Council-certified acid-free paper that
is **100% post-consumer recycled** (100% old growth forest-free), processed chlorine
free, and printed with vegetable-based, low-VOC inks, with covers produced using
FSC-certified stock. Additionally, New Society purchases carbon offsets based on
an annual audit, operating with a carbon-neutral footprint. For further information, or to browse our full list of books and purchase securely, visit our website at:
www.newsociety.com

 NEW SOCIETY PUBLISHERS
www.newsociety.com

 Mixed Sources
Cert no. SW-COC-001271
© 1996 FSC
FSC

FOR

Olivia Lynn Bernard

AND IN GRATEFUL MEMORY
OF THE
LIFE AND WORK OF

Dr. Mary Wilder Stoertz

1958 – 2007

Contents

Acknowledgments

*W*ITHOUT THE ENCOURAGEMENT, SHIATSU TREATMENTS, AND editorial help of my beautiful mate, Donna Lofgren, I might long ago have succumbed to creative sloth. She merits huzzahs, to say the least. Similarly, in various parts of the country, the Lofgren and Bernard clans need thanks for their nurture of a writer as much in the ozone as in their midst. I would single out Jonathan, James, and Celeste Bernard, my sons and daughter-in-law, who are as compassionate and intellectually alive kinfolk as you could hope to claim and love.

I am especially thankful for my long friendship with Jora Young. I want to acknowledge the many ways she has inspired my thinking and writing over the years. I am grateful she gave wholehearted support to this reprise of *The Ecology of Hope,* in which she played so seminal a role. Paul Croce, who rode the waves with me for more than a year, made substantial contributions to three chapters and helped broaden my perspective in many ways.

I have also profited more than I can write from the intellectual camaraderie of Rachel Cook, Erin Sykes, and Joe Brehm, who were extraordinary research assistants, and Sonia Marcus, Mark Mason, James Huth, and others in my classes and seminars in the past few years. It has been challenging and rewarding to sojourn with you while working on this project.

The folks by far most crucial to my recounting the stories in this book live in nine dispersed communities across the US. When I appeared on their doorsteps they offered warm hospitality, plenty of time to tell their stories, and unfailingly, often in the face of challenging circumstances, hope. I beg forgiveness if I fail to relay their experiences with the sensitivity they deserve. Special appreciation goes to Scott Miller, Michelle Decker, Tom Harris, Steve Parker, Larry Waukau, Dee Cobb, William VanLopik, Warner and Wendy Glenn, the McDonald family, Mark Appel, Freeman House and Nina Blasenheim, David Simpson and Jane Lapiner, Ken Young, Melissa Turner, Jane Braxton Little, Mike DeLasaux, John Sheehan, Lorena Gorbet, Steve Packard, and John and Jane Balaban.

At Ohio University, Ben Ogles, Mark Weinberg, Michele Morrone, Nancy Manring, Tim Anderson, and Ron Isaac each gave nudges of support when most needed. With help from Samantha Williams, Margaret Pearce and Katelyn Belleville of the Ohio University Cartographic Center expertly and patiently prepared the maps.

I am thankful too for the encouragement of Chris and Judith Plant and their fine staff at New Society Publishers. This is a connection going back two decades that I very much cherish. Kudos this time especially to Ingrid Witvoet and Diane Killou, my editors, who patiently endured countless technical hiccups and syntactical quagmires and compassionately guided me toward the finish line.

Many people read all or part of the drafts of this book. I offer salaams to Linda Blum, Ben Brown, Kim Criner, Paul Croce, Missy Crutchfield, Mike Dockry, Mitch Farley, Wendy Glenn, Seth Hadley, Tom Harris, Freeman House, Brian McCarthy, Loraine McCosker, Bill McDonald, John Preschutti, Tom Princen, Laurel Ross, Nathan Sayre, John Sheehan, John Tucker, and Ken Young. I thank these readers for the ways their comments helped clarify my thinking. That said, not one of these kind folks is due anything but gratitude. Blame for miscues and other failings is mine alone.

Ted Bernard
Shade River Watershed
June 2009

Introduction

A DOZEN YEARS AGO I SAT AT A TABLE IN A BOOKSHOP IN ATHENS, Ohio, signing copies of a book I had somehow managed to co-author. Curt Holsapple and Rich Purdy, the shop's proprietors — irrepressible jesters, bibliophiles, and communitarians in our little town — had kept their independent book business going despite the floodtide of big-box book retailers all about. On the day of the signing I remember feeling sheepish about being in the local literary spotlight, but I played along and greeted friends and colleagues I'd known for years who, for reasons I couldn't quite wrap my wits around, showed up on a chilly February workday to purchase endorsed copies of *The Ecology of Hope,* the launching pad for this book. Afterward, I got a coffee across the street and went back to class.

The years since 1997 have whipped by. As I look back, I realize I have come to a fuller appreciation of this small place where Rich and Curt's bookshop still thrives. And I've come to understand more deeply what community means across this troubled continent. Despite the hardships of sustaining community in small-town America, some places like Athens manage it. They all seem to have a strong sense of themselves and pride in and appreciation of their history and natural setting. They have a willingness to work through conflicts as a community. They have viable downtowns (called "uptown" in Athens). They support local businesses. They appreciate and promote the arts and nurture good public schools. In Athens, a town of just over 25,000 residents, there are not one but three independent bookshops (and so far no big-box competitors), not one but three newspapers, not one but several

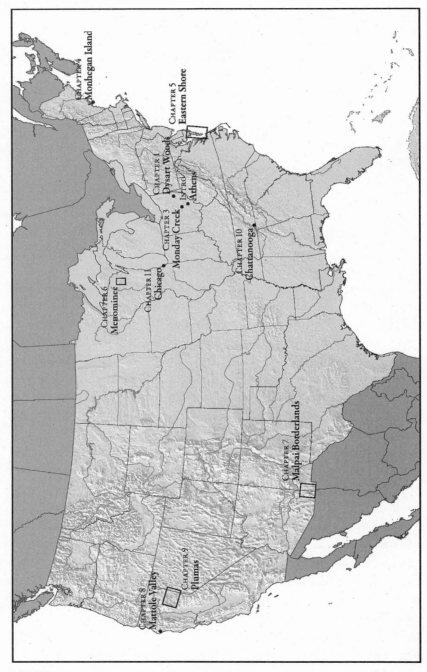

FIGURE I-1
Communities discussed in this book

dozen holistic health providers, two locally owned renewable energy firms, a thriving farmers' market, ACEnet, a nationally renowned catalyst of Appalachian economic development, three centers for the arts, and a music scene better than most college towns can claim (Fig I-2).

It's no wonder that Athens catches the eyes of the thousands of parents who bring their children to attend Ohio's oldest university and come back again and again to enjoy its quaint brick streets, its Georgian and Federal architecture and leafy neighborhoods, its pedestrian-friendly uptown, its bike lanes, locally owned gift shops, restaurants, bakeries, pizzerias, and coffee houses — including The Donkey, which serves coffee with a conscience, and a worker-owned restaurant, Casa Nueva. It's as if you've been transported to another planet and you fear that too soon you might be beamed back to the stultifying "real world" of sprawl and look-alike strip malls, decaying downtowns, crippling resource conflicts, and anonymity, with few opportunities for any kind of civic life.

If you open the liveliest of the Athens newspapers to the Letters to the Editor pages, you find extended exchanges that speak volumes about the enlightenment of this community: how to accommodate Ohio University, which is spilling out of its campus to foster condominium development on former pristine ridges; how to protect the town's green spaces and close-in family neighborhoods; how to restore the ecological health of the channelized Hocking River that flows through town; how to strengthen and sustain Ohio's oldest and most successful farmers' market; how to enhance the myriad nonprofits that work toward the betterment of the region — from the Chamber of Commerce to the Hocking River Commission and the Athens Conservancy; what to do about the plight of the impoverished rural people who have neither time nor money to enjoy the amenities of the town; how to improve the city-university bus system and the city's bike lanes and bike paths; and many more.

One such controversy in 2008 bowled over community members and environmental activists who love the forested hillsides and ridges that softly frame the city's historic architecture. Let's call it the viewshed crisis. One day in late May, Eastside shoppers looked southward across the river from the farmers' market at what appeared to be a tornado swath less than a mile away. Where once the view had been the forested

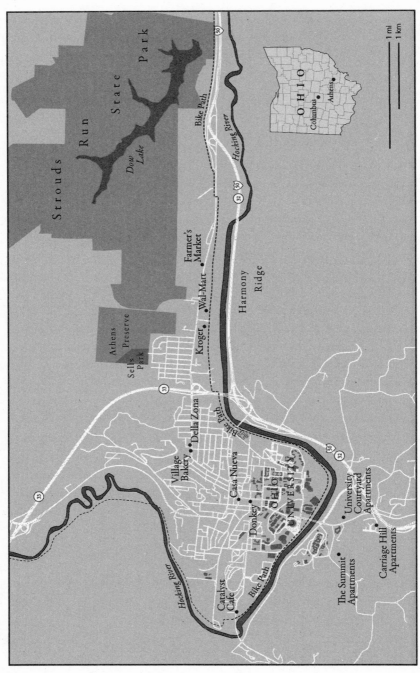

FIGURE I-2
Athens, Ohio

hillside of Harmony Ridge, 68 acres of forest had been leveled, not, as it turned out, by a force of nature but instead by a logging company. Though this was the landowner's right and though he required no permit, many people felt the aesthetics of their city had been seriously violated, as if a wrecking ball had toppled historic city hall in the middle of the night.

The timber was quickly removed and the owner filed for a permit to mine topsoil for fill dirt and to create some terraces, and put the land up for commercial development. That's when the ire of ordinary citizens and environmental activists led to a flurry of letters to the editor and not a small amount of venom aimed at the landowner, an Athens developer who had purchased the property from the county. A number of public meetings followed.

The clearcut land is outside city limits. With minimal zoning restrictions outside Athens, short of purchasing the property there would have been no way to halt the clearcut. Ohio has no forest practice law. However, as residents argued in letters and as the county planner later said simply, "Viewsheds don't stop at political boundaries."[1] On the property in question, the view has been altered and with it the ecological services the forest provided. Despite meetings, despite considerable lobbying of city, county, and state officials, and despite talk of legal action, nobody can put Humpty Dumpty together again. The mining permit was granted by the state. It is good for 15 years. An unsavory scar will long blotch one prominent Athens view.

Yet, as with many crises of this sort, creative thinking about avoiding future surprises and a renewed sense of community rose out of an ugly clearcut. More than 100 people attended one of several public meetings to discuss the issue with the developer and to identify on maps other backdrops that Athenians consider part of the city's viewshed. People came to discuss their favorite views, including a ten-year-old boy who wanted to save the view he currently saw from his grandparents' home. Others began to talk about putting viewshed land in trust and renewing the idea of a 30-mile circumferential trail around the city. "I sometimes would be awestruck on our shopping street," one Athenian told Loraine McCosker, who organized the meetings. "Asphalted parking lots devoid of vegetation juxtaposed against the forested hillsides. I would wonder, do people look up? Do they notice this incredible beauty and vitality?"[2]

The viewshed issue confirmed that yes, they did. In seeing the "good" arising from the "bad," Athens city councilor Nancy Bain said that this "event really galvanized people around the notion of protecting our viewsheds."[3] A task force appointed by the new mayor, who favors carefully planned development, is now at work on revising and updating the city land development ordinance.

In places like Athens, where people care about and dedicate themselves to nurturing historic and natural landscapes, where citizens, local government, and businesses often collaborate on projects to enhance the quality of life, you know you're not in suburbia anymore. Villages, towns, and city neighborhoods with a strong sense of place like Athens offer hope of successfully resisting the forces that lead to ugly so-called development, clogged freeways, and cookie-cutter neighborhoods with big houses on tiny lots, where curb appeal and the home theater are more important than the community.[4] To put it another way, places like Athens have a shot at a "deep economy" that draws on and gives back to native landscapes and the local talents and imaginations of people who intend to stay put and sustain their place for generations to come.[5]

Just such places captured Jora Young's and my attention and affection 18 years ago when we conceived of *The Ecology of Hope*, a collection of stories about communities tackling difficult conservation problems such as bad air, degraded rivers and streams, threatened species, decaying downtowns, and forests being clearcut at the expense of watersheds. We discovered that these communities, often in times of crisis, had built novel and effective organizations to arrive at good decisions that, with hard work and hope, trended toward sustainability. Reflecting on our choice of stories, Wes Jackson remarked that the "parochial" people who told them seemed exactly the role models the world needs. By parochial he meant "citizens of real places," who, though agrarian at heart, do not lack compassion or wisdom about the larger world and are "at home" in the work they do in their own watersheds and neighborhoods and villages. Often pitted against them are "the provincials," that growing and faceless crowd affiliated with institutions and economies of scale that threaten community. Jackson concluded:

> We have a long journey ahead of us. It is a journey to
> restore both culture and ecosystems. It is only one trip,
> so it has to deal with both forms of restoration at once.

*There is no 'how to do it' manual. We have to lay down
the path as we go. The dangers are subtle. The voices of
destruction are soft and inviting, but, make no mistake,
deadly .... They will willingly pervert, subvert, and
destroy nature's communities and human communities
because the reward for destroying such communion is
now, and ever shall be, power: the enemy of the parochial.[6]*

Although each story was distinctive geographically and historically
and each focused on different challenges, when faced with these
perilous "voices of destruction" they responded in similar ways, not so
much with angry protest and legal action but with subtle collaborative
partnerships that operated beyond the bounds of conventional social
and political structures. These partnerships enabled community-
minded parochials to do their work out of the mainstream and to
simultaneously pursue both cultural and ecological restoration. The
people putting their hands to these tasks were an unexpected collection
of everyday Americans — folk from the nonprofit world, householders,
working people, business people, bankers, farmers and ranchers, Native
people, local government folk, even resource professionals from federal
and state agencies. Their dreams and novel organizations gathered
stakeholders round the table, often including representatives of the
very provincial forces Jackson feared, to put aside historic differences,
to work collaboratively, and to arrive at decisions consensually.

Fresh and quietly revolutionary, these partnerships delivered
the beginnings of remarkable results: improved streams, better-
managed forests and rangelands, restored runs of salmon, sustainably
harvested lobsters, redeveloped urban riverfront, preserved barrier
islands, and restored prairies and savannas in the midst of a sprawling
metropolitan region. In all this, we saw a quest for sustainability. We
termed this whole thing "third-wave conservation." Even as we wrote
these words, we wondered: Are the experiments we turned up and
studied in the mid-1990s still thriving or not? What are the lessons to
tease out of them? What's happened to the third wave in the riptides
and crosscurrents of our globalized world? These are some of the questions
that launched this second look at *The Ecology of Hope* communities.

Part I sets the context. In the first chapter, I contend with the incredibly volatile situation in which we seem trapped: a scary combination

of ticking environmental time bombs and a world financial meltdown. These have been made significantly worse by a decade of weakened safety nets that should have helped protect us against the coupled disasters of the young century — tsunamis, killer storms, wildfires, melting glaciers, genocidal conflict, piracy of oil tankers, environmental refugee streams, poisoned food and toxic toys, and wobbly local and state economies, to mention a few. Using fossil fuels as a focus, I track the hard times each of the three waves of the conservation movement has faced and why these hard times have mounted and magnified and now challenge both the environmental movement and government as never before.

Chapter 2 looks at the half-full glass by telling about the promising and ongoing expansion, all across North America, of collaborative community-based projects, like the viewshed alliance in Athens, aimed at sustainability. In late 1992, when we launched the original project, there were just a few dozen such examples and none more than a few years old. Now there are thousands, tracked by hundreds of scholarly and popular articles, blogs, and websites — literally an embarrassment of riches, but generally one too fresh and unsorted to advance more than tentative hypotheses about what this bottom-up "parochial" revolution means. With Paul Hawken, I am cautiously optimistic about the recent flowering of bottom-up initiatives. He thinks it might be part of the planet's social immune system. "While so much is going wrong, so much is going right," he writes.[7]

As a geographer, I must add that complicated analytical and practical problems arise when a writer, myself included, tries to discuss vastly different levels of the planet's human and ecological hierarchies in the same breath, as it were.[8] How much influence can we ascribe to small, widely dispersed village-level narratives when transcontinental and global factors and processes push in the opposite direction? On the other hand, is it possible to imagine that local successes can have more profound and influential impacts on regional-level systems and even the global system that in many ways now control what happens at the village level?[9]

Part II is the book's heart. It takes the reader back to the signature communities and stories we told in 1997. Here we meet some of the same fishers and foresters, leaders and visionaries, community activists and resource professionals we encountered back then as well as many new conspirators. We also discover in virtually every case that other writers, scholars, commissions, and bloggers followed in our footsteps. It may be a stretch but these stories seem to be *causes célèbres* in America's quest to find better ways to manage local natural resources, build community, and truck down the road to sustainability. These documents and sources inform this project. But rather than being constricted by a rigid template, I choose to allow the uniqueness of each place to carry the narrative. As far as possible, the voices of those who related a decade-plus of history are the voices I wish the reader to hear.

The rural stories stretch across a vast scalar range, from 600-acre Monhegan Island, a story about setting limits, to the million-acre Malpai Borderlands in the Sky Islands of Arizona and New Mexico, where ranchers collaborate with government in one of the world's best known experiments in fashioning a "working wilderness" on rangelands. The stories also span a broad range of ecological and cultural settings, from the chilly northern coniferous and hardwood forests occupied by the Menominee Indian Tribe of Wisconsin, who've been native to that place for 10,000 years and can boast the oldest sustainably managed forest in the US, to the sandy soils and barrier islands of the Eastern Shore of Virginia, where African Americans and Euro-Americans arrived in the 17th century and currently struggle to balance economy and environmental justice. Between these extremes are stories about California watersheds and forest economies (Plumas and Mattole); about salmon restoration, water conservation, and survival (Mattole); and about a small watershed and its Appalachian region struggling to recover from the toxic legacies and social and economic disruptions of coal mining (Monday Creek).

In the urban set, Chattanooga and Chicago highlight both the intensity and the urgency of community-based experiments. Chattanooga, in overcoming a nasty history of air and water pollution, envisioned a renewed purpose and conceived an array of projects to revive both the spirit of the city and its quality of life. In 2007 and 2008, we returned to a dazzling river city few could have imagined fifty years earlier. But while air and water pollution are much lower, the word "sustainability" has fallen on hard times. Chicago meanwhile has been bent on saving, restoring, nurturing, and learning from remnants of Illinois prairie and savanna ecosystems that curiously have a wide, though diminished, distribution across that huge metropolitan region. From the impressive results of dozens of neighborhood-based restoration projects in the Chicago Forest Preserve District (which have revived thousands of human participants too) has sprung the Chicago Wilderness project, as far flung and visionary as the big shoulders of this mid-American colossus.

In the 1990s these stories, with their tentatively hopeful but fragile outcomes, seemed to counterbalance the more typical narratives of the times of environmental gridlock and gloom. Our stories not only cast light on "right relationships" between communities and their natural settings but also provided insights on how to heal polarities that divide communities. Now, a dozen years down the road, good news is if anything even more urgently needed, for the forces of destruction described above — the lust after land, labor, and resources driven by global capital and consumption — are even more daunting. As Richard Heinberg notes in a recent book about surpassing the peak production of many natural resources, turning successful community experiences into narratives that people can wrap their arms around is crucial, for "that is how we humans process and share our experiences of the world."[10] Bill Moyers writes that "the story that becomes America's dominant narrative will shape our collective imagination and hence our politics."[11] This, I believe, is why we must return to these unique places.

I have no illusions about the universality of these examples, nor can I confidently predict their fate in turbulent times. I am, after all, not blind to the ominous predictions of people with perhaps clearer crystal balls than my own. There are dozens of recent apocalyptic books written about what in its best light is being called "the great transition" and "the great turning" of the 21st century.[12] Of the direst predictions, one example is that of Sir Martin Rees, president of the Royal Society of Great Britain, who thinks our chances of surviving this century are no better than fifty-fifty.[13] Even highly optimistic best-selling author Paul Hawken admits that "the scale of environmental and social breakdown is vast [and] the warning signs are omnipresent."[14] Three years ago, Nobel laureate Al Gore wrote: "Some leading scientists tell us that without dramatic changes we are in grave danger of crossing a point of no return within the next ten years."[15]

My own sense is soberly sanguine. It derives not only from the hearts and works of the people in these stories but also from my long engagement with young minds who continue to come up with brilliant ways to tackle problems bequeathed by my generation. Author Pearl S. Buck observed that "the young don't know enough to be prudent and therefore they attempt the impossible and achieve it — generation after generation."[16] I do agree. I draw hope too from the long history of conservation in this country that produced such visionaries as Henry David Thoreau, John Muir, Rachel Carson, Aldo Leopold, and, I will say, some of the unheralded dreamers in the stories that follow.

Aldo Leopold, the great Wisconsin land prophet, most clearly laid out the path to circumvent the apocalypse Sir Martin and others now foretell. When Leopold looked at the world of the 1940s, he saw "a world of wounds."[17] To us who live in an exponentially more wounded world, his would have looked pristine with its unpolluted oceans and what seemed like limitless fish stocks, vast expanses of tropical forest, clear-running waters, and a stable ozone layer. Yet Leopold could see dangers just over the horizon. Ecologists, he wrote, must be like "the doctor who sees the marks of death in a community that believes itself well and does not want to be told otherwise." The doctor cannot easily cure these death marks. Leopold knew that "living on a piece of land without spoiling it" was not just a matter of better methods of conservation, or technology, or more education. The required therapy would be long and deep. "Success required more comprehensive ways of perceiving, understanding, and appreciating the relationship between people and nature. Success, in other words, required that we not simply change the land, but that we change ourselves."[18] Leopold proposed a land ethic that says simply a thing is right when it aims to preserve the integrity, stability, and beauty of the human-nature community. It is wrong when it does not.[19] These are still words to live by.

At the close of a compelling assessment of our current plight, James Gustave Speth, dean of the school of forestry and environmental studies at Yale, takes Leopold's advice to heart. All the positive developments of the current century, he writes, including grassroots conservation projects like many in this book, merely nip at the heels of the problem. The way out of "the problem," the only way out and our last best hope, he says, is a profound transformation of the way we regard the planet.[20] Just as Leopold advised, we desperately need an ethic that "enlarges the community to include soils, waters, plants, and animals, or collectively, the land."[21] The case for such an ethic, Leopold wrote, "would appear hopeless but for the minority which is in ... revolt against ... modern trends."[22] In Leopold's time such revolutionaries were few; today, as these stories show, their numbers and influence are growing, and so also may be a fragile kind of hope.

In Part III, I try to make sense of these stories. Taken together, I have to wonder: What do they tell us about the road to community sustainability and its tenacity and persistence? How do the stories array along a gradient of hope? Without spilling the beans at the front of the book, I can say the picture is neither complete nor totally rosy. This is no surprise. It has always been clear that the journey toward sustainability would be difficult. Why wouldn't it be? It demands monumental change: new perceptions of nature and of humankind, more guidance from nature, less anthropocentrism, less contempocentrism, less hedonism, less consumption and materialism.[23] It will oblige ecological literacy of us all, with our eyes fixed on the world of our children and grandchildren.[24] And it will demand that communities seek, above all, to restore well-functioning, resilient human and ecological systems.

And then there's urgency. The pieces of the sustainable world we seek must be snapped into place quickly. It is as if we have a 10,000 piece jigsaw puzzle splayed across the table with only fragments of a picture to guide us and the sands collecting rapidly at the bottom of the hourglass. Assembling the puzzle will require the best brains working from natural and social science platforms still being conceived, as well as a rediscovery of the ways people for hundreds of generations managed to live on pieces of land without spoiling them. Philosopher William Vitek thinks this is one of the most profound challenges ever to have confronted humanity: "We must change to a way of life as inconceivable to us as the invention of the modern factory or a heart transplant would have seemed to a peasant or professor in medieval Europe."[25] If this sounds impossible in the short term, it may be. My seven-year-old granddaughter's granddaughter may live in the world Leopold imagined. I hope so. In the meantime, we've got a long way to travel.

PART I

Hard Times

1

Hard Times

It was the best of times, it was the worst of times; it was the age of wisdom, it was the age of foolishness; it was the epoch of belief, it was the epoch of incredulity; it was the season of Light, it was the season of Darkness; it was the spring of hope, it was the winter of despair.[1]

~ Charles Dickens

I am at two with nature.[2]

~ Woody Allen

... poking around modern civilization's foundation and plumbing for two decades, I see cracks and leaks growing, and ever faster. I see that the past half-century's wonderful ride, an amazing and blazing run on the carbon bank of coal, oil and natural gas, is sputtering out. But not before we clog our carbon sinks, particularly the atmosphere, triggering global climatic disruption that is already under way.[3]

~ William Vitek

IF YOU HAPPEN TO BE DRIVING ACROSS EASTERN OHIO along Interstate 70 between Columbus and the Pennsylvania border, you would be deprived of natural wonder if you failed to make a brief detour southward near Barnesville to Dysart Woods. A heart-rending example of what Aldo Leopold called "tag ends" of wild landscape, Dysart Woods exposes the best and worst of our times and hints at why environmentalism just now seems tragically effete.

You are in the weedy Dysart parking lot. You find the trail head. After a short stroll through unremarkable second growth, the path drops into a ravine. It opens into something sacred, a cathedral of 400-

year-old trees that takes your breath away, especially in spring. There are few places in Ohio where you can interact breathlessly (and breath-fully) with a fragment of an ancient world that so bountifully offers itself to your imagination. Light translucent, sweet spring vapor at the ground, birds in the canopy, the oaks, beeches, maples, tulip poplars reaching the sky: you are awed by this little 50-acre patch of old growth. Here, in this green place, you can imagine a landscape of shelter and sustenance for Ohio's Native peoples and later, briefly, for pioneers from Pennsylvania, New England, and Virginia.

Exactly how Dysart Woods escaped the homesteader's axe and plow, the coal company's bulldozers and draglines, and the modern forester's clearcuts will never be fully known. Local legend is that the Dysarts saved it as a family hunting preserve. A remnant of a vast, mostly contiguous Ohio forest that in 1800 stretched across 25 million acres, Dysart now survives amid farms, towns, auto graveyards, malls, and mines. By some improbable accidents of history, the Dysart family and its descendants ended up preserving 0.0002 percent of Ohio's original forest. The property was bequeathed to The Nature Conservancy in the 1960s and then handed over to Ohio University for perpetual care.

Throughout the 1980s and 1990s, I dragged students to Dysart Woods. Sitting with them in the stillness, I could speak of the miracle of its preser-vation and how a forest like this stirs something deep in our humanity. I might call their attention to its enchanting soils and microorganisms, its plant and animal communities, and the pure aquifer beneath it. I might extol the scientific insights this forest could yield. Information gleaned from Dysart soils, I might tell them, could help fast-track forest regeneration, particularly on old strip mines. Perhaps I made mention of poet Wendell Berry's definition of hope wrapped up in cherishing Dysart-like places and fostering restoration of lands we love. He wrote:

> *The question that must be addressed, therefore, is not how to care for the planet, but how to care for each of the planet's millions of human and natural neighbor-hoods, each of its millions of small pieces and parcels of land, each one of which is in some precious way differ-ent from all the others. Our understandable wish to preserve the planet must somehow be reduced to the scale of our competence.*[4]

Would I speak of coal mining creeping to the edges of this place? Maybe not. But today, were we to venture to Dysart, I would have to tell the story of the mines. It begins with a legal conundrum.[5]

Here's the problem. Ohio University owns the surface of the Dysart property but Ohio Valley Coal Company (OVCC) owns its subsurface and all rights to its minerals, including a prodigious tonnage of bituminous coal. Environmentalists, Ohio University, the Ohio Department of Natural Resources (ODNR), and the coal company have been gridlocked in complex legal and political maneuvers for about 20 years. Unfortunately, in what I see as the dying decades of the fossil fuel era, the coal around and directly beneath the forest is worth at least $100 million. Against the intangible values of saving this meager bit of old-growth forest, OVCC, which is in the business of making profits from coal mining, has had but one directive: determine how best to extract what is legally theirs. Over the years of intense battle with the company, Ohio University and several environmental groups have seen themselves as the last line of defense.

From the mid-1980s, when the company first applied for permits to mine within what was meant to be a buffer zone surrounding Dysart Woods, the courts and the Division of Minerals Management of ODNR ruled largely in favor of OVCC as it mined ever closer to the old-growth woods. In late 2001, in what they viewed as a compromise, the company proposed to limit longwall mining to the edges of Dysart Woods and employ "room and pillar" mining underneath 14 acres of the old-growth part of the forest to access 2,400 acres on the other side. This would not damage the woods, they argued.[6] At length, the state issued permits for the company to do this mining — under the woods — using a series of extended, wall-like pillars with chambers ("rooms") between, where coal would be extracted. This method would yield about 50 percent of the coal directly under the woods and would, according to the company's theory, leave the surface intact. Appeals by environmental groups delayed things from mid-2002 to early 2004.

Much to the dismay of some faculty, many students, and several residents near the woods, Ohio University cut a deal with the company and dropped its opposition in 2004.[7] By March 2007, the Buckeye Forest Council, a statewide organization, and Dysart Defenders, a community-student group, had reached the end of their string of appeals. The courts finally granted OVCC permission to mine directly under the old-growth forest. In a battle of attrition, the coal company had outgunned the legal resources of both the university and the environmental organizations.

To those who cherish Dysart, the 2007 ruling was a chilling finale. Subsurface water disruption and pollution and surface subsidence, they feared and thought they had proven, likely would irreparably damage this "tag end" gem. With the demand for coal rising, OVCC prospers as Dysart coal finds its way to generating stations along the Ohio River, perhaps making the electricity for the computer helping me compose this chapter. It is not clean coal. In fact, there is no such thing as clean coal and admittedly I am part of the problem.[8]

The longer-term ecological fate of Dysart Woods is unclear. Brian McCarthy, an Ohio University forest ecologist, says it is too early to tell whether environmentalists' worst fears will play out.

> Cracks were noticed in the road. All the local wells of residents dried up as water was drained. Now, everyone is forced to have water trucked in and filled into carboys at the sides of their homes to use for potable water. There have been some very unusual tree deaths in the last couple of years, but directly linking this to mining activities is nearly impossible and remains simple anecdotal evidence.[9]

Ohio University has made no public pronouncements on Dysart Woods in five years.

The Choice

Dysart Woods, like much of the American native landscape, was "saved" late in the game. Most of the last bits of wild country had long become something else. The first wave of the conservation movement, rooted in the late 19th and early 20th centuries, evolved during wretchedly hard times for the continent's Native peoples and wild places. As the tragic genocidal Indian wars came to a close, with the bison almost exterminated, forests nearly decimated, and hillsides and streams in California blasted by gold mining, the American conservation movement was born. Advocating for the Sierras, John Muir, founder of the Sierra Club, fought to save the nation's last wild places. Gifford Pinchot, Theodore Roosevelt's forester, confronted robber barons marauding the nation's forests. Muir and Pinchot were both key personalities in what came to be called conservation, but they bitterly disagreed on how best to accomplish it. The country faced a choice between totally preserving wild country, even in the eleventh hour, or judiciously extracting natural resources, especially renewable resources, to achieve the greatest good for the nation's economic development. Tension between these two streams of conservation — the preservationism of Muir and the "wise use" of Pinchot — prevails to this day.[10]

I write at the conclusion of the momentous 2008 US presidential election. Of the many choices in this election, one involved the future of the Arctic National Wildlife Refuge (ANWR) on Alaska's North Slope.[11] Two viewpoints were put to the electorate about oil and natural gas beneath the refuge. On the one hand, preservationists (mostly Democrats) argued that the miniscule amounts of fossil fuels here would never compensate for damages to the vast, naturally functioning Arctic ecosystem that includes the continent's largest caribou herd and Native peoples who subsist in this remote corner of the continent. On the other hand, utilitarians (mostly Republican) cried, "Drill, baby, drill!" They argued that oil and gas under the refuge would help relieve the nation's dependence on foreign oil. Like utilitarians before them, they said this could be done in an environmentally sensitive way. The electorate chose the Democrat. But who can confidently promise that oil and gas will never be extracted there? Like Dysart's coal, the pressures to drill farther into the Arctic are unremitting. David Brower, a preservationist of the 20th century, put it this way: "[We] have to win again and again and again. The enemy only has to win once. We can only get a stay of execution. That is the best we can hope for."[12]

After more than a hundred years, despite much good work, first-wave preservationists and utilitarians have at best gained stays of execution, hardly diverting the industrial era's insatiable demand for natural resources. Whether at the hands of robber barons of the early 20th century or coal magnates of the early 21st, naturally functioning ecosystems have suffered. "Despite occasional success, overall we are losing the epic struggle to preserve the habitability of the Earth," writes David Orr.[13] Like a plummeting asteroid, the global economy is crashing against the natural Earth. It is virtually impossible to realize how much of "the abundance of wild nature ... we have lost."[14] The miracle is that some preserved and some well-managed lands and waters survive at all.

Thanks to first-wave conservationists, they are in the nation's National Park System and similar entities in every state, in the National Wilderness Preservation System, and in a few bountiful natural lands and waters privately held, like Dysart Woods.

Multiple-use forests, rangelands, and wildlife refuges, held and managed by federal and state agencies, are a legacy of the utilitarians of this first wave. Not by accident, ANWR was originally classified as multiple-use land. When people despair about the Arctic's wild future, their worries about it may be accurate but, in so despairing, many conflate the two streams of this early wave of conservation. Unless ANWR is reclassified as "untouchable" wilderness, it will surely ever be open to exploration for oil and other natural resources. As it stands now, it is a legacy of the utilitarian choice. If you like caribou, wolves, and polar bears and have compassion for the Gwich'in Nation and the Inupiat peoples, despair rather than hope is probably justified.

THE COMMONS

As the 20th century reached midpoint, mining again became a piece of the hard times driving the next wave of conservation. By the 1960s, daily fare in newspapers and on television included stories of fish kills in polluted rivers and along ocean beaches, raptors succumbing to pesticides, increasing incidences of asthma and other lung diseases in the smoggy air of cities, poisons leaking into people's basements from toxic waste dumps, collapsing foundations and poisoned drinking waters where coal was strip mined, and in extreme cases emergency evacuations of people from their homes. These were alarm bells sounding for decades of despoliation of the nation's commons — the air, waters, beaches, green spaces, and animal and plant species owned by no one but crucial to everyone's well-being. Freedom to desecrate the commons brings ruin to all, wrote biologist Garrett Hardin in his famous essay, "The Tragedy of the Commons."[15] The campaign to protect the commons fired up the second wave of the conservation movement.

During the administrations of presidents Nixon, Ford, and Carter, Congresses pressed forward with legislation to stave off a tragedy of the commons. This included the transcendent National Environmental Policy Act (1970), which amounted to an environmental bill of rights and responsibilities and created the Environmental Protection Agency.

Between 1970 and 1980, clean air and clean water acts, statutes to control and clean up toxic and hazardous wastes, and laws to regulate pesticides, protect drinking water, and reclaim abandoned mines sailed through Congress. Laws to protect wetlands, save endangered species, and safeguard human health were also put on the books. The 1970s were a golden age of environmental legislation. People believed that centralized agencies of federal and state governments, using "value free" science, would begin to turn things around.

Nongovernment environmental organizations, such as the Natural Resources Defense Council, arose to keep the system honest by taking environmental cases to court, lobbying for tougher regulations, pressing the government toward better enforcement, pursuing science in the cause of cleanup and protection, and pushing Congress for funds to support growing federal and state programs to protect the commons. Implementation of the new laws fell to resource professionals working in slow-moving bureaucracies, most of which also had a contradictory mandate: that of sustaining the American dream and its addictions to technological progress, economic growth, and the "hedonic treadmill" of material consumption.[16] The people's intent was often subverted by loopholes in rules, litigation, and political compromises between the economy and the environment.[17]

As with first-wave conservation, the second wave continues to offer some protections for the land, water, air, and human health. Generally speaking, our waters and air are cleaner than they were, say, in the mid-1970s, and the human health consequences of environmental pollution have been partially addressed. But there are serious gaps in laws and rules and persistent lapses in enforcement. Consider again the case of coal mining. One does not have to watch much television or browse the Internet long before encountering ads extolling the versatility and significance of coal in America's future. A series of 30-second television spots, aired during the 2008 presidential campaign, are the most recent version of "you cannot achieve the American dream without it." Here's the text of one of these spots:

> We wish we could say 'farewell' to our dependence on foreign energy, and we'd like to say 'adios' to rising energy costs.
>
> But first, we have to say 'so long' to our outdated perceptions about coal. And we have to continue to advance

clean coal technologies to further reduce emissions
including the eventual capture and storage of CO_2. If
we don't, we may have to say 'goodbye' to the American
way of life we all know and love.[18]

Beyond this public relations campaign, "big coal" has long convinced politicians, including President Obama, that coal is the bridge to renewable energy sources later in the 21st century.[19] Since coal now fires up half of the nation's electric power (89 percent in my home state of Ohio) and we have as much as 250 years' worth of it and few ready alternatives in the near term, this is unfortunately true.[20] Like it or not, coal mining and coal-fired electricity generation will be with us for a while.

Meanwhile, if our "outdated perceptions about coal" include that it is bad for the environment, the industry wants us to swallow the idea of *poof!* "clean coal." Looking toward a time when their carbon footprint will be regulated, they speak, for example, of liquefied coal and integrated gasification combined-cycle technology that would gasify coal underground, separate CO_2 and CO, pump them into the earth, and burn what's left in a combined-cycle gas turbine with little pollution. Such technology may be feasible in theory but in reality it is still decades away and perhaps ultimately too expensive. Even if it proves feasible, it will do nothing to reduce the carbon footprint of coal mining operations themselves, not to mention their inevitable impacts on waters, soils, and ecosystem services.

Because it is more efficient and much safer than underground mining, most of the country's coal is surface mined. In response to more than a decade of protest and environmental litigation back in the 1960s and 1970s, Congress finally passed the Surface Mine Control and Reclamation Act (SMCRA) of 1977. SMCRA is meant to prevent the landscape devastation by strip mine operations of the 1940s to the 1970s, many of which are abandoned and still eroding, still impounding millions of gallons of slurry and toxic water, often behind dodgy dams. So far, less than 20 percent of abandoned mine lands have been reclaimed.[21]

SMCRA requires companies to post bonds before mining to assure they will meet standards of reclamation and restore some semblance of surface drainage. Mines must also comply with other second-wave laws such as the Clean Air Act, the Clean Water Act, the Endangered Species

Act, and occupational health and safety regulations for their workers. Although SMCRA was riddled with compromise, it was meant to ensure that life would be more secure for people living near strip mines, that their houses would be repaired if impacted by blasting, that their communities and well fields would be protected, and that mines would be returned to something like the original grade with safely impounded water and established vegetative cover.

Section 522 of SMCRA offers protection to areas deemed by their importance to air and water quality or other natural assets as "unsuitable for mining." Because the decision to declare "lands unsuitable" was given to states where the provision has been heavily politicized, it has rarely succeeded in stopping mining. At Dysart Woods, "lands unsuitable" petitions in the 1980s were denied several times as mining encroached farther and farther into the buffer zone meant to protect the woods.[22]

As with many of the other 1960s and 1970s laws, SMCRA and associated environmental laws and precedents have proven to be ineffectual in delivering the protections they were meant to achieve. Individuals and communities have never seemed to be able to amass enough clout to match corporate America and its friends in political power. Never more so than now. In the waning weeks of George W. Bush's presidency, coal companies succeeded in convincing the outgoing administration to change a rule in a way that will significantly weaken protections to residents near coal mines. The rule, part of the Clean Water Act and in force since the 1980s, prohibits mining companies from dumping wastes into or near streams. Seems reasonable, wouldn't you think? Not so. One CEO told a reporter that "we're doomed if we can't fill dry ditches with overburden."[23] By "dry ditches," he was referring to headwater valleys, which may indeed be dry during some part of the year but are crucial to the well-being of rivers and people downstream.

Though this rule was not well enforced during the Bush years, it had been the single most effective means for residents to stop the abuse of dumping mine wastes into streams that would later flood and pollute their neighborhoods. On December 2, 2008, the Environmental Protection Agency, a weakened political tool of the administration, approved the rule change. Arguing that this change is illegal, opponents could take it back to the courts or the new Obama administration could begin to undo it. Either way, it will take many months, during which there are no holds barred out on the mines.[24]

Just when the Earth most needs decisive action, environmentalists of the second wave often find themselves mired in legal and legislative tangles like this. They ask: How long will it take to pursue this in the courts? How will we pay for it? How can we influence an administration in far-off Washington with dozens of big-ticket problems on its plate? To understand how frustrating questions like this are, I recommend the I Love Mountains website put together by a grassroots coalition of seven organizations in five Appalachian states. I Love Mountains aims to stop "mountaintop removal," a new form of surface mining that is more damaging than anything ever seen in the Eastern Coals Lands.[25] Their viewpoint is shared widely, for in the past two decades the scale of land wastage by surface mining for coal in Appalachia has ramped up by many orders of magnitude. Those who advocated for and wrote SMCRA could never have imagined what they would be up against in 2009.

Blasting and stripping for coal now occurs not only along the valleys and slopes of mountains but also across the very tops of the mountains. For good reason, environmental groups refer to this as "strip mining on steroids."[26] Despite many forms of protest and legal action, mountaintop removal is now the preferred way of mining in five Appalachian states (Kentucky, West Virginia, Tennessee, North Carolina, and Virginia). How vast are its impacts? The US Environmental Protection Agency estimates that 2,400 square miles of Appalachian forests will have been cleared for mountaintop removal by 2012. This is an area equivalent in size to the state of Delaware.[27]

Mountaintop removal begins with forest clearing. After that, up to 800 feet of what is called "overburden" (in reality, living soil and subsoil and the rocks from which they are derived) is blasted with dynamite, leveling the mountaintop. The overburden is trucked away or pushed into valleys in so-called valley fills, most of which were illegal until the current rule change. Huge shovels then gobble up the coal and disgorge it to a fleet of trucks that careen down the ex-mountain to washing and distribution sites. After mining, because surface waters (especially the headwaters of streams), topsoils — entire ecosystems, in fact — have been so disrupted, many mountaintops have proven irreclaimable. So even if SMCRA and associated laws had been well enforced, which they have not, the beast has clearly grown beyond their control.[28]

I can think of no better example of what former EPA scientist Patricia Hynes claims has happened to much environmental legislation of the second wave. She writes: "Environmental laws ... give the appearance of protection and sometimes the language of protection, but not necessarily the reality of it." Politics of the 1980s, 1990s, and especially those of the current decade (so far) continue to operate on the pretensions of unlimited resource capital and an ever-expanding economy. Even if the government intended to enforce the laws on the books (which it often has not done), such laws have not provided the environmental protection the public wants and believes it is getting. Hynes concludes: "For the reality of environmental protection, we need laws which have *ecological intentionality.*"[29] Such was the fundamental intent of Rachel Carson and others who inspired the second wave. But such has not been the outcome. And so, despite grassroots resistance, hard times in Appalachia continue and the second wave, while remarkably successful in passing statutes and launching the profession of environmental law, has not given us pathways toward sustainability.

The Ecological Way

Disillusionment with the current era of Earth pillage, that disillusionment so palpable on the I Love Mountains website and many other sites and blogs, propelled a third wave of conservation, "the ecological way." The people who want to halt mountaintop removal also propose alternative visions of restored communities in the inherent ecological diversity of these Appalachian Mountains. Based on an understanding of resilience in natural systems and a realization that we must restore and, if necessary, invent anew social and economic systems and human communities with corresponding resilience, the ecological way presumes that paths to more sustainable resource management and conservation and to sustainability itself are possible. Part of our reason for proposing a third wave in *The Ecology of Hope* rested on our confidence in the new collaborative grassroots organizations and shadow networks that had sprung up. When we wrote about this wave we could only say that its ultimate configuration was unclear, for the notion of sustainability then seemed to offer a range of possibilities and more than a little confusion. The new grassroots organizations and networks, though fresh and promising, were also young and vulnerable. Whether they would survive as the heartbeat of a third wave was still unclear.

With biologist David Ehrenfeld, we concluded that if the third wave were to flourish it would be "advanced by countless people working separately and in small groups, sharing only a common dream of life .... Nature will have entered their lives at an early age and will remain as a source of joy and as the measure of their best and worst efforts."[30] In looking back at the unfolding of this new wave, I must say that Ehrenfeld's phrase "best and worst efforts" catches my eye. The best efforts of people of the third wave, using nature as their template, are impressive. But, as we predicted, they have also faced mountains of resistance. Big bureaucracies, like the US Environmental Protection Agency that jiggered a rule with arguably calamitous consequences for rural life in five states, and faceless, placeless corporations like the coal companies that lobbied for that rule change still perceive nature as a commodity. These institutions, working within a damaged democracy, have sabotaged the ecological worldview that in the 1990s inspirited many communities. They have mired and delayed the movement, which is stuck in what Hazel Henderson called "the breakdown zone."[31] Like those before it, the third wave has run up against hard times.

I need not enumerate all the ominous tales of our "winter of despair" that envelop the world and might well resonate with Dickens were he with us. The Earth's vital signs are in a danger zone: human population and consumption stretch the capacity of the planet and tax the imaginations of the most inventive entrepreneurs to provide for even basic needs. Species are dropping left and right at many orders of magnitude faster than the background rate of extinction. Carbon dioxide and other greenhouse gases continue to mount. Groundwater is overtapped, rainforests are overcut, cropland is overcropped, the seas are overfished, human health is at risk, and on and on. I am not usually gloomy (after all, this book *is* about hope) and I realize there is more than a little crisis fatigue out there, but the facts tell me that, without a radical change of course soon, the world of my granddaughter could be unpleasant. Here are just a few of those facts:[32]

- Exposure of a fetus in the womb to chemicals in everyday plastics and pesticides may alter its genetic functions and increase its risks of disease.

- The UN reports that the number of low-oxygen "dead zones" in the world's oceans and seas increased from 149 to 200 in the middle part of this decade.

- Global carbon dioxide emissions more than doubled between 1990 and 2007 and the rate of increase is accelerating (350 parts per million is considered safe; we are close to 390).

- The "ozone hole" over Antarctica in 2006 expanded again to near record size.

- The World Wildlife Fund for Nature warns that birds are on their way toward a major extinction episode due especially to climate change. Some populations have already declined 90 percent.

- The International Union for the Conservation of Nature added 188 species to its Red List of threatened species. This list now includes one of every four mammals; one in eight birds; one third of amphibians; and 70 percent of assessed plants.

- The US wildfire season in 2006 was record setting. More than 96,000 wildfires burned a total of nearly 4 million hectares. The number of wildfires in 2007 was greater.

- Unabated global warming could cause damages that would consume 5 to 20 percent of global Gross Domestic Product.

- Arctic sea ice has thinned by half since 2001. Large areas of ice are now only one meter thick as the ocean and atmosphere continue to warm.

- An earthquake in Japan in 2006 caused leakages in one of its nuclear power plants, raising alarms about the risks of nuclear power and causing Japan to rethink its nuclear plans.

- In 2007 scientists moved the hand of the Doomsday Clock, which shows vulnerability to nuclear and other threats, from seven to five minutes to midnight.

It is obvious to me and many others that the global political-economic system is doing its best to sow the seeds of its own destruction.

When we wrote in 1997 that third-wave communities might help move us from the "breakdown zone" into a "breakthrough zone," we had no idea what was coming down the pike. George W. Bush's first few months in office in 2001 signaled even harder times for all three waves of the environmental movement. Areas designated as off-limits by the Clinton administration, such as the roadless parts of the national forests and the treasured red rock deserts of Utah, were no longer so. An energy plan, conceived behind closed doors and pitched largely to the coal and oil industries, set up the market for tens of thousands of SUVs and pickups (exempted, by the way, from fuel efficiency standards), and juiced once again what Vitek calls our "blazing run on the carbon bank of coal, oil and natural gas." By summarily rejecting the Kyoto Protocols of 1997, in 2001 the Bush administration walked away from more than a decade of international discussions toward stemming emissions that cause global warming. The President's Council on Environmental Quality became "a vestigial enterprise" and the EPA a weakened agency buckling under demands of industry lobbyists wanting less regulation.[33] Clinton's sustainable development initiatives, including two in this book, quickly became toast. "Never before in American history has a president so willfully delivered the government departments and agencies responsible for safeguarding America's air, water, and public lands into the hands of anti-regulatory zealots."[34]

Leaving aside America's bellicose responses to the September 11th attacks and the evolution of preemptive doctrines, leaving aside the resulting erosion of civil liberties, leaving aside Wall Street cronyism and levels of corruption and malfeasance that made the Grant administration look peachy — leaving aside all these things — what may be remembered even longer is the Bush administration's disdain for scientific evidence and reasoning, its deafness to warnings (including from their own CIA) about the seriousness of global climate change, and its arrogant confidence in so-called free markets and global capitalism. James Hanson, NASA's preeminent climate scientist who was repeatedly muzzled by the Bush administration, argued in testimony before Congress in 2008 that global warming science "has been corrupted in the same way that tobacco companies once attempted to blur the links between smoking and cancer." He said bluntly that CEOs of fossil fuel industries ought to be tried for crimes against humanity and warned

Congress that we have long passed what he considers to be safe levels of carbon dioxide in the atmosphere.[35]

As a new administration begins its work of repairing these damages, we live in volatile times. A weary environmental movement in the trenches also faces rear-guard action. America's hopeful new president must pull the country out of the worst economic times since the Great Depression. North America is still drunk on oil. Despite all this, communities across the country continue to cobble together pathways that are simpler and more sun powered, that enrich place and community, and that offer better futures for their children. These are the counternarratives we need to explore.

2

Striving For Home:
Community, Collaboration, and Sustainability

I have been thinking about stories of place in an effort to understand how the geography of mind adheres to the geography of earth.[1]
~ Scott Russell Sanders

If you don't believe in homecoming how can you get up in the morning?[2]
~ W.S. Merwin

Since community is in the struggle for community, no place gets it just right, or there would not be community.[3]
~ Carl M. Moore

The buzz of collaboration is all around the West. You can hear it being whispered by the grasses, moaned by the trees, gurgled by the fishes, hummed by the bees.[4]
~ Donald Snow

The key to sustainability lies in enhancing the resilience of social-ecological systems, not in optimizing isolated components of the system. If we examine [sustainability] through a resilience lens, it's clear that we still have a way to go.[5]
~ Brian Walker and David Salt

*H*AS HOMO SAPIENS EVER FELT AND ACTED AS IF IT WERE TRULY AT home? Some writers think our homing instincts are deeply embedded. To become more sustainable we simply need to restore the "sense of place" we presumably had before this hypertransient age. But the story is more complicated. Human history also speaks of restless generations, anxious to move on, looking for better places somewhere else. A certain placelessness, an appetite for wandering, an urge to migrate to a promised land are also in our DNA. Even cultures we think of as rooted, like the Amish, are only relatively so. As I write, a few counties east and west of my home the Amish are on the move as a consequence of population growth and land shortages. To be sure, they become more deeply and respectfully engaged in their new home than the average suburbanite, but they cannot shake the notion of occupying new space. "A vagabond wind" has swirled across America throughout our history and we are, in some senses, fortunate to have had the freedom to respond to this other deep urge.[6]

When we complain about being trapped in Podunk or on grandpa's farm, we may be feeling claustrophobic and fretting about stagnation. British writer Bruce Chatwin argues that the monotony of being stuck in place with what he calls regular work "weaves patterns in the brain that engender fatigue and a sense of personal inadequacy."[7] Cabin fever of this sort may rattle even the most rooted Amish farmwife. Though she may not bolt, many other North Americans can and will. Yet I dare say this does not contribute much to the countervailing winds of sustainability. What we must do, according to many sustainability gurus, is the opposite: engage in homecoming, stay put, sink roots, become a citizen, help make Podunk more resilient.[8] Gary Snyder, the poet, advises: "Find your place on the planet, dig in, and take responsibility from there."[9]

Our minds clearly embrace and map out the geography of what it means to be home. Perhaps, deep down, we inherently resist claustrophobia and long for home. If not, our identity may be at stake. "Without a fundamental realization of the question 'Where are we?' human meaning is not stable, and the logic of our own being collapses," writes bioregionalist Robert Thayer.[10] If we can find our way home, our bleak landscapes of placelessness may heal. Placelessness and its ugly outcomes, according to James Howard Kuntsler, result from "place abstractions" we carry in our heads — gentrified neighborhoods, suburbs, airport malls, theme parks. Kuntsler says these are not real, rooted places and that's why much of North America looks "like no place in particular"[11] and conversely why places like Athens, Ohio, feel real.

Tackling the world's environmental problems begins at home.[12] This does not imply returning to a mythical past but instead learning how to reinhabit the places where we live. Paradoxically, to do so may oblige that you sit with the national and international entities corrupting your place. Does that mean Wal-Mart and the Department of Transportation will climb into your bed? Maybe. But in the end, David Orr believes that sustainability "will not come primarily from homogenized top-down approaches but from the careful adaptation of people to particular places."[13]

Striving for home is a path toward better times, a reason, as poet W.S. Merwin puts it, for greeting the new day. At the scale of "home," we get to know our surroundings. We see and touch and smell seasonal change, moon phases, rainy seasons, droughts, blizzards, bees buzzing, and woodcocks bleeping. We come to understand the dynamism and intricacy of this natural system in which our home nests, as well as its relationship with things up the ladder, beyond home: aquifers, tides, floods, sunspots, and global warming. Although there are stable points and predictable cycles in these things, we come to appreciate that they are also unpredictable. Local events such as storms, lightning-set fires, and plagues of locusts roll in unexpectedly. Nature is ever in flux.[14] Once we have a grasp of this, we can perhaps find ways to adapt sustainably — that is to say, for the long-term benefit of our home and its people.

The social systems beyond our community — regional, county, provincial or state, and federal governments, financial systems, markets, trade regimes, cartels, nongovernment organizations — also operate according to somewhat predictable cycles in "experiential time." Their time frames are very much shorter than those of nature, or "ecological time." They frequently make decisions with nature as afterthought and they too are disrupted by surprises like human migration, fraud and other malice, market downturns, riots, revolutions, and war. Although the social capital on which such systems draw is theoretically unlimited, without careful planning accounts can be quickly overdrawn, especially during extreme "once in a lifetime" events, whether natural, technological, or both.

Given this, Hurricane Katrina's devastation of New Orleans in 2005 should have come as no surprise. As a category five hurricane striking a major city head-on, Katrina far outstripped response capacity. In spite of humanity's puffed-up confidence in information technology, early warning systems, and emergency response capabilities, we hit the wall with Katrina. An even scarier version of what happened is that, individually and corporately, our intelligence failed us. This version posits a widening gap "between our need for ideas to solve complex problems and our actual supply of those ideas."[15] This "ingenuity gap" implies we are neither clever enough to foresee and respond sufficiently to complex problems like Katrina nor humble enough to know our limits. If this is true, we must both lower the bar of expectations and work harder on building skills to tackle modern-day problems.[16] Catastrophe may lead to degradation or inspire new creativity. Aware of this challenge, "complex adaptive systems" theorists seek ways to tap a different kind of ingenuity — that of "resilience thinking" or designing social-ecological systems to stay intact and reorganize after Katrina-scaled crises of the future.[17]

COMMUNITY

Striving for home implies finding a community such as Athens with a resilient social structure and lots of social capital woven into complex networks occupied by smart and caring people. These communities have the makings of a deep economy with locally owned businesses, organic farmers, farmers' markets, locavores, craftspeople, cyclists, and purveyors of slow food. They strive for environmental and social justice. There are ample "third places" (neither work nor home) to gather and celebrate. Such communities retain some of their natural and historically significant landscapes and folks have a few notions about their bioregion and what happens beyond the bounds of their place. Just as they invest in social capital, they also work to enhance their natural capital by nurturing soils, waters, forests, steep slopes, and biodiversity. And they "wage" peaceable campaigns to save this sacred thing called community. As Moore writes in the epigraph for this chapter, community evolves in this "struggle for community."

Community, in this place-based sense, has been part of the American ideal since the time of Jefferson.[18] Jeffersonian public policy required informed citizenship, which enabled people to work toward the common good. Understanding and acting for the common good meant that individual rights might be trumped by the needs and survival of the community. In such a regime, Jefferson believed, citizens would have a natural incentive to shoulder responsibilities in the community's interest because indirectly it would be in their own interest as well. Partly because of our restless genes and partly because the Madison-influenced constitution favors a different paradigm, Jefferson's ideal community has never been fully realized. As we strive for home and seek a more secure and sustainable future, Jefferson's insights could not be more relevant.

Good communities enable people to live healthy and happy lives, to be secure, to have access to resources sufficient for their needs, and to achieve their full potential. In a real community, members share an identity and a core of common values, assume a degree of permanence in human relations, and bask in the identity and acceptance that radiate from their place.[19] Good communities also understand that conflict is inherent in living together and they invent and continue to adapt effective means of mediation and resolution.[20] Above all, when crisis comes, when nature or the economy slams their community with a surprise, they can marshal a commitment to respond not as atomized individuals but as people who "commune," who flash into action to protect their "commons," and who can conjure up new ways to enhance their resilience to future surprises.

What kind of citizenship does this imply? First, because the environment is a risky place, communities must try to avert some of these risks. This means "living off the sun" as much as possible by using nature's renewable resources and ceasing to mine the others.[21] It means saving species from threats and obliteration, for this is the natural capital on which we rely, and once it is gone we can't retrieve it. Averting risks also requires control of invasives that disrupt natural processes. It means planning according to ecologically relevant, rather than commercially relevant, time frames. And, in all of our personal and corporate dealings with nature, it begs humility of us. Let the late California poet Robinson Jeffers be our guide: "the greatest beauty is Organic wholeness, the wholeness of life and things, the divine beauty of the universe. Love that, not man Apart from that ... "[22]

Communities rooted in place are communities to die for. And they are rare in North America. Kuntsler observes that they have been "extirpated by corporate colonialism that doesn't care about the places from which it extracts its profits or the people subject to its operations."[23] Here again are the provincials of Wes Jackson. Back in Athens, small businesses and other citizens worry about the profusion of fast-food chains and big-box retailers. This may be just a phase, but it smacks much more of the corporate colonialism Kuntsler writes about. In Athens and in villages and towns across North America, the resilience of the local economy is being severely tested by the likes of Home Depot and Target.

Elsewhere, in the absence of real place-based community, as opposed to place-based marketing (think gated communities), people are deluded into thinking that other kinds of community will suffice. They argue that virtual communities (Facebook, Flickr, MMORPGs[24]), communities of shared interests (flea market devotees, llama keepers, financial planners), and communities of common norms (sociologists, Methodists, Deadheads), for example, build elaborate and sometimes lasting social networks. That may be so, but in my opinion these are faux communities in the sense that matters most. If we were to depend only on "communities without propinquity," there would be no chance of saving the planet neighborhood by neighborhood, which is what we must do.[25] Virtual communities, for all their pizazz, will not build "a bottom-up society, a community of communities that are local and relatively small,"[26] nor communities that promote the "ideal of local self-sufficiency."[27] Gandhi's concept of *swadeshi*, "that spirit in us which restricts us to the use and service of our immediate surroundings to the exclusion of the more remote,"[28] is perhaps retrograde but it strikes me as an appropriate target. Real communities can work toward it; virtual communities cannot.

COLLABORATION

Striving toward home by fashioning communities as foundations for planetary survival runs parallel to a home-grown social movement astonishing in its profusion and growth. *The Ecology of Hope* argued that this movement was picking up steam:

> *Across the planet, there is a quiet revolution underway. It is called many things: sustainability, biophilia, collaborative planning, community-based conservation,*

ecological restoration, ecosystem management, biore-
gionalism ... It is taking people away from a view that
the earth and its resources exist purely for humans to a
belief that humans are part of the living earth. It is
born of new stories ... it is our best hope for a future on
an earth in glowing good health, possessed of diversity,
integrity, stability, and wild beauty.

We believe the revolution is happening at the bottom.
It tiptoes into communities desperate for ways to escape
legacies of bad resource management. What emerges ...
are partnerships among conventional adversaries, collab-
oration between government and nongovernment
agencies, engagement of the private sector, deep
involvement of ordinary people. Pride of place and
confidence in a vision of a biologically and culturally
restored region propel a new kind of activism, based
not on resisting and finger pointing but on healing and
working together, on collaborations as creative and
diverse as the communities where they happen.[29]

What we intuited from literature, experience, and a bit of ground truth has since grown fast and continued to spread to places where desperate people working on tough environmental problems are doing desperate things. For example, some are sitting down with "the enemy" and figuring out how to work around the inertia of natural resource and other bureaucracies. Diverse and creative community-based collaborative groups now extend across the continent like a vast "populist conservation" archipelago.[30] Loose networks tie them together. While we could come up with just a few dozen examples in 1997, now there are thousands. If you doubt this, try typing "collaborative conservation" into your browser. What you'll get is over four million results.[31]

The community-based collaborative movement draws its energy from "local participation, sustainable natural and human communities, inclusion of disempowered voices, and voluntary consent and compliance rather than enforcement by legal and regulatory coercion."[32] The "buzz" around collaborative conservation comes partly from its unorthodoxy and flexibility. Collaboration, writes Donald Snow, "runs counter to the 'normal course' of environmental politics, counter to the course of most politics of any kind in the United States. Collaboration tends to

scramble ordinary political arrangements; it often requires a redefini-
tion of boundaries, a crossing of borders. Indeed, that scrambling is
one source of the immense power that lies latent in collaboration."[33] Such
power seems no longer latent. It is quite overt in countless ecological
restoration projects, land trusts, rangeland management partnerships,
community forests, firesafe councils, comprehensive plans, working
wildernesses, salmon groups, environmental justice initiatives, and
watershed councils. You can read more about each of these embodi-
ments of collaborative conservation in the stories that follow.

The literature on community-based collaborative conservation
grows so quickly and broadly it may amount to a fresh academic disci-
pline.[34] I am dubious, but I cannot claim to have read everything. What
I have read is empirically rich but as yet lacks coherent theory. The
possibilities seem boundless, for scholars come from many disciplines
and cross boundaries comfortably. Whether collaborative conservation
fits within political science or sociology or geography or corresponds to the
rubrics of political ecology, participatory democracy, shadow networks,
mediation and dispute resolution, common property theory, ecosystem
management, coordinated resource management, deliberative environmental politics, or sustainable development matters little. What
matters is that it generates lively transdisciplinary research that has
already accumulated enough case material to discern best practices and
prescribe performance outcomes, sure signs of policy wonks at work.

Given the legacy of gridlock, legal battles, influence peddling, and
distant ineffectual bureaucracies, it's no wonder that people in the places
they called home invented (and rediscovered) alternatives that, while
almost never excluding the government or the private sector, drew
upon the virtues of community, encouraged civility, welcomed engagement and dialogue, and believed in the absurdity that "nature knows
best." Collaborative groups jelled and invited everybody to the table.
They expected face-to-face interactions and openness in dealing with
their differences. They searched common ground. They demanded
transparency and fully expected to resolve issues short of formal mediation. In all these ways, collaboratives nurtured community and were
themselves strengthened by good community.

But rain falls on the parade. George Coggins, a law professor at the
University of Kansas and a self-described collaboration curmudgeon,

believes that devolved collaboration, especially that involving national lands and resources, is just another fad — a panacea based on faulty thinking.[35] He and others argue that collaboration delegitimizes conflict as a way of dealing with issues, puts more emphasis on local interests than national interests, is time consuming, especially if consensus is required, may cost more, redistributes power away from national environmental groups to local, place-based groups, may promote the norm that decisions are legitimate only when they are acceptable to all stakeholders, and may lead to "least common denominator" decisions that may result in poorer conservation outcomes.[36]

Well, yes. Collaboration, especially when it's based on consensus, stands guilty. In large measure, that's the point! Reduce conflict, be patient, bring power back home, and come up with win-win outcomes. Out of this, hopefully, will come better, more sustainable conservation (though, according to a recent government study, this is still an open question).[37] Larry Allen, a retired US Forest Service scientist I met in Arizona in 2008, states that in just a few years the Malpai Borderlands Group, which he advises, will be able to prove substantial landscape-scale success in rangeland restoration. He further argues that this would not have been possible had only one agency been at work. "One day soon, you're going to see a bright green triangle on satellite imagery of the Malpai," Allan says. "That will be proof of how much we've accomplished!"[38] If this success can be replicated across the whole domain of collaboration, it will be the measure of a huge paradigm shift and a beacon forward.[39] And that's not the half of it.

Paul Hawken, in his intriguing book *Blessed Unrest,* convincingly argues that this collaboration is part of a much bigger global movement that is highly diffuse, without orthodoxy or name, and largely out of the mainstream.[40] It is comprised of citizen groups trying to solve specific problems that will make little differences at the very bottom of the global pecking order. An example is working toward a fairer share of revenues from products, such as ginseng, exported from indigenously managed forests. The energy driving these small but ubiquitous groups unsettles the status quo. Hawken calls this quietly revolutionary situation "blessed unrest." I could not have named it so memorably, but such pot-stirring energy surely also fuels the engines of change in each of the stories you will soon read.

The goals and projects of the countless organizations in Hawken's "movement of movements" cluster around "security, the ability to support ... families, educational opportunities, nutritious and affordable food, clean water, sanitation, and access to health care." The movement has no overriding leadership nor any particular ideological posture. It is something so unique that social movement theory, conceptual frameworks, and history don't inform it. Like early abolitionists, people in the movement are doing what their hearts call them to do, and that is making their world a better place. They have no time for ideology or "branding."

To anyone who checks out Hawken's database, what is clear is that this phenomenon is huge — perhaps two or three million organizations worldwide if, as Hawken does, you include environmental, social justice, and indigenous peoples' groups.[41] Given our global information systems and the speed with which both good and bad news spreads across the Internet, what is truly surprising is that arguably the biggest social movement in history has gone unnoticed. Perhaps this shouldn't be surprising, for on second thought we do live in an oligarchic world in which "the powers that be" control resources, wealth, and information. They have reason to suppress success stories of small people doing big things. The profusion of organizations behind these stories, Hawken tells us, is an understory of ordinary people rebelling quietly against the power equations of our time.[42] In challenging the planet-wrecking crews on every horizon and listening both to the traditional wisdom of their people and to modern science, they will prevail. Like some colossal social immune system, people in the tens or hundreds of millions, working for the common good, will ultimately heal this good Earth. This movement, Hawken believes, gives us "wiggle room to dream."[43]

SUSTAINABILITY

To dream these smaller dreams is also to imagine the grand piñata of our times, the dream of sustainability. Though sustainability means something different to almost anyone you talk to and though it has been hijacked more often than any term I've ever tried to teach, in essence it still comes closest to describing what, in the midst of daily tremors from environmental foreshocks, we need most.[44] For that reason, I live with ambiguity and go on teaching about sustainability.

Ironically, it is the very vision that "sustains" me through these hard times. It contains enough kernels of hope to draw me back from the cliff's edge. Were I not teaching about sustainability, I would surely despair.

The way the term is used in this book is straightforward. Sustainability is nothing more than putting in place the age-old desire to live richly, equitably, and peaceably with each other and with our natural surroundings so that our "home" may offer itself to the imaginations and tables of generations to come. A more prosaic way of putting this is: "Sustainability is about *protecting our options.*"[45] It requires a new consciousness that will enable humans to live and work in ways that will not deplete social and natural capital and will ensure equity within and between generations.

Whereas sustainability had only recently broken into the public imagination in the mid-1990s, it is now a household word. It finds its way into hundreds of local plans and visioning exercises. It's at the core of mission statements, business plans, and a great deal of greenwashing. And while Washington has dodged global warming for most of this decade, towns, cities, and states across the political spectrum are setting Kyoto Protocol-like targets and talking about alternative energy futures, smart growth, mass transit, expanding green space, and planting trees as carbon sinks. The city of Cleveland recently hired a sustainability programs manager. One of the stated goals is to "institutionalize sustainability as a city value."[46] My own university is one of about 100 with a sustainability coordinator helping the institution better practice what it may be preaching.

Through the eyes of complex adaptive science, sustainability is about building resilience to the natural and human-induced surprises that inevitably, sometimes literally, wash across communities. Walker and Salt thus argue that resilience is the lodestone of sustainability. Resilience is, first, the capacity of a system (the "communities" in the stories that follow) to absorb disturbances while retaining basic functions and structure; second, the degree to which a system can "self-organize" on the rebound; and finally, the system's ability to build and increase capacities for learning and adaptation.[47] Though he would not have used these words, Aldo Leopold would have liked such a view. In 1948, he wrote that "many elements in the land community that lack commercial value ... are (as far as we know) essential to its healthy functioning ... the economic parts of the biotic clock will [not] function without the uneconomic parts."[48]

Hucksters in almost every walk of life trivialize this grand idea of sustainability and stretch it so thin you can see right through it. One example is Chevron's "power of human energy" advertising campaign launched in late 2007. Television spots, which have compelling imagery and a softly seductive male voice-over, are still running at this writing, almost two years later. They try to convince the viewer that people must join together to find alternatives to the global energy crisis and imply that Chevron is already doing it. Meanwhile, highly unsustainable images of sky-rocketing energy needs flash across the screen and there's no mention whatever of Chevron's profits, which have long depended on rising oil consumption, nor of the environmentally unjust impacts of oil production.[49]

So-called green advertising like this often misleads and usually omits much. But it also tells me that companies are beginning to see the handwriting on the wall. For example, Chevron, the fifth largest energy company in the world, made rich by decades of outlandish inefficiencies, trumpets a 27 percent increase in its own energy efficiency over a span of 15 years. Andres Edwards, who tracks these trends, writes, "The sustainability revolution's impact on business represents one of the greatest changes presently taking place in society." Companies realize, he believes, that "'business as usual' is destroying Earth's life-support systems."[50] Unlike its predecessor, the Obama administration actually gets this. Pushed by climate change, they intend to kick-start sustainable businesses. If they need models, they can turn to a spate of books that tell companies how to reduce their footprints and become more environmentally responsible.[51] As a bonus, they can also say, as Nobel laureate Al Gore often has, that most "environmentally friendly" initiatives also improve the bottom line.

Teaching about corporate sustainability raises a moral dilemma for me. At its root, the dominant system of growth-addicted global capitalism that determines the survival or demise of the Chevrons of the world is itself unsustainable. Growth of the kind this system rewards is morally unjustifiable, for it is often jobless growth, ruthless growth, voiceless growth, rootless growth, and futureless growth, all of which undermine community, despoil the environment, and increase gaps between workers and CEOs.[52] Does the capitalist system envision limits to this kind of growth? Short of calamitous collapse, never! On the other hand, I can think of other kinds of growth that are sustainable. Growth in human well-being, growth in creative expression, growth in organic food production, growth in happiness, and growth in peace, for example, pose no moral problems or limits if accomplished with happy, healthy, well-nourished, and appropriately educated children and grandchildren in mind.[53]

Changing the present system will require changing everything — from life's very purpose (it's not shopping) to the scale of the human enterprise to government and politics to architecture, transportation, education, energy — everything! As we stare across the chasm, hear the wailing wounded world, and imagine bleakness, we ask: Can we change all this before it's too late? History isn't reassuring.[54] As a graduate assistant for a conservation course required of all University of Wisconsin students seeking a secondary school teaching certificate, so often did I read their essays that I virtually memorized parts of the text we used. I found the book recently, a classic called *American Resources*, and I reread this startling paragraph I'd forgotten I'd memorized:

> *Since the time of the peak of uncontrolled spending of its resource capital, the United States has progressed some distance in developing a conservational attitude toward its natural environment. Many citizens now recognize the necessity for living within our resource means, and nearly every year brings new technological tools and some further strengthening of governmental organizations dealing with resource problems. Yet as this progress has been made, problems have grown too .... We have only begun to apply the design for a new age of stable adjustment to our environment.*[55]

As I prepare to teach another version of my class, Concepts in Environmental Sustainability and Leadership, I sit here wondering. If in the 1960s the authors of this book understood the imperative for "a new age of stable adjustment to our environment," can we now, 40 years later with problems vastly more challenging, ever hope to bring that new age into being?

And then I reflect upon sterling little communities like Athens and the others in this book and upon the "blessed unrest" of millions of other light-filled efforts across the planet (in spite of the global Goliath called "the economy"). And I tell my students to work toward better times. After all, sustainability, a noble goal like "a perfect union" in the American constitution, is a star toward which we sail. And like all journeys, it must start someplace. The stories of the communities that follow, I believe, *are* that someplace. Their narratives continue to give me "wiggle room to dream."

PART II

The Journey Back

3

Step Out Boldly:
Monday Creek, Ohio[1]

*Monday Creek was eaten up with acid mine drainage
and it was dead as a bag of hammers.*[2]

~ Mitch Farley

*Step out boldly ... the science is there and you can have
every possible skill set. But it's the people and their
boldness that will make the difference.*[3]

~ Mary Stoertz

*I've always thought of Monday Creek as a proving
ground for new ideas and concepts. It allows us to test
new and innovative ways ... of increasing public
involvement, improving water quality, and stretching
the boundaries of cooperative applied research.*[4]

~ Scott Miller

*M*ITCH FARLEY, MANAGER OF THE ACID MINE DRAINAGE PROGRAM FOR
the Ohio Department of Natural Resources, recalls being
incredulous 15 years ago when asked to help with a restoration project
aimed at a creek "dead as a bag of hammers" in the midst of the old
Hocking Valley coal fields of southeastern Ohio. His experience and
expertise told him that an attempt to save this creek was probably
futile. As recently as the mid-1990s, the US Environmental Protection
Agency had called Monday Creek "an unrecoverable stream."[5] (Figure
3-1) However, he found himself caught up in the enthusiasm and optimism of two early proponents, Mary Ann Borch, the watershed's first
coordinator, and Mary Stoertz of Ohio University — both personal
friends, both hydrogeologists. He took a chance, put aside his doubts to

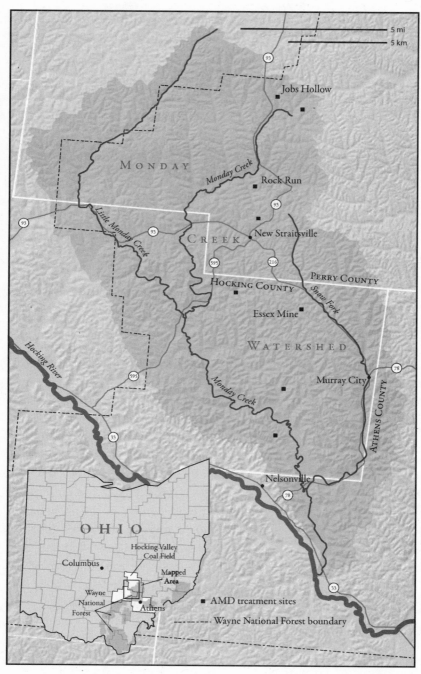

FIGURE 3-1
Monday Creek Watershed

throw his shoulder to the work of convincing his department of the project's worth, and teamed up with the hydrogeologists and Marsha Wikle, a National Forest Service ecologist, to launch the Monday Creek Restoration Project in the mid-1990s.[6]

My own connection to Monday Creek goes back to the mid-1980s, when I first took students into the watershed to see the pollution horrors of abandoned coal mines within a few miles of Ohio University's sublime campus. Years of seeing revulsion in the eyes of my students and the unconscionable poverty of watershed residents convinced me "an ecology of despair" was no longer an option here. So I too was enthused when I heard a restoration project was brewing. I attended an early meeting and saw that undeniable can-do spirit I had witnessed and read about during the launch of dozens of other collaboratives focused on conservation around the US and Canada. Despite this, it took some work to convince my co-author that a tiny restoration project in southeastern Ohio, with as yet unproven results, belonged in our book — especially since agencies of both federal and state governments then believed acid mine pollution to be beyond their water quality purviews and budgets.

What convinced us that the Monday Creek story was worthy was that it was conceived and cobbled together by a nongovernmental organization whose very purpose was community organizing and environmental renewal of Appalachian Ohio. Further, the wide-ranging and innovative collaborative partnership that formed to drive the project, its visionary leadership — the "four Ms": Mitch, Mary, Mary Ann, and Marsha — and its stunning early success in raising capital all seemed a fitting piece of the ecology of hope. Finally, we anticipated learning lessons about how to (and perhaps how not to) bring back a desperately degraded watershed and in turn uplift its residents. In other words, the story had a provocative mix that begged attention to all three elements of sustainability: a polluted environment at the bottom of it all, an economy gone south with the departure of coal mining, and serious environmental injustice foisted upon residents trapped in intergenerational poverty. If this project could succeed, we thought, it might model a trajectory for the wider Eastern Coal Lands of Appalachia. That one of the visionaries in this story, the late Mary Stoertz, could say with confidence that "we will step out boldly; we will gather the people around the idea of life in their creeks" convinced us that this was an example of the alternative body politic we sought — a body that rearranges assumptions about how bottom-up and top-down entities can work productively toward improving things in a beleaguered watershed.

In looking back, I now see that Mary Stoertz was spot-on about "life in their creeks," for what was once dead is now coming back to life, though it's still hard to say whether $6 million of capital projects have even begun to attend to a century of environmental injustice and the tens or hundreds of millions of dollars of opportunity costs and ecological services lost over the generations. "Keeping communities aware of what we're doing and working intensely with the schools and kids in the next generation who will benefit from a cleaner environment are crucial to holding up that original Monday Creek vision," a current leader and visionary reminded me recently. "We are not yet to the point where our investment enables us to think about whether a restored asset like a clean creek can be leveraged into more opportunities. We're not there yet."[7]

SWISS CHEESE AND SHOTGUN HOLES

Monday Creek watershed was in the very midst of the massive and prosperous coal industry of the Hocking Valley coal field. From the mid-1870s to about 1970, millions of tons of coal were taken from dozens of deep mines and, after 1940, some from surface operations. Folks here say the watershed has been shot through with buckshot. It's a land of Swiss cheese honeycombed with shafts, tunnels, and chambers that in some places cave in and others regurgitate immense volumes of underground water. Old mines, abandoned by the 1930s, underlie at least 20 percent of the 116 square mile watershed. Surface mines of the 1940s, 1950s, and 1960s scar an additional 4 percent. Household refuse, mine wastes and tailings, gob piles, rotting structures above and under ground, and acidic surface water impoundments bespeak disruptions of a century of mining. Underground water pollution contributes most to Monday Creek's sorry state. Beneath the watershed, where generations of miners (who later in life suffered black lung disease) once worked at great risk, the mines are now inundated with millions of gallons of water. In the presence of oxygen and bacteria, this water interacts with iron sulfides around former coal seams. Finding its way to the surface through seeps, fractures, shafts, and mine openings, acid mine drainage, which is dilute sulfuric acid with a load of dissolved heavy metals, causes Monday Creek to look orange in some places, turquoise in others, and barren gray-white elsewhere and to run at pH levels below 4.5, a threshold no fish species and few macroinvertebrates can withstand (Table 3-1).

Monday Creek is one of dozens of Ohio watersheds and thousands within the Eastern Coal Lands despoiled by coal mining and left to pollute rivers downstream — the Hocking and Ohio Rivers, in this case. The Ohio Environmental Protection Agency found 82 of the 107 miles of streams in the Monday Creek watershed severely impaired.[8] According to the US Bureau of Mines, Monday Creek is part of a much bigger problem. More than 10,000 linear miles of streams in Appalachia are polluted by acid mine drainage. This includes 1,300 miles of Ohio streams originating in 400,000 acres of abandoned strip mines and 600,000 acres of abandoned underground mines.[9]

The environmental injustices in this story show up in the taut faces of a people who long ago succumbed to the economic and social ravages of the region's coal mining past. Since 1910, the watershed has lost a third of its population.[10] It stands now at about 7,500. At least one fifth of these people live in poverty. Unemployment for all three counties of the watershed always runs higher than state averages.[11] College graduation rates are half those of the state average.[12] A history of broken promises by the government and by mostly defunct corporations leaves residents wary of outside initiatives. Forced to seek opportunities elsewhere, the

TABLE 3-1

Recovery Potential for Aquatic Organisms in Acidic Water

pH	Effect
<4.5	No fish whatever
4.5-5.5	Limited recovery for some trout, dace, and chub
5.6-6.0	Moderate recovery
>6.0	Further recovery with rock bass, small mouth bass, and darters

Source: US Army Corps of Engineers. *Hocking River Basin, Ohio, Monday Creek Sub-Basin Ecosystem Restoration Project: Final Feasibility Report and Environmental Assessment.* USACE, Huntington District, 2005, 21.

younger generation bails out or commutes long distances for work, leaving infirm and elderly relatives behind.[13]

In ways that startle outsiders like myself and most of my students, some parts of the region appear little better than they were in 1960 as described by Harry M. Caudill. Caudill, who spurred President John F. Kennedy to appoint a commission to investigate poverty in Appalachia and President Lyndon Johnson to make Appalachia the centerpiece of his War on Poverty, wrote: "As the nation moves toward the challenges of a new century and a world ringing with change, it cannot afford to leave huge islands of its own population behind, stranded and ignored."[14] In a conversation with high school student Cameron Blosser, we heard in 2005 how his generation is dealing with the social and economic marginalization that's still a part of Appalachian life. Of his schoolmates, he said: "They just want to get a job and as soon as they get enough money, they want to get out of here and forget this place even exists."[15]

WEAVING THE FABRIC OF COMMUNITY RENEWAL

Lead partner and organizational bedrock of the Monday Creek Project is Rural Action, a membership-based nonprofit dedicated to making things better for Cameron Blosser and future generations by focusing on community renewal in Appalachian Ohio. Rural Action conceives of watershed restoration as a key part of its work and something more profound than improving water quality. Speaking about the several watershed groups Rural Action oversees, its executive director Michelle Decker explains: "What we find from our body of watershed work is that, when people work together on improving water quality, the conversation moves fairly soon to matters that get right to our mission of social, economic, and environmental justice. Watersheds don't exist in a vacuum. Our strategy is always a holistic one."[16]

As Rural Action's oldest and most successful watershed project, Monday Creek has taught the organization many lessons, not the least of which is that place matters. They cannot imagine a whole and healthy human community, people living in a place of their own choice, if the lifeblood of that place is toxic and lifeless. Where waters run clear, almost by definition, a place sparkles with hope. Yet when survival is a daily struggle and a trip to the dentist can break the family budget, a person has neither time nor patience to think about alternatives to the orange stream running through the backyard. Rural Action's job, as they see it, is to help that person understand that for her community to be healthy, waters running clean and streams that are fishable and swimmable are important first steps.

Rural Action is one of thousands of organizations worldwide that work on watershed restoration and management.[17] Their basic premise is that most water quality issues won't be resolved unless the watershed becomes the basic unit of the imaginations and intentions of planners, managers, and activists. Robert Thayer, of the Cache Creek Watershed near Davis, California, puts it this way:

> 'One' cannot manage a watershed, only 'many' can, and the 'many' required to manage whole watersheds must talk to each other, see through each other's eyes, meet in real time and space, share common goals, build trust, and mutually undertake the work of keeping the watershed functioning. It is hard — but necessary — work, the kind that is likely to build rather than destroy community.[18]

This is why Rural Action sees watershed restoration as fundamental to its work and why its vision of "weaving the fabric of community renewal" is a third-wave beacon. "If, in addition to watershed work, we can build a better local food system, strengthen the forests and create jobs in sustainable forestry, focus on value-added forest products, be part of a transition to green energy, we will find our niche in the great transition," says director Decker. "As long as we remember that at heart we are talking about community renewal, we should be able to give more people access to these opportunities and, in turn, learn from them."[19]

First Steps

In 1997, the Monday Creek Restoration Project had less than three years under its belt. In that short time it had gathered 14 partners in a highly energized collaborative that included other nonprofits, a university and technical college, and several state and federal agencies, including the US Forest Service, which in Wayne National Forest manages 38 percent of the watershed. The project proposed to tackle a water pollution challenge never successfully accomplished in southern Ohio. To begin, it inventoried the watershed and wrote a watershed management plan. With community members, including students and AmeriCorps VISTA volunteers, it did stream sweeps and removed logjams, set up monitoring wells, planted trees, reclaimed a mountainous gob pile, got into the schools, and submitted a raft of proposals.

In getting this far, with Rural Action's steady guidance, the partnership acquired skills that would come in handy year after year: never losing sight of the vision of fishable and swimmable streams, learning how to work collaboratively, streamlining grant-writing, putting together environmental education programs, developing a watershed geographic information system, and delivering the goods on time. Like the watershed restoration projects of the Feather River in California (Chapter 9), in what should have been an exhausting trial and error process, instead of partner fatigue the project attracted new collaborators and sustained extraordinary energy levels. In moving boldly to clean up toxic waters, everyone seemed to have drunk from Mary Stoertz's quixotic cocktail.[20]

Poster Child

By 2008, the Monday Creek Restoration Project had become one of the premier watershed projects in the Eastern Coal Lands, where today many like-minded organizations are trying to improve ecosystems impacted by acid mine drainage (AMD).[21] The partnership of 20 represents a truly collaborative group of bottom-up and top-down players (Table 3-2). When we asked why this partnership had achieved such a high profile, Mitch Farley told us, "People know who we are precisely because we've been successful. And so we've become a poster child for acid mine drainage across the country."[22] In a matter of a decade, perceptions have come round 180 degrees: "We've done an about-face on what's possible with AMD," said a long-time mine reclamation specialist in the Ohio Department of Natural Resources (ODNR). "The proof is in what Monday Creek has accomplished."[23]

Before 1999, the US Environmental Protection Agency and ODNR believed streams impacted by acid mine drainage were essentially untreatable. In fact, the Ohio EPA designated Monday Creek biologically as "limited resource water with AMD" having either "poor" or "very poor" aquatic habitat that did not justify staff resources or grant monies to clean up. The Monday Creek partners, on the other hand, having seen good results in a similar Pennsylvania watershed, knew differently.[24] They were hopeful, but they didn't have much capital. Then, under pressure from coal field activists, the federal government redefined acid mine drainage as a nonpoint source of water pollution. This opened a new door for funding under Section 319 of the Clean Water Act.[25] In 1999, the Monday Creek Project applied for and landed the first of several EPA 319 grants. From there they began convincing naysayers that the waters of Monday Creek were in fact restorable.

The first step toward restoring Monday Creek was to determine exactly what was wrong with this watershed, and where. In a long and arduous process of field work moved forward by the US Forest Service,

TABLE 3-2
Monday Creek Restoration Project Partnership 2008

Athens, Hocking, Perry Counties Commissioners
Athens, Hocking, Perry Counties Soil and Water Conservation Districts
Community Action
Hocking College
Monday Creek Residents
Ohio Department of Natural Resources, Division of Forestry
Ohio Department of Natural Resources, Division of Mineral Resources Management
Ohio Department of Natural Resources, Division of Soil and Water Conservation
Ohio Department of Natural Resources, Division of Wildlife
Ohio Environmental Protection Agency
Ohio University, Department of Geography
Ohio University, Department of Geological Sciences
Ohio University, Institute for Local Government and Rural Development
Rural Action, Inc.
US Army Corps of Engineers
US Department of Agriculture Natural Resource Conservation Service
US Environmental Protection Agency
US Forest Service
US Geological Survey
US Office of Surface Mining

Source: Monday Creek Restoration Project (mondaycreek.org)

Ohio University's Institute for Local Government and Rural Development, the Ohio Department of Natural Resources, and the Ohio EPA, the Monday Creek partnership mapped sources of acid mine drainage and monitored water quality. Because of the extent and variety of nasty elements in the creek, the first order of business was simply taking stock and establishing baseline data.[26] "Once we had an idea of what was going on," explained Rebecca Black, Monday Creek's water quality specialist, "we could set priorities and improve conditions for life in this watershed."[27] The project then moved on to locate the most immediate problems and collaboratively developed plans to set priorities and attend to them as grants became available.[28]

With a 27-mile main stem and dozens of tributaries of differing water quality, all fed by thousands of seeps and openings gushing underground pollution — the Swiss cheese landscape — Monday Creek cleanup is a mind-boggling water quality and land restoration puzzle. The upper headwaters and Little Monday Creek and its tributaries, which flow over limestone, showed up as being "fair" to "good" warm water habitat and thus support a greater diversity of species than the rest of the creek. The upper watershed, which can support large-mouth bass and darters, serves as a refugium for the aquatic ecosystem of this region. But species there cannot migrate downstream across the wall of acidity in the middle sections of the watershed. Mitigation projects focusing on these segments would be the most cost effective and quickest way to improve downstream sections and allow life to return from both above and below mid-watershed.[29]

After much trial and error, the Monday Creek kitbag now includes a mix of passive and active treatments. Passive projects include filling subsidences, sealing gob piles with alkaline material, and treating seeps with labyrinthine channels and leach beds to reduce acid flow and lessen acid and metal loads. The proof that these kinds of treatments work is in the pH of waters downstream. After almost a decade of work, there are significant reductions in acidity. For example, downstream from the cleaned up and capped 13.5-acre Rock Run gob, the partnership's first major project, water improved from a pH of 4.2 before to 8.0 after the project.[30] Other passive projects have achieved similar improvements (Table 3-3).

As for active treatment, dosing, a technology imported from Sweden, adds a dry alkaline mixture (CaO) at regular intervals to the

TABLE 3-3

Selected Monday Creek Restoration Projects 1999-2008

Site and year	Treatment	Results	Partners	Cost/Funding
Snake Hollow 1996	Rectifed subsidences, installed leach bed, and neutralized gob pile	Eliminated subsidence cavities, reduced pH, regraded gob pile	ODNR, USFS	$986,000 USFS, ODNR
Rock Run 1999	Treated 13.5-acre gob pile with alkaline material, installed treatment ponds	Improved pH from 4.2 to 8	ODNR, EPA	$380,000 EPA 319 grant, ODNR
Majestic Mine 1999-2002	Closed a subsidence to limit water infiltration into underground mines, constructed open limestone channel to add alkalinity	Reduced flow from mine by 1/3	ODNR	$282,250 EPA, ODNR
Grimmett Property 2001-2003	Treated mine seep with WVU technology: J-trenches, channel installation, soil caps	Improved pH from 3.4 to 6.7, 100% decrease in acid loading	EPA, ODNR	$155,614 EPA, ODNR
Murray City Art Project 2001-2004	Seep treatment, installation of community art park around treatment site	Canceled		
Big 4 Hollow 2001	Treated major seeps with limestone leach beds, open limestone channels	Improved pH from 3.1 to 4.2; 41% reduction in acid load	USFS, ODNR	$322,124 ODOT, USFS, ODNR
Lost Run 2004-2007	Installed open limestone treatment channels and leach beds	Improved pH from 3.4 to 4.8	ODNR	$1,000,000 EPA 319 grant, ODNR

Site and year	Treatment	Results	Partners	Cost/Funding
Essex Doser 2003	Dosing technology – input of alkaline material	Treated upper part of watershed, improved pH from 2.3 to 6.8 for 6 stream miles	ODNR	$307,432 PA, ODNR
Jobs Hollow Doser 2005	Dosing technology – input of alkaline material	Improved 10 miles of Monday Creek	ODNR	$324,500 ODNR, OSM
Murray City Sub-sidences 2004	Closed 3 subsidences	Eliminated stream capture	ODNR	$43,022 ODNR
Happy Hollow 2004	Reduced acid flow via installation of limestone leach beds	Divert AMD away from recreational lake	USFS, ODNR, USACE	$81,988 ODNR
USACE Feasibility Study 2005-2007	Comprehensive study of watershed restoration projects	Feasibility study	USFS, ODNR, OU, MCRP, EPA, WVU, USACE	$1,000,000 USACE, ODNR
Shawnee 2008	Installed steel slag bed treatment system	To reduce acid load in upper watershed	ODNR, Village of Shawnee	$199,791 EPA, ODNR, OSM
WRDA projects 2008-2012	Preconstruction engineering and design and implementation of AMD mitigation at 1,600 sites	N/A (project commenced 2008)	USACE, entire partnership	$21,000,000 over 5 years USACE through WRDA 2007, ODNR local match $3,000,000

Sources: Mike Steinmaus, MCRP Coordinator. Interview (9 March 2005); Dan Imhoff, Ohio EPA. E-mail communication (1 August 2005); Mitch Farley and Paul Ziemkiewicz. "Abandoned Mined Land Reclamation Projects and Passive Treatment." Presentation to WV Surface Mine Drainage Task Force Symposium, 2005; US Army Corps of Engineers. "Draft Feasibility Report." 2005, 12-14; MCRP records; Mitch Farley, ODNR. E-mail communication (4 January 2009).

stream. The project has installed one Boxholm-style doser at the Essex mine and one wheel-style doser at Jobs Hollow. While these systems require regular maintenance and resupply of the alkaline mixture, a new system using steel slag, which has long-lasting alkalinity, has been installed near Shawnee to decrease reliance on the Jobs Hollow doser. If this system is successful, one doser may be relieved at considerable savings. Together with the passive installations and improvements, pH has been improved from 40 to 100 percent along about 10 linear miles of streams in the upper and mid-watershed and has brought some pollution-sensitive fish back to segments where few people now alive had ever cast a line. Biological assessments of the main stem of Monday Creek in 2005 revealed 22 species of fish. However, only 30 percent of them were acid pollution-sensitive (in other words, requiring a higher pH) compared to 48 percent in Little Monday Creek. Little Monday samples also revealed a healthy mix of macroinvertebrates that cannot yet survive in the main stem.[31]

The hard and expensive work of technically treating acid mine drainage in this landscape will be sustained over the next decade. In the first override of a presidential veto during George W. Bush's tenure, Congress passed the Water Resources Development Act of 2007. This includes some $21 million destined for cleanup of 289 mine sites in the Monday Creek watershed.[32] The preconstruction engineering and design phase, beginning in 2008, includes endangered species surveys, geotechnical investigations, and design of treatment systems for subwatersheds contributing the greatest amounts of AMD. Monday Creek coordinator Mike Steinmaus, reflecting on the long road to this grant, wrote: "When we take time to look at the projects completed, the positive public opinions, and the changes to the physical environment, we ... realize that hope and hard work can make a difference."[33]

Beyond the Dosers

While restoring stream quality to healthy warm water habitat is the end goal of these technical projects, it only begins to fulfill Rural Action's holistic vision of "a region of clean streams, healthy forests, thriving family farms, meaningful jobs, and lively towns that remember local history and celebrate their stories."[34] Whereas funding for water quality projects has been ample, there are no comparable sources for community work. The watershed coordinator, funded partly by the Ohio Department of Natural Resources, is theoretically meant to draw community into his work. In reality, just administering a multimillion dollar set of projects and holding together a collaborative with 20 partners is a full-time job. "Our work with Monday Creek communities has had to take place off the clock, on weekends often, and by being creative with volunteers," admitted Rural Action's Decker. "But the fact that we fund Mike Steinmaus's trips to community meetings and township trustee meetings and we have an office in New Straitsville demonstrates that we do not take community lightly."[35] "Community first, watershed second is the essence of what we are meant to do," said one partner, "but based on funding, you would not necessarily arrive at that conclusion."[36]

As for the community, participation over the years has come in fits and starts depending on particular projects. During the first few years, a local radio station hounded the project for spending thousands of dollars on stream cleanup instead of creating jobs or reducing flooding. Heated arguments and walkouts were commonplace at village council meetings. "We were not well perceived by local communities," one partner remembers. "We were outsiders."[37]

But persistence and patience among staff, partners, and community members have paid off. Community notions about the Monday Creek Restoration Project are generally positive these days (when such notions exist). Those aware of the project praise it highly, citing improvements in the creek, coordinator Mike Steinmaus's involvement in the community (including the volunteer fire department), the project newsletter *Up the Creek* that goes out to 700 addressees, and the Monday Creek Restoration Project's active participation in local culture and history festivals and organizations, including Little Cities of Black Diamonds, a group that promotes tourism and cultural events in the string of once-bustling towns of the Hocking coal field."[38] Longtime resident and friend of Monday Creek, Ron Eaton, noted that the Monday Creek Project has lessened traditional rivalries among citizens from different towns in the watershed.[39] "We've learned to work together," he said. Mike Steinmaus agreed: "People will work on projects together and then will say, 'Oh, yeah, I worked with that person, he's a good guy' ... and the community starts to come together."[40] Betsy Gosnell, a resident and volunteer, says that volunteering helped her "feel more a part of the community, not just the community where I live, Murray City, but the watershed community as a whole. Driving by the creek these days, I take pride in knowing that I am one of the many who are helping make the dream of cleaning up Monday Creek ... a reality."[41]

Steinmaus, an ebullient optimist, perpetually dreams up new ways to connect the project with residents. A recent brilliant example graces the Monday Creek office. It's a homemade bright red canoe, constructed and then paddled down the creek by teen participants in a watershed summer day camp. Very popular also are the annual watershed tours in the midst of fall foliage season. The same goes for spring tree plantings, work days to clear trails and creeks, summer potlucks, and canoe trips.[42] Partnering with Rural Action's Environmental Learning Program, the Monday Creek Project stages environmental education events in local schools and sponsors service learning projects for undergraduate and graduate students from local colleges and universities.[43]

Community outreach like this is a work of patience and tenacity. Progress is incremental. Some see it as diverting the real work of the partnership. Others seem unaware not only of these activities but also of the project itself.[44] For Steinmaus, the extent and variety of the project's community participation and outreach are crucial to its sustainability. He quite rightly argues that agencies, capital funding, and even Rural Action may not be here in the future. But residents will. Mary Stoertz once observed, "All this could be gone with the stroke of a pen. Then what?" Scott Miller of the Voinovich School of Leadership and Public Affairs at Ohio University, a participant in the project since his days as a VISTA volunteer, put it this way:

> The stream may be fishable and swimmable in ten years, but there is nothing to guarantee that it will stay fishable and swimmable unless we change people's perceptions. If the project completely walked away tomorrow, the communities here might easily backslide and adopt the same practices that got the stream into the mess it's in now.[45]

Looking back on almost ten years of community involvement, Steinmaus continues to argue that "this project is nothing without a holistic view that includes the watershed, the economy, and people's issues. If people can do something to improve their land, they will indirectly improve these waters. This can change the way they feel about the watershed." By participating in a wide range of community initiatives, Monday Creek accomplishes its goals, says Steinmaus, and this leads to "cross-community leadership that will serve the region well in the next generation and may produce a coordinator actually born here to take over the organization."[46]

Among natural resource agencies Monday Creek has the enviable reputation as a model for interagency collaboration and a proving ground for new ideas.[47] For many resource professionals over the years, the Monday Creek Restoration Project was their first experience in a watershed partnership with community people and nonprofits, folks from both state and federal agencies, and university types. For newcomers, the level of trust among partners and the partnership's collaborative spirit are a surprise and seem a clear legacy of "the four Ms" who began this journey. That all decisions in the partnership are still taken by consensus is another surprise. "Collaboration and consensus slow the process, which is not bad," said the Forest Service's Monday Creek liaison Gary Willison. "But it's important to stick to the idea of consensus on all decisions. Everybody's better off for it."[48] All this adds up to Monday Creek's hugely successful track record and its nationally renowned vision and accomplishments in tackling acid mine drainage. "Working with the Monday Creek Project has been highly refreshing," said ODNR's Mitch Farley. "It's rejuvenated my career."[49]

WITHOUT JUSTICE, IT'S NOT SUSTAINABLE DEVELOPMENT

Rural Action's transcendent mission for Appalachian Ohio certainly includes healthy watersheds as part of sustainable development. However, Rural Action's director believes that, in doing watershed work and work on other environmental and economic sustainability projects (such as light-touch forestry, promoting nontimber forest products, restoring the local food economy, tapping renewable energy stores, and exploring carbon sequestration), "we cannot lose sight of equity, environmental justice, and meaningful engagement of residents in all we do."[50] President Clinton's 1994 executive order on environmental justice mandated that federal agencies pay attention to environmental and human health in minority and low-income communities that are disproportionately exposed to pollution. Residents of Monday Creek are clearly suffering from a 180-year legacy of resource extraction that leaves them bereft of the fresh water and uncontaminated lands people in other parts of the country take for granted. And though this particular executive order has gotten little political attention in the first decade of the new millennium, it is nonetheless the bedrock of Rural Action's mission and a big part of the mandate for the Monday Creek Restoration Project.

Watershed residents have lived with orange streams all their lives and most have never had hope that things would improve. Ravaged streams seem to generate apathetic resignation. And as these streams were already trashed, it mattered little if somebody dumped household or construction wastes over a stream bank.

> During floods, people would stand on the bridges and drop bags of trash in the streams. They literally would do that ... and why shouldn't they? The streams were choked with plastic bags and trash ... the state had already made the decision that you could write off the stream. Historically people have often viewed waterways as sewers. [51]

As is common in marginalized low-income communities, this sense of resignation permeates virtually everything and everyone. Monday Creek resident Ron Eaton says he and his neighbors have traditionally seen the glass as half empty: "People around here are always complaining and generally negative and don't think that anything is going to work."[52] This legacy of hopelessness submerges any sense of community engagement that might naturally bubble up in more advantaged places with citizens who have time and resources for leisure and volunteering. This explains low turnouts, for example, at Friends of Monday Creek events. Despite this, coordinator Steinmaus is optimistic that the project will eventually bring the community together:

> There is an attitude of defeatism in these communities ... they feel like they have been left with nothing and that there is no one to help. The government programs wouldn't come; there were no jobs for them and the general attitude is that 'we're stuck.' Monday Creek works together to have them have a common goal to

improve the environment and economy ... now there is
less bitterness. Monday Creek has helped to spur that for-
ward. The ultimate sustainability test of the Monday
Creek Restoration Project will be how it is judged by
the next generation. In this sense, what is happening
now is very hopeful and a part of the larger dream to
breathe life back into the watershed community."[53]

To Rural Action's credit, Monday Creek and other watershed projects do, in fact, subtly raise expectations of a better future. Mary Stoertz
said, "The Monday Creek Project is injecting hope, it's injecting skills into
the community, and bringing a different way of looking at things."[54]
Cara Hardesty, coordinator of the Sunday Creek Watershed at mid-
decade, reflecting on a summer watershed camp for both Sunday and
Monday Creek kids, noted, "The adults here haven't had a lot of education and sometimes that's a problem. But the kids ... are learning and
enjoying the environmental education programs. That gives me
hope."[55] Cameron Blosser, the high school student whose despondent
voice we heard earlier, does not totally despair:

Used to be it was a unanimous vote that this area was
gone and that it was just a bunch of dying towns ...
and then they started working on them and fixing up
buildings and putting in sewers ... and trying to clean
them up, trying to save what's left .... I kinda think
maybe that there is some hope for them.[56]

Recent infrastructural improvements such as these, not explicitly
part of the restoration project but certainly contributing to a higher
quality of life, might be conceived as the beginnings of a renaissance in
what have long been conceived as dying villages. These include wastewater treatment plants and integrated sewage systems, the restoration
of historic landmarks and buildings, the cleanup of empty lots and illegal dumps, new village parks, thriving local history organizations, a
nature trail along a wetland in Wayne National Forest dedicated to a
local artist and writer, and murals and children's art enhancing town
centers.[57] Arguably these developments derive from the community
spirit the Monday Creek Restoration Project strives to foster. And while
poverty rates and graduation rates are still indefensible and there are
still too few opportunities to earn secure incomes anywhere near the

watershed, a successful (admittedly mostly technical) watershed project seems to make things just a little brighter on the streets of New Straitsville and Shawnee and along the trails in Wayne National Forest.

STEP OUT BOLDLY

Mary Stoertz, Monday Creek's muse during her foreshortened life, reminded Rachel Cook and me in a 2005 interview that the bottom line in this project is *boldness*. She called on her partners and on residents to step out boldly, to take risks, to go for the gold. To go boldly, I'm sure she would agree, is not to go blindly. The challenges Monday Creek faces are not unlike those we've seen in other watersheds — the Wolf (Chapter 6), the Mattole (Chapter 8), the Feather (Chapter 9), the North Branch (Chapter 10), and the Tennessee (Chapter 11). To endure, to be sustainable, a watershed project must have both working partners and friends and residents who can think long term, beyond, say, the grant that presently supports its work. This raises many questions. How can community organizing and development investment achieve the same level and importance as technical water quality fixes? How can residents take fuller ownership? What happens if sources of funding dry up? How can a fishable, swimmable, ecologically healthy watershed be sustained? What kind of economy is implied by environmental sustainability that starts with watersheds? To address these questions is to address the challenges most community-based watershed groups face. But here, where AMD treatment is likely to require many decades, they are even more complex.

Clearly, the Monday Creek Restoration Project has given the watershed new life. Without Rural Action's embrace of this project and a strong partnership with a winning history, Monday Creek would likely have been one of the last AMD-impacted streams in Appalachian Ohio to be restored.[58] Now, with steadily improving water quality and remarkably fast aquatic ecosystem recovery, it has become a success story known across North America. It may take longer for residents of the watershed to recognize this and it will surely require at least 20 more years of investment to really restore Monday Creek. That target, once unthinkable, now seems in reach. Then there is the question of sustaining treatment.

When I look at intangible things that are also meant to be a part of community-based conservation — things like enrichment of the sense of place to the point that people think of the place as "destination rather than devastation,"[59] planning for the long term, building a locally sustained group of collaborative operators and leaders that taps into local knowledge and leadership, and a dedicated and widely embraced commitment to ecosystem health — the results are less clear. As Douglas S. Kenny warns, as long as there is so much work to be done, work that requires hard-headed performance assessment, there is a clear danger of over-enthusiasm.[60]

In the end, as Steinmaus observed, it will be the residents of this watershed who will determine whether the project is sustainable. That will require work above and beyond the technical projects that will fall to Rural Action and to the communities themselves. Michelle Decker, surely a visionary leader able to sculpt such a future, is hopeful. She says, "If a bioregional framework can infuse our work in these communities, then we will succeed not only at reaching our water quality goals but also at achieving more equitable and sustainable development."[61]

As I take leave of the bustling Monday Creek Restoration Project office in downtown New Straitsville, having just talked with the effervescent Mike Stienmaus, knowing what I know about watershed work across North America, I too am cautiously hopeful that this creek in my own neighborhood may one day flow in glowing good health and that residents here will thrive and will fish and swim in its sparkling waters and picnic in the healthy forests that envelop them.

4

Into the Eighth Generation:
Monhegan Island, Maine[1]

The mystery and complexity of an island ... That it defies all but the faintest comprehension — even in a lifetime of intense, thoughtful experience — is a fact worth celebrating.[2]

~ Richard Nelson

From cowpats to South America, it is difficult to see what is not or at some time has not been an island.[3]

~ D.J. Mabberly

NO MATTER HOW YOU CUT IT, MONHEGAN IS SMALL. Among the islands in the Gulf of Maine occupied year round, it is the smallest at just under a square mile. Six hundred acres of hard-rock geology about 12 miles out to sea, born of isolation and struggling to remain partly so, Monhegan's wee dimensions are part of its essence. Compared to the other places in this book, Monhegan is microcosmic: 0.0004 percent of Plumas, 0.003 percent of the Menominee Reservation, and 0.008 percent of Monday Creek, the next smallest. How could such a speck have lessons to teach?

In 1997 we wrote that over the course of seven generations, people on Monhegan had made difficult decisions to set limits on resource use and ways of living. We detected no grand sustainability design, no visioning or strategic plan, nor any conceit about ways Monhegan might model a future others could copy. What we found was a hardy, understated, resourceful people living a good life in a difficult place. If they were prescient, their understanding of "the good life" was based on simplicity, tradition, self-reliance, common sense, and Yankee ingenuity. No less important were effective ways of working through conflict and, surely, awareness of the edges and small scale of their home. We framed Monhegan's story around the words of Maine island historian Philip Conkling, who wrote that "islands foreshadow the future for all communities."[4]

Setting limits is part and parcel of Monhegan life. One resident summed it up by saying that island people restrain themselves because they don't want to ruin either what tourists come to experience or what they themselves cherish. This seems to be what Thomas Princen calls "the principle of sufficiency" — that enough is enough, that limited consumption and disciplined resource use are part of the good life. Such wisdom has led to durable decisions that end up with fewer nasty side effects and in turn keep the enterprise from fouling its nest. Princen writes:

> ... go to an island like Monhegan and you will find that limited resources and limited ability to external-ize costs stare you in the face day in and day out. To act rationally you must find ways to survive by living within those limits, not by escaping them. With prac-tice and discipline you can even thrive.[5]

THE ISLAND SYSTEM

Islands have recently taken center stage in startling new ways. Global change in climate, with its sea level rises and ocean current shifts; the collapse of oceanic fisheries; egregious impacts of invasive plants and animals and technologies; the imposition of international tourism and other offshore activities — all these contribute worldwide to anxieties about the future of island life. Two decades ago, island states collectively began to worry, first, about their very survival and second, about whether a path to island sustainability could even be envisioned in these imperiled times. The United Nations Commission on Islands and Small Island Developing States, formed in the 1990s, argues persuasively that islands need special consideration:[6]

> Because they have many features in common that set them apart from other geographic areas, islands and small island states are increasingly recognized as a spe-cial category worthy of distinctive treatment. With the increasing rate of global change, [they] represent some of the most fragile and vulnerable resources on the planet.[7]

Monhegan is perhaps an outlier at the short end of the United Nations special category of island societies. Yet it is no less vulnerable economically, socially, and environmentally than others. And its human adaptations are as critical to its survival and sustainability as those of much bigger islands. Just as Sardinia and Hawaii can be understood as threatened though enduring "adaptive systems," so also can tiny Monhegan be seen this way. And they all have lessons to teach.

Island systems are ever changing. Over time they may display what are termed "stability domains," when the system is "steady as you go" for a spell.[8] From time to time, disturbances such as severe storms, economic hard times, disease, invasive plants and animals, or immigration threaten to unravel stability and take the system to a new, perhaps less stable, domain. If we could know something of the boundaries of these domains and of the forces that maintain them, then we would have an understanding of ways Monhegan has weathered disturbance and has, over seven generations, maintained the integrity of its life-sustaining functions. This is not simply a matter of knowing Monhegan's natural history, for human behavior, entrepreneurial activity, and creativity have also been part of the story for 180 years.

At the risk of disturbing a mental picture of Monhegan's solitude, imagine we are able to hop on board a helicopter and circle the island at a height sufficient to perceive it as a whole, including the land and surrounding waters, all the interacting ecological components, and the humans and their social and economic arrangements and built environment. Would this enable us to see the island anew? Might we identify key components and ask questions about the ways they interact? Would this be a way of making some sense of 12 years of change? And might it be possible to identify boundaries of "stability domains" and forces that have enabled the island system either to follow or to stray from a sustainable path? Let's try.

In its tiny expanse Monhegan compresses almost all the natural landscapes of mid-coast Maine (Figure 4-1). Flying above, we see a shoreline of rocky promontories, high cliffs, looming headlands, and offshore islands and ledges with seals and seabirds. Rising 160 feet above the Atlantic, Monhegan's headlands are some of the highest points along Maine's mid-coast. Just off the western shore are Manana and Smuttynose islands, treeless unoccupied humps that partially

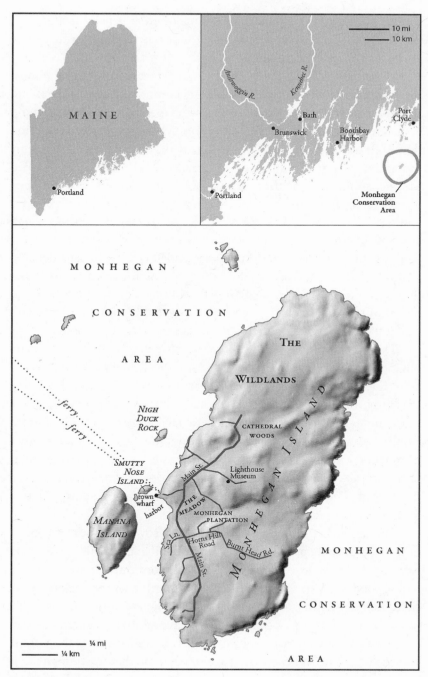

FIGURE 4-1
Monhegan Island

protect Monhegan's small harbor. Though there is usually shelter here, the harbor is described in cruising guides as "difficult and unsafe anchorage." There are no public moorings or marinas.

Monhegan is safely above the surf and so can withstand the most severe storms and potential sea level rises because the core of the island is an ancient crystalline ledge, averaging 66 feet above sea level. On top of it is a mantle of glacial till —the soil that supports the vegetation that appears to cover a large portion of the island. We can see tiny wetlands dotting the surface. At the center of the village (called Monhegan Plantation) there is one such relatively large bog, an open place referred to as "the Meadow." Recharged by precipitation, streams, and fractures in the bedrock, it is the sole-source aquifer for the island. You note that soils are sparse and shallow, yet there are gardens (with big compost piles nearby) and the village cemetery with burials beneath ground. (Later, you discover the cemetery has imported topsoil from the mainland.) Water pipes are mostly above ground. Sewage systems of various sorts attach to each house separately — or perhaps not. Along the shore, pipes seem to take sewage directly "overboard."

Thanks to choppy waters, the sewage disperses so that there are no obvious signs of marine pollution. (A lobster fisher assures us there's zero tolerance for messing up these waters since, besides being unsightly, it might be harmful to lobsters.) It is summer, so you can see cruise boats checking out seals and one farther out to sea looking for whales. There are no lobster buoys bobbing in the ocean around Monhegan in this season because the community does not fish their waters in the warm summer months. There does seem to be flotsam in the harbor. The air is clear on this day. Sometimes in summer it's so foggy you can't see the toes of your boots.

The vegetation you noted is mostly forest, covering about 75 percent of the island. Forty percent of this is mature. Red and white spruce and balsam fir dominate, but you also see red and mountain maple, alder, moosewood, quaking aspen, and white birch. Monhegan's walking trails, circumscribing and crisscrossing the island, disappear from sight into these woods. The most mature — Cathedral Woods, Lighthouse Hill, and Lobster Cove — are labeled on maps, known to tourists, and as sacred as they sound.

As you circle over the village again, you note that the human landscape is packed into the west-southwest third of the island. The rest is unoccupied. If you were to count buildings, you would discover 180 houses, the vast majority of which are single-family detached structures. Two large frame hotels, a schoolhouse, a church, a library, and a few small businesses are also part of the village as are fish houses, scattered along the edges of the harbor. In these structures lobster fishers socialize, store bait, keep their supplies, mend nets and traps, and meet to decide collectively when trap day (the opening of the season) will happen, to set limits on the numbers of fishers and traps, and to discuss how to deal with fishers from other harbors. During the winter lobster season, the fish houses arē departure points for lobster boats to head out into the icy waters.

Near the highest point of the village, at the end of Lighthouse Road, is the historic lighthouse, now a museum. Close by is the island's electric generating station with attendant diesel tanks. A small plume of smoke drifts eastward. A tower with radio antennas and a satellite dish brings modern telecommunications to the island, including high speed DSL and wireless Internet if one has a sight line to the tower.[9] Power and telephone lines from this hill extend to most but not all houses.

The unpaved road system is minimal (less than 2.5 miles overall) and similarly concentrated in the west and southwest. Apart from a few working pickup trucks parked near homes and businesses, there are no cars. (You must leave your car on the mainland.) Nor can you see any all-terrain vehicles, motorcycles, or jet skis. At the end of one of the roads is the town wharf from whence all ferry connections between Monhegan and the mainland happen. You note some 30 tourists disembarking from the mail boat and heading on foot up the road into the village, a daily phenomenon in midsummer. At the edge of the wharf are several dumpsters and an accumulation of gas cylinders.

What we see from the air are the macrocomponents of the island system. Invisible, of course, are commercial transactions, political and civic institutions, the knowledge base, the traditions and history that make this place tick. So to complete our look at this system, we must get back to the ground. Let's start with permanent residents. Of the more than 4,000 islands off the coast of Maine, Monhegan is one of just 15 occupied year round. In 2007, there were 75 year-round residents living in 46 households, virtually the same as reported in the 2000 census.[10] This is a decline of about 15 percent since the mid-

1990s. As in other remote places in this book, most island children leave Monhegan when they grow up.[11]

Those who survive year round are industrious, highly adaptable, and intriguing folk. They must balance individualism with the wary interdependence we've seen in other small, far-off communities.[12] After all, there is no supermarket or big-box retailer just down the block and the island has almost no public sector jobs and just a few businesses, many of which close in winter. But people do find work. At the time of the 2000 census, Monhegan reported full employment at 65 people, 36 of whom were self-employed. In addition to lobster fishing, which employed 21, there were no fewer than 11 other categories of work reported, some related to tourism (about 20 percent), fully one third in maintenance and construction, and some in services like education, health, transportation, and utilities (14 percent). These numbers reveal the economic necessity of diverse skill sets. If you are a boat captain, you are probably also someone who can fix pipes or electrical problems, do carpentry, and repair old pickup trucks and generators. Such versatility is the vital bridge between tourism in summer and lobster fishing in winter. Remarkably, this small, self-made village economy achieved a median family income 13 percent higher than that of Maine as a whole in 2000 (though low by national numbers — $45,179 versus $53,125).[13] Jan Kornbluth, proprietor of the general store, says year-round living "is not for the faint of heart. It will cost you, but you get paid for the effort."[14] Part of the pay back, as I've witnessed it, is knowing you can survive even when the mainland economy is in shreds (as it is at this writing).

Certainly being a jack of all trades is crucial, but there would likely be no year-round population without tourism, the principal source of capital and employment in summer. Tourists come to Monhegan to get off the fast track in a place that seems to have paused in an earlier time, with a stillness you can't easily find these days. Although some forms of adventure recreation like sea kayaking are possible, the visitors' guide warns that there are no shops plying to this interest and no kayak rentals. The same goes for biking, which is not allowed on island trails. So tourism is the rustic kind of a century or so ago. People come to paint and pursue other forms of art, long a focus of summer here, to walk the trails, to sit on the rocks and enjoy the island's natural areas and its teeming life along the shores and in surrounding waters, and to feast on home cooking as opposed to gourmet meals.

The tourist season is short and intense. Though it extends from the end of May to mid-October, the intense part is between Independence Day and Labor Day, when the resident island population on any given day jumps to about 400 in addition to as many as 250 overnight guests. Two hotels and a number of smaller bed and breakfasts and guest houses provide more than half the tourist beds. The rest are in cottages that residents and inshore owners rent out for periods of a few days to the entire summer. At the other end of the spectrum are folk visiting from the mainland for just one day. Excursions from Boothbay, New Harbor, and Port Clyde (the year-round port of departure) drop tourists off through the long summer days and retrieve them a few hours later. While on Monhegan, these so-called "day trippers" hike the 15 miles of trails, do nature cruises, visit artists' studios, and have lunch or picnic on the rocks.

The other part of the economy is lobster fishing. Though only about a dozen lobster boats operate out of Monhegan, fully half the island income comes from lobstering, an activity that complements tourism since lobstering happens in late fall and winter. Even in good seasons lobster fishers find it a challenge to scrape together a decent living. "Monhegan fishermen are not rolling in money or lobsters," a former shopkeeper told Tom Princen. "Almost without exception the people who live on Monhegan must work in some capacity during the tourist season."[15] Because the catch is taken when there is no demand on Monhegan, virtually all is sold on the mainland, where it then finds its way into national and international markets when prices tend to be at their seasonal high. Monhegan fishers adhere strictly to Maine Department of Marine Resources minimum and maximum size regulations and trap limits.[16] Their fish houses, summer-stacked traps and other gear, skiffs, and colorful buoys remind visitors that this is a working island culture, not a living history museum.

Of political and civic life, the most significant organization for the landscape is Monhegan Associates, a land trust formed in 1954 and run by elected trustees whose mission is preserving "for posterity the natural wild beauty, biotic communities, and desirable natural, artificial, and historic features of the so-called 'wild-lands' portions of Monhegan Island and its environs, as well as the simple, friendly way of life that has existed on Monhegan as a whole."[17] Together with a start-up gift of about 300 acres from philanthropist and summer resident Ted Edison, Monhegan Associates has acquired or otherwise put in protection about 65 percent of the island (480 acres), primarily outside the village in the contiguous, mostly forested tract we could see from the air. Monhegan Associates' bylaws are first-wave preservationist. They focus on what's not allowed and imply a hands-off approach to management. Through five-plus decades nobody has ever seriously suggested putting these lands up for sale, and hence there has been no possibility of runaway development or serious threats to Monhegan's "simple, friendly way of life".

Politically, Monhegan Plantation (the equivalent of a village or hamlet in other states) rules itself through a three-person board of assessors held accountable through annual town meetings operating according to "certain prudential rules" and of course to state fiduciary regulations. Plantation officers include a tax collector and municipal clerk (served by the same person in 2008), a municipal treasurer, and a road commissioner. One resident told us in the 1990s that "we've always had as little to do with the state as possible. If problems come up, we'd never call the state to ask if we were infringing upon this or that regulation or law. We simply took care of things ourselves in a time-honored and civil way."[18] Common law, as understood by residents and landowners, enables Monhegan to take care of itself, largely without interference of police or courts. (Though there is a constable, Monhegan is essentially crime free.)

When state zoning codes and federal clean water regulations imposed themselves from the 1970s onward on decisions about land use, the Meadow aquifer, and waste disposal, using Monhegan's "time-honored ways" people figured out how to use these laws to make good decisions for the community. For its part, "the state," especially through land use regulation, aquifer protection, and lobstering regulations and laws, has essentially helped Monhegan protect itself from itself. As Princen observes in the context of lobster regulation, where there is a long tradition of self-organization, "high government" can allow "low governance" to accomplish regulation more effectively.[19]

A LONGER VIEW: ADAPTATION OVER THREE CENTURIES

Before looking at what's happening on Monhegan as it heads into the eighth generation, let's first frame the 21st century in the context of adaptations over the longer term — the seven generations on whose shoulders present residents stand. Going way back, prior to the 1600s, though not settled, Monhegan was a summer fishery for Native Americans who canoed across the bay and camped near the present harbor. In the 11th century, Norse sailors probably visited Monhegan. Cabot passed by in 1497, as did many other European explorers from the early 1600s onward. Thereafter European crews regularly anchored near the island in summer, fished Muscongus Bay, and dried their catches on Monhegan's shores. For a time Monhegan and nearby islands were the most important European fishing stations along mid-coast Maine.[20] Monhegan was settled by the English in 1619, abandoned in 1679, and then resettled for good in the 1830s, when it became incorporated as a plantation. It soon had a population of 100, a schoolhouse, a church, pastures for sheep, swine, and cattle, and a year-round settlement that extends right to the present.

As a human-ecological system for more than seven generations, Monhegan has evolved through several periods (or regimes) of relative stability:

- **Self-Made.** Through most of the 19th century, an era of virtual self-sufficiency prevailed with most needs met by the sea and agriculture. Population averaged around 100 people. Some of the basic infrastructure evolved at this early time — a school, a church, the town wharf, the fishing economy, a tradition of home rule.

- **Fishing and Rusticators.** In the late 19th and early 20th centuries, commercial fin fishing and lobster trapping, together with the beginnings of rustic tourism and summer art, diversified the island's options. Robert Henri's Monhegan school in the early 1900s was followed by a steady stream of young painters including George Bellows, Rockwell Kent, John Marin, Reuben Tam, and Jamie Wyeth. Land speculators banked on continuing good times and subdivided most of the island.

- **Shocks.** An unstable time began in the late 1920s and continued into the late 1940s. Things began to come unglued. The Depression, serious declines in lobster catches, the collapse of ground fishing, and the onset of World War II all destabilized a domain that had endured for three generations. Land speculation failed and the island's human population declined. Monhegan came close to losing its winter community.

- **Release and Reorganization.** Hard times in the 1930s and 1940s led to the release of pent-up and dysfunctional arrangements (such as the 1920s subdivision plans). These became opportunities in the 1950s and 1960s. The island resiliently reorganized around a faithful and well-off summer community (including Edison); a recovering lobster fishery with a renewed commitment to the closed season; a famously creative period for landscape art; growing tourism based partly on land protection, historic preservation of the built landscape, and the quiet lifestyle; and a modest rise in population (to about 50) as escapees from the mainstream purchased or rented homes and businesses and infused the island with new energy and skills.

- **Partnerships.** Beginning in the 1970s, Monhegan and "the state" were thrust into partnership on a number of issues: land use, water quality, waste disposal, the lobster season, and trap limits. The year-round community, appreciative of the gifts of healthy lands, unpolluted seas, and record lobster catches, nonetheless declined. But then the island aggressively sought homesteaders by providing guaranteed loans for affordable housing. Between 1980 and 1995, the population increased from the mid-30s to the upper-80s. Still, the island struggled to meet thresholds of survival. Questions about the impacts of day tourists on Monhegan's lifestyle and waste streams arose as well as concerns over the conversion of fish houses to summer rentals.

"Partnerships," the regime we found in the mid-1990s, possessed enough steadying elements to outweigh the destabilizing ones that threatened to cross thresholds and upset the system's integrity. We wrote that Monhegan was sustained by a land ethic, "a great deal of luck" in Edison's gift, and a good measure of indigenous wisdom about how to set limits and how, through thick and thin, to sustain the basic structure and functions of a year-round community.[21] As Monhegan heads into the eighth generation, let's see whether this is still the case.

Into the Eighth Generation

Monhegan in 2009 looks very much as it did in the mid-1990s. The village is roughly the same size (eight new houses have been built), there are not many more businesses, artists still love it here, people still stroll serenely through these charming landscapes, the protected wild-lands still cover two thirds of the island, and interaction between summer and winter residents still defines Monhegan civic and cultural life. Beyond this apparent tranquility, as tourists and residents assuredly realize, are changes moving at warp speed at scales and magnitudes well beyond the island: globalization; runaway materialism; real estate bubbles; air, land, and water pollution; and climate change. They haunt us all. And they are no less threatening to Monhegan's social and ecological arrangements. In fact, as an island, Monhegan feels these pressures more quickly, more intensely, and with less ability to deflect them than comparably sized places on the mainland with their large hinterlands. As never before, these changes challenge the island. While Monhegan can do little about globalization or climate change, it does have something to say about issues that wash up on its shores and it can tap into long-held ways of low-impact living and setting limits on the natural resources that ground its economy. This won't be easy, for in almost all instances the future of the year-round community and thus the well-being of the eighth generation is at stake.

Contending with Limits Again .

If I were to have updated the Monhegan story in 2002 or 2003, I surely would have had to write about boom times. Monhegan had been redis-covered again both by upper-income people seeking summer retreats and by ordinary folk like me who can drink up Monhegan on a low budget by visiting for a day or two. Lobster catches were at record highs and some residents would have undoubtedly been happy to let the good times roll. Other year-round residents worried about being priced out of the housing market and the implied loss of community. The stark edges of this island and its finite resources were sounding alarms and begging the community to make choices.

A heated controversy in the middle of 2002 illustrates how close Monhegan residents found themselves to the edge of at least one threshold — that of domestic wastewater disposal, otherwise known as sewage. Had the conflict been adjudicated in the age-old manner offstage, probably only a small core of island residents would have known all the details, though surely it would have been widely discussed and more than likely it would have rested on the "unspoken but very real ethic of cooperation that tempers competition."[22] But this controversy was anything but offstage. Because state permitting was required, it broke into public view and the Maine Land Use Regulatory Commission was asked to hold a public hearing on the permit they had already issued. In this airing of island laundry we get a somewhat rare look at what happens when island people believe limits are being approached and how dreadful it is to confront those limits by denying a neighbor his slice of the pie, let alone forsaking one's own slice.

The brouhaha broiled up over property. A vacant and somewhat derelict waterside restaurant was purchased by a 25-year resident known to all, somebody who also owned a bed and breakfast and served as an agent for other rentals. He applied for permits to restore the restaurant to seat 90, add modern bathrooms, and convert the former second-floor dormitory space into four apartments. As with many old island structures, sewage from this building went straight to the harbor and he proposed that it would continue to do so. A revised "overboard discharge license" (a risible euphemism to landlubbers) was required by the Department of Environmental Protection (DEP). This is what set people off. Flushing two toilets a few times a day (as in the past) was one matter; six toilets, two of which would be in a restaurant with a summer turnover of a couple of hundred customers daily, was quite another. The harbor was already at the end of too many outfall pipes, resident Alice Boynton told the Maine Environmental Policy Institute. She said that besides stinking and being unsightly, the filthy beach conditions near the harbor could cause impetigo. Others claimed you could see the sewage floating in the harbor and around the beaches. More discharge, 3,300 gallons per day in this case, would mean more "floating baubles of unknown origin," despoiling the water and beach further.[23]

In his defense, the applicant argued that reduced seating in the restaurant (from 140 to 90) would more than offset any increase in wastewater flow from the upstairs apartments. Moreover, he promised that low-flush toilets would be installed throughout the building. "If we did not have a restroom, most likely the majority of our customers would go to the public restroom or back to their rooms at the Trailing Yew, Island Inn, or their house along the shore, where they all flush to Monhegan harbor." He recommended island-wide attention to this problem: "I think a good starting point for the harbor and the island would be to get the overboard lines down to the low-water mark where the permits require them to be. If there is more concern, perhaps we should look into possibly stopping unlicensed overboard discharges and seasonal discharges that are being used year-round."[24]

In a letter to the Land Use Regulatory Commission, Peter Boehmer, then editor of *New Monhegan News,* wrote that "Monhegan's history, culture, and appeal are mostly based on lobstering. Monhegan fishermen won't take short lobsters or breeding females because while such would result in the immediate short term gain of the violator, it would do so at the cost to the fleet as a whole." In this case, he continued, "the applicants stand to profit from changing part of the restaurant to apartments. That gain will come at lessening the quality of life for many Monheganites. Sustainability and quality of life are at stake."[25] People protesting this new business were obviously arguing that the limits of the absorptive capacity of Monhegan's inshore waters for sewage had already been reached. More subtly, they pointed out that, though one person might gain his fair share of tourist revenues, all would suffer the externalities of a filthy harbor and public health risks.

What happened? Today on this property one finds The Inn at Fish and Maine. The inn is run by the very applicant in question, still the owner of a B&B down the shore and a rental business, still resident on the island. It comprises four rental apartments upstairs and an internet café on the ground floor. No continental breakfasts are served to apartment guests; there is no restaurant.

The dispute about overboard discharge of sewage has not been resolved. There is still no comprehensive plan to deal with it or with island sewage in general. Legally, according to the DEP, there is no "grandfathering" of old systems. Even on islands, everybody is supposed to treat domestic liquid wastes before discharging them into the ocean. But there's little enforcement on the few islands where this does not happen. Treatment systems are expensive. More innovative solutions such as ultraviolet light systems are off in the future. The same goes for land disposal. Septic systems, the legal standard for rural places in Maine, mostly don't work on Monhegan because of its hard-rock geology and lack of space for leach fields. Moreover, septic odors in the tightly packed village would be anything but ideal. And a treatment system for the whole village is not feasible for many reasons. The crux of the matter is another nagging obligation to set limits. Monhegan may need once again to draw on the long traditions of the self-limiting practices and disciplines in the lobster fishery.

Behind this is the bigger issue of how much tourism is too much. Until pump prices of gasoline hit $4 a gallon and diesel for boats rose to more than $5 a gallon and the economy began to falter in 2008, Monhegan's tourism numbers kept rising.[26] As we saw, a midsummer day "full house" can come to about 400 people in houses and cottages, 250 in hotels and B&Bs, and perhaps as many as 300 wandering about for a portion of the day.[27] A thousand or so people in and around the village is a sparse density compared to any city you can name, but people come here to escape the city and soak up the quiet life. So besides the pressure such numbers place on water and waste disposal, not to mention all other manner of supplies and services, there is the question of tourist density. Might Monhegan tourists at some point be repelled by too many encounters with other tourists?[28]

Another more subtle trend is that the average time spent by cottage guests has been decreasing. In comparison to rusticator days and even to 20 years ago when visitors would spend a month or more, there are more short-term cottage rentals over the course of the season and thus, with rapid turnover (stays now average about one week), more impacts per cottage, not to mention more transience and less sense of community in summer. What Peter Boehmer wrote 15 years ago rings true today.

> The present summer community has no sense of history. This has brought a different value system. If we're not careful, success will cause us to change this place to accommodate the tastes and meet the expectations of these short-termers. Then we'll no longer have something unique to show.[29]

Then there is the fresh water supply for the summer population. Recall that the sole source of water on the island is the aquifer below the bog at the center of town. "The Meadow is a godsend," a resident told me in August 1998, "but like everything here, it has its limits." Sure enough, on that visit I and my workshop participants experienced water rationing. At our guest house there was no water in the middle of the day. "Part of the Monhegan experience," our hostess said. In 2004, partly to address such summer shortages, the pumps and distribution lines were upgraded to improve the efficiency of the system, which supplies two to three million gallons over the season. Despite this, in dry summers the Meadow is hard pressed to meet current demand, so conservation is a watchword. If you are a guest in summer, you will be reminded not to waste water. Residents Sherm Stanley and Robert Bracey told the Maine Environmental Policy Institute that summer tourism "just puts more strain on the town's finite water source."[30] As sea levels rise, water conservation promises to be even more significant, for if the Meadow aquifer is continually overtapped, intrusion of salt water could permanently despoil Monhegan's water supply.[31]

Dumpsters filled to the brim at the town wharf illustrate yet another challenge for Monhegan in the midst of summer. Everything that can be recycled is, and guests are strongly advised on Monhegan's visitors' website to pack out their refuse and return it themselves to the mainland. As costs have risen for transportation and disposal of solid wastes and recyclables, it has become clear that "businesses strain the system." Recycling coordinator Angela Ianachelli maintains that "they should pay more or do their own." But that has not carried the day, so overall disposal is a still an expensive Plantation responsibility. Every kilo of recyclable and nonrecyclable waste is taken back to the mainland and the town budget in mid-decade was about $30,000 for disposal.

Few tourists come to Monhegan without spending time in the island's magnificent wildlands. What of tourist impacts here? How much to manage this tract has challenged Monhegan Associates since they wrote the bylaws in the 1950s, assuming the best management was no management. This doesn't work because reliance on a hands-off approach leaves perennially unanswered questions about what to do about downfalls, trail maintenance and signage, limiting trail users, fire prevention, and invasives. Recommendations made by the Maine Forest Service in 1987 for more intensive management of the forest and trails were largely ignored by Monhegan Associates,[32] and in 1991 the Associates denied a resident's request for an evaluation of the ecological condition of the wildlands.[33] In the late 1990s, the small but damaging non-native deer herd was exterminated after a prolonged battle. By 2005, pressures from tourists and the fear of forest fire had built to the point that Monhegan Associates commissioned studies to address management quandaries at the time: invasives, fire prevention, and trail use.

One of these studies concluded that the old-growth parts of the forest were in fine condition ecologically.[34] In fact, some long-lost understory plants were making a comeback thanks to the elimination of the deer herd. In second-growth forests invasives like Asiatic bittersweet, black swallowwort, Japanese knotweed, dwarf mistletoe, and Japanese barberry had become ecologically disruptive. As for the trail system, which you can still explore without cost or impediment, Monhegan Associates was concerned enough to ask the Maine Conservation Corps to perform a full assessment of its status. Completed in late 2005, the assessment identified hundreds of trail maintenance needs from installation of bog bridges and water bars to construction of steps and better signage to keep people from trammeling the forest off the trail.[35] The price tag for these enhancements came to $300,000 and most of this work is still to be done.

In its short season, tourism puts pressure on everything, including the patience of those who work in tourist businesses. In reflecting on its current status, Sherm Stanley, one of the most memorable and distinctive voices in our 1990s visit to Monhegan, summed things up pretty well in 2002: "There's no way to keep increasing the summer guests on Monhegan without having an adverse effect on this small ecosystem."[36] A committee looking into Monhegan's future in 2005 affirmed this. The 35,000 tourists who visit in a typical season and their impacts on ecology, economic development, and community life, they concluded, are one of the island's "most pressing concerns."[37] However, recognizing that many businesses depend on this traffic from the mainland, the committee tabled discussion on the matter because "no solutions appear to present themselves," implying a reluctant recognition that the island's economy can ill afford to squelch day tourism.

Through six-plus generations, the limited number of guest rooms and summer cottages for rent and the lack of developable land curtailed mass tourism. Rustic tourism of the early 20th century prevailed. Today's tourism seems to threaten the ambiance that has long attracted people to Monhegan as well as systems, like water and sewage disposal, everyone depends on. Whether some kind of midsummer mass tourism line has been crossed is certainly debatable and very controversial, for almost all residents have some stake in this. It's nothing like Martha's Vineyard, where mass tourism has irreparably changed the island, but hundreds of people arriving on this very small piece of land each summer day surely do push the envelope. And so residents are beginning to wonder whether the goose that laid the golden egg might already be in the pot.

Which brings us finally to lobstering, the exemplar of restraint and respite, to use the language of University of Michigan scholar Thomas Princen, who offers a fine analysis of these intergenerational disciplines.[38] He writes that restraint and respite show up in very concrete ways: the off-season all fishers comply with, the insistence on old ways of trapping rather than more sophisticated methods, the limited number of boats fishing out of Monhegan, the practice of throwing back gravid and oversized lobsters during season (sometimes 90 percent of all trapped), and the agreed-upon trap limits per fisher. Rather than maximizing particular variables or being driven by greed or externalizing ecological costs, these elements sustain an economy grounded in "long-term ecological and social interaction." This would be a model, he believes, for the planetary economy of the future.

Though lobstering maintains its piece of Monhegan's economy, its practices have been challenged, to say the least, in the past 15 years. The most acrimonious assault ever on Monhegan lobstering began in November 1995, when five fully licensed fishers from the mainland village of Friendship "invaded" Monhegan's fishing grounds in its off-season and defied the island and the state to respond. The ensuing struggle, comprehensively covered by Princen, ended well for Monhegan in 1998, with the state upholding Monhegan's selective exclusion of other fishers from the 30 square mile Monhegan Conservation Area throughout the year (Fig. 4-1). What came out of this controversy, Princen writes, is that, in the eyes of the state, indigenous knowledge and practice achieved peer status with formal institutions, laws, and regulations in the management of fisheries.[39] What also came out of it is a vendetta that may take a generation to settle. According to Princen and to stories Paul Croce heard in 2007, a Monhegan lobsterman's boat was sunk in 2003 while docked at Port Clyde and his brother was beaten there on another occasion.[40]

Nonetheless, the off-season and home territory of Monhegan lobstering have held during these ten years. Had the supply of lobsters remained constant, we could end the story here. But the boom times of the early part of this decade (2003 was the peak) suddenly tanked, threatening Maine's $253 million lobster industry.[41] The Maine catch dropped 40 percent from 2003 to 2007, the sharpest decline in 50 years. Monhegan traps yielded so poorly that some fishers were at the point of bankruptcy. What caused this downcycle is still a mystery. Conjecture at this point includes overfishing (the Maine industry alone added a million new traps between 2003 and 2007), more deep water fishing of large lobsters (key brood stock for inshore fisheries), inexplicable but previously experienced natural cycles, and perhaps as yet unknown habitat changes associated with climate change.[42] Whatever the explanation, Diane Cowan of the Lobster Conservancy observes that setting limits like those of Monhegan should long ago have been standard throughout the fishery. "We should have been making the tough choices, putting lobsters in the bank. We don't want to fish on the edge of disaster."[43]

After four seasons of teetering on the brink economically, Monhegan fishers went back to the state in 2007 and requested an extension of their season from six to eight months, moving trap day to October 1st or thereabouts instead of December 1st. This would seem counter to the island's history of self-regulation were it not for a self-imposed agreement by Monhegan fishers to halve the maximum number of traps per boat. That accomplished, Maine fisheries biologist Carl Wilson, in cooperation with Monhegan fishers, designed an experiment to test the impact of this decision. The results surprised even the skeptics. The catch in 2007-2008 increased by 38 percent compared to the median of the previous three years. In the same period, numbers for the entire Maine coast were down 30 percent. This can only be explained by the scientifically long-known fact that over-harvesting lobsters ultimately consumes the "seed corn," the mature egg-bearing females and their mates.[44]

Wilson has taken his results on the road to Fisherman's Forums along the Maine coast, his subtext being "work smarter rather than harder." Using Monhegan data, he can now argue that fewer traps can result in at least equal harvests and a lot less money expended on equipment, fuel, and labor, not to mention the toll on the humans hauling up the traps. He says he is getting a good hearing but admits that it's always a tough sell when experiments challenge long-standing traditions. He hopes the story of Monhegan, where less became more, will lead to a more sustainable Maine lobster industry, especially as the 2008 harvest overall continued to decline.[45]

Resilience Thinking

Everything in this update so far assumes residents prefer "business as usual" with perhaps some tweaking here or there in tourism and lobster fishing. By this scenario, the resource-based economy is a given, though undoubtedly choices lie ahead, whether in finding alternatives to sewage discharge, limiting access to the wildlands, conserving water, or setting new limits on lobstering. And there's no guarantee the age-old dynamic of letting the edges of the island limit island decisions will succeed in a world that punishes communities for doing so. Even if you idealize this dynamic as one that leads to "sustainable" choices, you have to realize these systems have always been based on imperfect calculations about the future in the face of temptations to cash in on the present. The future is precarious.

Yet if we frame the story of this island as a tale of a dynamic system, perhaps a less precarious set of scenarios can be imagined to draw Monhegan back from threatening thresholds and to make it resilient enough to thrive even if lobster fishing and tourism tail off. This kind of resilience would offer new pathways to maintain the island and its ecological services for the long run.[46] Many Monhegan residents already know this experientially.

Sustaining the Winter Community

Foremost in the mind of virtually every Monhegan resident we've interviewed is sustaining a year-round community. To do this in 2010 will require fresh thinking. Compared to other populated islands in Maine, Monhegan possesses sufficient community infrastructure to keep it occupied year round, though it may be close to the minimum population threshold.[47] Projections from the Maine State Planning Office are not reassuring. They show Monhegan's population dropping below 60 by 2030.[48] But so far, so good. Two stores and the post office are open year round, Monhegan School chugs along (there were eight students, ranging from preschool to grade seven in 2007-2008), centrally generated electric power is sufficient for winter residents, ferry and mail boat service continues three times a week in winter, and an array of community organizations meet year round. On the other hand, the 19-year emergency medical service folded in 2007 and the mean age of the population is higher than that of most islands, emphasizing the difficulty of attracting younger residents.[49]

Among other things, sustaining a year-round population requires affordable housing. Thirty-year resident Doug Boynton believes this could be the critical variable that determines whether the island crosses the threshold nobody wants — a time when everything is shut down in winter. Here's the problem: rampant property inflation driven by the same forces that sent prices soaring elsewhere. With unwinterized basic cottages selling for a half-million, there are no starter homes for younger people. Those who already have a house are getting killed by rising taxes. Maine coastal property values, especially on islands with their limited land and unlimited mystique, are at an all-time high. Exorbitant mortgages and taxes convince year-round islanders they have no choice but to move to the mainland.[50]

On Monhegan, housing prices doubled between 2000 and 2007.[51] If these trends were to continue, properties would sell only to wealthy people interested in summer residence and people who want to live and work here year round would be outbid and squeezed out. Then who would maintain the island over the winter? "People year round are the stewards of this place," said one resident. Summer residents may take this for granted. But it cannot be taken lightly and may, in fact, be a threshold, as Boynton warns. After all, winter people nurture and maintain the setting that summer people enjoy. Without such nurturance, Monhegan's infrastructure would quickly crumble, as would its ambiance as a working port with a seven-generation history.

Here's resilience thinking, typical of the island's tradition of seeking prudent solutions that won't be catastrophic for their fragile tomorrows. In 2002, Monhegan residents formed the Monhegan Island Sustainable Community Association (MISCA), a land trust that seeks "to preserve the year-round culture ... by purchasing existing residential property on the Island and making it available to year-round Island residents at below-market prices in perpetuity."[52] MISCA draws on a tradition of lobster fishers giving preference to other fishers when selling their homes, a tradition seriously strained by the current cost of real estate. To drive home this point, counting on his fingers and naming each, a lobsterman said that between 2002 and 2007 five former lobster fishers' homes sold to summer purchasers at "astronomical prices."[53] If lobster fishers cannot live here in winter, what then? Half the island's income goes south.

MISCA will purchase existing housing rather than promote new development. As one of 11 such groups on Maine islands, MISCA raises funds to purchase properties. Then it sells them at prices indexed to the median family income for the nearest mainland county to people who sign a covenant to spend at least ten months annually on island, sell their houses to people who intend to reside on the island, and price them according to the same index. The owner buys the home and outbuildings; MISCA retains the land deed and holds the covenant. This almost surely means the new owner's investment will appreciate, but not at the rate the market has recently been generating.

Assuming MISCA's pool of properties accumulates, the scheme will ensure an affordable housing supply in perpetuity. More than a million dollars had been donated to turn around properties by the end of 2007 and MISCA properties housed 14 percent of the year-round community. MISCA also bought and partially renovated the old Monhegan Store, which houses a new business, the post office, a laundry, and two apartments, all crucial to the winter economy, and they brokered a lot-size rule change with the Maine Land Use Regulatory Commission to allow construction of a new house on land adjacent to a MISCA property. MISCA offers fresh thinking about the principle of sufficiency. Instead of letting the market rule, covenants are crafted to achieve the higher goal of a sustained year-round community.

Diversifying the Economy

With the lobster economy uncertain and tourism facing volatile oil prices and conversations about limits, diversifying the economy may be a way of bolstering year-round Monhegan. High though it may be, the cost of living could be relatively affordable for residents who come from pricier markets and intend to stay put on Monhegan and earn their living in the information economy. Because Monhegan has reliable broadband, a new possibility for diversifying the island economy presents itself. This is not fantasy. Take the Cash-Shea family. Chris Cash, a lobster captain, also works for a nonprofit organization that coordinates outreach initiatives for the National Science Foundation (NSF) in Washington, D.C. When working for NSF, she does not have to commute daily. Rich Shea, her husband, manages imports digitally for a Dutch firm. They live in a MISCA house and are fully engaged in Monhegan civic life.

Ted Edison may not have understood their lifestyle as "simple" or "friendly," but this is not 1954, when he helped craft the Monhegan Associates vision statement. In fact it may well be 21st century simplicity: no commutes, no automobiles, no costly accoutrements of corporate or public sector jobs, and quality time at home with family. Improbably perhaps, a Maine couple on an island way out to sea with a forbidding winter earns part of their keep without ever leaving home and so can live in the place that really grabs their hearts. In cobbling together jobs in the information economy, Chris Cash and Rich Shea are perhaps the year-round residents of the future. If their ways are picked up by others, they could stretch and diversify the economy and even reduce Monhegan's carbon footprint. For their part, they say what they've done is not extraordinary. Other long-term residents are skeptical about depending on an uncertain global economy. In classic Maine terms, they don't deny that "techno things" are gradually entering the scene and that there are opportunities in the wider economy, but they doubt such dependence will ever really sustain new folk. In light of the current global financial meltdown, they may be right.

Stretching the Tourist Season

As a stop along the Atlantic flyway, Monhegan is a birder's paradise with robust and diverse populations of pelagic and passerine birds, raptors, and waterfowl. On land, more than 110 species either reside on or pass thorough Monhegan on their routes north and south. Along Monhegan's shore, puffins, ducks, eiders, gulls, and terns live in great numbers. This diversity of birdlife has been part of Monhegan's charm for more than a generation but not until recently was it extolled to "birder" tourists — a niche also finding its way to Virginia's Eastern Shore (Chapter 5).

Bird watching is now a Monhegan attraction and it has extended the tourist season to October, when the fall migration passes over the island. Monhegan House, for example, stays open until October 5th and offers this on its website: "The island is known as a premier birding location for the many rare and unusual birds spotted during the spring and fall migrations."[54] Tours organized by Audubon, Wings, Elderhostel, and other organizations bring tourists from all over North America. Offshore, nature cruises cater not only to bird watchers, by taking them around the island's edges and to colonial nesting sites on surrounding unpopulated islands and ledges, but also to visitors who want to see harbor seals up close at their coastal haul-outs and watch whales in deeper waters. Such tourists are avidly recruited because they come off season and are environmentally responsible, low-impact visitors. Kristin Lindquist of the Maine Coastal Mountain Trust in Camden, writing in *Down East Magazine,* argued that Monhegan during the spring and fall migrations is every bit as rewarding a birding experience as places much more heralded. "Every time I step off the boat onto Monhegan, binoculars in hand, I know I have to be ready for anything. If you're not yet as crazed a birder as I am, one visit to Monhegan might be all it takes!"[55]

These three possibilities are not the only ones we collected. Creative and entrepreneurial people also talk of bringing alternative energy to the island to reduce costs and dependence on the diesel powered generator, of increasing workshops and conferences to even out the tourist season, and of conducting more educational tours of the wildlands aimed at specific market segments similar to the birding business. The arts are focused on a small number of galleries and a few summer events. More could be done to highlight Mohegan's distinguished arts history. Low-impact recreational tourism such as sailing and kayaking are other, though more controversial, options. The future, these resilient thinkers argue, need not be buffeted by forces over which Monhegan has no control. Philip Conkling of the Island Institute believes Monhegan equal to these challenges, though he recognizes it is tiring to be on the ground in the midst of intense forces of change happening well beyond the island.[56]

LEAVING MONHEGAN

In *The Ecology of Hope* we recorded visions Monhegan residents seemed to have about their lives and their future (Table 4-1). We inferred that these presented a modest though generalized scaffold on which to continue to build a sustainable community. Many if not all of these visions inherently expressed an understanding of limits. Staving off inappropriate development, sustaining community, fostering the lobster fishery, and protecting the human and natural environment all

TABLE 4-1

Mid-1990s Visions of Monhegan

The quiet island lifestyle is an essential part of Monhegan's future.
Keeping Monhegan the way it is for as long as possible will retain this lifestyle and its appeal to artists and other visitors.
Sustaining a winter community and all that goes with it is vitally important.
A healthy lobster fishery is crucial to our future as a year-round community.
The quality of the island environment, natural and human, is unique and fragile.
The quality of the natural environment affects everyone and is at the heart of all facets of our economy.

Source: Ted Bernard and Jora Young. *The Ecology of Hope*. New Society Publishers, 1997, 45.

speak strongly to a conservation ethic that recognizes the dimensions and capacities of this small speck of land and its surrounding waters. With the passage of more than a decade, I wondered whether Monhegan residents would still hold such visions dear and what else might be on people's minds and in their hearts.

In 2005, a visioning committee appointed by Monhegan Associates was asked to look into Monhegan's future. To get started they decided first to labor over a set of values. When they put these out for discussion, they told the community they had worked hard to come up with the appropriate language. Here it is:

> We believe that our support could be an important contribution towards preservation of some character- istics of island life, such as peace, safety, simplicity, and sense of community. We feel that we should work to sustain the environmental balance of the island with the least intervention practicable.
>
> We believe we need to work together to help to preserve the ecosystem of the entire island — its natural habitat as well as that of the town, and keep it safe, its air, water, and soil unpolluted, and its commercial devel- opment limited; and to support the efforts of the Plantation for sensible land use.
>
> We believe we need to honor and support the tradition of creative, independent, and entrepreneurial spirit in the Monhegan community.[57]

These few propositions, it seems to me, reflect the eighth genera-tion's view of what it will take to keep this island system on track to sustain the good life. They are not so different from those we found in the mid-1990s. They perhaps portend the next stability domain for the island — the domain of resilience. Hence they are imbued with hope.

When you leave Monhegan, you're hammered by the fast pace of change on the mainland with its commercial and residential sprawl, wasteful consumption, corrupted air and water, dysfunctional gover-nance, and social systems breakdown. None of this is lost on Monhegan residents, nor on their children who via television, the internet, and visits to the mainland are only too aware of the alternative frenzy. As I look back from the departing boat 15 years later, I still see a place that seems to have taken a deep breath sometime in the 20th century and decided to resist the forces that unravel community and its ecological services and to figure out ways to cope with the world of the 21st century without losing the integrity and good health of their home. Certainly there are elements of the modern world — satellite dishes, electronic gadgetry, fast Internet speeds, a modern phone system, electric power generated by diesel. No one would deny that these conveniences bespeak necessary adaptations to the 21st century. But in the eyes of that visioning committee, the gentle pulse of life, the limited commercialization, the native ecosystem, the town ecosystem, the sustaining land- and sea-based economic activities, and the inde-pendent, entrepreneurial, and creative spirit are what really matter. Then there is the midsummer fragrance of hollyhocks, conifers, wild blueberries, and sea air.

At the chapter head, Mabberly writes that almost everything can be seen as an island and in a certain sense I agree.[58] I also think, as Richard Nelson does, that islands are full of mystery and incomprehension.[59] What Monhegan reveals can conceivably be scaled up or repeated in locally adapted ways and possibly foreshadows the future. As I leave Monhegan, I think again that this is a seductive frame for this story. But then I hear the whisper of an old Monhegan salt a decade ago: "People come to this island thinking we are some sort of a legendary model. Well, we're not. We just do the best we can in our old ways."[60] Maybe "our old ways" with their limits and adaptability and self-reliance make for a pretty resilient model after all.

5

Ever Vulnerable:
The Eastern Shore of Virginia[1]

The developers and the conservationists are like elephants
fighting while lots of little people are hurt in the scuffle.[2]

~ Alice Coles

WHAT DO YOU GET WHEN YOU MIX A PENINSULA of pristine barrier islands and beaches on the seaside, significantly polluted waters on the bayside, aquaculture and agriculture in contention, and pressures to ramp up tourism of the kind you see from Miami to Maine? You get right into the battle between sustainable and unsustainable development at the tip of the Delmarva Peninsula. Like Chattanooga (Chapter 10), the Eastern Shore of Virginia was a Clinton-era poster child of sustainable development. And like Chattanooga, it has faced a history of tensions about the right balance among the economic, environmental, and social aspects of sustainability. As with many of our other stories, Virginia's Eastern Shore displays a mix of elements that juxtapose the best and the worst of community struggles toward sustainability. Now facing both the threat of more intensive development spilling across the bridge from urban Tidewater and environmental surprises associated with global warming, the Eastern Shore might see its 30-year journey toward sustainability derailed, or it might strike off in hopeful new directions.

LAND BETWEEN TWO WATERS
Two counties — Accomack and Northampton — are Virginia's only turf on this slender landmass between the Atlantic and Chesapeake Bay (Figure 5-1). For a place only 261 miles from New York, 186 miles from

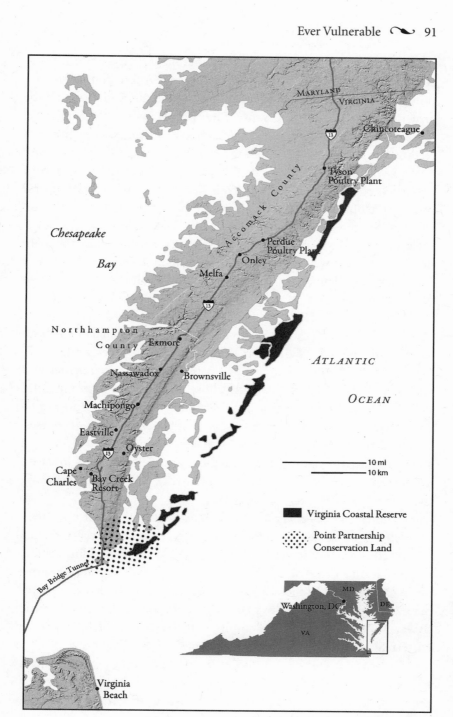

FIGURE 5-1
Virginia's Eastern Shore

Philadelphia, and 127 miles from Washington, D.C., the Eastern Shore is sparsely populated with about 51,400 people.[3] Although this population grew by about 5 percent between 1995 and 2005, virtually all the growth was in Accomack County. The two counties, in fact, differ in their attitudes toward growth. Accomack welcomes it and has grown in response to the poultry processing industry and expansion of NASA's research facility at Wallops Island. Accomack has the reputation of being more business friendly and less keen on restrictive zoning and other development restraints. Northampton has had virtually no population growth in the past decade and holds tenuously to protecting open space and limiting unsavory sprawl, especially along the main north-south highway, US Route 13. The main exception is the new 1,700-acre development of the peninsula's first golf resort in the town of Cape Charles.

Historically, truck farming and fishing dominated the economy and imprinted the landscape. Small 18th century villages dot both seaside and bayside. Farms on the order of 200 acres or less still predominate up and down the peninsula. Pristine salt marshes and barrier islands buffer the Atlantic shore and provide spawning and nursery habitat for fish and shellfish. Cropped fields and pastures, open space, and locally owned businesses, rather than dozens of golf courses, hundreds of beach condos, and strip malls with big-box retailers, tell a story of relative isolation and miraculous escape from mass tourism. The Eastern Shore is still a bucolic throwback of the rarest kind along the intensely developed Atlantic coast.

Although forests cover less than 25 percent of the landscape, they are picturesque backdrops to towns and cropped fields as well as crucial to protecting groundwater, breaking seaside winds, and providing resting, nesting, and roosting places for 250 species of resident and migratory birds. On the seaside, there is pristine habitat for waterfowl and shorebirds, especially during the biannual migrations along the Atlantic flyway. With the highest bird counts in the eastern United States, the Eastern Shore is a key stopover along a coast with precious few.

The seaside ecosystem is also of global significance with its intact barrier islands, 60 miles of sandy beaches and dunes largely unbroken by human structures and occupancy, and thousands of acres of salt marsh, coastal creeks, shallow bays, sea grasses, and lagoons. One of the last "coastal wildernesses" on the eastern seaboard, the Eastern Shore was designated a UN biosphere reserve in 1979. As such, it is also a working landscape. Before European settlers with their African American slaves arrived in the 17th century, Native peoples lived compatibly with this food-rich habitat. They burned, hunted, collected, farmed, and fished. The new settlers, by and large, followed suit and understood their own need for a clean environment to farm and fish. As one of our friends wrote in the 1990s, "If you intend to eat oysters from the marsh, you don't dump your chamber pot there."[4]

Farming is still the leading economic activity, with commercial tomato and melon operations, grain, livestock, and poultry grossing $225 million annually (2004), slightly more than one fifth of the total Eastern Shore's income. Tourism, the second major piece of the economy, brought in $178 million in 2004.[5] Fishing, once second to agriculture, continues to decline. Watermen who used to work out of dozens of small villages are now a dying breed as finfish and crab catches have absolutely tanked because of pollution, disease, and unsustainable fishing pressures. Fisheries are now at the point of commercial extinction, according to Citizens for a Better Eastern Shore.[6] On the other hand, commercial aquaculture for clams grosses about $50 million annually and is growing at 5 percent a year.[7]

For tourists, the charm of the Eastern Shore is a trip back in time through "small towns, along laid back country roads," with a background sun sinking "in a watercolor bay."[8] "Escape the crowds — escape to the Eastern Shore" is the tourist pitch that brings hundreds of thousands of visitors to the shore annually. The downside of this quaint image is a lack of opportunity and well-paying jobs, with persistent poverty. Compared to the mid-1990s, there are more jobs and less unemployment.[9] But the numbers are deceiving.[10] Two poultry processing plants are the biggest employers with about 3,000 jobs. Most of these pay minimum wages. An average poultry worker earns just $20,400 with virtually no benefits. The same is true for other major job categories. Vegetable and melon farming and poultry operations, which employ about 1,200 workers, pay median annual wages of just $18,500. Tourism employment for both counties is about 2,500, with a median income per employee of $10,400. For all categories of employment, including some 3,000 professionals in education, health care, government, and research, the median income in 2004 in Northampton

County was $31,847 and in Accomack County, $31,256, as compared to $51,103 for the entire state of Virginia.[11]

Overall, Accomack and Northampton counties are no longer the poorest in Virginia as they were in the 1990s, but they still rank in the lower quartile. Staying above the federally defined poverty level for a family of four in 2008 required at least $21,201.[12] Given that the main opportunities for work pay less than this on average, it is not surprising that both counties have much higher proportions of families living in poverty than the Virginia average. Accomack County is 83rd of 95 counties, with almost 25 percent of families falling below the poverty line; Northampton is 89th, with slightly more than 27 percent of families living in poverty. The state median is just over 9 percent.[13] As I survey these statistics, I see that this modest uptick in employment relates less to the sustainability efforts of the 1990s than to conventional economic development, especially in Accomack.

LATE 20TH CENTURY CRISES

Unlike Virginia Beach across the bay southward or Ocean City northward across the Maryland border, discount malls and parking lots have not inundated Eastern Shore dunes, marinas have not channelized creeks and estuaries, high-rise condos do not block views, and the wrecking ball has not obliterated all historic architecture. Despite a convergence of forces that could have converted the Eastern Shore to a mecca of mass tourism, so far this has not happened. We traced the history of these forces up to the mid-1990s in *The Ecology of Hope*. Here we need just a brief recounting to set the scene.

The story begins in 1967 with completion of the 17-mile Chesapeake Bay Bridge-Tunnel connecting Norfolk with the southern tip of the peninsula. At the time, it seemed as if droves of speculators would descend upon the Shore, even as the US National Park Service declared that "the best remaining seashore recreational opportunities in America" are right here.[14] A group of New York investors jumped on this. They purchased hundreds of acres of shoreland on three barrier islands at the tip of the peninsula, envisioning beach residences, shopping malls, a golf course, airport, clubs, hotels, and office buildings. The Eastern Shore was poised for a Hilton Head kind of boom.

Enter The Nature Conservancy (TNC), which had long had their eye on this pristine shoreline. With help from private foundations, they purchased and were given or bequeathed not only the three islands slated for development but also all or part of nine other islands northward. This string of purchases ultimately became the 38,000-acre Virginia Coast Reserve. Eastern Shore writer Curtis Badger predicted that this reserve would "give us a clue to the vastness of the great mid-Atlantic salt marshes before the bulldozers filled them and the developers paved them."[15] Indeed it did. With this grand gesture, The Nature Conservancy markedly altered the course of Eastern Shore development. Yet some residents in "the real economy" were not impressed, which surely reminds me of the Malpai story (Chapter 7). "TNC became the proverbial 600 pound gorilla, exerting an enormous influence on the Shore and especially on Northampton County .... [They] focused more on land acquisition and preservation than [on] any real or diverse economic opportunities and livable wage employment," remembers a county executive.[16]

By the 1980s, in fact, the everyday economy was seriously hurting. Farmers and watermen struggled to make a living. Land-rich, cash-poor farmers could no longer compete with Midwestern and Western agricultural regions. And if times were bad for farmers, they were even worse for watermen. Overfishing, disease, and pollution led to catastrophic declines in their catches. In 1989, a virus took down virtually every crab on the seaside. Fishing income had dropped from a third of total revenues along the Shore in the late 1960s to about 6 percent in the late 1980s. By the early 1990s, the Eastern Shore began to show up as one of Virginia's poorest regions, with significant parts of the population, especially African Americans, living in substandard housing and having little or no income. Incredibly, 12 percent of the houses in Northampton County in 1990 had no indoor plumbing. Unemployment in 1994 stood at 9.3 percent. Some 15 to 20 percent of African American males were jobless.[17]

Such were the tough times we encountered on our first visit in 1994. On the one hand, there was TNC, a respected national conservation organization providing a sophisticated, science-based level of protection to the seaside sufficient for it to become the core of a UN biosphere reserve. On the other hand, there was an economy straining under burdens of farm and fishing failures, a seriously polluted bayside, and significant numbers of desperately poor mainly black people with few opportunities to rise out of poverty. Just as we arrived, these two worlds converged.

A recreation plan in the mid-1980s set the tone for an array of initiatives to capitalize on the remoteness and ecological integrity of the Shore. The plan required collaboration among TNC (the largest landholder on the Shore), state and federal agencies, and local businesses and community organizations. Their focus was low-impact recreation and ecotourism. In 1991, TNC, Citizens for a Better Eastern Shore, and the Northampton County chapter of the NAACP formed an economic forum that met for more than a year, putting aside differences and collaborating on a development plan that would uplift the Shore's economy without threatening its roots. It was the first time representatives from all sectors of the economy and all segments of society had ever collaborated on such a scale. Their 1992 *Blueprint for Economic Growth* focused on retaining the unique sense of place, protecting and wisely using its environmental assets, building civil society, and uplifting people as well as on business and industry.

In 1993, with leadership from Northampton County's board of supervisors and county administrator Tom Harris, the region got grants to translate their plans into a sustainable development action strategy that, unlike the *Blueprint,* proposed to depart from conventional economic development to pursue sustainable development. Public visioning sessions, workshops, and consultants helped a task force refine the strategy and insert it into Northampton County's plans for the future.[18] That same year Tim Hayes was appointed director of sustainable development. He went right to work bringing competing interests together with the aim of making sustainability and sustainable development household words. Hayes told Eastern Shore people, "We've just got to figure out how to live off the bountiful dividends on this peninsula without drawing down the principal."[19]

In 1994, I attended a workshop on green commerce led by Paul Hawken. More than 200 residents were there, including elected officials and staff of both counties. They appeared to be highly animated by the prospects Hawken awakened. They could see how these could be applied to the Shore and they came up with dozens of new sustainability ideas. That convinced me that these people "got it" — got the connection between a healthy environment and a healthy economy. In August 1994 the Sustainable Development Action Strategy received the Presidential Leadership Award from the National Association of Counties.

With grant funding through 1997 and high profile visits by officials of the Clinton administration including Vice President Gore, they began putting plans on the ground. These included a Sustainable Technologies Industrial Park; an Eastern Shore Heritage Trail; proposed zoning ordinances to preserve compact villages and towns; protection of water quality; a birding festival; expansion of the aquaculture industry; niche marketing of produce and seafood; and a heritage crafts collective. The Nature Conservancy, meanwhile, looked on from the periphery and continued their long-term ecological research on the Virginia Coast Reserve and surrounding waters, capitalized the Virginia Eastern Shore Corporation to develop and market products of the Eastern Shore, partnered with the Virginia Eastern Shore Economic Empowerment and Housing Corporation to upgrade and add to housing stock for those with lower incomes, and offered conservation easements to protect seaside farms and open the Shore to commercial shellfish farming. John Hall, then Virginia Coast Reserve director, said "The challenge ... will be to distinguish activity from progress, to balance excitement and terror, and to prevent the community from getting disillusioned." Thinking about all these initiatives, he concluded, "We need a bunch of small successes."[20] For his part, Northampton County's sustainable development director Hayes said, "Sustainable development is understood to be our future. We have a consensus to go forward."[21]

After my second stint on the Eastern Shore in the mid-1990s, I remember thinking that this place might provide a window on a more sustainable future for seaside places in North America. County administrator Tom Harris had just told me, "What we've got here is very hopeful." And Hall, TNC director, firmly believed that "this place has a chance to get it right." I took this back to my co-author and together we wrote that Eastern Shore collaboration and sustainability initiatives amounted to a resilient and hopeful blend of light-touch economic development, ecological conservation, and attention to the downtrodden. It seemed a storybook example of communities collaborating toward sustainability.

THE SHORE THESE DAYS

That was then. By 2008, the Sustainable Development Action Strategy was a piece of ancient history that had been "hijacked by folks who sought grants for something else," a focus group told Paul Croce.[22] The focus group was comprised of members of Citizens for a Better Eastern Shore, a 20-year-old nonprofit described by an outsider as "the Shore's landed gentry" or "the haves." In their view a piece of that "something else" was the Sustainable Technologies Industrial Park (STIP), a high profile project meant to be the crown jewel of the imagined sustainable economy.[23] In the view of the county administrator at the time, STIP was a critical piece of the Sustainable Development Action Strategy, which itself was clearly focused on economic opportunity, social equity, and environmental stewardship. In the fullness of time, and in spite of the initial influx of a half-dozen sustainable businesses, by 2003 STIP appeared to have failed. Despite investment of more than $9 million, the park never sustained more than two tenants. It was sold to a private developer in 2004 for more money acre-for-acre than the county originally paid for it, but in almost a decade of trying, it had attracted very few jobs.[24]

Sara Nosanchuk's analysis of why STIP faltered concluded that the rush by county leaders to capture grant monies was partly to blame. Some of STIP's problems could have been averted, she wrote, had "the leaders of the collaborative decision making process let the community shape the direction of the Action Plan rather than steer the community in the direction of the STIP without complete buy-in."[25] On the other hand, she believes STIP was a success in creating and implementing a new model for the economy with ecological integrity at its heart. The model unfortunately did not take, or perhaps was deliberately undermined by opponents.[26] Like many county industrial parks across the US, it now sits virtually empty.

As for The Nature Conservancy's efforts in "sustainable development," the Virginia Eastern Shore Corporation, their initiative to create and market Eastern Shore products and services, also folded, having burned through 86 percent of its initial capital in the first two years of its life (1997-1999).[27] Among its notable missteps were Hayman Potato Chips, which made sweet-potato chips but could not source enough sweet potatoes for profitability; ecofriendly seaside farms and waterfront homes aimed at the hyper-rich; and a $3.5 million restoration of Cobb's Island Station as an upscale inn to anchor high-end tourism. Although Cobb's Island Station was never operated as an inn, it was sold to a nonprofit organization for $4.1 million with a protective conservation easement. The Ford Foundation, a funder of some of these ventures, was pointed in its critique. It wrote that the concept, business plan, and execution of the Eastern Shore Corporation were all seriously flawed.[28]

On a trip back to the Shore in 2009, I could almost hear reverberations of these popping balloons as well as a "great sucking sound," to use Ross Perot's image, as sustainabililty champions rushed to other places. Gone were many of the visionaries of the 1980s and 1990s: people like Hayes, Harris, Hall, and Hall's TNC boss, Greg Low. Nor had Paul Hawken, William McDonough, and other cutting-edge thinkers ever come back. Some collaborative operatives were still around but had disengaged or had become disillusioned by factionalism: people like Jane Cabarrus and Alice Coles, activists in the African American community, and Phil Custis, a farmer we interviewed in the 1990s. Among these, Custis is most pessimistic about keeping unsavory development off the Shore. "Real estate speculation and local politics are a real mess." he asserted. "Back in the nineties, we who wanted to protect this open space were the dog and pony show for the sustainability crowd. But we were never fed. They got all the funding."[29]

Citizens for a Better Eastern Shore (CBES), a group with a few dozen members in the 1980s, now claims 1,000 members. It is populated by civically active residents, retirees, and others who seem to be partly a local government watchdog and partly a collection of advocates for protecting the quaintness of Eastern Shore landscapes, lifeways, and property values. "Sustainability language isn't much used these days," CBES spokesperson Denard Spady said. A CBES critic believes that the group gives lip service to low-impact tourism, which does not impact the property values of its membership and provides only minimum wage hospitality jobs for the "have nots."[30]

What seemed a remarkably pervasive, broad-based collaborative spirit to provide a pathway to sustainabililty and make decisions with that vision at the center has at best splintered. "There were really too many planning processes, driven by government requirements and mandates," wrote 1990s Northampton County administrator Tom Harris. "It would have been better to have brought the various plans under the umbrella of the Sustainable Development Action Strategy ... but by 2003, the political will for the Strategy also seemed to dissipate."[31] Collaboration, so crucial to successful pursuit of sustainability, seems to have seriously broken down. Meanwhile, opportunities for the rising generation have not improved. "There are more jobs, yes. But good opportunities for young black and white kids with education are few and they are leaving this place in droves," developer Bill Parr told Paul Croce.[32] "There are no demographic indicators that show hope for the bottom of society," he said.

Does this mean sustainability is passé here? Or do the principles live on, though the word itself is toxic? The only way to answer these questions, which of course are pertinent to many of the stories in this book, is to chronicle the details of what's happened in the past decade or so. In doing this, I have come to see a region that clearly struggles, issue by issue, to nurture and protect its historic landscapes and economies; to help those at the bottom of the heap; to grasp opportunities in low-impact tourism and other noninvasive economic activities; and to fend off development that could topple its efforts to sustain environmental quality and level the playing field for the least advantaged residents.

Beaches, Islands, Marshes, Fields, and Woodlands

Singer James Taylor, of "Fire and Rain" fame, launched his summer 2008 tour in Virginia Beach with a benefit concert for migratory songbirds. Migratory songbirds? Yes, believe it or not, they've got a friend in James Taylor, a staple on the concert tour since the 1960s. On that June night, he drew a huge audience of boomers who helped him raise $200,000 for the Southern Tip Partnership across the bridge in Northampton County. The Partnership aims to protect stopover habitat for passerine birds and waterfowl as they fly north in spring and south in fall and also to attract tourists who like to keep bird lists. The partnership came into being in 2006 when TNC and four state and federal agencies signed a memorandum of understanding to acquire, protect, and restore migratory bird habitat on the Shore. Together they now hold and manage some 24,000 acres around the Bay Bridge's Eastern Shore terminus. This has been a universally popular collaboration. In 2008 the Partnership received the Virginia Governor's Gold Environmental Excellence Award.

Even farmers have bought into it. Thomas H. Dixon, a landowner who sold his 82-acre farm to TNC in 2005 to become part of the Southern Tip, said, "This is one of the most important environmental and economic projects on the Eastern Shore." It is also an economic boon, in his judgment, "because of the increasing number of birders coming to the shore as tourists."[33] Virginia Coast Reserve director Steve Parker, who has brokered TNC's role, believes the Southern Tip Partnership is a significant piece of the peninsula's low-impact tourism strategy. He told me that "this is the number one tourism initiative now on the Shore and it is helping us convince other farmers to protect bird habitat on their lands."[34]

Compared to the needs for stopover habitat along the Atlantic flyway, the relatively miniscule amount of land protected on the Eastern Shore might be dismissed if the plights of migratory songbirds and some species of waterfowl were not so dire. As a piece of TNC's role in regional environmental sustainability, this land is crucial. And it demonstrates that, after more than 30 years on the Shore, TNC is not giving up its place in the biodiversity bucket brigade. On broader community and economic sustainability issues, TNC may have had to step aside, but in protecting songbird and waterfowl diversity and shoreline habitat they are still in their element.

Beyond this partnership, TNC's Virginia Coast Reserve (VCR) continues to be the ecological heart of the Eastern Shore. Now comprising 38,000 acres, the VCR includes land on 14 of the 18 seaside barrier islands. Its significance has been recognized not only by the United Nations as one of 500 biosphere reserves but also by the US Department of the Interior, the National Science Foundation, and the Western Hemisphere International Shorebird Network. Beyond the VCR, TNC has played a constructive role in extending protection to other key bits of habitat. In addition to the VCR, more than 76,000 acres are now protected by conservation easements (which comprise 22,000 acres of the total) and by state and federal agencies in parks and reserves. TNC's acquisitions have meanwhile shifted to the bayside while its seaside activities focus on research and education.[35]

In an extended conversation with VCR director Parker and Michael Lipford, executive director of TNC in Virginia, I came to understand that while TNC is still unquestionably a force to be reckoned with they see themselves differently than in the 1990s. Back then, they told the world that they had come to realize that their reserve could not be detached from the Shore's history and economy with its race tensions, failed real estate speculation, crumbling towns and villages, and abject poverty. "As a big player on the landscape, it was hard for us to ignore some of these things," Parker said. "We originally got involved in the substandard housing issue around issues of land and water. The African American community was hugely disadvantaged and they are as big a part of the community as we are, so the engagement to improve their living conditions, including their lands and waters, was natural."[36]

The Nature Conservancy in the 1990s preached "biosphere reserve thinking." Greg Low, the TNC vice president who brought this kind of thinking to the Shore, declared, "There is no way that the Conservancy or any other conservation organization could buy enough land to buffer and preserve a system as vast and complex as this. Balance between long-term preservation and sustainable human use must originate with local people and local government."[37] Even today, Conservancy literature reads:

> *Because people are a vital part of ecosystems, the Virginia Coast Reserve partners with local communities as they seek to make informed land-use decisions. The Conservancy also helps local officials identify development approaches that preserve local character, history, traditions and, ultimately, vital natural systems that sustain all life on the Eastern Shore.*[38]

When we left the story in 1997, TNC had taken some big leaps of faith, working not only on housing but also in the Northampton Economic Forum, with other nonprofits on social and economic challenges, and with the county on sustainable development. Among the biggest leaps was TNC's creation and capitalization of the Eastern Shore Corporation, the holding company alluded to earlier that would launch private-sector ventures ranging from tourism to specialty foods to arts and crafts and real estate. Hardly the epitome of biosphere thinking, these ventures were aimed primarily at the upper end of the tourist spectrum, a sector long part of TNC's Rolodex. During its short life (1997-1999) of promoting local products, seeding ventures like clam farming, and launching a number of real estate ventures and building restorations, the corporation seriously overextended itself. It went bankrupt in 2000, leaving egg on the faces of Eastern Shore entrepreneurs, bankers, and The Nature Conservancy itself.[39]

Such unexpected negative outcomes for what it deemed to be sustainable economic ventures forced TNC to reconsider its strategic role on the Shore. Twenty-one-year veteran Virginia Coast Reserve director John Hall resigned in 2001 as did the CEO of the Eastern Shore Corporation. TNC decided it needed to recoil from economic sustainability ventures like these. "Compatible economic development may create as many problems as it solves," concluded TNC's own assessment of some of its projects — especially loans to the clam industry that led to oceanic pollution. The then TNC president Steven J. McCormick admitted that his organization was inexperienced in running businesses, blurting to the *Washington Post* in 2003, "We don't tend to think like a business."[40] William Weeks, who ran TNC's autonomous Center for Compatible Development, which fostered the Eastern Shore Corporation, closed up shop and resigned. Biosphere reserve thinking apparently had dropped off the screen.

Yet if one looks back with detachment, it's possible to conclude that with more oversight and planning, more time given to community buy-in, and less hubris, "compatible development" seems close to the aims of economic sustainability. In that important sense, it is regrettable that TNC was forced to retreat as a player in the Eastern Shore's quest for sustainability, even though its current focus on "understanding how the barrier island system ticks and assessing and conveying the importance of the ecological services it provides" is surely important.[41] TNC now works through the Anheuser-Busch Coastal Research Center at Oyster (partnering with the University of Virginia) and the Virginia Institute of Marine Sciences at Wachapreague (partnering with the College of William and Mary). In addition to conducting research to understand keystone parts of the marine system, these labs also work on applied matters like oyster production, bay scallops introduction, and sea grass restoration. "This research will help these two counties become more resilient to disturbances that are sure to come and will help broaden livelihood opportunities for people who want to make their living on the water," TNC's Parker explained.

Significant to this work has been the Seaside Heritage Program of the Virginia Department of Environmental Quality.[42] Working with funds from the federal Coastal Zone Management Act, more than $1 million has been invested since 2002 in helping the seaside recover from the storm and disease calamities that killed sea grass meadows, once vital to the production of scallops, oysters, and blue crabs. By focusing attention on seaside ecosystems and productivity, the Seaside

Heritage Program will help build artificial oyster reefs, restore sea grass beds, and protect several species of beach-nesting birds. And finally, with an eye toward ecotourism, this program has developed a water trail for kayakers and canoeists, with new shoreline access points that will open portions of the VCR to low-impact paddlers.

In looking back, both Parker and his boss, Michael Lipford, tried to make the case that TNC's early work in biosphere reserve thinking, bringing people together to talk about development and environment, had paid off, especially in Northampton County, "where natural assets are at the top of their list of values as reflected in the comprehensive development plan, in the current members of their board of supervisors, in landowners willing to put their land into protection, and in green businesses started here." Lipford asked, "You see what I mean? You cannot trace an unbroken link from, say, the Northampton Economic Forum to the current comprehensive development plan, but a kind of land ethic has evolved here and it can be seen in many facets of Eastern Shore life."[43]

Sifting through a bit of spin from an organization whose reputation perhaps needs burnishing, I can see their point. TNC has undoubtedly helped promote ecologically-based thinking about what it means to have a protected shoreline, to secure fresh water supplies coming from an aquifer vulnerable to salt water intrusion, and to restore a marine environment for those who love seafood and those who make their living from it. The Nature Conservancy and its work with partners is a long way from being done, Parker and Lipford say. "The good news is we're not going anywhere. We and our partners will be in relationship here for the long term. TNC is back to what TNC does best, which is working with public and private partners to protect the goods and services provided to both natural and human communities."[44]

The Economy, the Environment, the People

In the eyes of the dreamers of the 1990s, sustainable development first required uplifting the peninsula's desperate economic situation and its social consequences. In 1993 Tom Harris, the new Northampton County administrator, was told he had entered a "community of hopelessness," with highly entrenched factions pursuing their own special interests and inviting inappropriate development while half the population suffered in poverty.[45] In the next five years, he attempted to lead the county into a visioning process to pull up the region in the short term while extracting promises for the long term that would enhance rather than exploit the ecological foundations of the region's economy. Many residents came to understand that the intersection of the economy with the region's environment required a new kind of awareness. It meant understanding that the two were interdependent and that limits would need to be set to provide sufficient fish and shellfish, agricultural production, fresh water, jobs, and a high quality of human life in perpetuity.

These principles were articulated in the Sustainable Development Action Strategy, which sadly was destroyed by just the factionalism it was meant to transcend. "TNC and others allowed ... the collaborative to become fragmented into a number of splinter groups, thus diffusing the overall impact of the Strategy just when vision, unity, focus, tangible progress, and real employment opportunities were so urgently needed," remembered Harris.[46] As for Hayes, he moved on in 2003, when "it became clear that the general thinking of elected and appointed local leaders was that 'sustainability' and 'green development' were merely fads whose time had passed."[47] Ironically, offshore the Strategy had become a widely copied and lauded model for county-level sustainable development.[48]

Now 15 years later, tensions between the economy and the Shore's environmental quality continue to be "ground zero" in heated debates about land use, transportation corridors, and zoning; the threat of high-impact tourism; jobs; education and a future for the rising generation; affordable housing and real estate inflation; and the environmental impacts of both aquaculture and agriculture. These tensions were aired in 2007 during two planning summits conducted by Virginia Tech to develop a comprehensive plan for Accomack and Northampton counties. And they are evident in the plan itself as well as in month-in and month-out contentious county-level decisions about water, land, housing, and tourism.

Unlike the 1990s, no single forum or task force with sustainability in the back of its mind and collaboration in its heart provides a platform for these debates. However, if the political will could be mustered, then cutting-edge thinking about sustainability and bottom-up consensus-based practice might be fused into the existing two-county planning process. Such a process would first have to overcome the demons that unraveled the Sustainable Development Action Strategy a decade earlier. These include: insufficient community buy-in; mission creep driven by federal and state funding agencies; other centrifugal forces that pulled partners away from collaboration and toward their own parochial modes of operation; an ambiguous relationship between TNC and the county; and the absence of committed leadership such as was provided in the 1990s by Harris, Hayes, John Nottingham, the county supervisors of the time, and others. Attending to the many frayed relationships and the overall bad taste of "sustainability" as remembered by present leaders and community activists will be a difficult job, but not an impossible one.

Meanwhile, the Eastern Shore stares directly into the face of pressures that surely recall all the reasons sustainability made sense in the 1990s. Consider these items from recent news clippings:

- **Sustainable Technologies Industrial Park languishes** (2004): The covenants, conditions, and restrictions regulating building and operating in the park to ensure that its uses would be ecologically sensitive, economically viable, and socially just "amount to social engineering." "Those are things that make it very difficult to market," allege two Eastern Shore leaders.[49]

Backstory: As noted earlier, STIP under the county industrial development authority had failed by 2004. What was at stake then (and is still) is whether a private developer could use the park for other purposes (say, residential development). Some argue that the covenants, conditions, and restrictions prohibit doing so profitably. Since the park was funded partly with federal grants, it seems unlikely that all of these stipulations will be removed. On the other hand, what's wrong with development that is ecologically sensitive and socially just?

- **Second-home development on agricultural lands** (2005): Though the Eastern Shore has the reputation of being "Virginia's Vegetable Garden," it now seems to specialize in importing well-heeled home buyers. Housing projects are scattered across the peninsula, especially in Accomack. "The idea of sprawl and just gobbling up farms — there are a lot of people that don't like it," said Northampton County board of supervisors chairman, Richard Tankard.[50]

Backstory: The 1,729-acre Bay Creek Golf and Marina Resort is a new and previously unprecedented venture in Cape Charles of the kind envisioned in the 1970s. It is seen by some as the thin end of the wedge of mass tourism mixed with Hilton Head exclusivism. The project was built on former farmland. As of 2008, it had sold more than half its planned 2,700 housing units. Related is the toll structure of the Bay Bridge-Tunnel. Despite public protests in 2001 by a group called WE DECIDE and others, the Bay Bridge-Tunnel Commission lowered round-trip tolls from $20 to $12 for people making the trip back and forth in 24 hours or less. This opens the lower Shore real estate market to Urban Tidewater commuters and second-home buyers. Just 23 miles away are 1.6 million people.

- **Shellfish farming confronts waterfront development and agriculture** (2007): "Two of the biggest economic engines on Virginia's Eastern Shore these days — shellfish farming and waterfront development — are headed for a showdown."[51] In the absence of sufficient regulation of agriculture and other Shore land development, the aquaculture industry cannot survive. Creek closures because of storm and agricultural runoff jeopardize millions of clams on the leased creek bottoms.[52]

Backstory: Clam and oyster farming are a $50 million-a-year industry on the Eastern Shore. Michael Pierson, a biologist who heads Cherrystone Aquafarms, the largest Eastern Shore clam farm, has repeatedly said that the burgeoning aquaculture industry will fail without clean water. Both agricultural runoff (mainly from poultry farms) and housing developments with new roads and added storm water and sewage threaten shellfish farms. Resolving these conflicts has so far proven impossible for the planning commission and in the absence of a crosscutting collaborative partnership, the dispute festers.

- **Limit the season on blue crabs** (2008): A professor of marine science faced "pointed criticism" from watermen over a decision by the Virginia Marine Resources Commission to close the lower bay crab sanctuary to fishing a month earlier than usual to allow stock to replenish from an historic low in 2007.[53]

Backstory:Because of declines in shellfish populations, 65 percent of watermen were forced to leave the business between 1998 and 2008. At a public meeting reviewing this decision, one waterman still in business said, "The waterman always has to take the brunt." He further complained that Virginia regulates watermen but doesn't deal with

upstream causes like agricultural runoff, storm drainage and preda-
tion. Unlike Monhegan (Chapter 4) setting limits in troubled times is
proving to be difficult on the Eastern Shore.

- **State mandated water quality plan** (2008): "Farmers and
  watermen have become worried about increased waterfront
  development along the myriad coves and creeks where shellfish farming has taken off." When Governor Kaine asked the
  Department of Environmental Quality to draw up a set of new
  regulations that would allow growth while protecting water
  quality, the news "created a political storm on the Shore."[54]

Backstory: The governor is walking a fine line between a bayside real
estate market that before the 2008 meltdown was booming and the
resource-based industries that need a healthy environment and are at the
heart of the Shore's economy. Ways to buffer new development at ecologically nonthreatening densities are desperately needed. A wide-open real
estate market in Accomack gives rise to these conflicts. Northampton
zoning codes to save open spaces and promote smart town growth are
better, but creeks and coves in both counties are nonetheless at risk.

- **Indoor plumbing waiting list updated** (2008): The indoor
  plumbing rehabilitation loan program provides zero-interest
  loans to residences without indoor plumbing. The Northampton-
  Accomack Housing and Redevelopment Commission maintains
  a waiting list of low- and moderate-income citizens eligible for
  these loans. Demand exceeds available funds.[55]

Backstory: The good news is that the percentage of homes lacking
indoor plumbing had fallen from 7.4 percent in Accomack and 12.2
percent in Northampton in 1990 to 2.6 percent and 4.6 percent respectively in 2000. Even so, about 650 homes await indoor plumbing and
many of the residents cannot afford loans. Most are African American
or Hispanic.[56] The Bayview and Sawmill housing projects have
provided Eastern Shore low-income residents almost 500 new affordable housing units in the past 15 years. Bayview single family "rent to
own" houses replace despicably rundown former rentals. There are also
community facilities and a 100-acre adjacent site meant for agriculture
and conservation.[57] Although many goals of the Sustainable Development
Action Strategy were never met, working toward housing equity is

largely a success story. Still, "African Americans sense that the good life is being snatched from them."[58] Large numbers of residents in Northampton County have been critical of the county's processes for handling housing needs and of job opportunities for low-income people.[59] Some in the black community believe that zoning codes hurt them. Among the most outspoken is Alice Coles, the driving spirit of Bayview, who believes this masks the underlying "moral economy" of the Eastern Shore in which African Americans are a peasant class stuck at the bottom. Zoning cannot fix this historical structural inequity, she says.[60]

These clips by no means depict all of the economic and social tensions on the Shore. Nor do they foretell what changes may ensue in the troubled global economy in which climate change will play a big role. If you talk with Shore residents and decision makers, you hear anxieties about the future that make it clear the Shore faces new vulnerabilities while its institutions seem less capable of envisioning how to deal with them. Referring to Northampton County in 2007, one resident preferring to remain anonymous said, "County government has really stumbled recently, even having to postpone elections. People seem to be playing special interest politics and forgetting the needs of the community."[61] This reminds me of the situation Tom Harris stepped into 15 years ago.

Meanwhile, community organizations (such as the NAACP and the Bayview Citizens for Social Justice) continue to press for social and environmental justice. It is also true that civic society has given rise to other new environmental organizations. Some of these are NIMBYs ("not in my backyard"); others have narrow interests such as putting more land in trust or promoting Eastern Shore arts and crafts; still others actually seek some aspects of sustainability, like the Eastern Shore Farm Market Alliance. Not one of them, as far as I can determine, has either the reach or the intent to bring back the precious moments of the mid-1990s, when sustainability drove conversations about the Shore's future. That the words "sustainability" and "sustainable development" have become loaded should not mean that efforts to rebirth their noble intentions should cease.

The Way Forward

How could this rebirth happen? A place to start might be the Eastern Shore Comprehensive Economic Development Strategy. In mid-decade, with help from the Eastern Shore Regional Partnership, a cross section of citizens came up with this vision of their homeland in 2020:

> The Eastern Shore of Virginia is a rural community, with thriving towns and villages and lots of open space, parks and trails ... a prosperous region where all residents share in our economic well-being. We are proud of the abundance of safe, affordable housing throughout our region .... Our industrial parks attract industries which do not deplete our natural resource base or pollute our air or water. We have a sustainable, diversified economy .... We are a haven for artists. Our region is also a great place to retire .... Tourists are attracted ... because of our clean environment, open spaces, and natural resources .... Our natural resource base is well managed: we have prosperous agriculture and aquaculture industries ....[62]

This sounds almost like some of the language of the 1990s. It even uses the word "sustainable" once. From this view of the future, five strategic goals, dubbed "landmarks on the road to prosperity," emerged at two public meetings in Accomack and Northampton (Table 5-1). About 375 citizens participated.

TABLE 5-1

2007 Eastern Shore of Virginia Comprehensive Economic Development Strategy

Strategic Goals

Create a positive environment for the growth of seven industry clusters by providing necessary public infrastructure. Industry clusters are: agriculture & food processing, aerospace, tourism, seafood & aquaculture, education & research, studio businesses, and retiree services.

Offer opportunities for lifelong learning and skill development related to the seven industry clusters.

Develop a regional identity that celebrates the Shore's competitive advantages and connects the communities of the region.

Attract or grow businesses that provide living wage jobs and don't harm the environment.

Recognize the importance of historic towns and villages and develop strategies to stimulate their revitalization.

Source: Eastern Shore Regional Partnership. *Eastern Shore of Virginia Comprehensive Economic Development Strategy.* 2007, 9.

These goals set the table for an action plan that focuses on people, places, infrastructure, and business and industry. Although most of the action items and projects in each of these categories are written in the language of conventional economic development, without too much stretching many could be refocused toward a society that tries to detach itself from the fossil fuel, consumption-driven way of life that now undermines the Shore's resilience and threatens to impair its ecological services and biodiversity. If you are thinking about sustainability, especially promising are the plan's emphasis on human development (though couched timidly in a narrow conception of the job market); its promotion of low-impact tourism; its recognition of the importance of renewable resource-based agriculture and aquaculture (both of which are now dependent on fossil fuel inputs and neither of which is close to "natural" or "organic"); its advocacy of broadband expansion and the improvement of water and wastewater infrastructures; its recognition of the need for downtown revitalization; and its attention to the connection between land use and water quality. "This would be a place to start," said Accomack County administrator Steve Miner, "but I'm struck with how little attention there is to sustainability compared to central Virginia where I came from."[63]

A plan, of course, is merely a proposal for the future and many plans do nothing more than collect dust. What of the present? What's on the ground now may provide a sturdier platform for trying to scramble a few passengers on board the sustainability express. In the realm of tourism, for example, you could focus on the Southern Tip Partnership and its connection to bird conservation and birding tourism. The Eastern Shore Birding and Wildlife Festival has been a successful event for almost 20 years, attracting a few thousand visitors in mid-September each year with consequent economic spinoffs in food, lodging, and other retail services. In the same vein are the Eastern Shore Loop and the Eastern Shore Heritage Trail, both of which are safe cycling routes, and the Seaside Water Trail for paddlers.

Each of these ongoing ecotourist activities brings in a portion of the more than $100 million tourism sector and they are high-dollar, low-impact kinds of tourism. Few of these dollars, however, now lift up people in the lower economic rungs. They create a few jobs, but almost all pay minimum, nonbenefited wages. Brenda Holden, whom we first met in the 1990s, is a senior extension agent for Northampton County.

"Tourism is OK as a part of our economy," she says of current developments, "but who really benefits? There are now no black-owned gas
stations or hotels or bed and breakfasts. The lack of black access in
tourism is both an economic and a cultural issue. I'm afraid that
tourism is not going to save this area."[64]

When you ask about residuals of the sustainability era, besides ecotourism and the recognition by almost everybody that the Virginia
Beach kind of development is not the way to go, people always mention
a few successful ecofriendly private sector ventures. These include New
Ravenna, a company that makes mosaic tiles marketed nationwide and
employs 450; the Blue Crab Company, which wholesales gourmet foods
(some from the Eastern Shore) and employs 25; and the several
successful aquaculture farms and organic farmers, which promote
better land use and a healthier Shore, and export Virginia produce and
clams worldwide. None of these is really the outcome of collaboration
toward sustainability *per se*. On the other hand, the Eastern Shore of
Virginia Farm Market Alliance is. It promotes local enterprises that sell
fresh produce, garden plants, seafood, and wines. It also coordinates
weekly farmers' markets at Chincoteague, Exmore, Cheriton, and Cape
Charles. Though not presently tied together formally, these entrepreneurs could be the foundation for a more integrated bottom-up
sustainable business plan.

Sweet Life on the Shore [65]

If you are a bird watcher, the Eastern Shore might be your North
American nirvana. In winter, you can watch marsh hawks and kestrels
soar over the marshes and woods while you sense the days lengthening
toward spring. In March, you can sit at the marsh edge to mark the
arrival of glossy ibises, egrets, willets, snow geese, swans, and other
waterfowl up from the south. They move on. You stay. In May, you
spot ospreys rebuilding their massive nests to fish and to fledge. By
summer, more than a hundred kinds of songbirds, black ducks, blue
herons, and hawks become daily companions as heat and humidity
oppress and greenhead flies buzz and bite. When the leaves begin to
turn, you search the northern horizon for willets and ducks and geese
that stop awhile before winging southward. Birds will etch your days
on this little peninsula.

Repeating itself for millennia, this sweet life of sea and marsh, wind and tides makes human folly seem of little consequence. On a windswept beach by yourself, you ask, who cares whether sustainability initiatives once fell on hard times? Who cares whether, in the tiresome boil and bubble of politics and speculation, folks here do or do not rise to a new vision? Who can even predict what will happen to the barrier islands or the Bay Creek Resort in the long term? Who can say whether the Perdue Chicken plant will still want cheap labor out here, away from city eyes? When all has been spoken, all that can be said is said, you know that these marshes and beaches will offer themselves fall after fall, spring after spring. Assured of such wildness in easy reach, you smugly imagine the Shore to be forever.

Of course, it's not. What is forever is change. And coming to the Eastern Shore is BIG change. Wrought by global warming and sea level rise, by human suffering and the post-petroleum plunge, by capital markets gone amok and pensions down the drain, change is coming. Whether on this particular shore or some other, the wee window on the world that was once the barrier islands is fast closing, like it or not. If people of the Eastern Shore of Virginia hope to live and prosper in the face of such gut-wrenching disruption, they must reattach themselves to the opportunities and limits of their little peninsula. They must fashion something long lasting and resilient.

This will surely require another tack at building community, at setting sights on the long distant future of grandchildren and great-grandchildren, at reconnecting deeply and gathering all the forces of good and abundance that now exist: local food and shellfish production; a diverse local food supply; the presence of a vibrant arts community that may lead people once again toward a more civil and lasting local democracy; local energy production; small business and crafts development; pertinent education; energized retirees. It will require collaborative institutions, open and inclusive communication, trusted ways of resolving differences, and responsive local government. Call it sustainability or call it survival. Whatever you call it, it will require people of courage and tenacity ready to redesign their "life place" so it is as fit for egrets as for humans of all kinds and fulfills the needs of all life: clean air and water, food and shelter, peaceful and purposeful dwelling.[66]

6

Millennia of Resilience:
The Menominee Indians of Wisconsin

Resilient systems absorb shock more gracefully and for-give human error, malfeasance, or acts of god.[1]

~ David W. Orr

When you look at our history, you have to conclude that we're a fiercely resilient people. Our small size and our geography sandwiched between bigger tribes forced us to be good negotiators. We have always been inde-pendent, but we also learned how to live at peace with our own people, with neighbors, and with this beauti-ful forest.[2]

~ Verna Fowler

ONE MONTH BEFORE I ARRIVED AT THE MENOMINEE INDIAN Reservation in the summer of 2007, a tornado ripped a 12 mile-long swath across the northwestern part of the reservation and continued onward another 25 miles through the adjacent Nicolet National Forest (Figure 6-1). Packing winds of 150 miles per hour, the storm toppled and shredded big trees and everything else in its path. In a matter of minutes it had turned prime stands of maple 150 years old into matchsticks.[3] The storm flattened 14,000 acres of forest overall, at least 3,500 acres of which were in Menominee Forest, the focus of the Menominee economy for 140 years. Fortunately, no human settlements were in its path, but people agreed it was the worst storm in at least a decade.

As they assessed damage to the forest, the Menominee quickly discovered they would need to salvage many million board-feet of

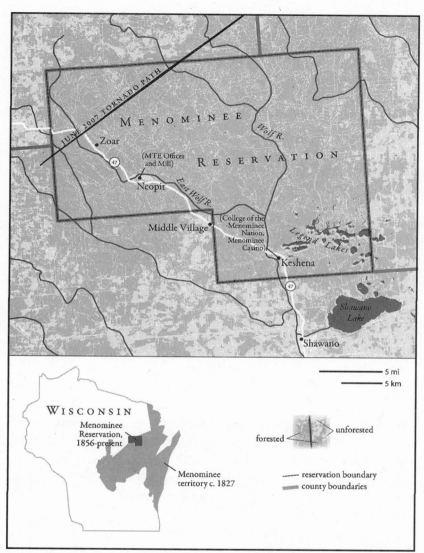

FIGURE 6-1
Menominee County, Wisconsin

downed trees, a cut that would be two or three times what they deem to be sustainable. Time was of the essence because, as most hardwoods begin to decompose in the warm weather of summer, they stain. Since about 75 percent of the downfall was the vulnerable white-wooded sugar maple, staining would seriously degrade the value of these logs.[4]

The challenge was to get them to the mill quickly, where they could be watered to forestall staining.

When the storm hit, Menominee Forest manager Marshall Pecore was in Montana at an Indian forestlands conference with Menominee Tribal Enterprises (MTE) president Adrian Miller. They made their apologies and jumped on the next plane. Within 24 hours, they were back at MTE headquarters plotting their response. While others flew over the area to assess the tornado's wake, GIS project forester Paul Crocker created a preliminary map using satellite imagery. Aerial reconnaissance and groundwork helped refine the map. His colleague, forester Mike Waukau, remembers many hours of compass and pace surveillance along roads intersecting the swath. "From the imagery, the aerial work, and our ground-truthing, within a few days of the storm we had a good map for the salvage plan."[5]

Meanwhile, Miller asked the Bureau of Indian Affairs for a rapid response in preparing the environmental assessment required of Indian trust lands and he declared an emergency that led to the suspension of a tribal ordinance requiring interviews, paperwork, and delays in hiring extra crews. Forest manager Pecore called every logger he'd worked with in the previous few years. Clearing a tornado-damaged forest, "a forest of jackstraws at the center," in Pecore's words, is risky both to men and machines, so MTE's emergency response plan kicked in, which includes opening seven heliports for quick evacuation of any injured workers and mandating a refresher safety course for all operators.[6] In less than a week, the environmental assessment had been completed ("The Bureau listened to us this time; lots of times they don't," said Miller), most access roads opened, 35 logging outfits contracted, and a second shift hired at the mill.[7] Ecological damage appeared to be small, although some red-shouldered hawk nesting sites were obliterated and several historic logging camps, homesteads, and burial sites were in the path.[8] David Grignon, director of historic preservation, advised loggers to respect each of these sites.[9]

Northeast of Menominee, woods hit by the tornado in the adjacent Nicolet National Forest also lay silent that summer. Months later, with the Menominee forest half cleared, downfall in the Nicolet lay "decaying in a quagmire of bureaucratic entanglements."[10] The Forest Service, of course, can never be as nimble as the Menominee. But the kicker here is that their quagmire may ultimately swamp the Menominee. "With lots of pine down there, we're presented with a possible infestation problem," said forester Pecore. Downed pine attracts pine bark beetles. These then infect standing timber. The infestation spreads. "Hopefully, the Forest Service will salvage their timber quickly enough so we don't experience a multiplier effect in our forest," but as of late spring 2008 tornado downfalls had still not been fully cleared in the Nicolet.

Tornado downfalls in Menominee were fully harvested by March 2008. Ninety-eight percent of the downfall was converted to wood products: 30 million board-feet of saw logs and 40,000 cords of pulp wood.[11] The MTE marketing department found customers for everything. About 270 loggers and three dozen second-shift millworkers earned additional wages. Some of those earnings helped strapped families and multiplied across the reservation. By the new season of 2008, Menominee foresters were back to their management plan, determining a much smaller "normal" cut and, as they have been doing for more than a century, telling the mill just how much lumber and just what species they should expect in the new season. By 2009, the great tornado swath of 2007 had begun its miraculous process of regeneration and the berry picking that summer was the best in years.

By ripping open a gash in the forest, a devastating tornado provided the most recent test of Menominee resolve. A dozen years ago, Larry Waukau said of Menominee forestry that "with new information, we adjust our management."[12] The information presented by the tornado of 2007 was, first, that storms like this are anything but unprecedented. "You see two or three in your lifetime. Everywhere you go in the forest, there's evidence of storms. Plot out the hummocks, which are root mounds, and you can trace the history of windstorms," observed Marshall Pecore, a man who's walked these woods for more than 35 years.[13] Second, Menominee foresters know that surprises like severe windstorms are part of a natural regime of disturbance. "This is how the forest turns over and is reborn."[14] Without disturbance, these forests would in a sense be "unnatural," they say. And third, the Menominee fully understand that their culture and economy, long connected to the forest, must be as supple as nature in dealing with disturbances. Dating from deep wisdom given by elders long ago, their lifeways are rooted in beliefs that humans are an integral part of the natural environment. Disturbance by wind or fire may look bad at first, but it can yield good things, Pecore says. "No fire, no berries; no fire, no sweet grass; no storms, no pines."[15] To this, one might add, no disturbance, no opportunity for learning.

One afternoon I drove out to look at the tornado damage along Route 47, the main north-south state highway. What I saw was the aftermath of a stunning natural disturbance that, by any human reckoning, showed nature's capacity to inflict change quickly and conclusively. Standing there in the stillness of a devastated forest, no birdsong to be heard, I reflected on the salience of Menominee adaptation. Who can deny Menominee pluck? I asked myself. Through a turbulent history these remarkable people are indeed "fiercely resilient." In nature, being resilient is the ability to self-organize, to sustain stress without losing control over its historic structure and function, to learn and adapt, and as David Orr writes, "to absorb shock gracefully."[16] Social and economic systems connected to natural resources — like the Menominee Tribal Enterprises forestry department and mill — must be similarly adaptive and ready to learn. In that still forest in mid-July 2007, millennia of resilience echoed across the tornado swath, calling the Menominee to bounce back, as they always had.

WILD RICE PEOPLE

The Menominee (the "wild rice people") probably descended from late woodland cultures of the upper Midwest in early postglacial times. They once ranged from the upper peninsula of what is now Michigan westward to the Mississippi and eastward to Lake Michigan — a territory of about 9.5 million acres of rolling, poorly drained land with birch, oak, maple, basswood, cedar, hemlock, and hickory forests covering its vastness. Grassy outwash plains, swamps, and lakes created ecotones for the rich bounty that yielded the foods, shelter, clothing, and medicines they required: deer and caribou, fish, nuts, berries, roots, maple sugar, construction timber and firewood, and, of course, wild rice. The Menominee language for the calendar months reflects their millennial interactions with these lands: sturgeon month, sugar-making month, strawberry month, rice-threshing month.

Beginning in the mid-17th century, they began to encounter Europeans: first explorers, then trappers, and inevitably French, British, and American homesteaders. Disease and brutal encounters with these interlopers reduced their numbers by two thirds and forced them, treaty by treaty, to cede all but 0.025 percent of their land. Yet unlike other woodland tribes, the Menominee successfully resisted attempts to relocate. In 1848, Chief Oshkosh and other leaders stubbornly refused to move to Minnesota and in 1854 signed a treaty establishing their current 235,000-acre reservation. The remaining 2,000 souls then paddled up the Wolf River to settle into the small, heavily forested portion of their once vast domain.

Interactions of this small band of dispirited Indians with the rapidly evolving and aggressive white society pressing its borders is a long saga that constantly tested Menominee mettle. Through it all they were unwilling to part with any portion of their small reservation and faithfully obeyed the instructions of their elders to keep the forest intact while using it wisely. They became one of the few tribes of the northern forests to hold fast to communal tenure, fight assimilation, and resist depredations of the timber industry that had laid waste to the rest of northern Wisconsin.

In 1890, in partnership with the Bureau of Indian Affairs (BIA) and the newly formed federal forestry division, the Menominee convinced Congress to allow them to cut the forest using a controlled regime under the supervision of federal foresters. The ensuing act established an allowable cut of 15 to 20 million board-feet per year (still the annual target), with profits going to the hospital, the poor, and a tribal trust fund. The Menominee thereby launched the first statutory sustained-yield forest in the country and one of the largest and oldest tracts in the US managed this way. By 1950, they had become a relatively wealthy tribe with a high literacy rate, a modern mill, an electric power generating station, a garment factory, a sewage treatment plant, schools, a hospital and clinic, and a community center. The majority of civil service and administrative jobs were filled by Menominee and household income on the reservation was comparable to white households in the area.

Then came a shock: the Termination Act of 1953, Congress's attempt to assimilate Native Americans and free them from federal supervision and control. Almost overnight, Menominee prosperity and cultural well-being melted down. Historian Nicholas Peroff called this act "one of the most ill-considered congressional experiments in the history of national Indian policy."[17] It certainly proved so for the Menominee. For the next two decades, life on the reservation became insufferable as tax revenues fell, the hospital closed, tribal enterprise bonds were fore-closed, mill earnings plummeted, and social services collapsed. By the mid-1970s, Menominee County had the highest rates of unemploy-ment, lowest family incomes, lowest number of high school graduates, and most substandard housing in Wisconsin. The government's deci-sion to terminate the tribe had "reduced the proud, independent, self-supporting Menominee Nation to a poor, disorganized group of citizens dependent on federal [and] state support for survival."[18]

Menominee Enterprises Incorporated (MEI), the tribal business operating the mill, was saved from bankruptcy in the 1960s by entering a joint venture with a private development company. This venture led to the unthinkable act of selling 5,000 acres of prime Menominee land at Legend Lakes to non-Indians. A line had been crossed. Tribal members, especially those living in Milwaukee and Chicago, vehemently objected and by the mid-1960s, a determined resistance movement, led by an organization called Determination of Rights and Unity for Menominee Shareholders (DRUMS), demanded return to Menominee control of MEI, cessation of land sales to nonMenominee, new programs to save Menominee culture, and federal reinstatement of the tribe.

A protracted legal and legislative struggle through the 1960s and early 1970s hardly looked promising and people became skeptical. "People said we're never going to be restored because it's like unscram-bling eggs," remembers educator Verna Fowler. However, the miracle did happen. In 1976, the tribe was reinstated with full self-determina-tion and return of the reservation to federal trust.[19] "So eggs can be unscrambled?" I asked Fowler. "Yes, it can be done. Look at us."[20]

The Menominee Nation now elects its own legislature, maintains its own courts and law enforcement, and is fully in charge of reservation infrastructure. The reservation, like the national forests, is held in federal trust. Never again, without congressional approval, can any part of it be sold on the open market. And miraculously, the Menominee were able to use but not abuse their precious forest throughout these bleak times.

Menominee Tribal Enterprises, MEI's direct descendant, now manages the forest and its milling operations. Overseen by a 12-member elected board of directors answering to the Menominee Indian Tribe of Wisconsin (MITW) through the tribal legislature, MTE struggles with at least two inherent tensions: that between MTE and tribal government and that between MTE and the "sovereign people," the Menominee forest watchers. Of the first, MTE president Miller noted that the relationship is at times adversarial, but he says his people can get beyond contention. "We just have to stop listening to our egos and listen to the Spirit instead; that's the significance of our culture as tribal people."[21] Of the second, Lisa Waukau, chair of the MITW legislature, said, "The reality is that each and every Menominee owns the forest, so the people pay close attention to the way it's managed. When those trees are cut, they better be used as prudently as possible or we'll hear about it."[22] She and others agree that everybody has ideas about how mill revenues should be spent and is not hesitant to express them and that inevitably tensions will bubble to the surface. Yet no one, *no one*, ever advocates liquidating the forest or moving away from the long-held practice of sustained-yield forestry.

FROM SUSTAINED YIELD TO SUSTAINABILITY

When we wrote about the Menominee 13 years ago, we highlighted their powerful history of stewardship and we were told of plans to diversify forest and mill operations by adding value to forest products. We saw a two-year college with an Institute for Sustainable Development on the drawing board. The bingo hall of the 1980s had become a casino in the 1990s, yielding revenues to help the tribe. And we saw an open 2,000-acre housing tract recently purchased from adjacent farmers to provide housing without encroachment on the forest. Larry Waukau told us, "We're good at sustained-yield forestry. We have to move toward sustainable development."[23] Tugging against these 1990s elaborations of Menominee land philosophy, we also noted levels of substance abuse that troubled leaders, below-average educational performance, high unemployment, and suffering inherent in intergenerational poverty, much of which could be laid on the doorstep of the tribe's termination history. What exactly is the mix 12 years down the road? Have the Menominee moved from sustained yield to sustainability?

The Forest

When I walk in this profoundly beautiful oasis set starkly in a checkerboard of dairy farms and rural sprawl, I am transported to a time when ancestral Menominee wandered from Lake Michigan to the Mississippi River without ever being far from the verdant cover of their northern hardwood forest. Though the forest, to my eye, appears pristine, it is in fact one of the most intensively managed forests in the country, having yielded 2.5 billion board-feet in the past 150 years. Yet, miraculously, 11 of the 16 major forest types of the region flourish here; the aquatic ecology of the clear-running Wolf River, a national scenic and historic river, harbors the historic fish and invertebrate species mix; deep-woods-nesting birds like the hooded warbler, the bard owl, and the red-shouldered hawk may still be heard; native mammals except wolves and cougars are abundant; and there are few invasive species.[24] The value of standing timber and the forest biodiversity are greater now than when first assessed in 1908.[25] And it is just such facts that draw the world to this award-winning example of ecological coherence and sustained-yield forestry.[26]

A dozen years down the road, there's no doubt the Menominee forest — the single most important element of Menominee life — is, if anything, more sustainably managed than when we first walked through it. Still based on long-term rotations (aspen 60 to 80 years; white pine, maple, and red oak 150 to 180 years; hemlock up to 350 years), in a certain sense "the forest takes care of itself; the garden grows," assures Larry Waukau.[27] But increasingly it does so through a sophisticated blend of indigenous knowledge and western science that aims ultimately toward self-regulation. The management system is not unique but the Menominee time frame is. The system is based on the Kotan habitat-typing system using ground-cover indicator plants. In the past ten years it has been extensively refined and fully plugged into the Menominee GIS system. "We have honed it down since the 1990s," says Marshall Pecore, adding, "We are now tying in other ecological elements — habitat types ideal for wild rice, for wildlife, and important cultural and medicinal understory plants. That's the next stage for this system."[28] Of course, in the old days, "people constantly in the forest already inherently knew most of this. This is what our tribal people knew from age-old experience here."[29] When it comes to habitat types and management of this forest, science and ancient wisdom flow as one.

Back in the 1990s, foresters knew that about 50,000 acres were out of sync with the objective of matching tree species with the best habitats to yield both quality and quantity. The long-held practice of single-tree selection (in force since the early 20th century) resulted in maple domination because maples prosper in several habitats. Though this may be good from a marketing standpoint, science says that such dominance makes the forest more vulnerable to disease and stunts smaller trees in the understory. By careful management of natural regeneration, the areas in which species are mismatched with habitat types have now been halved to about 24,000 acres. This has required use of controversial management techniques like small clearcuts (so-called shelterwood cuts), the application of herbicides, and pruning the overstory (for example, removing young aspen to release white pine). People still express dismay when they see clearcuts or signs warning them away from tracts where herbicides have been sprayed, but in the long run they understand that "if we use habitat types to manage our forest ecologically, it costs less and yields more."[30] As for herbicides, "until we can get our fire program up and running, we need to use that herbicide tool to hit our goals on white pine and maintain diversity."[31]

The fire program of the near future will involve controlled burning during a small window in spring, a traditional practice used as recently as a century ago. Clearly on its way back — as in Monday Creek (Chapter 3), the Malpai (Chapter 7), the Mattole Valley (Chapter 8), and Plumas (Chapter 9) — prescribed burning will soon be part of forest management here as well. "The Menominee alive now have only experienced a landscape in which single-tree selection and uneven-aged management are the practices," observed Marshall Pecore, "but ecologically these are largely foreign to this forest. We've had 140 years of this kind of management compared to thousands of years of fire yielding patches of even-aged stands. Which should we be doing, really?"[32] If it were possible to ask elders of the mid-17th century, the answer would be "burn carefully." They undoubtedly knew that "there's something in the environment conducive to laying a cool fire on the ground in spring."[33] And because both the BIA and the Forest Service are themselves embracing prescribed burning, there seems little doubt it will soon return to the Menominee forest.

Meanwhile, there has been no change in the care with which the forest is harvested. Light-touch logging assures minimum secondary damage. All loggers must attend training and be recertified following Soren Erikkson's "game of logging" timber harvesting system.[34] The woods are off-limits to logging during the wet late winter and spring. MTE foresters carefully monitor logging operations to assure minimal damage to standing trees, use only of designated roads and skidding trails, and adherence to equipment restrictions. These high standards do not discourage logging contractors; rather, there are always more bids than can be accommodated.

Ecological services of the forest are thus sustained. These include protection of the Wolf River and its tributaries as well as wetlands; protection of soils, groundwater, and habitat for animals, birds, butterflies, and insects; preservation of ecological corridors and connectivity to the adjacent national forests; and sustained provision of nontimber forest products such as wild rice, maple sugar, ginseng, medicinals, and berries. The Menominee forest is thus the best example in Wisconsin of what this forest ecosystem looked like 200 years ago.[35]

Clearly, the forest continues to be synonymous with what it means to be a Menominee. It's still the "integrative glue that bonds our people."[36] Among the teachers during this round of visits, forester Jeff Grignon gave new voice to the essence of sustainable forestry here.

> My work in this forest comes from the heart. It's not a paycheck. If I wanted to make money off the forest, I'd still be in the woods marking or logging. I will do what is right for the forest and not worry about what happens next.[37]

Menominee Tribal Enterprises: Certification and Diversification

MTE took pride in the 1990s as the only Indian wood-products industry with Forest Stewardship Council (FSC) certification and only the second timber operation in the whole country to have been FSC accredited. We rightly made a big thing of this in *The Ecology of Hope*. It therefore came as a surprise to hear that MTE had suspended its participation in the certification program in 2003. Why? They explained that the high cost of audits and the unfulfilled promise of higher prices for certified products made it hard to justify. Instead, MTE issued a declaration of self-certification, explaining to customers that, though "we're not opting for the 'Good Housekeeping seal,' nothing whatever has changed in the way the forest is managed and harvested."[38] Customers generally bought into this argument, but MTE marketing specialist Bill Schmidt made it clear that FSC certification was never totally on the back burner. "We're getting some interest in it again, especially from the paper mills, so we may want to revisit our decision and we're willing to do that."[39] In 2008 MTE completed a process of recertification through FSC.[40]

If the forest is the heart of Menominee identity and cultural history, for the past generation MTE has been its circulatory system. It is still the biggest employer and the source of the best jobs on the reservation. What has happened since we were last here, however, is a patch of managerial instability leading to criticism from many corners, including the tribal legislature. Between 2001 and 2006, the MTE board went through five presidents and several iterations of board leadership. Persistent tugs of war between the board and the tribal legislature added to the mix and seem to have temporarily sidetracked good ideas. This pattern is partly the age-old ebb and flow of local politics and partly a byproduct of changing times.

MTE must operate in ways mills outside the reservation do not. Rather than being market driven, its business plan is ever mitigated by the forest's sustained-yield plan. The forest drives the mill. And its copilot is the social contract to provide living wage employment, a benefits package, and distribution of excess profits through so-called annual stumpage payments (about $200 per enrolled Menominee in 2007). The Menominee have lived with these stipulations for a long time, but the current globalized marketplace and the decline of the Great Lakes timber economy present new challenges.

Interviews with MTE managers, board members, salespeople, and forest personnel all convey a sense of confidence that diversification of the business is the way to adjust to these times. "We absolutely need to diversify," exhorts tribal chair Lisa Waukau.[41] So far, though, only baby steps have been taken (such as sorting and bundling of milled wood before sale), though the MTE strategic plan says clearly that diversification of the business and therefore of revenues, and broadening the customer base regionally, nationally, and globally are necessary. "These will enable the company to be financially as well as ecologically sustainable in this new marketplace," asserts Miller.[42] Foremost in his mind is development of biomass energy generation using byproducts now partly left in the forest and partly sold to paper mills and landscapers, an idea that dates back to the energy crisis of the 1970s.

Many think biomass makes sense. "Tribes across the country are talking biofuels," says Forest Service planner Mike Dockry.[43] In the frenzied 21st century search for alternative fuels, biomass is again viable. If a biomass-powered generator can be developed, other projects such as cogeneration of heat for nearby schools and a tree nursery would follow, or so thinks Miller. He argues also that, with biomass-generated electricity, mill operations would also be cheaper as would the production of new value-added products such as coffins, pellets, landscape materials, pharmaceuticals from lignin, and juvenile furniture. So instead of marketing only raw logs, chips, and a limited range of finished products as is now the case, a diversified MTE would capture far greater value per board-foot and create jobs that would multiply benefits across the reservation.

Some of this could happen soon. In early 2008, MTE issued a request for proposals for the development of a 5 to 20 megawatt biomass energy facility. Venturing $50,000 of its own capital, MTE sought a partner to provide financial services leading to a plan that would enable MTE to start biomass energy generation to support local economic development and produce electricity. [44] MTE is thus finally moving toward a goal, talked about for three decades, of multiplying the possibilities of diversified forest-product-driven sustainable development. Though far-fetched in the minds of some critics, there is precedent. The Confederated Tribes of Warm Springs in central Oregon already operate a small biomass generator and, working with the Forest Service and the BLM, they are now constructing a bigger one.[45]

A Symbol of Hope: College of Menominee Nation

Just after crossing into the Menominee Reservation from the south, you see signs for the College of Menominee Nation (CMN). A quick right takes you into a compact green campus — the site of a couple of temporary structures when last we visited. Now a handsome complex of low-rise energy efficient buildings, including two classroom halls, a campus commons, a cultural learning center, and a new library, the campus is graced by grassy hummocks, old-growth pines, wildflowers, rock outcrops, and an archaeological site. This new campus is the fruit of sensitive planning by campus planner Joel Kroenke and his Menominee advisors. Kroenke said that as the college develops, "we carefully try to incorporate existing natural features and to restore those lost. We want this campus to showcase what the Menominee are most known for — good land management."[46] To this end, a serpentine interpretive walking trail weaving through the campus offers a carefully laid out introduction to the natural history of the Menominee Nation.

Once inside the college, I found myself drinking up a celebration of Menominee culture in the atrium of Glenn Miller Hall, the heart of the campus, where a stunning carved bear reveals the story of Awaesah, the bear later to become human who stepped out of the Wolf River eight millennia ago. In the campus commons, photos document a century of Menominee history and high above the entrance is a large logo, depicting the five clans of the tribe — wolf, bear, eagle, moose, and crane — carved from a piece of Menominee forest butternut. "By gradually incorporating cultural elements in our buildings," says Kroenke, whose enthusiasm spills across the site plans and building elevations spread before us, "our students and our community will be reminded of their rich traditions and history."[47] In the new library, an archive of the evolution of sustained-yield forestry and of the history of termination and restoration is being gathered. "The strengths and values from our history are being conveyed by this college," CMN president Verna Fowler explained in a long conversation about the visions of the tribe manifest here.

Though there's no intent to minimize the forest in this place, Fowler hopes that the Menominee will come to be known "as much for the quality of our education as for our forestry."[48] President since the college's inception in 1992, Verna Fowler is a visionary with her feet firmly planted in this reservation. She was born in South Branch and raised in the shadow of the mill in Neopit. From her parents she learned the importance of education and participation in local politics. After earning a PhD and working in a range of educational settings, she emerged as the natural choice for president of the budding college. "She's the most politically astute leader you could hope for," said Melissa Cook, director of the college's Sustainable Development Institute.[49] So linked to the evolution of the college, Fowler's stature is mythic and people sometimes have thought of the place as Fowler College, "perhaps cynically," she says, "and there are still doubters out there, but mostly it's embraced as an important part of our future and a symbol of hope for Indian people."[50] In 2008 the college won the campus sustainability leadership award from the Association for the Advancement of Sustainability in Higher Education.[51]

The tribe allocates $300,000 per year to the college, a small but symbolically important part of its budget of $11 million, which is meant to show its commitment to higher education. Enrollment at the main campus and at a fast-growing satellite in Green Bay includes students from the nearby Oneida tribe as well as from 20 other tribes in the upper Midwest and Great Plains. From a beginning of fewer than 30 students, there are now 500, of whom almost 80 percent are Native American.[52]

As a two-year institution, CMN encourages its students to transfer to four-year degree-granting universities and colleges beyond the reservation. "When you leave this reservation, you enter an entirely different nation," said Fowler. "If we're going to survive as a tribe, we have to understand how mainstream society functions, how their government operates, how they think. Our students need the larger worldview; we'll soon be doing business in China. We are not going to learn these things if we stay on the reservation."[53] Thus, the signing of a transfer agreement with the University of Wisconsin in 2007 made Fowler particularly happy, for it smoothed the way for CMN students to transfer into the UW system. She and her counterpart, UW provost Patrick Farrell, see this as beneficial to both institutions: Menominee students will gain access to one of the most distinguished and comprehensive statewide systems in the country and UW students will gain more exposure to Native Americans.[54]

Even more impressive is the place of sustainability in the curriculum here. Every student must take a course on sustainable development that focuses on the Menominee model of sustainability, encompassing the six dimensions of life that draw from the Menominee sense of place: land and sovereignty, natural environment, institutions, technology, economics, and human perception and activity. A sustainable development major and majors in natural resources and sustainable forestry are among CMN's 20 degree programs. And woven throughout the college's curriculum, research, outreach, and service activities is the work of the Sustainable Development Institute (SDI), conceived by Fowler, Larry Waukau, and the then tribal chairman Glenn Miller in 1993.

The Sustainable Development Institute builds on the tribe's long history of sustainable silviculture and expands upon this to economic and social sectors beyond the forest. "Sustainability, in its contemporary sense, is no stretch for this tribe," director Cook says. "So when we say we're putting forth sustainability education as a focus and trying to run the college accordingly, Indians, with their deep pool of indigenous knowledge, easily plug in."[55] The staff includes Menominee historian Cook, a geographer, two communications and technical specialists, and a forester, all of whom have as their mission "threading sustainability throughout the tapestry of the college."[56] Beyond the curriculum, SDI runs workshops and conferences, assists the tribe with planning (for example, the recent sustainable energy plan), and hosts a legion of visitors from all corners.

In the story of the tornado, connections between Menominee forestlands and those of the adjacent Nicolet National Forest were painfully manifest. While the Menominee quickly turned downfall into board-feet, the Forest Service found itself gridlocked. Disease organisms threatened as pines decayed and managers on both sides worried about the longer-term health of the lands they manage. This story is not unique, for of the 562 federally recognized American Indian nations, 302 have significant acreages of forest and many of these forests border lands managed by the Forest Service and other federal agencies. Just like forests on federal lands, those on Indian lands must deal with the coming threats of climate change and wildfires, air and water pollution, and fragmentation. They also must deal with a complex land tenure history, high population growth, and increasing demands on forests by tribal institutions.[57]

To focus explicitly on the interdependency of Indian and federal forests, in 2003 the Forest Service and the Sustainable Development Institute joined hands in a unique collaboration they called the Center for First Americans Forestlands (CFAF), and they symbolically based it at the college rather than in a federal building. CFAF serves American Indian tribes and their foresters and land managers, Indian allottees of forest lands, reservation communities within and/or adjacent to national forests, communities of interest,[58] and tribal colleges and universities. The Forest Service embraces the partnership and collaborates in its programs of research, education, policy analysis, and technical assistance. Indirectly, CFAF aims to attract qualified Indian applicants for careers in the Forest Service.

The central focus of all forest programs is sustainability, "perhaps better understood by indigenous peoples than by the Forest Service," said Mike Dockry, the Forest Service planner who coordinates CFAF. "The relationship between tribes and the federal government hasn't always been the best, to say the least, so having this center in a relatively neutral place is a big advantage for this partnership."[59] In tight federal budget years, he will need all the advantages he can muster, for his main assignment is "figuring out how to do good projects in partnership." With youthful enthusiasm, he's set out a busy program of workshops, internships, and research that brings in the expertise of the Forest Service on scientific and policy questions that challenge MTE and its forestry department. "The key to success," he believes, "is working closely with the community to find out what they really need from us."

Of course, the Forest Service has long preached sustained-yield forestry and understands the modern notion of sustainability, but Dockry thinks the Menominee concept of sustainability has something to teach the Forest Service, for the concept applies not only to the forest and forest products but also to the entire life system, human and nonhuman. "I've shared the Menominee sustainability model widely with my Forest Service colleagues, for it has broadened my own concept of sustainability. What we can contribute together to thinking about sustainability in forests could be hugely important. Tribes like the Menominee have success in managing their lands and this may be a real incentive to the Forest Service."[60] Forestry, of course, will always be part of the picture, but Dockry thinks the tribe can capitalize on its expertise in forest ecology and forest management and its understanding of sustainability to grow a knowledge-based economy. "If you want to study and really understand sustainable forest management and what it means long term, particularly for indigenous lands, where do you come? Who do you think of?" he asks. "This college and their center can be globally known for this."

Challenging Community

The challenges we saw for the people of the Menominee Nation in the 1990s — poverty, unemployment, lifestyles from the outside world threatening traditional values, assimilation, and squabbles that become political skirmishes — are still there. Menominee County is Wisconsin's poorest and is the 38th most impoverished in the US (out of more than 3,000 counties). Unemployment on the reservation in November 2008 was 9.6 percent, compared to 5.6 percent statewide.[61] "No work means a poor self-image and a temptation to break the law," said Larry Waukau.[62] But there are relatively few jobs on the reservation and getting work in nearby towns is difficult. "We run up against prejudice outside the reservation, even if the job is only flipping burgers," said Dee Cobb, a staff member of Bridges Out of Poverty.[63] "There are limited jobs on the rez and many families are only a few hundred dollars away from catastrophe. All it takes is for their car to break down." Ultimately, it will be education that will make the difference, predicts Cobb. A mother of five, after years of working in Milwaukee she returned to the reservation to pursue a degree in tribal legal studies at CMN. As a person retooling in mid-career, she is upbeat about her future. CMN graduates, now scattered across the reservation, are far less likely to live in poverty than those with only a high school education.[64]

On the other hand, like Dee Cobb, many Menominee I interviewed see threats to Menominee lifeways on all fronts. For instance, Mike Waukau, the young MTE forester who helped respond to the tornado, said:

> The church and assimilation caused us to turn our back on old ways. Most people now don't even know about these old ways and cannot speak our language. We've got to move forward and we do need a good education to do this, but we must not lose touch with who we really are. Sadly, kids nowadays here are caught up in the outside world. They can tell you more about Puff Daddy than Chief Oshkosh.[65]

Initiatives emanating from the MITW office of cultural programs try to counterbalance the seductive influences of television, computers, video games, and the social pathology of kids hanging around with nothing to do. Language classes for people of all ages and immersion camps for children focus on traditions and lifeways and take kids into the forest. The game of lacrosse, for example, which originated here long ago, is played in the old way, kids learn to dance and drum, and the wild rice harvest has been revived . "We try to challenge outside influences here; that's our business," said Rebecca Alegria, director of cultural programs for MITW.[66] Schools also give focus to Menominee history and forestry. Lisa Waukau, now tribal chair, taught high school for years, and was always "kicking around ideas drawn from tribal history and politics."[67] Forester Jeff Grignon takes kids into the forest every year to plant trees.

Others believe population pressure to be a continuing threat. With so much of the reservation in forest and therefore off limits, housing is very limited in the three main towns. More land is needed. Tribal chair Lisa Waukau boldly warned: "Those who live among us who are not Menominee must understand we are a sovereign people. If you have land, realize you're just temporarily here until we can get that land back for our people." How would this happen? Waukau thinks that ultimately casino revenues will fund the purchase of land contiguous to the reservation, which would then be placed in trust. She admitted she's thinking especially of Legend Lakes and the corridor between Shawano and Keshena, now in farms and other rural land uses. Were this to happen, it would surely be a tasty bite of poetic justice: casino revenues, derived largely from non-Indian gambling, would bloodlessly return to its rightful owners land lost in a tragic history of displacement, conquest, termination, and questionable treaties.

This leads me to the gaming sector of the Menominee economy. In the 1990s, the Menominee Casino helped restore community services and infrastructure lost during termination. Today, as one of about 400 Indian casinos in the US, it continues to remit a percentage of its profits to the tribe (averaging $9 to $10 million annually in the mid-2000s and reaching a high of $13 million in 2007). Unlike many tribes, the Menominee do not distribute a per capita share of profits, so revenues flow to health services, education, law enforcement, and other tribal administrative expenses. One can see the fruits of such investments in the tribal buildings, the roads and sidewalks, the clinic, and the schools. The upgrading of community facilities we wrote about 13 years ago is still much in evidence. The casino also contributes about $700,000 annually to nonprofit organizations on and off the reservation, to community events like the annual pow-wow, and to promotion of local tourism.

If gaming for Indians these days is the modern equivalent of the buffalo, then there's no doubt the "herd" is huge. In 2006, Indian casinos nationwide generated revenues of approximately $22.6 billion, or almost 25 percent of all earnings by the industry at large.[68] Gaming in Wisconsin is a wee portion of this and it is nowhere near saturating the market, according to James Reiter, the Menominee Casino-Bingo Hotel general manager. The "buffalo" here is the relatively modest Menominee Casino, which employs about 550 people, almost double the number at the MTE mill.[69]

With only about 20 years of history, the casino has been vastly expanded to become a resort, adding some 170,000 square feet to the gaming and lounge/restaurant areas, upgrading the adjacent hotel, and adding convention space. Slated to be complete in late 2009, this $75 million project aims at significantly increasing revenues and profits and thus improving the distribution of benefits for the tribe. A potentially sustainable link back to the forest will be a spa that uses forest products. As North American woodland Indian representatives in a consortium to develop and market spa products, the Menominee will contribute product lines from their ecosystem such as wild rice lotion and products using ginseng.

Whatever one may think about the gaming industry, the casino is neither going away soon nor ceasing its steady subsidy of the tribe. Whether it is a sustainable economic activity is quite another thing, no matter the tiny linkages to the forest or to local ecotourist activities in which casino visitors already engage (for example, rafting on the Wolf River and visiting the logging museum). What does seem fruitful is the prospect of continued investments to sustain the tribe in the long term and lead to social and environmental justice in education, health care, and tourism. Beyond that, the casino must strive for better working conditions. Most needed, according to CMN president Fowler, is jobs paying living wages, not now the case with many of the gaming floor positions. General manger Reiter admits that part-time jobs (comprising about 40 percent of the workforce) carry no benefits package. "This is disheartening but we must compete in the open market," he says.

Fowler thinks, "It's then our role to push them to create better jobs. And more importantly, to bring up the skill levels of our people so they won't have to choose between minimum wages without benefits at the casino or nothing. We cannot condone work that perpetuates poverty."[70]

Perhaps an even bigger casino is the answer. The Menominee are in the thick of planning an off-reservation casino near Kenosha in southeastern Wisconsin that will dwarf their present facility. This project, estimated to cost $808 million, has been in the mill since 2004, when the Menominee signed an agreement with Dairyland Greyhound Park to obtain exclusive rights to purchase the track and its assets. Together with the Connecticut-based Mohegan Tribe, which runs one of the country's most successful Indian casinos, the Menominee will build a Las Vegas-type casino-resort and update the current racetrack and facility. When fully developed, it will employ 3,000.[71]

Legal action by the Potawatomi Tribe, which has long operated a casino near Milwaukee, halted the project for three years, but these obstacles were resolved in 2008 along with various legal clearances from the BIA and the EPA. Then, in January 2009, the outgoing secretary of the interior informed the tribe that their application had been denied. The tribe promised a quick appeal of this decision, claiming it "was not based on the law, but on an illegal guidance memorandum which the Tribe currently is challenging in federal court."[72] If the decision is overturned and the new casino goes forward, it will significantly raise the stakes and challenge the Menominee to remember the wisdom of their chiefs who spoke of keeping all pieces of the ecosystem intact, including the ancient Menominee culture. Is it possible that casino planners could have such a worldview? "Yes, definitely," says tribal chair Waukau. "We will control the way this will be run and we need the benefits to purchase land and provide health care for all Menominee. Are those not pieces of the sustainability puzzle?"[73]

THE SECOND PATH

When we reflected on what we discovered here more than a dozen years ago, we found enormous cause for hope. It is no less true now. With a blend of science and traditional practice, the forest is a paragon of sustainability. It pays for itself day-in and day-out by sustaining ecological services such as pollination, clean water and air, fish and wildlife habitat, and habitat for berries, sugar maples, and ginseng to thrive. More directly, of course, it also provides jobs and benefits to several hundred MTE employees and supplies the country with certified products from a sustainably managed forest. Diversification may finally begin to happen. As the regional wood products and pulp and paper economy shifts, the Menominee are proving their resilience once again.

Climate change is always the elephant in the room, and here foresters are only beginning to confront it. There are pathogens knocking on the Menominee forest door — emerald ash borers, spruce budworms, and root rots, for example — that by everyone's reckoning will spread farther in a warming world. "Our forest will be subject to more opportunistic diseases and invasives and its species composition will undoubtedly change," said Marshall Pecore. "But by keeping the ground diverse, it will adjust, partly on its own, partly with our help."[74]

The potential of College of Menominee Nation seems without bounds. In the words of a University of Wisconsin vice president, "In ten years, this college is going to grow into a major regional center."[75] With a green campus having sustainable development as its centerpiece and with a center focused on sustainable forestry for Indian country, the only drag on the college's future might be demographic. So far, Indian young men have not flocked to its doors; fully 70 percent of its students are women. Larry Waukau, our wise and good friend, sees trouble here, a sign that Menominee men more generally are failing to step up to the plate. "If you have disenfranchised people in society, be they men or women, what do you expect society will become?" he wondered. "Our society must somehow escape that trap."[76]

On the other hand, other tribal elders and leaders, without hesitation, always responded to my question about the rising generation (Do you see a teenager around here who could be sitting in your place twenty-five years from now?) with words like those of MTE president Miller, "Oh, absolutely. There are all kinds of gifted kids here; all they need is stamina and staying power."[77] Jeff Grignon, Mike Waukau, and Chris Caldwell, with education and experience in the world beyond the reservation, are such gifted men, all in their thirties, all with impressive stamina, wisdom, and hope. In 2007, Daniel Blackowl was an 18-year-old on his way to study meteorology at University of Wisconsin-Madison. For his peers, he had this advice: "Keep up your grades, don't let the nightlife of the rez slow you down, and if you set your mind to do something, you can do it."[78]

Here are the people who give elders the hope of achieving a new knowledge-based society. The Center for First Americans Forestlands believes this possibility naturally arises from the forest and its long history of sustainable management, while others envision an even wider horizon: becoming a global center for the exchange of information and skills on the blend of indigenous wisdom and science. They see the Menominee as a burgeoning hub for appropriate technology and the application of information science and technological innovation to a range of land and resource issues — nontimber forest products, ecological services, carbon sequestration, land-use planning, campus sustainability, and successful self-governance that blends Indian ways with American democracy.

With a new flush of casino revenues in the near future, the land base for such visionary thinking could expand and investments in education, health care, ecotourism, sustainable energy, and historic preservation could be vastly increased. Should even a portion of this happen, the Menominee will open new vistas for Native people and in fact for all of us. But the future, according to many Menominee, is not simply a matter of technology. Elder Eddie Benton Benai of the Lac Courte Oreilles northwest of the Menominee writes that the rush to technological development has everywhere led to a seared Earth. The other road, the spiritual one, is the slower path Native people have long traveled. "The Earth is not scorched on this trail. The grass is still growing there."[79]

A forest people who have long walked this second path, the Menominee know how to love rather than scorch their trail. Now they seem poised to apply this wisdom to a spectrum of other activities that can only broaden their prospects for sustainability. This is the unique narrative of these people: to be ever mindful of lessons from nature, to work with change and not be a victim of it, to learn, to evolve, and to thrive.

With a passion I can only describe as soulful, tribal chair and elder Lisa Waukau told me: "We've been here since the glacier retreated. We were the old copper people; we followed the mammoth here."[80] As a resilient and vigilant people, the Menominee now engage a fiercely changing world. Their resiliency, their wisdom of living in and with their vibrant forest, and their history of placing the common good above

the individual will serve them well. As they resourcefully and confidently absorbed the shock of the tornado that ripped across their
forest, so also have they sustained themselves for many millennia.
Today their homeland is full of promise and makes ordinary
Menominee proud to live here. More than one elder said something
like this: "The more people here travel off the reservation, the more
they appreciate that it's good to come home." Home indeed!

7

Gathering the Borderlands:
The Sky Islands of the Southwest

We are gathering these Borderlands together,
Mesas, arroyos, and valleys as far
as our eyes can see,
Blue mountain range upon mountain
range forever,
Turning towards dawnlight, then
into the evening West,
As far as pale North sky circling South,
to where vaqueros
Come crossing horseback by the
broken mesas in Mexico.[1]

~ Drum Hadley

*A*LMOST 14 YEARS HAVE SLIPPED BY SINCE WE LAST SAW the Sky Island Borderlands and crossed the big valleys that stretch beyond the eye to "blue mountain range upon mountain range" — an exhilarating vastness that stirs the soul in ways words cannot capture. The Borderlands are home to dozens of sensitive and threatened species, a few endangered species, and almost no invasives.[2] Missing from the native mix are grizzly bears, beavers, and wolves, but there are pronghorns, mountain lions, bighorn sheep, the rare Gould's turkey, and the occasional jaguar. Though not wilderness statutorily, this vastness is surely one of the wildest and least populated places in the lower 48 states. It is also caught up in the historically risky and often controversial cattle business and ever at the edge of devastating drought. In the eyes of rancher and poet Drum Hadley, folks here are "gathering these Borderlands together" to sustain lifeways that will ensure this unique

138

place, with its open spaces, ecological diversity, and historic *vaquero/cowboy* culture and economy, will remain perpetually so.

The Malpai Borderlands Group (MBG), which Drum Hadley helped found in the early 1990s, has worked hard toward these ends and has become celebrated for its vision and success. A nonprofit organization governed by a board of directors, MBG is managed by its executive director Bill McDonald and a staff of five. The group's annual operating budget is $142,000. In 1997 we concluded that the Malpai Borderlands Group was too young and untested to know whether it would succeed in protecting this great wilderness from the risks it faced, and it was too soon to tell whether its plans for ecological restoration would work.

In 2008, I returned to the ranch of Warner and Wendy Glenn for the annual meeting of the Malpai Borderlands Group to find out whether they had succeeded in fending off the fragmenting forces of the "New West"; whether they had found ways to restore the grasslands, riparian gallery forests, eroded arroyos, and dried springs that flourished here before 1870; and whether they had managed to protect not only the ranching economy but also the creatures of the wild mountain canyons. What follows is a story of "hard-headed folk" meeting crises with determination and grit and straying neither from their 15-year vision nor from the "radical center" where change improbably happens.[3]

MYSTIQUE OF THE BORDERLANDS

> *The roundup crew of the San*
> *Bernardino Ranch*
> *Had been asked to do two days*
> *of work in one day.*
> *The cattle buyer needed to have the steers*
> *In the shipping corrals of Agua Prieta,*
> *But it was one day earlier than planned.*
> *The vaqueros were spread out*
> *through the shimmering distances ....*[4]

Drum Hadley and others on the roundup crew at the San Bernardino Ranch back in the 1970's, were part of a cowboy culture now mostly gone. Back then "the shimmering distances" of the San Bernardino

Ranch south of the border symbolized a transborder cattle economy. Cattle reared on grasses in both Mexico and Arizona found their way to the corrals of Agua Prieta, the Mexican city a few blocks south of Douglas, Arizona. Butchered beef returned to the US market.[5]

"We have lived in an integrated society and economy," Gerry Gonzalez, district conservationist for Natural Resources Conservation Service, told me in his office in Douglas. "Ranches here and in Sonora are much alike and draw from the same workforce. Center pivot irrigation systems from Arizona are dragged south to be rehabbed in Mexico. Ranchers from both sides shop at Wal-Mart in Douglas."[6] Like most border regions in the US, "social and cultural life, commerce, family, and friends are spread on both sides" and until recently people have been able to almost ignore the border.[7] "No border," writes Alan Weisman of earlier times. "Only rivers and mountains crossed this country ... the lay of the terrain and the flow of the water was north and south. No line running east to west. The land here was inseparably one."[8] By Malpai program coordinator Peter Warren's reckoning, the Malpai Borderlands Group gained international prominence "because we're part of a border society. The group's planning area does not formally extend to Mexico, but there have been many ways we connect to ranches to our south. The mystique of being on the Mexican border is a big part of the story."[9] Drum Hadley put it this way: "The border is where hard gringo practicality has blended with a more romantic, older non-mechanistic view of how men should live."[10]

These Borderlands comprise a high plateau with valleys at elevations of 4,000 to 5,000 feet that stretch northwards from Sonora and are broken by parallel north-south mountains rising to about 8,500 feet. The Sonoran Desert to the west and the Chihuahuan, both lower and drier, to the east are biogeographically part of the same province. Rainfall, which can be as high as 20 inches annually in the mountains and averages about 14 inches annually across the valleys, is highly variable and may drop to 4 inches some years. Evapotranspiration is ten times rainfall.[11]

Domain of the Apaches into the mid-19th century and then hammered by Texans with huge herds of longhorns in the 1870s,[12] this harsh land comprises myriad ecological communities often subsumed as "desert grassland." Grasses were the dominant vegetation a couple of hundred years ago. Now they cover about 60 percent in the Malpai region but only about 20 percent in the Southwest as a whole.[13] So, except for the ponderosa pine-clad mountain tops (the "Sky Islands"), perhaps "desert scrub" or "thorn scrub" more accurately describes the present vegetation and associated biota.[14] Diamond A Ranch, the largest in the Malpai region, harbors 60 plant communities with at least 954 plant species, 80 species or subspecies of mammals, 320 bird species, and 52 species of reptiles and amphibians. Though desert in climate, in biodiversity this region "defies comparison to any other like-sized piece of North America."[15]

Ranchers in the Malpai Borderlands Group live in a pyramid-shaped area of about 1,500 square miles in southeastern Arizona and the boot heel of southwestern New Mexico (Figure 7-1).[16] Through the eyes of a natural resource professional, the Malpai Borderlands are a land tenure nightmare. The Chiricahua Mountains are almost all national forest and national park lands. The San Bernardino Valley is predominately State of Arizona land; the Peloncillo Mountains just east are a mix of public and private, while the Animas Mountains, one range further eastward, are wholly private. Everywhere else what you've got is a confounding mosaic of private, state, and federal lands. Five federal agencies and two states have built elaborate bureaucracies to oversee rangeland, forest, recreational areas, and water resources, and until the Malpai ranchers organized, they often worked at cross-purposes or at best without good coordination.

As for the private lands, some Malpai ranches are owned by families like the Glenns, who go back to the 19th century; others are worked by relative newcomers like Drum Hadley, who arrived in the region in the early 1970s. Ranchers in the Malpai Group — some 35 families — own or lease about 60 percent of the land.[17] All raise livestock. As lands in this part of the country go, despite the ownership maze, there is ecological contiguity. Apart from an 18-mile stretch of paved road, there's no fragmentation by highways or small holdings or big fences or towns. Telephones, fiber optic cable, and electrification, which did not get to most of this area until the 1980s and 1990s, have not seriously impeded wildlife or cattle movements.[18]

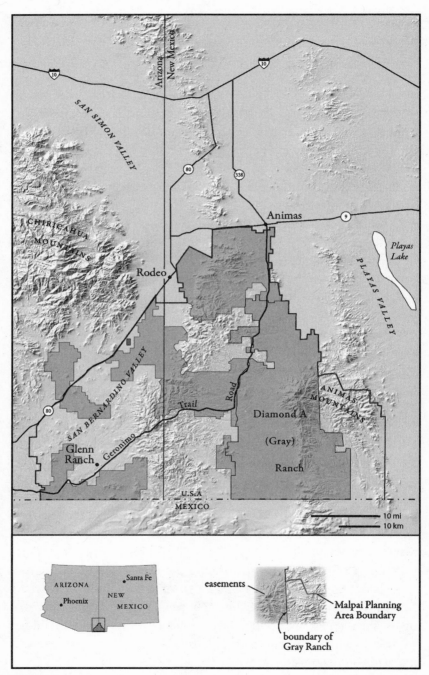

FIGURE 7-1
The Borderlands

Our Lands in the Belly of the Beast

Take them; invite them out to lunch.
Subdivisions in mountain valleys,
Wild running rivers, country ways
of livelihood,
Deer, cowboys, mountain lions, javelina,
Don't get attached. It's money. It's property.
It's real estate. It's things.
Take them; invite them out to lunch.[19]

The threat of subdivision of the open range into "real estate" is the single most significant undercurrent in this story of so-called rugged individualist ranchers banding together to create an organization that is all about community. Across the "New West," the raw calculus of the real estate market renders land held by ranchers worth far more as ranchettes for those seeking mountain valleys and deer than for raising calves.[20] "It's no contest, no matter the pay-back time," said Don Decker of the Natural Resources Conservation Service (NRCS). "Overnight, we could have a Sun City East here."[21] Alarmist? Perhaps. The Sky Islands are more than two hours from Tucson, El Paso, and Albuquerque. But perhaps not. At the northern edge of the Malpai planning area, halfway between Rodeo and Animas, New Mexico, there's evidence of folks who conceivably might invite ranchers out to lunch.[22]

Portal-Rodeo Realty
SUNDANCE ESTATES
10-40 Acres —
TERMS AVAILABLE

Rich Winkler, a strapping 42-year-old high school teacher with a ready, open smile, helps keep the family ranch near Animas going. He tells me his ranch is already on the front lines. "On a daily basis, people are looking at you through their picture windows, disturbing your privacy. Encroachment is right up to our borders."[23] Beyond the loss of privacy, fragmentation into ranchettes implies loss of the ecological cohesiveness of this country, abused in many ways to be sure, but in a far more natural state than, say, condo country around Albuquerque.[24] Winkler observes that roads to ranchettes bring traffic and dust; that folks put up high fences around their places and let loose their pets and their exotic landscape plants and pests, all of which threaten this desert ecosystem in ways ranching doesn't. And that's not to mention the pressure subdivisions put on scarce water resources.

"We are seeing a lot of new building on the fringe of our working area," wrote Wendy Glenn. "Soon the only places left for quiet hikes, hunting, scientific studies of the wonders of nature, and just enjoying the quiet landscape will be these few places, like the Malpai Group working area, that have been fortunately protected from subdivision."[25] A decade and a half ago, ranchers here intuitively knew what was coming, knew that saving their region from becoming "Sun City East" required sustaining their own ranches and the patchwork of supporting and buffering public lands. From this, they've come to explore the makings of a "New Western Range" where the *vaquero*/cowboy culture can mix with conservation biology.

According to Malpai adviser Nathan Sayre, the "New Western Range" will have big livestock ranches and vast open spaces that are essentially undomesticated, like the Malpai of the present. His term for this, borrowed from Arizona photographer Jay Dusard, is "working wilderness."[26] Whether this term resonates or not ("It's kind of odd but good as any," says Malpai executive director McDonald), it is a basic premise of the Malpai Borderlands Group, who resolve that they will work "to encourage profitable ranching and other traditional livelihoods, which will sustain the open space nature of our land for generations to come."[27] The concept has taken hold across the West as ranchers try to sustain the West's essence.[28]

What else besides the threat of subdivision was going on here in the early 1990s to catalyze Malpai ranchers — neighbors but rarely collaborators — to seriously organize? The answer can be summed up briefly as fire, endangered species, range wars, and the potential loss of the biggest ranch in the region. Together with the specter of ranchettes on all horizons, these got the ranchers' attention and they began to think more about the land and its future and less about the things that divided them.

Fire

What to do about fire on the landscape tapped into ranchers' long experience and "indigenous" knowledge that included a healthy respect for the natural lightning-set fires that happen across the Borderlands every summer and the human-set fires of aboriginal Americans over the centuries.[29] They understood that displacement of grasses by woody shrubs like mesquite was not simply an outcome of grazing practice or climate swings. They knew that fire deters the spread of woody species and gives grasses space to get established and dense enough to dampen mesquite germination. But fire here, as elsewhere in the West, had been routinely suppressed for a hundred years by local, state, and federal governments, allegedly "to save the range." In the absence of fire, brush species have taken over, and as ground cover has become more and more devoid of grasses, the country can no longer even carry a fire. The ranchers inherently understood that if you take fire away from this landscape, you can kiss the restoration of grasslands goodbye.[30]

Endangered Species

These open spaces and their sparse livestock densities also enable survival of species threatened or endangered elsewhere. Of the few sightings of jaguar in the US in the past 20 years, for example, two have been in Malpai of lone males up from Mexico seeking "who knows what?"[31] "It's no coincidence that where large wild landscapes are protected, that is where jaguars show up," wrote Wendy Glenn in 2007.[32] Similarly, both of the known sites of New Mexico ridge-nosed rattlesnake habitat in the US are in the Malpai. The Fish and Wildlife Service lists six endangered and 15 threatened species in the Malpai planning area. Species listing and the declaration of critical habitat under the Endangered Species Act are controversial among ranchers, for they can prohibit or forestall some aspects of their ranching operations while federal and state agencies, in trying to comply with the Act, become gridlocked.

For example, concerns about the New Mexico ridge-nosed rattlesnake and the lesser long-nosed bat have hamstrung prescribed burning in recent years. "The first times we tried to burn, the agencies came up with thousands of reasons why we should not burn, all having to do with endangered species," recalled Bill McDonald.[33] By the same token, declaring the Borderlands critical habitat for the jaguar (which two environmental organizations have sued the Fish and Wildlife Service to do), would in the eyes of Malpai ranchers be counterproductive.[34] To put it more bluntly, they believe it would backfire and hasten "the end of any jaguar activity in the United States."[35] For its part, the Fish and Wildlife Service thinks that designating critical habitat is unwarranted as there is no breeding population of jaguars north of the border now.

Range Wars

Another tense element in the mix in the early 1990s was a nationwide push by environmentalists to remove or significantly reduce livestock on public lands. Like Redwood Summer in the Pacific Northwest, the range war brewing across the West in the 1980s and early 1990s was polarizing and tense. The "Cattle Free by '93'" movement to end public lands grazing pitted protesters who'd never set foot on a ranch against long-term ranching families tied to the land and, in many cases, dedicated to restoring it. Among other things, environmentalists argued for curtailing the subsidized livestock economy by raising grazing fees on public lands. The idea got traction in the early months of the Clinton administration and in 1993 the federal government released a draft schedule of much higher grazing fees. Ranchers like those of the Malpai who depended on public lands for half or more of their pasture looked at the new fee schedule and said, "no way!"

As livestock associations beat back the proposed fees and the Sagebrush Rebellion got a new lease on life, environmentalists assailed western ranchers, alleging that livestock accounted for 90 percent of western riparian devastation and 59 percent of the deterioration of public rangelands, that livestock release too much methane, that they despoil rivers and campgrounds, and that they ruin our arterial health.[36] So it's not surprising that The Nature Conservancy, one of the country's biggest environmental organizations, would be seen as the enemy in the early 1990s when it arrived to "save" a big piece of the Malpai region — Gray Ranch.

Saving Gray

Named after a long-gone Texas Ranger who owned part of it, Gray Ranch (now called Diamond A) takes up about a third of the Malpai

Borderlands. Once a half-million acres, 322,000 acres of Gray Ranch became available for sale in the late 1980s when its Mexican owner let it be known that he would be willing to break it into smaller holdings. As it was one of the biggest and most biodiverse tracts of unfragmented privately-held land in the Southwest — land that included the entire Animas Mountain Range — ranchers and conservationists could agree that keeping Gray Ranch intact was crucial. Absolutely no one could imagine success here (whether focused on saving ranching or on nurturing the rich species mix) if the region ended up shaped like a doughnut with a giant hole at its core.

The Nature Conservancy (TNC) moved into the breach and in 1990 purchased the ranch, their first acquisition in a far-reaching national program called the "Last Great Places."[37] It was never the intention of TNC to hold on to Gray for long; they simply could not afford to. They immediately began seeking buyers. In doing so, "all possibilities were on the table," John Cook, the TNC officer overseeing Gray, told author Dan Dagget.[38]

That the ranch might become a National Wildlife Refuge, for example (a real possibility), with the potential of 65,000 visitors a year (also real), sent chills through the ranching community.[39] "The Conservancy might as well have announced that they actually were going to plop down three Manhattans in the Animas Valley," wrote Dagget.[40] Later, TNC's idea of subdividing the ranch into three management areas, each owned or managed by a different public or private entity, seemed equally absurd to the ranchers.[41] All in all, as Malpai ranchers wondered about how best to ensure their future, uncertainty about Gray Ranch further fed the crisis atmosphere of the early 1990s, an atmosphere that forced both the ranchers and TNC to think in ways neither had thought before.

AN EXPANDED WORLDVIEW

The Borderlands are where change occurs.
Where one is becoming another
And where one life is left and another is found.[42]

Among many moments of insight during my recent days in the Borderlands, I will long remember what emerged from a group interview around a dining room table late in the day. Present were Reese Woodling, a recently retired rancher and Malpai board chair; Ray Turner, board member and retired US Geological Survey ecologist now working at the University of Arizona Desert Laboratory; Larry Allen, retired Forest Service scientist, board member, and natural resource consultant; and Peter Warren of the Arizona Nature Conservancy, who is also program coordinator for the Malpai Borderlands Group. In response to questions about the most significant happenings in the past decade or so, the group circled round the idea of a changing worldview. After awhile, Peter Warren summed it up as "helping change what it means to be in ranching." He continued:

> We've had rich exchanges with Maasai from Kenya, with pastoralists from Mongolia, people from Brazil, and ranchers from all over the West. This has expanded the worldview of people involved in ranching here and has changed people's attitudes and perceptions about their role in conservation at a time when the society at large might be thinking that ranchers are only involved in destructive activity on the land. To turn that around and say, "No, you're doing beneficial work" just changes the whole attitude about how people feel about ranching. I'd call this a big success.[43]

I came to understand that such an expanded worldview is an underreported piece of this story and one of the reasons behind the sophistication Malpai ranchers have brought to collaboration. As Sarah McDonald, 24, the sole representative of the sixth generation of McDonald ranchers, had told me the day before, "We're more flexible than had the Malpai Borderlands Group never been formed and much more able to garner support from the wider world." To that, her dad concluded, "We hope so."[44]

John Cook and TNC counsel Mike Dennis and the ranchers became trusted collaborators in keeping Gray Ranch intact and ensured that both ranching and conservation would be well served. This is a key narrative in the Malpai mythos and an important precondition for the emergence of the Malpai Group. After all, Gray was not just vast but having been neither overgrazed nor fire-suppressed it was also an ecological gem. Gray Ranch was purchased in 1994 by a local foundation with the intent of perpetual management of the property as a cattle ranch. TNC holds a conservation easement on the ranch that prohibits subdivision, ensures the land will be maintained in at least the condition at sale, and promises to maintain monitoring plots to assess range conditions. No stock limits were stipulated.[45]

"We didn't sell the Gray to a cattle rancher," said John Cook. "We sold it to an institution with a charter, a board of trustees, and nonprofit status — an institution that has agreed to own the ranch forever, to never let it be developed, and to continue a very extensive monitoring program in perpetuity to ensure that the conservancy's goals are being met."[46] Now in the hands of folks the ranchers knew and trusted, Gray Ranch came to embody the soul of the matter: that all these lands would be managed according to a land ethic that enabled ranching to be part of a grand and wild landscape with fire and natural diversity and open spaces sufficient to sustain the economy and sense of place Malpai ranchers hold dear.

The Malpai Borderlands Group built their organization around this acquisition. With help from Drum Hadley and Jim Corbett, a Quaker pastoralist and activist from nearby Cascabel, ranchers and environmentalists first gathered at the Glenns' Malpai Ranch (hence the name "Malpai"). Jim Corbett's role was seminal. "With his Quaker background, Jim was instrumental at the onset. He took us in a consensual direction without making it obvious."[47] From there, the Glenns, McDonalds, Magoffins, and others joined hands to envision a better future and to work tenaciously and collaboratively on the looming threats of subdivision and fragmentation, resistance to fire, endangered species designations, and range wars. "What these guys wanted was fire back on the land, the ability to deal with agencies at the table, restoring their lands, preserving their livelihoods, and the possibility of easements. To us at The Nature Conservancy, these hopes seemed eminently reasonable," observed John Cook.[48]

As Bill McDonald thinks back, he recalls that:

> We were fortunate to have an individual with some means and some contacts in the environmental community who was interested in collaboration toward our purpose. Drum Hadley was the driver behind the scenes. There are lots of landscapes where a wealthy

person has a ranch in the middle, but mostly these
people don't have much to do with their neighbors.
Drum was an exception. So we got involved on a very
personal basis beyond the fact of our roles — me a
rancher from a family who's been here a while; Drum,
a wealthy neighbor and newer rancher; John Cook and
Mike Dennis, officers of a large environmental organi-
zation. Soon those roles fell by the wayside and we
were just people trying to get something done. When
you can get to that level, you can accomplish much.[49]

Indeed, by any typical set of performance outcomes, much has
been accomplished in the 15-year life of the Malpai Borderlands
Group. A contentious life of range wars and wrangling with the agencies has been replaced by another of collaborative accomplishment. As
Drum Hadley knew well, in the Borderlands when "one life is left ...
another is found."

The Malpai Borderlands Group was legally born in 1994 as a
private nonprofit organization. Although collaboration models in the
West usually have not taken this form, it has turned out to be a brilliant
choice for the Malpai. "It created a center and structure that at the
onset was not attempting to be 100 percent collaborative. The board
came up with the bylaws, *then* reached out to partners. Agencies were
encouraged to participate but could not be part of the board."[50] This
got them off the launching pad with deliberation and comparative
speed as well as very explicit goals:

> *... to restore and maintain the natural processes that*
> *create and protect a healthy, unfragmented landscape*
> *to support a diverse, flourishing community of human,*
> *plant and animal life in our borderlands region.*
>
> *Together we will accomplish this by working to encour-*
> *age profitable ranching and other traditional*
> *livelihoods, which will sustain the open space nature of*
> *our land for generations to come.*[51]

To accomplish these goals meant first, bringing as many as possible
of the 50 or so landowners on board, and second, pursuing a long and
tedious effort to find consensus on sustaining the ranching economy

in the region (as opposed to "submitting to the whims of specula-tion"[52]), returning fire to the landscape, and collaborating with government agencies on management of the ecological diversity of the Borderlands.[53]

That consensus was reached on these primary issues in less than two years might suggest a smooth path. In fact, it was bumpy.

> *I expected to have some resistance from some ranchers but I didn't expect them to go underground with it, to start spreading falsehoods and rumors to try to undo us. It got really nasty for us in those early years. But after awhile, they realized they weren't going to beat us. We really were doing just what we said we'd do. We weren't going to take away anybody's lives or give over everything to The Nature Conservancy. And people with conservation easements were still on their ranches. So that resistance died away and we were able to get things done.[54]*

The resistance that "died away" within the Malpai planning area is now mostly history, partly because Malpai has delivered tangible things to ranchers — easements, better working relationships with government agencies on whom they depend, collaborative watershed work, cost sharing with the NRCS Environmental Quality Incentive Program for wildlife-friendly fencing, and prescribed fire, to name a few.[55] What remains is suspicion outside the Malpai Group area, where there are still hard feelings. One Malpai rancher put it this way: "As Malpai has become successful, people out there have become more bitter. I feel the anger of some of those people I know. When somebody is successful, you know, people look at you with jealous eyes."[56]

Protecting an Unfragmented Landscape

> *As far as the eye can see, the distances*
> *cling to each spoken word*
> *As each word clings to the distances*
> *and tries to take them in.[57]*

Once Gray Ranch (Diamond A) was protected by a conservation ease-ment, the task was to offer the same protection to other ranches to keep them intact and fend off subdivision. Recall the deal The Nature

Conservancy cut in selling Gray. The lynchpin was the easement protecting Gray's conservation values in perpetuity. Under a conservation easement, a landowner agrees to limit land uses that might degrade a property's conservation value. Normally held in perpetuity by a third party, a conservation easement changes neither ownership rights nor the ability to sell or bequeath the property. However, the easement travels forever with the deed. The trick for the Malpai Group was to convince ranchers to give up some of their rights for the sake of ecological integrity and coherence and to raise funds to compensate ranchers for the current market value of these relinquished rights. Another way of putting this is that ranchers must secure the equity value of the subdivision potential of their land in exchange for the overriding community goal of protecting a healthy, unfragmented landscape with distances "as far as the eye can see."

Whether one sees the glass as half full or half empty, the Borderlands landscape has surely benefited from conservation easements. "We have *half* of the private land in the San Bernardino Valley protected! Very few places in the West can say, 'Our goal is to protect a whole valley and we're already halfway there.' However, another way to look at it is that we've still got half to go and there are no guarantees that we'll finish the job."[58] If one includes Diamond A and other ranches in New Mexico, of 480,000 acres of private land in the Malpai more than 320,000 acres are now in conservation easements with an additional several thousand acres added in late 2008.[59]

Cobbling together funding for conservation easements spurred an innovative program that has been copied elsewhere, called "grassbanking," which is the exchange of development rights for an equivalent value in forage. The Malpai Borderlands Group, leasing pasture from the Diamond A ranch, raised funds to offer easements to ranchers strapped for dry-season forage on their own holdings. By 1998, five ranchers with 17,400 acres had placed easements on their properties that granted them three to five years of grazing in exchange for subdivision rights. While their ranch rests, ranchers agree to work with the NRCS to develop and implement a grazing plan.[60] Rest, in theory, improves forage, which then will enable fire, sustain grass, and ultimately increase ranch revenues (not to mention the ecological benefits of enhanced wildlife habitat, less soil erosion, and better ground-water reserves).[61]

Although the grassbanking program has had no participants since 1998, it is still an available tool for staving off fragmentation.

Meanwhile, the Malpai Borderlands Group has successfully raised millions to pay other ranchers cash for their easements and Drum and his son Seth Hadley have easements on their ranches, through The Nature Conservancy in collaboration with the Animas Foundation. Keeping the program going is capital intensive and "is our biggest challenge to pull off," said financial director Mary McDonald. "I stay awake nights worrying about it. Lots of donors don't want to give money for easements and we can't keep going back to the same sources."[62]

Back to the half-full or half-empty glass. On the one hand, "at any given time, one of those families without easements could sell their ranch outright in the middle of our area, which would then compromise all contiguous ranches," Peter Warren told me. "The easement program is a huge accomplishment, but we've still got 150,000 acres to go."[63] On the other hand, some of this acreage may never need easements by virtue of being surrounded by ranches with them. The McDonalds' ranch is one example.

In 2007, a ranch with an easement south of Animas sold roughly at market value for about $2 million. What attracted the buyer, who was an outsider, was that his new ranch and those of his neighbors all had conservation easements. In other words, easements did not discourage him or seriously depress the selling price. "That rancher paid more for this property than cow/calf production could bring in over twenty years," said Don Decker of the NRCS.[64]

Enabling a Flourishing Community of Human, Plant, and Animal Life

> The Borderlands was a time and a place
> When men and women still knew
> Where they came from and who they were,
> And that milk came from off a cow
> Instead of a supermarket, and meat
> From the butchering of an animal.
> They knew that under all the world's paved places
> There was earth ....[65]

The Malpai Borderlands Group's success rests firmly on the presumption that resilient rangeland ecosystems require resilient communities with a strong sense of time and place and a clear knowledge of where their food comes from. No small part of their track record is built on what is expressed as a "hunger for community" in the Borderlands. "You know, the rugged individualist is not the full story. For generations we have also been neighborly," rancher Bill Miller told Jora Young in 1994. "We just revived the traditional practice of neighboring."[66] Don Decker, the NRCS range management specialist who returned to work here in 2004, told me he was surprised at the level of trust. "Despite what you hear about crusty ranchers, these people have found ways to meet and make decisions using consensus. It comes down to being neighborly and to trust between neighbors." [67]

When I brought up the usual tension one sees in the West between rugged individualism and community with John Cook, who has worked with the group from its beginning, he nimbly responded that community now trumps self.

> The Malpai Group was way ahead of its time. When the door to this community opened and my boss encouraged me to walk through it, I found Malpai to be one of the few places at the time where there was true community and leadership that understood what to do with it.[68]

Thinking about the evolution of this community, Bill McDonald remembers a time in the mid-1990s when "we got to the point where this group and what it was trying to do took precedence over all the little petty things that tend to break up groups like ours. I mean, there were people in the group who couldn't stand each other, but they came to work together because they knew they needed to."[69] Without any prompting or sentimentality, people I interviewed readily described this relinquishment of ego for the sake of their region as "the Borderlands community."

How did this return to neighboring happen? "Well, it comes down to good leadership," Reese Woodling, current chair of the Malpai board, said. "We have Bill McDonald. Most groups don't have a Bill McDonald as their visionary and leader." "Bill McDonald is the man," agreed Mark Apel of the University of Arizona Cooperative Extension Service, who's worked with McDonald for 15 years. Indeed, McDonald has earned a national reputation for his vision and wisdom in steering this organization. And it's true that few collaborative organizations can claim such leadership.[70] But to be successful, visionaries and leaders require collaborators at many levels and all agree that ranchers and partners in this extraordinary experiment are committed for the long haul. "What has not happened," ventured Peter Warren, "is that we've not had folks in the group who lack long-term commitment to make it work. Everybody here has pulled their share of the load and agreed to keep doing it."[71] McDonald says plainly, "We were extremely lucky to have some of the right people in the right place at the right time."[72]

Water and Earth

Beyond cattle, the basic pieces of restoring a flourishing community of plant and animal life in the Borderlands are water, earth, biodiversity, and fire. Bringing back the *ciénagas*/wetlands, restoring riparian corridors, and helping the water table recover are the projected outcomes of watershed work. Such restoration will help stem erosive forces that have left bare expanses and deeply cut arroyos — in essence, it will save the Earth for ecosystems to heal the Borderlands and preserve its unique biodiversity.

The watershed restoration program formally got underway in 2003 with grants from the Fish and Wildlife Service, the BLM, and the Claiborne-Ortenberg Foundation. In restoring "induced meandering" on incised channels, Malpai ranchers have constructed more than 2,500 small baffle and rock structures in gullies and draws. These capture sediment, increase infiltration, help natural revegetation, and control erosion. "With induced meandering we hope to manage erosion and deposition into stable patterns that will allow vegetation to grow and prosper out on the range."[73] By 2008 more than 15 miles of river courses had received such treatments. In addition, Josiah and Valer Austin, who own a ranch just outside the planning area in the Chiricahua Mountains and several other ranches adjacent to the planning area's southern boundary in Mexico, have installed tens of thousands of such structures in the watersheds that course through their properties. By all accounts, their work has been an inspiration to watershed restoration in the region.[74]

Biodiversity

Biologists estimate that in the surrounding Apache Highlands region there are 4,000 species of plants, 104 species of mammals, 295 species of birds, and 136 species of reptiles and amphibians, not to mention insects and other invertebrates.[75] Instead of continuing to fear that this biodiversity, particularly those species listed under the Endangered Species Act, might inhibit ranching, the Malpai Group argues that "if there's an endangered species ... and it is coexisting at the present time with grazing, then there's no reason why it shouldn't continue to be that way."[76] Warner Glenn, who spotted and photographed both jaguars seen in the Malpai, revealed his finds to the world in the belief that if these animals can wander through these mountains "it must mean we're doing something right."[77] On the other hand, the nexus of fire, grazing practice, drought, and other influences such as migration through the area of people crossing from Mexico raises questions about how best to restore and protect the plant and animal communities across this vast landscape.

The Malpai Group believes that if the ecological structure and natural processes are sustained, so also will be species, endangered or otherwise. The government, however, in enforcing the law, is forced to focus on species and, if they are designated endangered or threatened, to protect them from all harm, including habitat degradation. And here's the rub. As soon as the Fish and Wildlife Service defines and designates critical habitat for a listed species, the government is obliged to provide regulatory oversight of all human activities.[78] This is why ranchers cannot see a happy outcome of a critical habitat designation for the jaguar. As noted above, more than any other activity, fire has been the stumbling block. If a prescribed fire kills an endangered animal species on private land, no matter the long-term ecological benefit of the fire, this will be construed as a "take" and is punishable as a felony.

Over the last 15 years, the Malpai Group has had to grapple with the interaction of prescribed burning, construction of stock tanks, lion hunting, and the fate of four high-profile endangered species: the Chiricahua leopard frog, the lesser long-nosed bat, the New Mexico ridge-nosed rattlesnake, and the jaguar. In each of these cases, doing nothing was not an option, so finding an appropriate course through the thicket of ESA regulations and the risky business of risk assessment was necessary, case by case. So far, each of these species has survived management interventions. In the case of jaguars, which are now merely transient, a proposed ban on lion hunting with dogs was deemed unnecessary but the "critical habitat" designation looms.[79] As to dealing with possible conflicts between ranching and jaguars, in 1997 the Malpai Borderlands Group established a jaguar depredation fund to compensate livestock owners who can prove livestock loss to jaguars. As of this writing only one payment has been made.[80]

A "biodiversity breakthrough" that has taken more than five years to accomplish occurred in 2008 with the release of a Habitat Conservation Plan (HCP) for the Borderlands. If this passes successfully through various stages of public review and comment, it will, at long last, articulate Malpai Borderlands Group activities and the Endangered Species Act and provide an agreement that ensures compliance even during implementation of large-scale projects such as burning, watershed work, and water impoundments on private lands. Thereafter, it will not be necessary to go through the cumbersome case-by-case approach of the past. "When it becomes a signed, formal agreement, the HCP will prove to be an invaluable tool for achieving landscape-scale conservation in the Malpai Borderlands for years to come."[81]

Along with its agency partners, the Malpai Group played no small part in pushing for and brokering this agreement. Their resolve and willingness to work with state and federal governments and scientists to resolve the many intricacies of the plan point toward continued workable decisions on land management activities in endangered and threatened species habitat. This could not have been imagined 15 years ago, when most ranchers could think of dozens of ways they'd like to squash the Endangered Species Act and its enforcers. Now executive director McDonald says, "Relations with the Fish and Wildlife Service exceed those of any other agency."[82]

Fire

Founders of the Malpai Borderlands Group understood that putting fire back on the landscape required crafting a new relationship with state and federal agencies. Obstacles were legion. Now there's plenty of evidence of accomplishment. TNC ecologist Jonathan Adams writes that the Borderlands is one of the few places in the US where replication of natural fires on such a grand scale has been attempted with success.[83] Having contiguous ranchers, government agencies, rural fire departments, and fire scientists all at the table led first, to far-reaching fire plans, second, to massive prescribed burns, and third, to agreement to let natural fires run their course as long as ranches and public infrastructure are not threatened.

The Malpai Group's most active fire program is on the Diamond A (formerly Gray) where wildfires and prescribed burns have happened on more than 400,000 acres since 1989. In 2005, a big burn of 17,000 acres, overseen by the US Bureau of Land Management, brought fire to lowlands north of the Animas Mountains. In summer 2008, more than 42,000 acres burned, 98 percent of which were naturally ignited. These fires make the Diamond A "one of the few places in the Southwest where fire is playing something close to its natural role in the landscape."[84] Just outside Diamond A, one of the largest prescribed burns ever attempted in the US, the Baker II burn in 2003, covered 48,000 acres and required multiagency and landowner collaboration and oversight. Its purpose was to "reestablish a natural fire regime and improve hydrology in the Peloncillo Mountains where fire had been absent for many years."[85]

Prescribed burns and decisions to let natural fires go are now taken under two programmatic fire management plans that took more than a decade to hammer out. Among other things, the plans designate where natural fires should be allowed to burn, where they should not, and where prescribed fires should be set. What distinguishes the Malpai Group's role here is both their determination to bring fire back to this landscape and their willingness to stay at the table with the agencies. The original memorandum of understanding on fire required consensus among nine federal, state, and local agencies. "This was just slow, hard work," John Cook said when thinking about the tenacity of the Malpai Group. The benefit has flowed two ways. Fire experience in the Malpai, says US Forest Service district ranger Bill Edwards, "has really changed Forest Service attitudes toward fire. Before, it was suppression largely; now what we're looking at is 'appropriate management response,' where we could have full suppression on one flank, fall back to a holding action on another flank, and letting a natural fire burn on another."[86]

"Fifteen years ago, ranchers here would rail at the Forest Service and other government agencies. That's all changed. We are collaborators now, though there are still ranchers in the area who don't always get along with these agencies. Overall, we are slowly winning more and more people to our side, not only in the working area but farther out as well."[87] The Nature Conservancy's Peter Warren, whose job is to head up relations with state and federal agencies for the Malpai Group, concludes: "We've set the marks for what's possible in field management of big fires and how to protect endangered and threatened species through a programmatic plan."[88]

Reflecting back on what we heard in the mid-1990s, the Malpai Group realized that to achieve their goals they had to include and respect the interests and ideas of agencies with vastly different histories and experiences. This was partly what moving to the radical center was all about — moving to a place of neither more regulation nor laissez faire ranching.[89] The vast and complex fire program is squarely in that radical center and it "shows it's possible to have collaborative relationships in places where people were once polarized and litigious."[90]

Whether frequent fire on this landscape has been successful in bringing back the grasslands is another matter. Partly because the Borderlands have suffered through a long drought during most of the Malpai Group's history, grasses have germinated poorly. In the McKinney Flats study, which explicitly looked at the impacts of fire on herbivory, grass abundance plummeted on all plots, no matter the treatment (fire, fire with grazing, grazing alone, or no management). "This shows that severe drought swamps every other management system. You can't improve the range if you don't have rain."[91] McKinney Flats, on the other hand, along with other sites, apparently also reveals that livestock grazing itself may dampen shrub encroachment (as range manager Alan Savory has long argued), lending further credence to the view that totally removing livestock will not in itself help rangeland restoration.[92]

Science

From its beginnings, the Malpai Borderlands Group decided that peer-reviewed science — "the best science available" — would be the basis for resource management decisions.[93] As it turned out, one of The Nature Conservancy's most important early contributions was providing access to this unfamiliar world of ecological science (as opposed to range science) and ultimately raising the profile of science with ranchers. A Science Advisory Committee helps review projects and provides credibility to the overall program.[94] Even so, science outreach is still necessary. Ben Brown, current Malpai science coordinator, says one of the most important aspects of his role is to "make science safe and nonthreatening for ranchers. As such, we don't ever tell people how to manage their ranches; what we share is information derived from plots, some of which may have management implications."[95] The Malpai Group sponsors annual science conferences that are attended not only by scientists and agency professionals but also by ranchers. "Science is helping the ranchers in this area to do a better job of managing the land, though now we can't precisely document the outcomes."[96]

The Malpai science program has worked at developing baseline data to understand trajectories of change involving fire, livestock grazing, and grassland restoration. To do this, a series of 100 by 200 meter plots has been systematically monitored across the MBG working area. Data are accumulated, stored, and processed by the USDA Agricultural Research Service in Tucson. "Although this data set has revealed interesting patterns, because it lacks controls and has no corresponding weather information, statistically we haven't been able to draw conclusions, say, about the relationship of fire on a grand scale to brush prevalence or to grass recovery," Brown said. The results thus have generally not found their way into peer-reviewed journals. "This is disappointing because we have failed to meet our own standard."[97]

While the recognition of shortcomings here is commendable, the way the Malpai Group has responded is more important. They will not abandon their monitoring. Instead, they will sharpen its focus, first, by concentrating on a few sites where site dynamics are unknown, and second, by collecting information and performing rapid range assessment on a smaller but broader array of sites more evenly distributed across the planning area. At the same time, they realize their science so far has not answered key questions about the "whole landscape" and their impacts on it. So the Malpai Borderlands Group will ratchet the preponderance of their research upward to the scale at which ranching happens. They will use both aerial photography (dating back to 1946) and satellite imagery to identify trajectories of change in the structure of ecological communities and will try to specify signatures of management actions such as controlled burns and watershed restoration. If this program garners funding, it will become a major part of Malpai science and will "enable us to move our focus from individual plots on ranches to the landscape level."[98]

In *The Ecology of Hope* we set forth attributes that signal sustainable lifeways. Among these were a good working knowledge of the ecosystem, a commitment to learning, acceptance of change, and a long-term investment horizon. Each of these is manifest in the Malpai Group's decision to alter the course of their science program. They realized they needed to change; microscale science wasn't answering many of their questions. Their flexibility shows organizational resilience. Also, they have been and obviously now are impressively dedicated to learning. Further knowledge of ecological site dynamics at the scale of research plots is still needed. This can ultimately be applied to "pasture-level" grazing decisions, pest control, smaller prescribed burns, watershed structures, and reseeding. But that's not enough. They also need mesoscale information to understand what kinds of prolonged change are happening over the entire planning area. And so they are willing to invest resources over the long term to fathom patterns and drivers of change and achieve what they describe as "a viable land ethic," a term brought to them by Jim Corbett that means ranching in a way that sustains "the health and unreduced diversity of the native biotic community."[99] What I see in Malpai science mirrors the most laudable and perhaps the most replicable elements in their quest for sustainable life in the Borderlands.

What the Future May Hold

> I am this day when the first Summer rains
> Have come after all these months of dryness.
> Arroyos, rippling, grasses growing, birds ...
> All the cow country singing a different song.
> I am all that stayed waiting ...
> after all that you wanted was gone.[100]

What do you see when you look 15 years down the road? I asked folks in the Malpai. What do you fear? Will "all the cow country" be "singing a different song" as after the first summer rains? In fielding those questions, *nobody* responded with anything but optimism that the Malpai Borderlands Group would travel further down the path to sustainability. Against all odds, to use Nathan Sayre's words, a legacy of futile polarization has been eclipsed by grassroots collaboration. Success has built on success and swirled around again to spawn still more success. "What we've got here is nothing but positive," Ray Turner, an insider, asserted.[101] Bill Edwards, looking through the lens of the US Forest Service, observed that the "bonds that have developed could never have happened if a government agency had started this. At the root is a community trying to preserve its way of life and the love of this place."[102]

Framed as an example of community-based conservation, the accomplishments of the Malpai Group are impressive. Gathering ranchers around a crystal clear mission that struck common ground with environmentalists and agencies has reinforced and strengthened their sense of place, built community, opened doors for collaboration, and put the Malpai in the national spotlight. As a consequence, half the private lands are protected by conservation easements, thousands of watershed and grassland restoration projects now stem gullying and erosion, prescribed and controlled natural fires have returned to over 400,000 acres, a resilient science program tries to fathom how best to restore and sustain these high-desert ecosystems, endangered and threatened species populations are protected, bighorn sheep and falcons have been reintroduced, and two fire plans and a Habitat Conservation Plan guide future projects.

It is impossible to say definitively whether these 15 years of collaborative conservation are yet reflected on the Borderlands landscape. Many hot issues are wrapped up in this relationship: cows, brush and grass, arroyos and erosion, ranchettes and fragmentation — issues crucial to the future of the region and of the Malpai Group. Larry Allen, the retired Forest Service coordinator instrumental in bringing the Forest Service into the Malpai Group, said, "I know that empirically we can't prove these watersheds are healthier for our efforts. But I think they are. Proof of that is that we've got jaguars coming into these lands that haven't been seen here for a hundred years and we've got aplomado falcons and bighorn sheep."[103] If he's right, the new Malpai monitoring system ought to show the Malpai planning area as a glowing green garnet.

Long ago Wallace Stegner wrote: "When [the West] ... fully learns that cooperation, not rugged individualism, is the quality that most characterizes and preserves it, then ... it has a chance to create a society to match its scenery."[104] The Malpai Group and its collaborating partners are taking a shot at such a society. They believe that working together on the common ground of conservation and ranching, an inconceivable ground only two decades ago, will build community and sustain the lands of the spectacular country they love. It has worked so far.

But their work is far from done and nobody underestimates the obstacles out there: climate change that augers very poorly for the Southwest and more pointedly for the Malpai Group's crusade to fight brush encroachment and bring back grasses;[105] unprotected ranches and the capital required to put conservation easements on them; the solidarity, organizational capacity, and generational turnover of the Malpai Group; the precarious economics of the cattle business; and an increasingly tense border with Mexico, with proposed security fences and stepped-up enforcement that adds roads, crisscrossing Border Patrol vehicles, and perhaps undocumented immigrants and drug war refugees.

Though daunting, apart from climate change each of these challenges also offers opportunities, according to people I interviewed. John Cook of The Nature Conservancy is confident that the group will be able to continue to raise the funds needed. "I mean, this could be jaguar habitat soon and that would attract tourists from all over the world. I am confident this will enable us to raise money despite the competitive philanthropic market."[106]

Of solidarity, organizational capacity, and the group's age profile, MBG folk say, "We've managed so far and have laid the groundwork for new people to keep the organization going."[107] The demographics of the most active ranchers certainly portend generational turnover of land in the next couple of decades. Will the next generation want to ranch? Sarah McDonald, of the rising generation, says, "There's a lot of interest in people my age in returning to the land. Down the road, what we do may not be what our parents have done. Perhaps we'll go for niche branding of beef. There will be a different look in the future ...."[108]

The push/pull of the Mexican and US economies continues to send a stream of immigrants across the border. "Where a single hungry Mexican might appear at my door for food a few years ago, now whole families come begging," rancher Suzie Krentz told me.[109] In the Malpai, this flow adds to landscape litter, is a risk to human life (these ranches, after all, are "wild'), and may even influence fire ecology. The Malpai Borderlands Group takes no position on immigration but they have confidently used their collaborative experience to engage the Border Patrol by including them in meetings, by sponsoring a border field trip in 2007 for the local US congresswoman, and by trying to explain how new roads and fences along the border have the potential to backfire. Sadly, the more the border is "sealed," the more likely it is to become a conflict zone, which is not good for humans, cattle, or wildlife.

Despite or perhaps because of these challenges, the Malpai Borderlands Group seems likely to thrive in its noble mission. It is organizationally strong and cohesive and more financially stable than many community-based groups. It has a tidy endowment with the intent to increase it further ("We pretend it's not there," Mary McDonald said) and an enviable record of tapping the worlds of philanthropy and science for its projects, easements, and networking. The Diamond A and the Animas Foundation are invaluable and reliable partners. Then there is grit. "I would never bet against these people," John Cook said. "They've been here since before statehood and they can roll with the punches. They know how to survive."[110]

And finally, there's the lifestyle they want to protect. After all, what this tiny group of ranchers and its partners want to sustain are those icons of the Borderlands — the *vaquero*/cowboy way of life and the Borderlands mystique. For this reason alone, it is hard to deny the Malpai éclat. Though the people who do the tedious work here refuse to be romantic, the ranching life is not to be taken lightly. The aura of a Borderlands ranch that infuses every corner of the Glenns' spread and stretches to blue horizons is somehow so authentically American as to be a haunting metaphor in these times for dreams lost and, in certain ways, dreams yet to be realized.

8

Healing Relationships, Healing Landscapes:
The Mattole Valley, California

Our movement is contributing in some small way to a larger societal shift in which we reward restoration more than we reward destruction.[1]

~ Jeremy Wheeler

As a species, we have become a population of refugees, longing for homes we remember only faintly, as we remember dreams. The process of reconstruction and immersing ourselves in our own specific places at times resembles the effort to recreate the memory of a victim of amnesia.[2]

~ Freeman House

*I*N THE SUMMER OF 2006 I FOUND MYSELF IN TRACY KATELMAN'S spacious office in Old Town Eureka, about 60 miles north of the Mattole Valley. A professional forester and proprietor of Forever Green Forestry, Tracy makes her living in forest assessment, management, and fire safety. She has lived and worked extensively in the Mattole Valley. Despite her work as a forester and her credentials, some folk still connect her with the turbulent early 1990s, when she arrived here for Redwood Summer, the protests that brought the plight of old-growth redwood forests to the attention of the world. "Redwood Summer will ever be part of my identity," she admits.[3]

In the polarized world of northern California two decades ago, Redwood Summer protesters saw "locals" as the enemy. "Locals" included ranchers, fishers, millworkers, and families whose livelihoods were dependent on the natural resources of this wet and cool part of the continent. Industrial timber, a deeply embedded segment of the economy, built towns like Eureka, Arcata, and Scotia, ran mills, owned the staging and shipping infrastructure, and provided plenty of jobs. Millworkers, loggers, and those who serviced them were a big segment of the workforce. Ranchers, with ample tracts of forest, were their allies.

On a crystalline morning, in the shade of a small barn in the lower Mattole Valley a few days after I spoke with Tracy, Sterling McWhorter talked with me about the ranching economy, the threat of fire, the fast-recovering forests, and the difficulty of raising a family here. As manager of the McWhorter family partnership, a 4,000-acre ranch owned by the family for three generations, Sterling, with his seven siblings, battles uncertain cattle markets, crippling inheritance taxes, threats of subdivision, and what they see as an unfriendly regulatory environment.[4] Described by others in the Mattole as a property rights advocate, Sterling McWhorter, who's about the same age as Tracy, is extolled for his generosity and humanity, his community spirit, and his willingness to work hard.

In the days of Redwood Summer, McWhorter would likely have been stereotyped as a "good old boy," a guy who surely wouldn't hang out with the likes of Tracy Katelman. And by the same token, Katelman would have been seen by most ranchers as a "hippie homesteader envirofreak." These were the polarities of this region less than two decades ago, bespeaking lifestyles and assumptions people had about each other. In the late 1990s, the Mattole Watershed Alliance, a promising collaborative that tried to bridge the rancher-homesteader divide, blew up. For the next several years, ranchers and homesteaders retreated to their separate camps.

Tracy Katelman and Sterling McWhorter may not be perfect archetypes of this polarity, for each spends some of their life out of the valley and neither necessarily speaks for their elders. And it surely is unfair to stereotype and oversimplify their many-layered lives, occupations, preferences, and opinions. Yet how each has changed over the past dozen or so years is a story worth telling. Each is now a collaborative leader who not only honors the first generation of Mattole visionaries and community organizers but also inspires new ways of pursuing "reconstruction and immersion" in this remote California valley where home is no longer a distant dream.

One such new way is the Buckeye Conservancy, formed in 1999 as a collaborative organization without explicit connections to previous natural resource conflicts. Depicted on its website as a North Coast organization of family farmers, ranchers, forest landowners, and resource managers dedicated to ecological and economic sustainability of natural resources and open space, the Buckeye Conservancy has a membership of 200 households, who own some 300,000 acres in Humboldt County (not all in the Mattole).[5] Sterling McWhorter is chair of the Conservancy's board. Tracy Katelman helped the Conservancy write a ten-year plan and devise ways to change California forestry regulations to favor family landowners.

Compared to the heated timber wars of Redwood Summer, the Mattole has chilled. Gone are the angry confrontations, the complete isolation of ranching and homesteading communities, and the animosity and caution bred by separation. Everywhere I went I heard of bridge people like Tracy and Sterling, of collaborations like the Buckeye Conservancy, of events like Grange pancake breakfasts and farmers' markets that bring folks together, and of stunning stream and creek restoration, water conservation projects, and an epic struggle to save salmon. Twelve years down the road, the Mattole still manifests the power of collaboration toward sustainability.

THE VALLEY

The Mattole River drains a compact watershed of about 300 square miles amid the coast ranges of northern California (Figure 8-1). It is California's westernmost watershed. The Bureau of Land Management (BLM) owns about 22 percent, some of which is in the newly-designated Northern California Wild Heritage Wilderness. The remainder is a mix of working ranches (about one third of the watershed), rural residences, and areas protected by conservation easements (about 7 percent overall).[6] About 3,000 residents make their lives here on some 900 separate parcels.[7]

The Mattole flows north, empties into the Pacific just south of Point Mendocino, and like all northern California rivers has long been the spawning destination of coho and chinook salmon and steelhead trout.

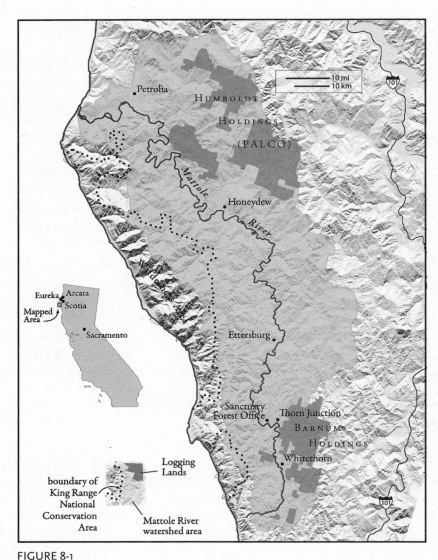

FIGURE 8-1
The Mattole Valley

Beneath the offshore waters of Point Mendocino, three tectonic plates come together and make the Mattole Valley one of the most tremulous places in the US. When the builders of Highway 1 along the California coast encountered this mountainous and tectonically alive terrain, they plotted a course eastward to avoid the place. This left a 60-mile stretch of coast inaccessible and undeveloped — a "lost coast" just a mountain range away from a Shangri-la of incomparable beauty: the Mattole Valley, a place, one could say, left alone thanks to those tectonic plates.

The climate here is the cool variant of Mediterranean. Throughout the winter low pressure systems roll in from the north Pacific and bring 100 inches or more of rain. During this damp, frost-free winter, salmon and steelhead fight their way upstream to spawn in the river of their birth. As winter yields to spring and precipitation subsides, eggs hatch to fry that then mature as fingerlings in the shady pools of the upper watershed. They migrate downstream. Some head out to sea. Others become juveniles in the river during the warm, dry summer. By November they're ready to swim into the Pacific for the next four or five years. But first they must wait for the river to swell enough to break through the sand bar that closes the estuary in late spring.

This cycle of seasons and salmon stretches back at least 5,000 years and surely provides a sublime setting for humans. People who live here now often use the word "paradise." Before 1850, Athapaskan-speaking Mattole and Sinkyone peoples claimed this paradise as theirs. Like their neighbors, they were fishers, hunters, and gatherers who fashioned their lives around acorn production, the controlled burning of the forest and prairie, and the bountiful seasonal gift of salmon and steelhead. We know few details of their lifeways, for they disappeared quickly and tragically when settlers in the late 1850s expropriated land and dealt brutally with the Natives. By 1862, almost all the indigenous people of the Mattole Valley had been slaughtered. The few survivors were shipped to reservations, where they and their language soon became extinct.[8] "In the span of eleven years, a culture and people which had been in place for hundreds or thousands of years was completely decimated."[9]

Settlers brought cattle, sheep, hogs, and a market driven economy to the valley. Isolated though they were, they found ways to respond to the needs of fast-growing California. Oil wells near Petrolia in the late 1860s raised hopes of quick money but the oil proved insufficient and the boom fizzled. A bustling agricultural economy, based on crop agriculture, orchards, and livestock, carried the valley through the latter decades of the 19th century and well beyond. Fertile soils and ample rainfall brought good harvests and settlers cobbled together a rough-hewn prosperity. They built a school and churches. Commercial opportunities, such as

sawmills and gristmills, a slaughterhouse, and a tannery, brought entrepreneurs to the valley and created supplementary income for ranchers.

Abundant runs of salmon and steelhead handsomely supported
offshore commercial fishers and local river fishing. The size and scale of
these runs were fabled, especially of the king (or chinook) salmon,
returning without fail every November as resplendent 35-pound
adults. During their exuberant runs, horses spooked at crossings and
people could scoop salmon from the river using pitchforks. As with the
indigenous peoples, but with none of their rites of self-regulation, the
coming of the salmon brought the community to the river to celebrate
the wondrous cycle of spawning, death, and rebirth.

Up to World War II, the Mattole had a diverse and relatively self-
sufficient economy that required hard work, survival skills, and no
small measure of ingenuity. Sterling McWhorter's grandparents would
have known how to frame homes and barns, lay out fence, get water to
house and livestock, tinker with wagons and plows, rear and care for
livestock, deliver babies, fish and hunt and clear forest, and selectively
burn to expand pasturelands. They had also brought with them inad-
vertent guests. For example, European grasses marched in on the
hooves of their livestock. Non-native species quickly displaced native
bunchgrasses, but with little tolerance for the long, dry summers they
utterly failed to provide summer feed. To feed stock in summer, the
flatlands had to be plowed and put to exotic species of hay.[10]
Troublesome plants like Japanese knotweed and scotch broom somehow also spread across the pastures and forest edges. Just as Native
peoples had altered the landscape over many generations, so also did
the Euro-Americans, though at comparative warp speed and with
much more profound ecological impacts. And the biggest changes were
yet to come.

After World War II, loggers came into the valley. In 1947 more than
three fourths of the watershed was forested with old growth: redwoods at
the headwaters, Douglas fir in the lower valley. Newly developed bulldozers gave loggers access to steep slopes and serious logging and
milling began in the 1950s. Between 1950 and 1970, eight sawmills
operated out of Honeydew alone. It was a feeding frenzy:

> It came out fast ... all in the space of [a] single genera-
> tion. No one paid any attention to what anyone else

*was doing. There was no awareness, really, that a whole
watershed was being stripped of its climax vegetation
all at once .... The trucks taking timber out of the valley were so numerous and frequent that their drivers
had to agree on one route out and another one in.*[11]

According to rancher Sanford Lowry, the logging boom was partly
the result of an ad valorem tax on standing timber levied by California in
the 1940s.[12] Lowry's father was burdened with more than $1,000 in addi-
tional annual taxes on his Bear River ranch. "This was ample incentive for
everyone to sell off timber as fast as they could." So it was sold cheaply at
about $2.50 per 1,000 board-feet (compared to $350 per 1,000 board-
feet now), and this opened the Mattole for the expansion of ranching.

Lowry says "gypo loggers," mostly from Oregon and two or three
times removed from the buyers, did the cutting. Working on very
narrow margins, they logged badly, cutting roads up and down slopes,
skidding in the creeks, doing the job as cheaply as possible. To the
ranchers' dismay, they left the landscape a wasteland and virtually all of
this happened before passage of California's 1973 reforestation act.
Once the timber was cut, the land became "stump meadows" for cattle
and sheep. Sterling McWhorter recalls his family having regrets about
how that logging was done. Had the ranchers themselves logged, he
says, "There's no way they would have done it like that."[13]

Yet logging provided good jobs. A generation of men made their living
in the woods and mills, and many of them came from ranching families.
By the late 1980s, the big stands of big trees were gone: 91 percent of the
old-growth forests had been cut.[14] Loggers moved on and took most of
the jobs with them. What they left behind was an exposed, steeply slop-
ing landscape, subject to frequent tremors and quakes, in one of North
America's wettest places. "For anyone who knows anything about accel-
erated erosion, this was a formula for disaster," said geomorphologist
Thomas Dunklin.[15] The soil quickly found its way into the Mattole.

To make matters worse, in the 1960s and 1970s a number of ranchers,
especially in the headwaters, subdivided their holdings into 40- and 80-
acre tracts for newcomers. Each property required a road or long drive-
way. Most were roughly hacked along steep slopes with inadequate drainage
and culverts. In the heavy winter rains they would wash out. These roads
were contributing tons of sediment to the river and its tributaries.[16]

SALMON GOING DOWN

The Mattole had been prime salmon and steelhead spawning habitat for several thousand years. Now it was choked with sediment. Severe storms in the 1950s and 1960s changed the river "from a cold, stable, deeply channeled waterway enclosed and cooled by riparian vegetation to a shallow, braided stream with broad, cobbled floodplains, warm in summer, flashy in winter."[17] The river of the 1970s mocked the one the indigenous peoples called "the Mattole" or "clear water."

Places where salmon and steelhead lay eggs and pools where young fish mature — cool, clean gravel beds — were buried in mud, especially those in the lower and mid-Mattole. Trees that once provided shade along the riverbank were gone. Modern Mattole inhabitants who had participated in celebrating and feeding upon the once spectacular runs were alarmed. "We could see that the rivers here were in trouble," said rancher Lowry.[18]

Mattole king salmon runs, reckoned to be more than 30,000 in the mid-1960s, had dwindled to a few hundred by the late 1970s. Though forces at sea undoubtedly contributed to the decline, a group of homesteaders were convinced the river's bad health was even more important. Without places to spawn and summer-over, the salmon would have no chance whatever. The Mattole king salmon was the last genetically wild salmon along the California coast. Saving them became an urgent community mission. Like first responders, a small group of volunteers rushed to the scene of the disaster — the river itself. They formed the Mattole Salmon Support Group (now called the Mattole Salmon Group or MSG) and pledged to restore the run. Though ranchers were never systematically excluded, most were never included either and some came to think of the MSG as a kind of exclusive club.

In *The Ecology of Hope* we told the story of their early work, which included a unique hatchbox program to improve hatch-to-fry ratios, diverting some downstream migration of juvenile fish in spring to cool pools where they could spend the summer, engaging school kids in rearing and releasing fish, monitoring stream conditions, building the best database in California, obtaining state and federal funding, and working with a wide array of partners in government and the community to stabilize populations of salmon and steelhead. Between 1982 and 1996, more than a half-million community-nurtured king salmon were released to the sea.

A lyrical and thought-provoking account of these years is Freeman House's memoir, *Totem Salmon*. [19] House concluded in 1998 that it was impossible to know whether restoration projects had stabilized the salmon runs. The same can be said today. As if to punctuate his plaintive conclusion, the coho was listed as threatened under the federal Endangered Species Act. Seven years later, the chinook was also listed. In the late 1990s, a survey by the National Marine Fisheries Service found some fifty coho juveniles in pools in Mill Creek, a Mattole tributary, a hopeful number for an endangered species. House writes:

> No one will ever know if it was the introduction of juvenile fish into the creeks, or the restoration and maintenance of habitat, or the protection of the ancient forest, or a combination of the three that has resulted in the presence of coho here. No one much cares. Human hands have been applied in ways that resonate with the resilience of the recovery of the wild. [20]

This simple and profound insight is at the heart of community-based conservation aiming at sustainability. If we humans can find ways to intersect with that "resilience of the recovery of the wild," we will have discovered a way human systems can support ecological integrity and dynamism, and this would be a way toward sustainability.

What's happened with salmon in the past decade in the Mattole is a story of both resilience and the ecology of the possible. Three elements stand out. First, the Salmon Group itself matured from a largely volunteer effort to a full-fledged nonprofit with professional staff, a full-time executive director with degrees and experience in fisheries, and a cadre of AmeriCorps watershed stewards. With an annual budget of $350,000, MSG receives funding from the California Department of Fish and Game (DFG), the federal Bureau of Land Management, the National Oceanic and Atmospheric Administration (NOAA) Fisheries, the California State Coastal Conservancy, and others. As in the past, MSG finds its work thwarted at times by rule-bound state agencies and officials "who should have been acting as our partners in salmon restoration but often far more resembled our adversaries." [21]

Second, the work of MSG toward salmon recovery continues unabated, though with significant changes. Of these, surely the most profound is termination of the hatchbox program in 2003. That year the California DFG decided to suspend all citizen-based hatchbox programs in the state, claiming a serious risk of genetic bottlenecks. This decision was based on what was known about salmon genetics at the time. "We didn't put up much of a fight," remembers MSG cofounder and long-time hatchbox advocate, David Simpson. "We understood that in five years the decision would be reviewed."[22]

In 2004, a series of papers by the same geneticists DFG had used to ban hatchboxes recanted some of their findings.[23] As of this writing, the issue is unresolved and the work of MSG, legendary along the salmon coast of North America, carries forth resiliently but without hatchboxes. Their work these days includes habitat improvement projects in the estuary and tributaries, annual spawner surveys and databases (begun in 1981), monitoring summer populations of steelhead (since 1996), estuary temperature and dissolved oxygen monitoring (since 2001), channel monitoring, diversion of chinook juveniles to constructed pools in early summer, and continuing engagement of schoolchildren in salmon releases.

Of the diversion of chinook, Simpson says, "We fight tooth and nail with DFG about this diversion. They think nonintervention is a better policy. It may be in some cases. I don't think it is here. The alternative is a shallow, ecologically unhealthy, too warm estuary, which kills chinook juveniles in summer."[24] This disagreement is a problem. DFG, after all, funds some of the work of the Mattole Salmon Group. At the same time, the federal government, now actively on the scene because of the coho listing, favors more intervention.[25] "So here we are, a community group, caught in a turf battle between government agencies," says Simpson. Yet MSG's work has so impressed the US Fish and Wildlife Service that they have provided additional funding under the Endangered Species Act. MSG has thus partly influenced federal policy toward coho restoration.

Finally, and importantly, after almost three decades of community-based salmon recovery, population trends are "at least not negative."[26] MSG's long-term monitoring, itself a highly systematic and important element of conservation here, may indicate stabilization of the runs. MSG believes that "by conducting salmonid population monitoring and analyzing trends ... we [continue to] add to local and scientific understanding of salmon populations and life history strategies. We will develop restoration projects based on cumulative [data] and create adaptive ways in which humans can help preserve these magnificent fish."[27]

What have they learned?

- **Poaching:** The advent of the salmon group spelled the end of poaching. "We could quantify declines of the run at the headwaters, so poachers who used to argue that there were still a lot of fish in the river were shown to be wrong. Twenty years later, people are fully aware of the precarious state of the run and it would be a huge breach of what people consider acceptable community conduct to take salmon or steelhead from this river."[28]

- **Tributaries:** A series of channel monitoring projects in the upper Mattole measure stream cross sections and profiles, substrates and sediment, degree of shading, and amount of woody debris. Baseline data like these enable MSG to track the impact of habitat improvement and restoration projects.[29] Examples of the latter, accomplished on dozens of tributaries over the past ten years, are stabilizing banks using rock riprap, building structures with log downfalls to create scour pools, and making wing dams to create deeper pools. Because the stagnant lower river is still a problem for juvenile salmon in summer, a series of pilot dams are meant to "create a network of cool, deep pools that will enable the estuary to nurture thousands of young salmonids through the summer, as it did before sediment from human activity turned it into a shallow, over-heated summertime death trap for salmon."[30] Continued funding from DFG and other state and federal agencies sustains estuary restoration.[31]

- **Salmonid numbers:** As to the recovery of the salmonids, former MSG director Ray Lingel summed up the situation as "fish on a roller coaster."[32] Partly he was reflecting on the excessively dry summer of 2002, when the upper river dried up and thousands of coho and steelhead were stranded in isolated pools, and partly he meant to represent the generally uncertain state of the runs. Better rainfall and therefore spawning and survival rates at mid-decade gave hope for improved runs, but at the time of this writing (early 2009), the MSG reported that the threat of losing both species of salmon is still "very real and very urgent."[33] Compared to the rough estimates of the early days, current data include trap-mark-and-release of downstream migrants, in-stream fish counts (by diving), and measurement of redds (egg sites) per stream mile. From these data, it appears that chinook runs are barely holding their own, while coho numbers and steelhead are lower. Given that all three runs were almost extinct here in the 1970s, these observations could be taken as hopeful, especially since the federal government is at work on recovery plans for all three species. But offshore risks prevail. Though neither commercial fishing nor sport fishing is permitted from San Francisco northward, at sea are drift nets, trawlers, and sea lions. The Mattole Watershed Plan perhaps best summarizes the cautious hope people have:

> The salmon are still here, and their populations, though still only in the high hundreds or low thousands, seem stable. In addition, there are reaches and tributary streams in the watershed that are still healthy, and which function both as fish refugia and as reference ecosystems for restoration.[34]

Freeman House elected to call his memoir of the first two decades of salmon restoration *Totem Salmon,* bringing to mind the powerful symbolic role of salmon in the lives of the Native peoples and, in fact, of more modern Mattolians as well. "Salmon," he writes, "who spend most of their lives hidden from us in the vast oceans, return to instruct us and feed us." What instructions are salmon giving? For one thing, salmon are calling for help. Salmon groups like MSG have sprung up wherever salmon once ran, from the Sacramento River all the way north to Alaska. The best of these, House thinks, are drawing inspiration from a mystical creature that speaks across species boundaries. "We are related by virtue of the places to which we choose to return," he writes.[35] The significance of place cannot be overestimated in the many successful conservation efforts of the Mattole community. If such inherent human/salmon connections to this place were palpable a decade ago, they are more so today, for hundreds of Mattole adults and school children have participated in the work of salmon restoration.[36] Those who wrote *The Mattole Watershed Plan,* a collaborative project of the Mattole Restoration Council, the Mattole Salmon Group, and others, must agree, for it begins with these words:

> We consider ... the Mattole River watershed — the 300
> square-mile slice of heaven that we call home — a natural

point of focus defined by where the salmon call home,
and the source of water that powers our lives.[37]

"Salmon are an integrating element," reflects Tracy Katelman. And salmon restoration, she says, "gives us hope that one day there will once again be enough salmon in northern California rivers for a revived fishery."[38] Can runs in the tens of thousands ever happen again? David Simpson thinks so, but perhaps not in his lifetime, which is all the more reason for MSG's collaboration with other community-based groups and agencies to continue restoring the riverine habitat.

HEALING THE WATERSHED

Mattole Restoration Council

In a 1990s documentary about the Mattole, Janet Morrison, a restorationist of the era, observed that salmon not only live in streams, they also live in watersheds.[39] This is the primary rationale for the Mattole Restoration Council (MRC), launched in 1983 with help and encouragement from the Salmon Group. At the time, MRC described itself as a coalition to restore and sustain the healthy functioning of the natural systems of the Mattole watershed. Its basic purpose has not changed in 25 years, though today their vision is grander and is a fine articulation of restoration toward sustainability:

> We look forward to a time ... when 'restoration' will no longer be needed ... and the watershed and its human communities are healthy and self-sustaining. We seek to educate ourselves regarding the natural processes at work ...; to learn about best land management practices; and to share with our neighbors what we learn. We hope that over time, a common understanding of these factors will help to shape broadly held community standards that will sustain the natural endowment of this place for future generations .... We will apply what we learn by undertaking cooperative projects in watershed restoration to enhance those processes, healing the landscape as we heal our relations with one another.[40]

It wasn't always so. In its early life, in addition to landmark data collection and systems mapping, stream stabilization, and serving as an umbrella for related organizations and land trusts, MRC took controversial positions

on logging and logging practices. This confrontational environmentalism arose from the fevered Redwood Summer. When the California
Department of Forestry and Fire Protection (CDF, now CalFire) began
to push new, highly restrictive "sensitive watershed" regulations in
1991, the emotional brushfires exploded into a big blaze. Tensions were
so unbearable and fears of losing local control so great that ranchers
and environmentalists, including MRC activists, landed together at a
highly charged public meeting about the regulations in April 1991.

One meeting led to another and after a few months, a group calling
itself the Mattole Watershed Alliance coalesced and agreed to describe
itself as "a diverse group of residents and landowners working together to
improve the health of their watershed and their quality of life through
communication, cooperation, and education."[41] As long as they talked
about how to make the Mattole a healthy and productive place, barriers
between them softened. Rancher Stanford Lowry had high hopes. In
1996 he said, "When you get right down to it, everybody who lives here
— the ranchers, the enviros, fishermen, the timber companies — are
neighbors by virtue of sharing the same place. If we don't manage our
affairs, someone else will."[42]

Despite noble intentions, when we left this promising alliance in
1997 it had already begun to crumble. Whenever logging practices and
land use issues came up, consensus collapsed. Meetings petered out and,
with all its baggage and fragility, the Alliance passed from the scene by
1998. Restorationists and ranchers backed away. MRC went back to
watershed restoration, the ranchers formed the Buckeye Conservancy,
and the controversial concept of "sensitive watersheds" was dropped by
CDF. "Sensitive watersheds," remarked Claire Trower, a homesteader of
some 30 years, "was a disaster that set us back a good ten years."[43]

In 1997 MRC operated on a budget of about $336,000, much of
which was paid in wages to staff and independent contractors for rental
and operation of heavy equipment and for consultation.[44] Funds came
largely from government agencies. Membership was in the dozens. All
staff, including the director, were part time. Today the annual budget
exceeds $3.5 million, 85 percent from fee-for-service contracts and
grants from 19 different agencies and foundations.[45] Membership has
grown. Now some 300 households bring in $70,000 from membership
dues and contributions. Once it was hard to find board members. Now

it's not. The diverse board includes foresters, homesteaders, naturalists, fish ecologists, and ranchers. The board oversees a payroll of 28 full-time and 120 seasonal staff.[46] As the biggest employer in the valley, MRC attracts eager, mostly college educated, restorationists to their full-time staff. Though many come from outside, some, like the Good Roads, Clear Creeks Program director Joel Monschke, are natives.[47] The seasonal crews draw young people who want summer work. They, in turn, learn about restoration, generally become passionate about it, and begin to think of it as a potential career. Up to a third of these people have grown up in the valley.[48]

Much of the credit for MRC's recent success is given to Chris Larson, its executive director from 2000 to 2007. With a degree in conservation biology from Cornell and a few years' experience in a small watershed south of San Francisco, he replaced retiring director Freeman House, who at the time had qualms about Larson's youth and inexperience. "Here was this guy replacing me who was 40 years younger than I and he saw this position as a career move. It was very puzzling. But he's worked out very well."[49] Indeed, Larson understood the director's job to be not simply a career move but also a life's work toward a time when "we can move beyond restoration." By that he means a time when human management and the structure and function of ecological systems are more fully in harmony.[50]

Larson is praised as both a visionary and an effective and inclusive day-to-day leader. MRC bookkeeper and board member Claire Trower called him "a brilliant leader, a grant-writing fool, a guy who's quick on his feet, a guy who can relate well to all kinds of people. To the old-timers here, he doesn't come across as a fanatical environmentalist."[51] How did he manage this? Tracy Katelman thinks it's because he partied with the "good old boys" at the local hangout. Inclusivity and leadership like this, hallmarks of sustainable collaboration, are rare. Chris Larson himself says that it boiled down to spending one-on-one time with ranchers, listening to their concerns, and not focusing on differences. Such personal interaction in people's kitchens "provided no opportunity for diametric oppositional politics" and therefore served good political ends for both sides.[52]

MRC's diverse projects and collaborations reach the length and breadth of the valley. They are steeped in a tradition of service and grounded in the idea of thinking like a watershed. Their success and resilient spirit make them a model for watershed groups across the Pacific Northwest."[53]

Present and Future Forests

The Wild and Working Forests program, one of MRC's biggest, engages landowners in forest management that combines timber harvest for sale with good conservation practices. The program now focuses on fuel reduction and fire safety projects for landowners, helping them prepare costly forest management plans, especially in riparian corridors.

Fire safety brings folks to the table who normally wouldn't be together. Following the catastrophic southern California wildfires in 2003, suddenly in the Mattole there were meetings in people's living rooms attended by professionals from CDF, the BLM, volunteer fire departments, MRC, and landowners. From this came concrete plans to educate, to thin hardwoods, to cut shaded fuel breaks, and generally to gird the landscape against big fires. Ranchers began to see MRC in a new light. "They couldn't believe it; we were talking about cutting trees," said Chris Larson. "But nobody in our group saw it as a radical departure from our long-term mindset."[54] Fire safety has proven to be an effective bridge across many divides and has provided common ground on which to build consensus. "Part of the work is to get a plan done, but subtly it is also about forming networks," pointed out Tracy Katelman, who helped Mattole residents write two plans.[55]

MRC has now helped almost 50 landowners fortify their properties against catastrophic fire. "This starts with the landowner and we try to listen and respond accordingly and thereby generate good will," said Larson. "This enables us later to ask ranchers for help with sediment control and riparian planting projects on their land. And that becomes a win for everyone without any compromises."[56]

Meanwhile, Mattole forests are quickly recovering from the massive clearcuts of the 1950s and 1960s. The combination of extensive riparian and upslope tree planting, natural regeneration of Douglas fir, and the departure of industrial timber now reframes the conversation about a merchantable timber harvest. "We are less than a generation away from substantial harvest potential," predicted David Simpson. But the idea of "working forests" has been a hard sell to those who remember the denuded Mattole of the 1970s as well as to others who don't want to see any trees cut. Many believe that working forests must be part of the Mattole's future and foresters think that selective forestry can improve the condition and diversity of the forest. It comes down to how to provide landowners the right incentives to derive income from trees without resorting to unsustainable practices.[57]

An initiative called Mattole Forest Futures may be just the incentive needed. It will promote collaboration between MRC and landowners to perform most of the expensive environmental analysis for a timber harvest plan in exchange for a promise of low-impact forest practices. Forest Futures brings MRC and landowners together with the Buckeye Conservancy, the Institute for Sustainable Forestry, the University of California Cooperative Extension Service, and registered professional foresters. While this is a first step, the question being pursued is a long-term one: How is it possible to make it affordable for people to manage Mattole forests?

Almost everyone agrees the ultimate solution is a change in California's forest practice law, originally written for industrial timber, to provide small landholders the option of a one-time-only timber harvest plan that could be periodically updated using some kind of "EZ form." This would reduce the incentive to clearcut and subdivide just to pay for the plan (currently at least $30,000).[58] It would also enable landowners to watch the timber markets and respond accordingly. For the Buckeye Conservancy this is the number one priority, but so far the California legislature, under heavy lobbying, has failed to bring a bill to the floor. While Conservancy executive director Johanna Rondoni works hard to build coalitions in Sacramento, her members wonder: "'Why are you in bed with the Sierra Club? They're just using you.' I look at it the other way," she says. "We want them on board to get something our landowners really need. That's what collaboration is all about."[59]

Mattole Forest Futures is built around collaboration toward the far horizons between ranchers and organizations with expertise in habitat conservation and forest economics, policy, and management. The goal is to create resilient, profitable land management plans for income and for conservation. Possible sustainable outcomes include keeping big ranches intact; creating jobs for restorationists, foresters, and loggers; providing income for strapped ranchers; and tweaking the centralized resource management institution, in this case CDF, toward more sensible and sustainable regulations.

Roads and Sediment

MRC's 1989 plan, *Elements of Recovery*, estimated that 76 percent of the Mattole's most serious erosion originated with roads.[60] In 1996, I hiked along some gullied and virtually impassable roads in the BLM's King Range and then was taken to one that had been recently decommissioned. Only a year after being regraded, mulched and planted, it was almost impossible to see the road's trace and our guide told me that almost no sediment was deriving from that former road. Since 1996, more than 15 miles of BLM roads have been "put to bed" and at least an equal amount on private and other conservation lands, particularly in the upper watershed. To drive home the significance of this, MRC helps school children adopt a decommissioned road site. Classes plant trees on the site and learn about long-term restoration and community service.[61]

Removing roads is one thing. Fixing those still in use is another. The Good Roads, Clear Creeks Program (GRCC) aims to identify and survey problems on all legacy logging roads and homestead access roads in the watershed by 2011. With state, county, and foundation support, GRCC had reached 25 to 30 percent of its goal in 2007. On private property, landowners must consent to the survey and ultimately approve the work plan if their road is a high priority site. The survey and engineering are grant funded and therefore free to the landowners, who are encouraged to think of road improvement as helping salmon habitat. Given this, few refuse. "Many folks have wanted to do something, anything, for the fisheries," says JJ Hall, one of the MRC landowner liaisons.[62] Overall, this program has prevented tens of thousands of cubic feet of sediment from entering the Mattole and its tributaries, especially in critical spawning habitat in the upper watershed. Like fire safety, the program is successful because there is a congruence of interests. MRC improves habitat, landowners have improved roads, and salmon spawning is enhanced.

MRC Far and Wide

As the premier community-based conservation organization in the valley, MRC is the "go-to" place for an even broader set of activities focused on that elusive long-term target — a time when restoration will no longer be needed. These activities range from coordination of the 30-year Mattole Watershed Plan[63] to ongoing programs of education in the watershed's six public schools; to promotion of sustainable stewardship of wild and working landscapes; to invasive species removal; to improvement and application of the Mattole geographic information system; and to continued monitoring of industrial harvest plans in the watershed.

Among these many programs, perhaps that aiming most toward the longer term involves education and related projects to promote sustainable land use in the valley. The schools program is broad and includes not only hands-on experience in watershed restoration and beach cleanup but also activities to raise awareness about consumerism, packaging, environmental practices of local companies, and integration of MRC education programs with those of other nonprofits like MSG. Ecological education director C. Moss says:

> *You cannot save the world, but neither can you cease from trying to. Community matters. All over the watershed, there are people — long time ranchers, loggers, native peoples, back-to-the-landers, environmental restorationists, foresters, fishermen, firefighters, gardeners. etc. — who each, in their own way, realize that they may not be able to save the world at large, but they're sure going to give it their best shot, locally. These folks ... are full of wisdom .... I say pass along your knowledge to the generations coming up.*[64]

Saving Water, Saving Fish

Why, in a place that receives 100 inches of rain a year, would anybody need to worry about water conservation? There are two answers to this question: increasing rates of river water extraction and exceptionally low flows over several years. In the late 1990s, people monitoring fish began to notice low flows in the upper watershed. In August 2002 they awoke to find no flow whatever, seeing only disconnected pools and stranded populations of juvenile coho and steelhead. In 2004, the same thing: the river stopped flowing for three weeks. Juvenile fish died each time. In fact, with further checking, it became clear that some stretches of the upper river had ceased to flow in each of the years between 1997 and 2006, except 2005.[65]

Residents of upper river communities wanted to know why. All the restoration and salmon recovery programs would count for nothing, they argued, if summer habitat ceased to exist. Eric Goldsmith of

Sanctuary Forest, the main conservation nonprofit in the headwaters, promised answers. He asked hydrologist Tasha McKee to look at historical data and to measure flows. Her research showed that: a) rainfall seasonality (rather than raw amounts) had affected flows and b) water extraction by residents of the upper watershed in the dry season was just enough to stem flows in dry years.

> We found that the 0.06 cubic meters per second people draw is enough for the river to go into negative flow pretty quickly in dry years. That finding was huge. We realized human water use, though not the cause of drought, does make a difference during drought.[66]

This answered one set of questions and in turn raised others. What should residents who depend totally on river water for their households, gardens, and livestock do? Should upper watershed residents have to pay for solutions while lower Mattole residents still have full extraction rights? Who does, in fact, have water rights?

Trying to keep the river flowing to save fish catalyzed a new set of collaborations, led by Sanctuary Forest, the lead partner in the Upper Mattole River and Forest Partnership, which holds most of the headwaters acreage of old-growth redwoods. Together with MSG and MRC, Sanctuary Forest organized community water education workshops in 2002 and 2003. More than 100 residents showed up for each. From these came two basic strategies: use stored water in summer and conserve water all year long. Storage options include roof catchment systems, tanks to store water extracted from the river in winter, and ponds. Conservation includes the obvious household and garden means of saving water as well as drought tolerant landscaping. Beyond these strategies, McKee argues that MRC's Good Roads, Clear Creeks Program and the rapid natural regeneration of the forest will ultimately enhance groundwater recharge and retention and therefore help extend upper river flows in the longer term, assuming no further extraction and no sudden climate change.

Still to be answered are questions of upper-lower Mattole equity, extraction rights, how to pay for expensive storage systems (the recommended Australian-built storage tank costs $6,300), whether ponds make ecological sense (they provide habitat for non-native species like the bullfrog), and how to write forbearance agreements by which owners of storage systems give up withdrawal rights seasonally. Most of these questions had not been answered definitively at the time of my last visit, but I was able to see an example of a 40,000-gallon Australian storage system near Whitethorn, filled from the river in winter, detached in summer, and sufficient for the needs of a small household with an extensive organic garden but no livestock. Residents said they were more than happy to relinquish their rights to withdraw water seasonally to benefit the salmon and their community. "We are discovering the mortality of the river. Beyond the needs for the fisheries, having the river dry up is of no use to anyone at any level."[67] By the summer of 2007, the mantra for Mattole headwaters residents was: fix leaks, stop tank overflows, irrigate efficiently, and pump safely.[68]

This comprehensive and quick response to a water crisis — at least for salmon and steelhead — attracted attention beyond the Mattole. California's Department of Fish and Game, in the midst of writing provisions for the California Coho Recovery Act, found this model worth copying.[69] They included language that recommends use of public funds to provide incentives to landowners to reduce summer water usage, establishing the principle that taxes can legitimately subsidize storage systems on private lands. In thinking about this, Tasha McKee saw something bigger.

> This is really about cultural change, about how people live on the land. What we're talking about here is a voluntary program by which landowners embrace the idea of changing their water use. And they get help to set up a system that will enable them to do that. That helps the fish and it becomes a way of life for people. If you live by a river, you realize it's a shared resource. It's a powerful binding force.[70]

SURPRISES FROM BEYOND

Like other stories in this book, the Mattole, though isolated, is by no means self-sufficient. Four members of the Mattole Self-Sufficiency Group, an organization focusing on ways the Mattole can return to a locally self-sufficient economy and culture, sat down with me one summer afternoon in the expansive Grange Hall between Petrolia and Honeydew. They spoke about community supported agriculture, the farmers' market, the historical society that's brought people of all kinds together, a local currency called "petols," and the "Mattole potluck," to which people must bring only items grown and created in the valley (including salt distilled at Mattole Beach by coordinator Ken Young).

The Group got started in 2005 with the idea of resurrecting a 1990s project called "Mattolia," in which residents of the valley imagined their grandchildren's world.[71] Essayists in the vividly prescient book from this project explored pathways to self-sufficiency, diversity, simplicity, and community by "dreaming indigenous."[72] What this might mean in the frenetic world of the 21st century needed further exploration. When they got to thinking about how people in the Mattole live today, it struck them that the society beyond the valley, with its macroeconomy they had come here to escape, was in fact their mother ship. "In reality, we're in extreme suburbia," remarked Laura Cooskey, "because we depend on our cars much more than those in town do. We really have to rethink this, to do something about it, because the world is changing and the time is now."[73] For the moment, what the Mattole Self-Sufficiency Group does is gently bring people on board through programs that educate about self-sufficiency. As people grapple with volatile oil markets, something like this (often called "voluntary simplicity") is happening all over North America.[74]

For remote places like the Mattole to rethink the ways they depend upon systems at scales beyond them raises issues mostly beyond the scope of this book. Yet unless localities can respond nimbly to the profound changes rolling in from the world beyond them, they and their local sustainability efforts are not likely to survive. Of this, C. Moss, MRC's director of ecological education, noted: "I find myself worrying more and more about the future ... and wondering what the point of environmental education is when it feels like the best we can do is put our finger in a huge, leaky dike."[75]

Mattole friends, who gladly boasted about their conservation accomplishments, also had plenty to say about that leaky dike — the impact of a globalized world on the lives of locals highly committed to their home. Here's a small sample of their concerns:

- **Global Climate Change:** Elders House and Simpson believe the valley must pay close attention to the predictions of global climate models. The prospect of warmer winters and hotter summers may tip the scales toward the demise of salmon and steelhead. More severe storms may undermine restoration projects and disrupt access into and out of the valley. And the seasonal water scarcity may be exacerbated in longer, drier summers. Of restoration and climate change, Freeman House asks: "Given the inevitability of climate change, what should be our target for restoration? Restoration to what? In a warmer time 5,000 years ago, there were virtually no salmon here. Is that the prospect?"[76]

- **Industrial Timber:** Most of the big timber operations are leaving Humboldt County. Only Pacific Lumber (PALCO) and Barnum Timber Company now hold land in the watershed. What PALCO does with its 18,000 acres is enough to keep MRC forest practices review director Ali Freedlund alert. "It is still painfully clear how important it is to protect the current stream buffers because it is just those areas that PALCO hopes to open up for timber harvest ...." New road construction proposed in a Barnum timber harvest plan raises questions about that company's intentions. Do they plan to subdivide and sell land after the harvest?[77]

- **Real Estate:** California's pre-2008 real estate boom vehemently thrust its way into the Mattole. Land prices have since dropped but are still higher than they were a decade ago. Up to late 2008, ranches and ranchettes were being purchased as soon as they came onto the market, mostly by outsiders who see the Mattole as the ideal place either for first or second homes or for land speculation. Some 75 percent of the ranches in the lower valley have changed hands in the past decade. People have three fears about this. First, who in the rising generation of ranchers and homesteaders, not to mention restorationists, can afford land costing millions? Second, subdivision seems inevitable and, as in the Malpai (Chapter 7), everyone sees this as a threat to Mattole landscapes and ways of life. Johanna Rondoni, the Buckeye Conservancy director, predicted that kids of the present generation of ranchers will conclude: "We love this ranch, but what are we to do with prices this high? When we inherit it, we'll have to subdivide it."[78] As ranchers sell out, "local knowledge of how to live on the land and how to manage it is being lost," says Tracy Katelman.[79]

- **Marijuana:** Humboldt County, including the Mattole, has long had an underground agricultural sector in which the smoke of pot mixes with the fragrance of greenbacks. The marijuana economy brings an estimated $15 million annually to the valley and as much as $130 million to the county.[80] It is, by most accounts, the number one revenue source in the Mattole. Until recently, Mattole landholders of all kinds grew a few plants, exchanged marijuana in the nonformal, largely local economy, and worried little about getting caught.

> *You could visit someone's homestead and they might not have store-bought beer to offer, but they could always roll you a joint or share the pipe. In the past, marijuana money has subsidized volunteer work for restoration and other kinds of community service. There are a lot of positive benefits you don't see because it's an underground economy.[81]*

This income also provided "a kind of illusory freedom for people who came here in the seventies, eighties, and nineties to live out the 'Mother Earth dream' with thousands of dollars coming in from an illegal agricultural endeavor nothing else could touch."[82]

What's changed about this is the incursion of megagrowers with elaborate under-the-lights indoor facilities and the passage of California's medical marijuana law in 1996. Both threaten to undercut the price, which could make a big difference to some Mattole households. Even more serious than the environmental and social costs associated with big operations (for example, diesel spills into creeks, speed labs, and "other extensions of the outlaw economy"[83]), the reclusive marijuana subculture and reckless growers undermine community and make people nervous. Freeman House believes another impact is that the marijuana economy seems to override the restoration movement. "Maybe it's just human nature that people's loyalties will drift toward big bucks," he says. "But nowadays there's little connection between marijuana income and restoration projects."[84]

- **Rising Generation:** In thinking of the future, Mattolians usually come around to fretting about how few of their kids settle here. Land prices are prohibitive, the restoration economy (as in most places) is grant- and contract-funded and thus unpredictable, local schools have been failing for a number of reasons, and the call of the world beyond the valley is seductive. Most children of the activists of the 1970s and 1980s went off to college and set up elsewhere. A few, like Joel Monschke, bring their education home (in his case, degrees from Stanford and Berkeley). But overall, the work of saving salmon, planting trees, stabilizing habitats, decommissioning roads, teaching kids, and building GIS systems is done by young folk from elsewhere, many of whom also move on. Ranchers' kids move on too. "It's difficult for them to think about committing to this way of life," says McWhorter about ranching and the future of his own kids' generation. The generational angst I witnessed in the Mattole is everywhere. The transfer of knowledge, energy, humility, patience, and perks enjoyed by an aging first generation of collaborative leaders and workers is fitful at best. Almost everyone knows solutions lie somewhere off in the misty future when a healthy environment, a vibrant culture, and plenty of family-wage income opportunities bring self-sufficiency back to the valley. But even the Mattole Self-Sufficiency Group is uncertain about how to get there.

Despite challenges from within and beyond the valley, the Mattole strikes me as one of the most hopeful of case studies. Two decades of experience with collaborative conservation, steeped in the particulars of this beautiful, remote valley, present a lively array of collaborations. Groups with crosslinking memberships range from a vibrant historical society to a land conservancy founded by ranchers, and from a restoration council that is the valley's biggest employer and a renowned group keeping salmonid runs alive to an innovative partnership that holds conservation easements to protect the last big stands of redwoods. From community supported agriculture, organic gardening, and a farmers' market, to continued work on forest certification and restoration of all kinds, collaboration rules. And, to my great surprise, in a grand Grange Hall there's a small and deeply thoughtful group discussing self-sufficiency in a post-petroleum world.

The possibilities the Mattole presents rest not merely on these collaborative networks and an awareness of coming times. Twenty-plus years of hard work have yielded an impressive record of accomplishment.

With help from the Buckeye Conservancy, ranchers have organized toward sustaining the ranching life. This includes conservation easements and light-touch forestry as well as lobbying for changing California's timber laws. There are now healthy segments of the river offering refugia for fish and the rest of the aquatic system. The upper and mid-Mattole are fast returning to their pre-1950 cool, deeply channeled essence with overarching riparian trees and stabilized vegetated slopes

Every summer the Good Roads, Clear Creeks Program fixes bad spots, aiming to get to them all by 2011. This has significantly reduced sediment loads in the upper watershed, the same locale where residents and a collaborative of collaboratives is helping change the culture of summer water use to keep the river flowing. Meanwhile, Douglas fir are recovering faster than memories of Redwood Summer recede and the MRC is aggressively coordinating projects to control invasive species such as knotweed and scotch broom. Ranchers, whose pastures are impacted, are fully on board, for these plants make range management and fence maintenance nightmarish. And the two-decade tradition of engaging children in salmon and watershed restoration continues in all six schools in the Mattole.

Thinking about its own future and that of the valley, the MRC speaks of organizational resilience by building an endowment, aggressively diversifying, doing more fee-for-service work for landowners, working further on effective coalitions in the valley and statewide, and devising a range of carbon sequestration strategies to respond to climate change that could "fundamentally reorient the economy in a way that has never happened before."[85]

This history of collaborative conservation aimed at making the valley a better place both for salmon and for humans has lifted veils and dissolved barriers. Ranchers today know about conservation easements and techniques of restoration just as homesteaders raise livestock, grow vegetables and fruit, and are active Grange members. Sterling McWhorter operates heavy equipment under contract with MRC and Tracy Katelman does professional forestry for the Buckeye Conservancy. In many ways, they are on the same page. They foresee a working landscape that protects vulnerable slopes, keeps people here and ranches intact, and helps the river restore salmon and steelhead habitat. Who would have guessed this possible back in 1990 in the heated times of Redwood Summer?

9

The Eyes of the World Are Upon Us:
Plumas County, California

> *There might be a place of land. It would have a snow
> mountain to the north, a blue-grey expanse to the east,
> ridges and canyons to the south, and a broad valley to
> the west that leads to further mountains and finally to
> the edge of the world. This land might have great
> meadows, beautiful parklands, bare granite ridges,
> and splendid fast streams and rivers. It might be some-
> one's home.*[1]
>
> ~ Gary Snyder

TUCKED INTO THE EASTERN EDGE OF NORTHERN CALIFORNIA, THE
mountain landscape in this story is shrouded in thick, highly productive forests. Snow covered Sierra Nevada peaks, rising to about 9,000
feet, look down upon these forests, "great meadows," and "beautiful
parklands." "Splendid fast streams and rivers" rush westward, tumbling
swiftly through rocky riffles and rapids (Text Box 9-1). They collect
behind dams and eventually spread across the broad Sacramento Valley
and southward toward central and southern California. This lovely
corner of the Earth is indeed "someone's home" — good people who
care deeply about the future of their mountain redoubt (Figure 9-1).

When Rachel Cook and I drove up through the canyons to Plumas
during a sparkling July week, we unexpectedly found ourselves in the
cross hairs of heated debates about community sustainability. How
much logging should be done in the forests? How much should be
protected as wilderness? How can communities be girded against big
forest fires? Are big saw mills the industry of the future? At what point
do collaboratives that are not inclusive fail to serve the community? Where

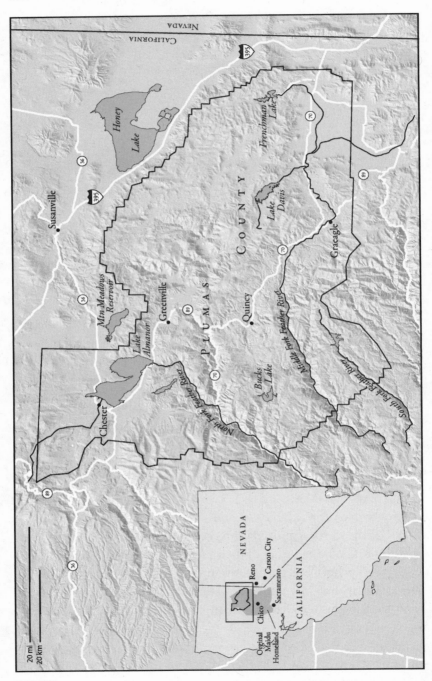

FIGURE 9-1

Plumas County, California

are those jobs you promised ten years ago? How can water become the region's economic engine? How can land speculation be contained? Is ranching viable? How should controlled fire be reintroduced to this landscape? Can endangered species recover? These questions swirled through the atmosphere we found in 2005. Now, four years later, as the full force of the economic meltdown strikes the Sierras, anxieties swirl even more intensely in these exceptionally hard times.

Long in the collaborative conservation spotlight, Plumas has become notorious. "Notoriety is both a blessing and a curse," said Plumas County attorney Michael Jackson. "It has brought us where-withal to do our work but also has tended to make us radioactive."[2] Some people, like Jackson, are willing to take the heat; others work quietly on the sidelines and shy away from the "radioactivity" that inevitably comes with prominence. Few would disagree with Maidu elder Lorena Gorbet, who told Rachel and me that "the eyes of the world are upon us."[3]

Plumas Prequel

Were we able to flash back to the 1990s, we'd see Plumas as a model for successful collaboration in the mountain West. The backstory reads like a handbook on why collaborative conservation was so desperately needed and why it seemed so promising. By the 1960s, work in the woods and a dozen sawmills were mainstays of an economy dependent mainly on harvests from the region's national forests. Responding to rising demands for wood products, Plumas National Forest and adjacent Lassen National Forest became the most productive national forests in the country. A "get out the cut" mentality in the Forest Service and the widespread practice of clearcutting fed the mills and supercharged the economy. In the late 1980s over 400 million board-feet rolled into mills in northern California every year.[4]

In their rush to claim the big trees, logging companies and the Forest Service ignored expanding stands of white fir and other conifers that crowded the understory, competed aggressively for nutrients and soil moisture, comprised a deadly array of ladder fuels, and threatened overstory trees with disease and insect damage. Deadfall and duff accumulated on the forest floor. The threat of catastrophic fire loomed on every horizon.

Meanwhile, in the 1970s and 1980s new people drifted into the mountains — back-to-the-landers and urban refugees, entrepreneurs and retirees — people with different expectations and a fresh appreciation of the region's amenities. By the mid-1980s, newcomers began to demand a halt to clearcutting, an end to logging in old-growth forests, and absolute protection of spotted owls.[5] They were not alone in making these demands, for by 1990 logging practices and levels of timber production were clearly not sustainable. As attitudes changed, logging and milling, long the lifeblood of Plumas, began to hemorrhage. Environmentalists challenged every major timber sale on public land. Workers were laid off and companies went bankrupt. A plan to list the California spotted owl as a threatened species held up timber planning at the same time that the Forest Service was being downsized.[6] Timber harvests declined by two thirds between 1991 and 1995.[7]

With layoffs, foreclosures, and sinking tax revenues, the community went into free fall. Fear and despair led to finger pointing and recrimination. Loggers said their jobs had been scotched by an owl. Environmentalists claimed the owl was the last gasp of old-growth forests. Families of woods and mill workers alleged that suits in office towers — timber magnates and environmental elitists alike — were strangling their families. Citizens bemoaned budget cuts for schools, roads, and other local services. Everyone blamed the Forest Service. As in the Mattole in the early 1990s (Chapter 8), people got sucked into a timber war.

Out of this steaming cauldron emerged the Quincy Library Group (QLG), a now-famous collaborative partnership of elected officials, the timber industry, environmentalists, and other citizens that aimed to stabilize things. They devised a plan to provide timber for the mills, improve environmental quality, protect the spotted owl and wilderness, stem erosion, and reduce fire risk. They took their plan to the Forest Service. After four years of unrelenting bureaucratic hassle, they threw up their hands and went directly to Congress.[8] A bill was passed by both houses and signed into law in 1998.[9] At long last, in the eyes of the QLG and its supporters, logging and landscape restructuring could begin in earnest. Wrong! For many reasons the QLG has been unable to accomplish its ecological vision and politically has been a "divisive attempt at peace."[10]

Working out of the limelight beginning in the mid-1980s, the Feather River Coordinated Resource Management partnership (the

Feather River CRM) completed three dozen stream restoration projects and was hailed as one of the most successful watershed groups in California. In 1997, Jora Young and I heaped praise upon both the community stability proposal of the QLG and the accomplishments of the Feather River CRM. While these organizations were not perfect, we sensed that in crisis this community had fashioned a promising though surely daunting set of tasks and had embraced a new spirit of place. John Schramel, the Feather River CRM visionary, said that "our job is to reach consensus and get something good done for the watershed. And, by golly, we get there one way or another." Speaking for his colleagues in the QLG, Jackson told us in 1994, "This is a community that hopes and understands that its best days are in the future."[11]

Well, the future has come. Looking back over two decades, I see successful restoration projects and fire protection efforts that inarguably have enhanced the natural resources on which the region depends. I see a huge collaborative experiment with the Forest Service constantly in court and possibly on the ropes. And, as the one remaining sawmill closed its doors in May 2009, I see an economy again in crisis. A teller of tall tales could not have conjured a more complex plot to illustrate what this book is about. Hard times and hope play tag across these wondrous landscapes while the future of 20,000 people hangs in the balance.[12]

A SENSE OF TIME

A sense of time lies thick and heavy on such a place.[13]

~ Aldo Leopold

The now familiar question raised by the stories in this book is whether local solutions framed in what Aldo Leopold called "experiential" or human time (about two decades in this case) can be sustained long enough to have an effect in "ecological time," that requiring more decades or even centuries. Ecological time, lying "thick and heavy" on these Sierra landscapes, will surely have something to say about that. Ecological time will measure how well people have helped restore resilience to the river systems, the forests, the upland meadows, and especially to the humans dependent on these resources (see Text Box 9-1).

Three collaborative initiatives frame our narrative about what's happened in experiential time since 1997. Two of these date from our

TEXT BOX 9.1
Waters, Forests, and Meadows

- **Waters:** The Feather River watershed covers 3,200 square miles of northeastern California. Its headwaters convey snowmelt and rain to an elaborate series of reservoirs, including Lake Oroville (with a capacity of 3.5 million acre-feet), the keystone of the State Water Project.[1] On average, 2.3 million acre-feet of Feather River water are released to urban, industrial, and agricultural users downstream. At the extreme, Feather River water irrigates fields and fills swimming pools 500 miles south of Plumas. The Feather River system also powers hydroelectric turbines that meet about 3 percent of California's peak energy demand.[2]

- **Forests:** On west-facing slopes, where up to 60 inches of precipitation fall annually, a wet coniferous forest flourishes. This is a complex blend of ponderosa and sugar pine, Jeffrey pine, Douglas fir, and incense cedar, with red and white fir at higher elevations. Downslope, California black oak and canyon live oak fill the valleys, and willows, California hazelnut, dogwood, and maples grow.[3] In these forests 80-year-old trees can still be found but most of what is referred to as "old growth" averages 50 years in age. Into the 1990s, these forests yielded as much as 400 million board-feet of saw logs every year, one third of the output of all Sierra forests.[4]

  On leeward desert-facing slopes eastward toward Nevada, precipitation is 30 inches or less annually and elevation drops precipitously. Less distinctively zoned by elevation, these forests comprise mixed Jeffrey pine, ponderosa pine, and white fir at upper elevations and a mixed evergreen forest and black oak woodland at lower elevations, often bearing an open, park-like appearance.[5]

- **Meadows:** Alpine valleys are among the most extensive in California. They comprise about 20 percent of the Plumas landscape. Once covered by sedges, wet meadow grasses, and willows, they served as sponges to absorb and slowly release rains and snowmelt in spring and early summer. Subdivided into ranches in the late-1800s, they were degraded by upstream erosion, invasive species, and ineptly managed grazing. Alpine meadows are still predominantly ranchland, and ranching comprises about 10 percent of the Plumas economy.[6]

---

1 lakeoroville.water.ca.gov (15 March 2009).

2 Equivalent to 1,400 MW peak power. cpuc.ca.gov/cfaqs/htm (15 March 2009).

3 Sierra Nevada Research Center. *Plumas/Lassen Study: 2004 Annual Report.* University of California, Davis, 2005.

4 *Status of the Sierra Nevada, Summary of the Sierra Nevada Ecosystem Project.* University of California, Davis, 1996, 5-6.

5 Michael G. Barbour. "California Upland Forests and Woodlands" in Michael G. Barbour and William Dwight Billings, eds. *North American Terrestrial Vegetation.* Cambridge University Press, 1988, 131-164.

6 cfbf.com/counties/?id=32; labor.ca.gov/cedp/pdf/Plumas.pdf; fedstats.gov/qf/states/06/06063.html (15 March 2009).

earlier time here (the Feather River CRM and the QLG). The other is a project of the Mountain Maidu Indians, who in the 1990s decided that one way of combating the social ills of their tribe and the hard times brought on by the sagging timber economy was to return to their venerable traditions.

Each of these collaboratives swims against countercurrents deriving from both the local political economy and the big institutions at regional, state, federal, and global levels. In almost every instance, the Forest Service plays some role. How could it not? The Forest Service oversees management of 75 percent of the county in the 1.3 million-acre Plumas National Forest. Protected from fire for a century, this forest is made up of unhealthy combinations of species and structures at high risk for wildfire. It is also critical habitat for sensitive and threatened species. And national forest watersheds control the destiny of millions of water users downstream. So it's impossible to tell the Plumas story without taking account of a huge federal bureaucracy that "cannot turn on a dime, [is] ever buffeted by shifting political winds, and, after all is said and done, has no legal mandate to choose its own direction."[14]

COUNTERCURRENTS

> *Recreational development is a job not of building roads into lovely country, but of building receptivity into the still unlovely human mind.*[15]
>
> ~ Aldo Leopold

As the first decade of the 21st century draws to a close, the last of Plumas County's sawmills has shut down, several timber operators have gone out of business, and, in the face of an 18 percent unemployment rate, young people have fled the county.[16] Though jobs in agriculture, forestry, and related occupations still comprise about a third of the workforce, real estate speculation is putting the resource-based economy at risk.[17] With vast acreages of pasture and irrigated forage and hay, highly productive forests, and enough water to slake a million thirsts, at first glance Plumas should be able to forever sustain an economy based on renewable resources. The truth of the matter is that for almost two decades this community has been a human-ecological system poised to topple. As I write in 2009, this has never been truer.

To complicate matters further, "recreational development" in the guise of golf has invaded the northern Sierra. In 1993, there were four golf courses across the entire northern Sierra; by 2009, there were 11 in Plumas County alone. Many of these new courses are magnets for resorts featuring million-dollar condominiums and homes. I wanted a firsthand look this new phenomenon, so one afternoon Rachel and I drove around golf-focused Graeagle, a mini-version of Tahoe or Squaw Valley. We saw views across lush irrigated fairways framed by forested slopes. We drove past a big private clubhouse. We saw huge homes under construction and we wandered around trendy shops, galleries, and boutiques. We mused at how far a cry such resorts seemed from the struggling former mill towns and their unemployed workers just a few miles away. We remembered Leopold's image of the "still unlovely human mind."

"Golf has become a sort of religion," quipped Plumas Corporation CEO John Sheehan.[18] In 2006, Plumas County was ranked 15th on a list compiled by *Golf Digest* of the hottest retirement destinations for golfers in the US.[19] Realizing this, The Nature Conservancy (TNC) has been scrambling to cut off potential new golf developments that would further threaten the biodiversity of the region. "We are into preemptive thinking," said Greg Low, Northern Sierra project director for TNC. "If we can quickly purchase or otherwise protect lands of unique biodiversity, we can then fine-tune strategies to keep them open and ecologically productive for the longer term."[20]

The golf boom and tourism development around Lake Almanor pumped up the value of Plumas real estate by 91 percent between 2000 and 2007,[21] but then the bottom dropped out in 2008.[22] Despite this drop, the average wage earner in Plumas is still unable to find affordable housing.[23] Equally significant is the difference between the environmental values of people who live in golf resorts and those of locals who depend on forests and other natural resources for jobs. "The second-home people basically don't want to see trees cut," Plumas County supervisor Bill Powers told us. "We are in a financial crunch in the industries that used to sustain us. We cannot produce the timber the industry demands and we know we can't sustain the level of industry we used to. People want amenities from forests rather than timber."[24] California's 1990s land boom, with all its upsides and downsides, had finally washed into Plumas.

EXPERIENTIAL TIME: 1997-2009

> *... a system of conservation based solely on economic*
> *self-interest is hopelessly lopsided. It tends to ignore,*
> *and thus eventually to eliminate, many elements in the*
> *land community that lack commercial value, but that*
> *are (as far as we know) essential to its healthy func-*
> *tioning. It assumes, falsely, I think, that the economic*
> *parts of the biotic clock will function without the*
> *uneconomic parts.*[25]
>
> ~ Aldo Leopold

Water: Sustaining Natural Capital

What if, in the next few decades, water rather than timber became the most lucrative export of Plumas? Though this may seem far-fetched, a trend is already underway. Downstream users across the West have begun to recognize they have a vested interest in the ecological services afforded by upstream health. This idea is, of course, not new. It dates back to John Wesley Powell, who after traveling across the arid West in the late 19th century "sought to integrate resources, communities, and sociopolitical institutions together in arrangements organized at 'hydrographic' scales."[26]

Now, almost 140 years later, Powell's insights may come to pass. The hydrographic scale in this case is virtually all of California because the Feather River, as a component of the California State Water Project, sends water across the state, each year providing 2.3 million acre-feet to users downstream. As urban and agricultural users multiply in California, this water is ever more crucial. Folks in Plumas argue that reliable delivery depends on maintaining and improving the condition of the Feather.[27] In the early part of this decade, resolution of a complex legal case between the California State Water Project and water contractors (known locally as the Monterey Agreement) obliged an $8 million payment to Plumas County by water contractors in Santa Barbara County (500 miles south of Plumas) for Feather River watershed improvements.

The Plumas Watershed Forum, established in 2003 as a collaborative partnership of community groups, Plumas County officials, the California Department of Water Resources, and State Water Project contractors, disburses funds from the Monterey Agreement.[28] As of

2008, the partnership had allocated some $5 million to resource conservation districts, the Forest Service, the Plumas Corporation, and Feather River College for creek and meadow restoration, aspen grove restoration, QLG project monitoring, groundwater research and monitoring, and a variety of other outreach, education, and capacity-building efforts.[29] The Monterey settlement was a one-time award that some in Plumas called a rip-off. "It was insultingly low," one resident told me. But Jim Wilcox of Plumas Corporation thinks it will become a template for the future. "This classic north-south California battle will never cease because water is the one indispensable commodity we share. And here we are in the driver's seat."[30]

The Feather River CRM is known throughout the world for its accomplishments and willingness to innovate.[31] For more than 20 years it has cobbled together agreements and funding to do its work. Everyone I've talked to finds the work of this watershed group meritorious — a promising sign that grassroots watershed restoration is not only possible through thick and thin but can be sustained over the long run, perhaps in ecological time, and can make big differences downstream. By 2008, in its 23 years in partnership with 23 public and private organizations, the Feather River CRM had completed 97 projects totaling 43 miles of stream restorations and 3,800 riparian acres.[32] Between 2004 and 2012, the partnership will have invested some $16 million in watershed-focused work.

John Schramel, the retired teacher who helped dream up the collaborative group in the mid-1980s, attributes its persistence and success to four factors: a high level of collaboration, an ability to learn and adapt, a supportive home base in the local community development organization (the Plumas Corporation), and exceptional leadership in the person of program manager Jim Wilcox.[33] Greenville resident and journalist Jane Braxton Little agrees. "It is a positive force in this region in its work with ranchers, other landowners, agency folks, the private sector, hydrologists, and heavy equipment operators. It maintains its focus, has no political pretensions, and applies adaptive management to four to six projects each year."[34]

Among the most innovative of its recent projects is meadow rewatering, a program of alpine meadow restoration so successful that demand far outstrips the group's capacity to do it. Based on early-1990s experiments in Nevada, the program takes streams out of their unnaturally incised channels in upland meadows and puts them back into their former courses.[35] The Feather River CRM first tried the concept in 1995 and within a year they began to see "a mind-boggling raft of benefits," Wilcox said:

> *The water table comes back up to the surface. With incision, meadows had converted to sage grass but with this new technology, wet meadow vegetation, dormant in the soil for decades, bursts to life. Sage retreats up the hillsides and is replaced by willow and meadow sod. Now all the stresses of annual floods are spread across a whole meadow; there's no super-high velocity erosion on the channel. The fishery comes back right away and so do waterfowl.*[36]

To this, they have added an element called "pond and plug." After relocating the stream, this technology rids the meadow of former gullies by refashioning them into ponds that become attractive fishing, swimming, and picnic sites, as well as sources of water for livestock. People are so drawn to the idea of ponds in their meadows, they forget the ponds are a byproduct of channel and meadow restoration, says Wilcox. So far dozens of these projects have been completed and the technology is spreading. "Channel incision is not just a Feather River problem; it's an issue throughout the Sierras."[37]

Restoration work has significant conservation outcomes. Stream monitoring below restoration projects shows lower, more natural water temperature profiles; increased fish reproduction; far less sediment; improved habitat for aquatic life and waterfowl; and persistence of channel restorations through big and small floods. In such tangible accomplishment Wilcox himself is regenerated. "You'd think I be jaded after so many projects, but when a project is going through its first runoff, its first spring, it's just so enlightening to watch the landscape burst to life."[38]

What was impressive to us when we first trekked along trashed and restored streams with Jim Wilcox in 1994 was how well the Feather River CRM was working at the time. We noted that old hippies and fourth-generation ranchers, high school students and resource professionals, backhoe operators and college teachers had come together and that all these people were laying the groundwork for profound cultural change. Fifteen years later, I am even more convinced. "Collaborative community-based watershed efforts can be extraordinarily productive. They work because all stakeholders are at the table. You listen and they listen and together you develop a sense of how the project can become better and how you all can reduce the potential for conflict down the road,"[39] said Wilcox.

Forests: A Top-Down Outcome of Bottom-Up Activism

As one of America's most "notorious" natural resource-focused collaborative groups,[40] the Quincy Library Group is in a class of its own. Out of a desperate situation in the 1990s, a group of tenacious citizens did something no other community had done.[41] First, they envisioned and agreed upon specific ways to stabilize their local economy and move the surrounding national forests toward greater fire resilience and ecological integrity. And second, after being spurned by local and regional Forest Service officials, they boldly took their plan to Congress. Their efforts paid off in the passage of the Herger-Feinstein Quincy Library Group Act (HFQLG) in 1998, which initially was a five-year pilot project to carry out a modified version of the QLG community stability proposal of 1993, funded through the Forest Service at about $26 million per year.[42]

HFQLG implants a landscape-scale series of plots to test fire reduction and ecological prescriptions in Plumas National Forest and parts of Lassen and Tahoe National Forests. The fire strategy involves thinning the forest using a network of Defensible Fuel Profile Zones (DFPZs), which were to have been put on the ground between 1999 and 2004. However, because of the listing of the California spotted owl and a flood of litigation over both the owl and the manner of thinning, almost nothing had happened in the core areas of the plan by 2004.

While the community waited for results, the QLG fielded brickbats from every corner and they and the Forest Service were taken to court on virtually every piece of the plan.[43] Realizing this, Congress extended the act twice. It is now scheduled to conclude in 2012. After seven years of legal snags that would daunt the most dedicated community activists, in 2005 a federal judge ruled that thinning could commence in Meadow Valley, one of the largest pilot tracts. Failure of the last legal challenges in early 2006 opened the door for a major piece of the plan to get underway. A joyful photo on the QLG's website shows members toasting this decision with champagne, but a year later veteran county forester Frank Stewart admitted that lawsuits had in fact not ceased. "We've got through the analysis; now we're again stuck in litigation," he said.[44] This continues to be so.[45]

The QLG plan was patterned partly on the long record of sustained-yield forestry by the Collins Companies in nearby Chester.[46] Covering 1.53 million acres, it envisions an all-age, multistory, fire-resistant forest to "more closely mimic the historic landscape of the Sierra."[47] Sensitive areas consisting mainly of spotted owl habitat (160,000 acres) have been deferred from harvest. Using the Collins prescriptions of group and single-tree selection and riparian protection, 1.4 billion board-feet were meant to be harvested by 2009.[48] Because less than half of the fuelbreaks were in place by the end of 2008, this target has not been achieved.[49]

Gales of praise, controversy, and criticism have buffeted the HFQLG plan, many the inevitable outcome of a bottom-up group — the QLG — telling a top-down organization — the Forest Service — what to do. As QLG members have consistently noted, a gale is what you often get when you venture into uncharted waters. Their early decision to limit conversation to items QLG participants could agree on has enabled the group to hold to its purpose. But the decision has also rained down incessant controversy that threatens to unravel this purpose. Debate about whether the QLG has reached beyond its jurisdictional grasp is covered elsewhere and is beyond our purpose of assessing progress toward sustainability.[50] Suffice it to say that the heated atmosphere we found in 2005, which still prevails, raises questions about whether the QLG can claim to have calmed anxieties in what was, in the early 1990s, a highly polarized and economically troubled community[51]

Conservation Outcomes

Throughout this book I have been trying to test the idea that collaborative community-based conservation can help communities edge down the road to sustainability. In Plumas forests, the case is difficult to make because the biggest and most promising project has been hamstrung during much of its life.[52] Organizationally, the QLG-Forest Service legal tussles with environmentalists are a nightmare. I'll leave that for later

(Chapter 12). Here let's stick to the conservation goal of infusing a radically different kind of silviculture across great swaths of three national forests. On this, my conclusion is that it is way too early to say whether HFQLG has come close to achieving its objective of restoring a fire-resilient forest approximating "pre-settlement" conditions.[53] As of this writing, here's what one can say:

FIRE AND OWLS

Among the most significant and hopeful accomplishments of the QLG has been raising awareness of fire and forest fuel loading within national environmental circles, in the Forest Service itself, and across the communities of the northern Sierra.[54] Equally impressive, the QLG proposed a system of fuelbreaks that the Forest Service could support and implement. As the Maidu (and now science) know full well, low-level fires burned regularly in the aboriginal forest and have been absent for a hundred years. One day they must be reintroduced, but this cannot happen until fuel loads are reduced. A system of fuelbreaks is a first step toward this goal.[55]

Fuelbreaks in the HFQLG plan are called Defensible Fuel Profile Zones (DFPZs),[56] thinned strips about 0.25 mile wide. When implemented, they will form an irregular, sinuous network along roads and around wildfire hotspots, camps, and communities. By removing undergrowth and small trees, clearing deadfall and most snags, and thus defusing fire ladders, DFPZs are meant to prevent fires from crowning and to bring fires already in the crown back to the ground. By removing some medium and a few large trees (so-called thinning), the canopy will be opened. Riparian areas are not touched and most large trees are spared.[57] At HFQLG's conclusion, there will be 200,000 acres of DFPZs, covering less than 20 percent of the forest.[58] Later, thinning operations will move to tracts between DFPZs, using single-tree and group selection in a 150 to 200 year rotation.

Rob MacWhorter, deputy Plumas Forest supervisor in 2005, took Rachel and me to see a DFPZ. In the field, he explained that "pulling apart the canopy" will definitely bring fires to the ground and do less damage to the big trees. "There's tons of evidence for this," he argued.[59] We hiked through fairly open tracts, climbed atop stumps, looked up at the partially filtered sun, and watched machines thin out pole-sized firs. As laypeople, we couldn't judge the efficacy of this system, nor could we reconcile a virtually opposing view offered by John Preschutti, a forest activist, on a field trip three months earlier. Fires in the three seasons since those field trips seem to bear out the Forest Service-HFQLG view of the value of DFPZs. However, fires that have burned more than two days have broken through DFPZs to rage wildly through unthinned tracts.[60]

Forest activists like Preschutti, who have repeatedly taken the Forest Service to court, argue that thinning the canopy is the wrong strategy. "A closed canopy reduces growth of brush, while logging the larger, fire-resilient trees increases the long-term fire danger," they say.[61] The fuelbreaks, which they argue are "barely shaded," create hotter, drier conditions at the floor, which they believe will lead to greater fire severity. "Cutting the fire-resistant older trees out of a fireproofed forest runs counter to everything we understand about forests and wildfire."[62]

Despite the criticism, the HFQLG plan continues to win in court. In the end it may well significantly refashion parts of the forest from its present dense, brushy stands to an open, multistoried structure — the hypothesized "pre-settlement" situation in which low-intensity fires were widespread, crown fires rare, and an open, park-like appearance was overstoried by big trees.[63] Scholars, foresters, and most residents agree that such restructuring is crucial to the well-being of people and to ecosystem diversity and viability throughout the Sierras.[64] Not all agree with the means and scale at work here or the threshold size of trees cut. Nor is there consensus about whether these thinning prescriptions will actually make the forest "fire safe," whether they will lead to "pre-settlement" conditions, or whether they are good for the spotted owl and other critters.[65] We will one day know what works from this experiment and what does not. In the meantime, one must hope that good monitoring will enable adaptive responses in which bad ideas are modified or thrown out, and that the most cataclysmic of dissenting opinions — that the forest will be more fire prone — does not turn out to be true.

As for the California spotted owl, the mitigation plan in the HFQLG Environmental Impact Statement initially prohibited thinning or timber harvests in designated spotted owl habitat. The QLG appealed this decision in 1999, arguing that "the viability of the spotted owl — the very thing the mitigation was designed to protect — would be threatened because of the increased likelihood of fire."[66] Further, they said the prohibitions would prevent the HFQLG fuelbreak strategy from being tested on a landscape scale as mandated by the bill. Despite the appeal, the Forest Service (in this case, in opposition to the QLG) held its ground until the Meadow Valley decision in 2005, which opened some owl habitat to thinning. The Sierra Nevada Protection Campaign (now Sierra Forest Legacy), one of four plaintiffs in the Meadow Valley suit and subsequent appeals, argued that the plan did not account for cumulative impacts of logging on owls. The judge denied their argument and ruled that both the specific and cumulative effects of the project would be less harmful to the owl than a catastrophic fire.[67] According to a recent Forest Service study, this may be so. Within two years of thinning, owls have returned to reproduce in DFPZs. After fires, DFPZ-treated areas also show less severe large tree damage, which means that owl nesting sites survive.[68]

ROADLESS AND RIPARIAN AREAS

The HFQLG bill protects all riparian zones and sets aside 350,000 acres of roadless areas as "wilderness." According to Mike Yost of the Sierra Institute for Community and Environment and a member of the QLG, no other Sierra national forest has such protection.[69] These "wilderness" targets have weathered challenges and remain off-limits to logging. John Sheehan, another QLG member, says such protection is unique. "Think of it! No harm to riparian areas throughout our three forests; no large trees cut; a huge wilderness area. These are big accomplishments."[70] On the other hand, fire management in this "wilderness" looms large. Forests here are as fire prone as any others, but they cannot be thinned under provisions of HFQLG. If they're not thinned, it is impossible to claim that forests overall are protected from catastrophic fire, and they and their wildlife and ecological services could be devastated. "We haven't made any progress on this issue," says Sheehan.[71]

COMMUNITY STABILITY

Between 1998 and 2009 the flow of sawlogs from the three national forests has been less than half that predicted in the HFQLG bill. This means that the economic prescription of having logs from landscape restructuring pay for perpetual thinning is untested. In anticipation of a steady flow of pole-sized logs, Sierra Pacific Industries downsized its Quincy plant and planned to run full shifts. To offset the low output of national forest logs, it shipped in timber from private lands, sufficient to keep about 150 mill workers on the payroll in early 2009 (down from 350 in 2005). But even at mid-decade, mill workers and their families were nervous about the plan and the security of their jobs. Former Plumas County supervisor Rose Comstock told me, "People will say to me, 'QLG was supposed to create timber jobs, but nothing ever happens. We're not getting anything out of QLG. Why are we continuing with this?'"[72] With the Quincy mill now closed, this skepticism has morphed into anger and despondency.

When we asked questions about whether the kind of industrial forestry at the heart of HFQLG is sustainable, QLG members argued that, yes, a predictable flow of logs from the national forests would lead to a "base-level of economic stability," which in turn would attract private investors in the industry to expand their businesses and "refuel the economic engine that has long driven this place."[73] "If you take the timber infrastructure out of the equation, you do not have a sustainable community nor a sustainable environment," said Comstock. Michael Jackson, the QLG lawyer, told Plumas County supervisors in early 2009 that if the QLG were to fail, half the county's population would move away. To this, supervisor Sherrie Thrall said, "Plan B is an unsustainable economy basically."[74] John Sheehan, CEO of the main community development organization and a QLG member, fully agrees. "Mill jobs are the best jobs to have because they provide family wages. When they disappear, it's devastating to the community — at every level, ranging from Girl Scouts to Little Leagues to churches to choirs, they're all negatively impacted." As to the future, he says, "I still believe that the forests and forest economies are sustainable."[75]

Curiously, QLG folk we interviewed this time did not mention molding a future timber industry after Collins Companies' sustainable forestry, as originally planned. Although a representative of Collins usually attends QLG meetings, the intention to achieve sustainability, as Collins defines it, with limits on logging, single-tree selection, and a focus on production of FSC-certified products, seems to have been sidetracked by disagreements on how to get to that point. Jane Braxton Little, the writer who has followed the QLG from the get-go, told us that one of her "big disappointments has been that [the HFQLG plan] has truly excluded innovative responses to the general reduction in logging happening on national forests in the West." Over a cup of coffee in Greenville, she ticked off job-creating small businesses doing noninvasive thinning and harvesting nontimber forest products that should have been part of their plan. "We should have a sort mill. We should have equipment available to rent. We should have cottage industries to build furniture, mill fencing, and make building timbers. None of this is happening."[76]

Sadly, the economy of Plumas County in early 2009 approximates what we found in the early 1990s, with fewer family-wage jobs, skyrocketing unemployment, and a bursting real estate bubble. In a March 2009 *New York Times* story on the mill closing, QLG member Linda Blum, whom we interviewed in the 1990s and again in 2005 and who is among the most avid of QLG proponents, admitted that the plant closure is a bad sign. "It is a big hit on the community of Quincy, but it is also a big hit for the future of these projects," she said.[77]

THE QLG AND THE FOREST'S FUTURE

Although the QLG has deliberately never had a board, a bank account, or officers, at stake are hundreds of thousands of acres, tens of millions of federal tax dollars, and the well-being of northern Sierra residents. With so much at stake, it is no wonder the QLG is "radioactive." QLG meetings are technical and legal; they touch on issues a casual visitor is not likely to understand. It's not surprising that people who drop in feel alienated. Linda Blum explained, "We *are* somewhat inaccessible because there's so much information to master. If somebody new wants to jump on this train now, they're going to have to run to catch up. We're not about to stop."[78] "It's a hard group to break into and members seem reluctant to turn things over," agreed Mike DeLasaux, a University of California extension forester who advises the group.[79]

One cannot deny the QLG's solidarity and persistence, its ability to suffer the boredom that goes with collective decision making, and its tenacious focus on a small cluster of issues.[80] The QLG's core group has stayed the course for what its members see as the greater good. Those we interviewed believe this to be their major accomplishment. Rose Comstock, the former Plumas County supervisor, perhaps spoke for all:

> Typical milestones people mention are spotted owl
> habitat protection, wilderness, fuel reduction, saving
> mill jobs. But equally important, I think, is our staying

power, our persistence. We knew we had a piece of the
truth and that it would go to battle with us.[81]

The QLG holds fiercely to that "piece of the truth," a vision some like Jackson and Sheehan still find hopeful. As global warming puts Sierra forests at greater risk for catastrophic fire, the QLG can argue that recent fires would have been far less severe had their project been on schedule. A case in point was the Moonlight Fire in September 2007, which burned 13,000 acres scheduled to be protected by DFPZs but tied up in litigation at the time. The outcome was a charred landscape offering no habitat for spotted owls and no timber whatever.[82] A blogger noted the irony of this tug of war between the QLG and environmentalists: "The ultimate experiment of 'cooperation' with environmentalists has failed .... And the forests will continue to burn. And people will keep losing their jobs."[83]

ECOLOGICAL TIME: THE MOUNTAIN MAIDU

In the spring ... the old squaws began to look about for the
little dry spots of headland and sunny valley, and as fast
as dry spots appeared, they would be burned. In this way
the fire was always the servant, never the master .... By
this means, the Indians always kept their forests open,
pure and fruitful, and conflagrations were unknown.[84]

The Mountain Maidu Indians are the indigenes in this story. For hundreds or perhaps thousands of years, they lived in ecological time at the margins of upland meadows in oak groves where there were ample fresh water and acorns, the mainstay of their diet. In those days, the forest was far from primeval. The Maidu cultivated oaks, farmed camas bulbs, harvested wormwood (*Artemisia* species), and pruned willows and maples. They cut pathways through the forests and, with fire as their servant, annually burned the understory. Their forests were so open that early explorers described them as parklands. "This wasn't just some natural forest where 'natural' means people aren't part of it," noted Maidu ecologist Ferrell Cunningham.[85]

Modern Maidu describe their traditional low-level fires as "cool burns."[86] Such fires were set so regularly that huge conflagrations almost never happened. Scientific study of pre-settlement fire in Sierra landscapes confirms this view, with ample evidence of low-to-moderate severity fires across much of the landscape and only rare occurrence of high-severity fires of more than a few acres.[87] Because the relative roles of fire and forest product harvesting have so drastically changed over the past 150 years, "the glory and beauty of this lofty, roadless landscape can today only be appreciated by an act of imagination."[88]

With the gold rush of the mid-19th century, the Maidu were driven off their land, hunted for bounties on their scalps, and wasted by white men's diseases. In 1800 there were 20,000 Maidu; by 1850, only 2,000; in 1900, just 204.[89] Abandoned with neither land nor federal recognition as a tribe, the survivors relinquished but did not forget their traditional lifestyle. Today, at about 500, they are 2.5 percent of the population of Plumas County.[90]

Although the Mountain Maidu people make up a small proportion of the residents of modern Plumas County and their current access to natural resources is tiny compared to that of the QLG, their engagement with this landscape over thousands of years should grant them special sovereignty. Unfortunately, it doesn't. As with most California Indians, the Maidu, as a so-called nontreaty tribe, have virtually no access to a land once theirs. In the wake of their virtual obliteration, treaties granted survivors small tracts, but miners and loggers lobbied against them and they were never ratified. Except for one small *rancheria* (a ranch-sized "reservation") near Greenville, the Maidu as a tribe are landless. They receive no assistance from the federal Bureau of Indian Affairs.[91]

In response to this plight and a range of other problems, including alcoholism and other substance abuse, suicides, family and community dispersion, and collapse of the logging industry in which many men worked, the Maidu formed a Cultural and Development Group in 1996. It aims to preserve Maidu language and culture, to encourage economic development, to protect sacred sites, and to rediscover threads of relationship to the mountains and valleys of the northern Sierra. These purposes wrap around reengagement with the land.[92]

In 1998 Congress funded a series of stewardship demonstration projects to test alternative techniques to reduce fire hazards on public lands.[93] With a deep history of stewardship of this place and a need for income and activities to replace the faltering logging economy, the Maidu were awarded a contract by the Forest Service in 1998. Their project was the first in which Native Americans proposed to apply their traditional ecological knowledge (TEK) to managing national forests.[94] Besides the Forest Service, the Maidu are partners with eight other organizations of Native peoples from the wider region.[95]

Traditional ecological knowledge is an old wave washing freshly across a diminishing sea of indigenous peoples around the world. It encompasses a body of past and present interactions and practices that tie "the people" to their land and resources. "Traditional ecology describes the lifeways of people who have been created with those lands, people whose stories, songs, foods, medicines, and even languages have shaped and continue to be shaped by their environment."[96] Managing a tract of 1,500 acres in Plumas National Forest is an opportunity for the Maidu to regain touch with their own traditions and wisdom about the animals, plants, rocks, and waters that once provided their subsistence. They will focus first on oaks, maples, willows, medicinals, bear grass, and various bulbs. They will blend traditional knowledge with modern technology by developing an inventory of the plants and animals. And they will be allowed to try out their own ways of thinning and controlled burning to make the forest more fire resilient.[97]

Even before contractual obligations with the Forest Service had been straightened out, the Maidu were at work. They visited sites across their stewardship tract to sit and engage in conversation with the land. "We talked to our relatives and sang to them, listening for what they require," explained elder Lorena Gorbet.[98] Formal work began in 2004 with thinning on 36 acres to protect a Maidu-run campground and part of the town of Greenville. Later, this work, accomplished by Maidu-owned companies with light equipment extended to areas around residences near Greenville and to a dump transfer station. They also transplanted cluster-lily and camas bulbs and gray willow shoots, pruned oaks to encourage acorns, and began to burn small areas using "cool burn" methods. Such fire won't harm rhizomes and burrowing animals and leaves islands around protected plants.[99]

This unusual partnership between a rigid bureaucracy and an intuitive, ecologically timed management system has been a learning experience for both parties.

> *Even when the new partners communicate in English, they often speak a different language. Agency officials talk of written objectives, formal business plans, and budgets.*

The Maidu depend on less-bureaucratic tools, insisting
they must talk to the trees and wildlife to see what changes
they want and need over long periods of time.[100]

These differences struck Gorbet as a difficult paradox: "We've done
TEK for thousands of years, but the Forest Service is giving us only ten
years to validate it under this contract."[101] From the Forest Service
perspective, deputy MacWhorter said, "This is a great concept but
working through the details has been rough. Not a lot of tools have
been given to the Forest Service to make this kind of collaboration
happen."[102] On the other hand, there's a good prospect of adapting
some Maidu practices, particularly the timing of burns and techniques
of meadow restoration. "This is a tremendous opportunity to add value
to our work and for them to teach us. Kudos to the Maidu for sticking
with us." Whatever may happen with this particular contract, Maidu
patience with the Forest Service and Forest Service openness to traditional ecological knowledge are hopeful symbolic acts.

For their part, the Maidu know their work must show the Forest
Service tangible results, so they appointed a "western science team."
This is a group of eleven scientists, including both a Forest Service
botanist and Maidu ecologists Ferrell Cunningham and Tommy
Merino, who know plants in their indigenous contexts. Using GPS, the
team has pinpointed 30 monitoring plots and 30 photo points to revisit
each season, some where traditional ecological knowledge is applied to
management and some without any management whatever. With help
from the Pacific West Community Forestry Center, a participatory
monitoring program was begun in 2006. Local people (including
Maidu students from Feather River College in Quincy) have been trained
to map and monitor these plots. Data will be collated and displayed
using GIS technology.[103] Though the project has yet to produce results,
the western science team has built community capacity and helped
create a TEK workforce. It has thus become a bridge between an
anxious, results-oriented federal agency with a short-term mandate
and a Native people who can think and work in ecological time.

Here lies the hope of the Maidu piece of this story. Returning to
the land from virtual obliteration, a handful of their people are, in a
sense, baptizing a small tract of these overwrought mountains. "The
plants are coming back and the people are coming back to take care of

them," said Lorena Gorbet.[104] By taking advantage of an opportunity to apply their wisdom, they now have a chance to demonstrate what it means to live harmoniously in this place, as they did for thousands of years. Those days, of course, can never return. The genocide, injustices, and resulting climate of despair could not have been imagined by his ancestors, writes Farrell Cunningham, "but the point is that these things exist within Native California in our time and we must, all of us, deal with them."[105] That is what the Mountain Maidu of Plumas are trying to do.

LOOKING BACK, LOOKING FORWARD

The sad feeling is gone from this land.[106]

~ Lorena Gorbet

Of all the stories in this book, none presents a more confounding picture of the ambiguities and promises of collaborative community-based conservation in these times. In comparison to the mid-1990s, there are, on the one hand, economic and political tensions that threaten the future of the forests; there's land speculation that has opened a Pandora's box of unsavory options; and there are unemployed working people, aging activists, rich second-home golfers, and QLGers and environmentalists poised to throttle one another.

On the other hand, the meadow and watershed restoration projects are spectacularly successful. Water royalties footing the bill for watershed restoration and providing a promising new income stream may revive the trek toward sustainability here. Then there are several new forums for collaboration and the Forest Service has slowly adapted to bottom-up directives. The reemergence of ancient and powerful ecological wisdom may itself be a foundation for sustainability. Then imagine a range of sustainable possibilities largely untapped: organic farming and ranching, alternative energy, ecotourism, and information technology, not to mention the possibility of a genuinely sustainable wood products industry. In the gloomy shadows of global recession, these are faint rays of hope.

The media focus on the Quincy Library Group conveys the impression that this is the whole Plumas story. This is understandable, for the scale of the experiment is audacious and its stakes are enormous. Policy analysts, forest practitioners, and taxpayers wonder whether better conservation can possibly come from a citizens' group waltzing around with a maladroit and cautious federal agency. To this extent, the QLG is unique as a force for change in the Forest Service. Will this opportunity for reinvention be long term or temporary? The answer lies in how resilient both parties prove to be in putting their pilot projects on the ground, whether they can achieve Collins-type sustainable forestry, and whether current QLG participants can pass on their experience and expertise.[107]

Fifty years down the road, I can envision a partially restructured forest that is more fire resilient, multistoried, and open. What will happen in the longer term, when thinning is no longer so critical, is anyone's guess. It is possible to imagine a day when logging per se will no longer be the crux of the Plumas economy, and this may have little to do with HFQLG. Across the West, people already deem other things from national forests — nontimber products, watershed protection, wildlife, ecological services, and recreation — as more significant than timber.[108]

Perhaps the Maidu will restore some of their domain over this forest in years to come. Perhaps a Maidu forest will yield not only nontimber forest products but also an environment to enrich ecotourism, buffer climate change, and restore the spirit. Before the Europeans came, the Maidu sustainably produced resources like gooseberries, acorns, porcupines, and camas bulbs. Few people eat these things nowadays, but other forest resources, including mushrooms and medicinals, offer promise. Beyond that, the Maidu offer their Earth-consciousness and sense of time. If the good people of Plumas can be attentive to this wisdom, ecological time may finally prevail. The world is watching.

10

Blowback on Sustainability?:
Chattanooga, Tennessee[1]

Sustainability has lost credibility. Instead of calling ourselves the sustainable or the environmental city, we call ourselves the best mid-sized city or a progressive or successful city.[2]

~ Bruz Clark

As far as sustainability in Chattanooga, the city has made leaps and bounds in the past two decades.[3]

~ Melissa Turner

There has been a blowback on sustainability because people fear policies will drive away business. Catch phrases change, but interest in the high quality of life remains.[4]

~ Ron Littlefield

PICTURE TWO CHATTANOOGAS (FIGURE 10-1). THE FIRST, A PRIME tourist destination in the southeastern US, is the one I chose to visit in my first days in the city since the mid-1990s. Though I didn't, I could have stayed at the Hilton Garden Court Hotel or one of several others virtually on the riverfront downtown(with room rates around $160 per night in 2008). Within a few blocks of these hotels, you can go to a Chattanooga Lookouts baseball game, spend the better part of the day at the Tennessee Aquarium, take your kids to the Creative Discovery Museum and the IMAX theater, stroll eastward a few blocks to the Hunter Museum of American Art and the Bluff View Arts District, go to a 2,500 seat Cineplex on the site of the old Bijou with adjacent restaurants and businesses, or amble across the half-mile

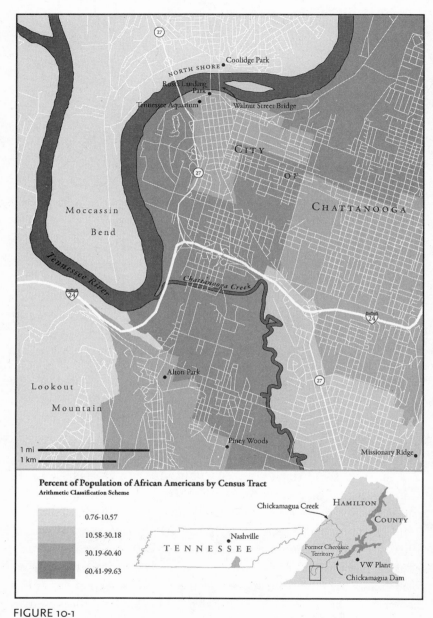

FIGURE 10-1

Chattanooga, Tennessee

pedestrian-bikeway, Walnut Street Bridge, into the North Shore neighborhood (where "hip meets history") for an ice cream at Clumpy's. As the sun is setting, you might then climb aboard the Southern Belle for a river cruise and a southern fried chicken dinner on the Tennessee River.

On succeeding days, I tried to experience the other Chattanooga. It began with a tour of the compelling Chattanooga African American Museum on East Martin Luther King Boulevard. Here you get a clear picture of the triumphs and struggles of 36 percent of the city's population.[5] You encounter African American icons with a Chattanooga connection from "Queen of the Blues" Bessie Smith to baseball hall-of-famer Willie Mays. From there you can take a bus along seedy Rossville Avenue, a sixties strip of derelict businesses, old Baptist churches, used car lots, pawn shops, brick buildings of unknown use, and the post-molten edges of industrial brownfields.

If you get off the bus and walk westward across Chattanooga Creek, you come upon a scramble of land uses and sensations. This is South Chattanooga: old factory and foundry sites surrounded by chain link fences; historic buildings like Howard School, the first African American high school, and African Methodist-Episcopal and Baptist churches; weedy ball diamonds and basketball courts in small parks and school-yards; pocket neighborhoods of early 20th century bungalows with dead cars and tippy front porches; overgrown lots; and truck terminals. Smack in the middle is Alton Park, an incongruous new neighborhood of smartly painted single-family homes with screened porches, pretty lawns and gardens, off-street parking, streets with curbs and drainage, and prosperous looking, mainly African American, families. This small set of redeveloped blocks offers a window into what could be for South Chattanooga, a reflection of Chattanooga's burst of "sustainability energy" in the 1990s. Looming at the edge is north-flowing Chattanooga Creek, an EPA Superfund site, now mostly detoxified but in the minds of folks who live here, still an ominous health hazard. "Lots has been spent cleaning up this place," we're told, "but not much of this money has improved our lives."[6] This is a gritty reality tourists never see.

Championed in 1996 as a national model by the President's Council on Sustainable Development and often cited in the literature on American urban renaissance, Chattanooga was recently ranked as one of the top US mid-sized cities by *Outside* magazine and featured in

Bicycle, American Hiking, and *Southern Living* magazines. Writing in *Southern Living,* Kim Cross called Chattanooga a splashy river town that's experienced "an utterly inspiring turnaround." "Chattanooga," she writes, "proves that a vision, a plan, and a community that cooperates can make big dreams happen."[7] Dreams, as these outdoorsy magazines see them, are wrapped up in the fabulously successful Riverbend — a nine-day music festival in June that attracted a half-million visitors in 2008; the glitzy downtown museums and aquarium, restaurants, hotels, and building restorations; the new Ross's Landing and greenway along the waterfront; and abounding outdoor adventures, including the Tennessee Blueway, a 50-mile stretch of the Tennessee River for paddlers that passes right through Chattanooga's restored waterfront.

In *The Ecology of Hope* we concluded that Chattanooga was providing a blueprint for a sustainable urban America. Using a simile that surely pushed the envelope, we wrote that Chattanooga was to the sustainable cities movement what Florence had been to the Renaissance. After all, David Crockett, home-grown prophet and great-great-great-grandson of *the* Davey Crockett had told us, "Our goal is to be a defining place, a living experiment for breakthroughs in sustainability. If humans are ever to figure out how to live sustainably on the Earth, it is in places like Chattanooga where we will find the way."[8] He used the word sustainability pointedly and often, and as we toured the city and talked to movers and shakers and doubters, we got caught up in his (and many others') fervor and lauded the highly effective marketing of this city as an environmentally sustainable, clean, and friendly place to live.[9]

On our return some 12 years later, that coherent vision of the future has dimmed and the word sustainability isn't much heard. As we near the end of the first decade of the 21st century, I am led to wonder how much of Chattanooga's indisputable and often dazzling development is really sustainable. Have environmental cleanup and economic development taken the city farther down the path to sustainability? With huge areas of downtown given to parking lots and garages and suburban sprawl that stretches way north and east of the city, the car dominates. On hot summer days, photochemical smog builds in the valley. Is so much dependence on the automobile really sustainable? How much current development meets the needs of the least empowered at the lower end of the income spectrum? I wonder whether Chattanooga's renaissance has strived toward equity. And I wonder whether the highly inclusive and successful visioning process survived the decade to continue to give voice to ordinary folks in the neighborhoods.

If you pose some of these questions to Chattanooga residents, you get dramatically varied views. There are those who see sustainability as a hollow concept, perhaps grasped by visionaries who imported the idea but never fully embraced by power brokers. "Sustainability hit the wall as a concept in 1997," Crockett himself said. "The old industrial people felt threatened by it."[10] And whereas environment ranked as the second most important issue in people's minds in the 1990s, according to Chattanooga State Community and Technical College president James Cantanzaro, now it is not in the top five.[11] People lament the retreat of visionaries and with them the idealism and rhetoric that so inspired the city to dream big dreams in the 1980s and 1990s. "The David Crocketts are missed," mused Sandra Jones, director of the African American Museum.[12] Gone too is Chattanooga Venture, the organization that catalyzed the sustainability vision and brought thousands of people into rebirthing a city deemed America's most polluted in 1969. Although Ron Littlefield was elected mayor in 2004 to return the city's focus to the neighborhoods, many feel that the grassroots spirit and honest dialogue that infused Chattanooga two decades ago have mostly dissipated.

Among cynics, one hears that Chattanooga's new face is not for ordinary and low-income citizens, who can't afford the price of a ticket to the city's magnificent aquarium, go to a baseball game, attend Riverbend music festival, or even take the time to stroll along or paddle the river. Nor are the upscale downtown developments (including LEED-certified new buildings) and sprawling new suburbs accessible to those who work for low wages in tourism, a booming element of Chattanooga's current personality. Theirs is the reality of places just off Rossville Avenue.

Though the term sustainability has perhaps become tainted, many initiatives begun in the 1990s have borne fruit and have spun off into new ventures. This leads *EnviroLink Southeast* editor Melissa Turner to portray sustainability as having made leaps and bounds in the past two decades. At the urging of Mayor Littlefield, who helped lead the visioning process in the 1990s, the city signed the US Mayors Climate Protection Agreement in 2006 and gave birth to a multifaceted Green Committee, which conducted a well-attended public forum in 2008 on ways to achieve climate protection targets. Although curbside recycling has had to be curbed, a controversial budgetary move that infuriated some residents, more collection centers have been added, recyclable volume has increased, and in collaboration with the nonprofit Orange Grove Center, more disabled citizens have been hired to sort and ship recyclables.[13]

Two new magnet elementary schools sit on formerly decayed or underutilized sites downtown. These are meant to attract residents into the heart of the city. Half their $16 million price tag came from the private sector.[14] There are also the Chattanooga Slow Food Convivium; Chattanooga Recycled Fiber, a packaging manufacturer that depends wholly on recycled material; Collins and Aikman, producing cradle to cradle floor coverings; TMIO Corporation, which produces smart and efficient ovens; EarthCraft certified green homes in downtown neighborhoods; Take Root urban tree planting; and many other green initiatives associated with the 21st Century Waterfront Plan.

CITY OF THE RIVER

Chattanooga, a metro area of 485,000 people, is now and always has been a river city. It was founded in the 1830s on the Tennessee River site of a trading post and ferry crossing known as Ross's Landing. Across the river, the lands to the north were part of the Cherokee Nation, whose ancestors had lived near the river for thousands of years. But within a heartbeat of the coming of whites, the Cherokee were driven from their home by the federal government and sent along the infamous Trail of Tears in 1838. For generations thereafter, Chattanooga had no indigenous people. By 1860 it had become a modest but thriving settlement of 2,500, sending agricultural produce southward to New Orleans and producing textiles and tobacco for national and international consumption.

Civil War battles, Union occupation, and Sherman's March combined to crush Chattanooga's economy and set back its urban evolution. Those were bleak years. But by the 1880s, with a combination of entrepreneurial capital and a river location, Chattanooga had reinvented itself. Like Birmingham, it had become a center of heavy industry with Appalachian coal fueling factories and foundries, making captains of industry wealthy, providing work for an industrial proletariat, and spewing forth prodigious amounts of soot and gray-air to despoil vistas and corrupt the lungs of a largely blue-collar population. As before the Civil War, Chattanooga's economy again became tightly linked to nearby Atlanta (90 miles to the south). Historian William Hull writes that "Chattanooga can almost be thought of as the biggest town in North Georgia."[15] In the Depression years, Chattanooga became the seat of the Tennessee Valley Authority (TVA), which tamed the river with dams to improve navigability, generate power, and lift Appalachia out of poverty, an outcome that to this day has been elusive. TVA still employs about 2,000 in a vast office complex downtown.[16]

The city came through the 20th century with an amalgam of Appalachian rural immigrants, African American blue-collar workers and professionals, post-Civil War northerners, and a small white southern elite who made their money as managers, professionals, and industrial capitalists. Divided by topography and Interstate Highway 24, white and black Chattanooga inhabited two different worlds. Neighborhoods south of I-24 were predominantly black; those upslope, white. Black residents suffered environmental, social, and economic injustices associated with their valley locale and bottom-rung status and even in recent times have perceived themselves to be mostly excluded from the sustainability vision.[17] Meanwhile, the neighborhoods on the ridges and mountains prospered and became somewhat separate exclaves, turning their backs on an increasingly troubled city.

By the 1960s, three generations of industrial effluents dumped into the naturally humid air of the Tennessee Valley had made Chattanooga a despicably polluted city. "People had to turn their headlights on in the middle of the day. Daytime had turned to dusk. Particulates were so thick your nose would blacken."[18] Better-off folks on Lookout and Signal mountains and along Missionary Ridge in their leafy Victorian estates and sprawling suburbs lived above the inversions that trapped the foul air. Workers in the valley could not escape. Their neighborhoods were perpetually choked with the worst air in America. And Chattanooga Creek, where their children played, ran across what would become a Superfund site.

Revision of the Clean Air Act in 1970 forced the city to do something about its air in the midst of a recession and the loss of 11,000 industrial jobs. Bad air was the symptom of something much bigger: the failure of society to manage the technological and organizational apparatus of the Industrial Revolution.[19] Reflecting back on wastelands left by old industry and deindustrialization, on a decaying and crime ridden downtown, and on Chattanooga's polluted waterways and blighted inner city neighborhoods, David Crockett said Chattanooga had suffered a massive urban coronary arrest.

As it turns out, this was just the crisis needed to catalyze new kinds of thinking. With funding from the Lyndhurst Foundation, Chattanooga Venture was born in 1984 to conduct a city-wide conversation about urban cardiopulmonary resuscitation and new visions for this beleaguered city. Modeled on a process used in Indianapolis, Chattanooga Venture organized visioning sessions that engaged citizens from all parts of Chattanooga. Part of their purpose was to unify what had become at least five Chattanoogas, fragmented by topography, history, zoning practices, mobility and opportunity structures, and race and class.[20] In less than a year, Chattanooga Venture circulated Vision 2000 — a broad set of goals to propel Chattanooga into the new millennium. Citizen task forces went to work on revitalizing downtown, improving substandard housing, raising expectations for education, expanding green spaces, and dealing with air and water pollution. An inclusive grassroots spirit infused this early work.

In less than ten years, $800 million of new state, federal, foundation, and private investment flowed into Chattanooga. By the early 1990s almost all of Vision 2000's goals had been successfully tackled and, as Chattanoogans travelled the country telling their story, ideas and grassroots energy kept flowing. More grant money in 1993 sustained this extraordinary momentum with Revision 2000, which led to still more goals and projects to achieve the dream of becoming America's environmental city.

This is the Chattanooga that swept us away in the mid-1990s. What had been achieved with crosscutting community participation, inclusive of but separate from government, was dazzling. Chattanooga seemed unique in its ability to raise private sector capital for its projects, the outcome partly of old wealth and family foundations such as Lyndhurst, Benwood, Caldwell, and MacLellan lodged in the city.[21] The signature project was the $45 million Tennessee Aquarium on the river — the anchor of downtown renewal. From there Chattanoogans renovated many downtown historic structures, restored the Walnut Street Bridge as a pedestrian and bike way, bought electric-powered buses built in Chattanooga to serve downtown workers and tourists, created Riverbend music festival, built a world-class children's museum, introduced the concept of magnet schools, engaged in neighborhood revitalization like Alton Park, began to implement the River Park and Riverwalk, started cleanup of polluted creeks, refurbished abandoned industrial sites, and set aside green space in the Tennessee River Gorge. We encapsulated this activity by writing that the city had returned to its roots as a river town, not as some transient marketing ploy but in a deeper way. The city had reconnected itself to the river as its very lifeblood.

Chattanooga's Clinton-era renaissance projects brought environmental sustainability to the fore. "Environment was a vehicle for us to learn about ourselves as a community," said activist Monty Bruell. "At either end of the socioeconomic spectrum the issue is felt because the rich have high quality of life needs and the poor are dealing with the worst environmental quality problems."[22] "Environment" obviously meant different things to different people, and therein perhaps lies the disconnect between sustainability as cutting-edge urban form and sustainability as equity. When these extraordinary visionaries embraced sustainability, they certainly took the environment and the economy into account and were aware of structural inequities in Chattanooga's population, but even in 1997 many of their projects fell short of either social sustainability or environmental justice, a fact that admittedly got eclipsed in our bedazzlement with the accomplishments of the era.[23]

CHATTANOOGA 2008

What of Chattanooga a decade-plus down the road? Though the word sustainability seems somewhat *verboten* these days, it is still possible to find it on Chattanooga websites and it is still partially discernible, at least for projects that impact the city's environment. However, it is not possible to say whether principles of sustainability today infuse the behaviors and decisions of politicians and other leaders in this city. The visionaries of the 1980s and 1990s have mostly left public life and taken with them the collaborative spirit and creativity that made this a city oft visited by internationally known sustainability prophets. This is more than a conceptual setback. Chattanooga's visionaries were extraordinary and apparently irreplaceable people with long-term horizons. With such horizons they had an ethic of asking first, "What's the right thing to do for the long term?" and second, "How can we accomplish that?" Of course, the crisis that catalyzed them — a city in coronary arrest — is no longer a driving force. Still, the sustainability ethic, the creative energy, and the dialogue with cutting-edge thinkers have been displaced by pragmatic implementation of disparate projects, a familiar brew of development with environmental compromises, and a leadership without much time for engaging in the exciting, highly promising, and even more urgent sustainability conversations of this decade. Despite this, much good has happened in Chattanooga, and many of the best projects ride the crest of those two earlier decades of exceptional thinking.

A Genuine Place

Writing about the sustainability of urban places, Timothy Beatley, a professor of sustainable communities at the University of Virginia, believes that reinforcing and vitalizing a city's sense of place enhance the city's resilience.[24] Urban form that permits walking, provides an abundance of "third places" (not work or home) for gathering, invests in walkways and bikeways, promotes inspiring architecture and interesting design, and sponsors public events that celebrate place contributes to resiliency and thus sustainability.

> Places that provide the spaces, reasons, and opportunities for people to come together, to share their passions, hopes, and troubles, will be healthier, stronger places and places where people trust and care about each other. And the more involved and engaged we are, the more likely we are to care about our communities and to be committed to working on their behalf in the future.[25]

For more than two decades, strengthening and sustaining place has been a signal quality of Chattanooga's journey. By the reckoning of Beatley and many other new urbanists, it has been the right way to go. And so also was it for us in 1997 when we were moved by words on a plaque at the Chattanooga River Plaza:

> Most of all this is Our place. Chattanooga, Tennessee — Our scale, Our history, Our forms, Our ideas, Our river and mountains, Our festivals, Our ideals. Our energy. Ours is what will make a genuine place — belonging to, loved by, and cared for by the citizens of Chattanooga.

Of the array of recent projects, one can see that most continue this legacy of strengthening Chattanooga's place authenticity, which visionaries of the 1990s understood would be the heart and soul of their renaissance. This part of the search for sustainability continues with impressive accomplishments, including:[26]

- **The 21st Century Waterfront Plan:** Begun with public meetings and a design charrette in 2002, the waterfront plan was meant to complete the city's return to the river by fully connecting the community to the river, creating a 24-hour waterfront, and fast-tracking funding. The city raised $200 million to implement the 129-acre plan on both sides of the river. It celebrates history at Ross's Landing (Chattanooga's birthplace) and commemorates the Trail of Tears with a stepwise waterfall framed by a series of inlays created by Cherokee artists. The plan connects and integrates earlier downtown projects such as the Hunter Museum, the Walnut Street Bridge, and the Tennessee Aquarium. Rerouting River Parkway enabled the creation of an expanded marina, waterfront taxis, and parks, as well as riverfront businesses and residences. Across the river are mixed-use neighborhoods and restored wetlands with an interpretive boardwalk. Moccasin Bend Gateway includes an interpretive center, water taxi access, and entry to the Moccasin Bend Unit of the Chickamauga and Chattanooga National Military Park. Completed on schedule in mid-2005, the plan also helped fund expansion of the Tennessee Aquarium, the Hunter Museum of Art, and the Creative Discovery Museum.

- **Riverwalk, Tennessee Riverpark, Coolidge Park:** Extended, enhanced, and completed in 2005, Riverwalk, part of the Tennessee Riverpark system, is an 11-mile hiking/biking trail starting at Chickamauga Dam. It weaves through riverfront green spaces including Ross's Landing Park, and ends up at Coolidge Park, a 39-acre site with a riverside stage, a restored carousel, and a huge fountain with sculptures of fanciful animals. There's also a multipurpose pavilion, a canoe/kayak launch, a floating restaurant, curving walkways, green meadows, river overlooks, and an adjacent wetland.

- **Tennessee Aquarium Expansion:** Opened in 1990 as the nation's largest freshwater aquarium, the Tennessee Aquarium has long been the centerpiece of downtown renewal and a raft of educational and community events. As part of the 21st Century Waterfront Plan, a $30 million expansion of the aquarium added a new building called Ocean Journey and a nearby IMAX theater. With completion of the building in 2005, the aquarium now covers nearly 200,000 square feet and includes freshwater as well as marine exhibits, including penguins.[27]

- **Public Parks Expansion:** Over 39 acres of new parks were added to the city's system by the 21st Century Waterfront Plan. These include Ross's Landing, First Street Park, and Renaissance Park on the north shore of the Tennessee River across the Market Street Bridge from downtown. Renaissance Park has forested and wetland interpretive sites, hill overlooks, and recreational and historic features.[28]

- **Electric buses:** A symbolic piece of urban renewal and compelling icons of Chattanooga's clean air in the 1990s, Chattanooga's electric buses still ply the central city. According to the Chattanooga Area Regional Transportation Authority, since 1992 they have recorded over 11.3 million passenger trips and an estimated 1.9 million miles, saving some 65 tons of pollutants.[29] Originally manufactured in the city, new buses are sourced elsewhere as Advanced Vehicle Systems, the manufacturer, went out of business in 2003. Though a new company is again producing electric buses on a very small scale, so far they have not supplied Chattanooga.

- **Creative Discovery Museum:** One of the premier children's museums in the US, the Creative Discovery Museum hosts 260,000 visitors a year. As part of the 21st Century Waterfront Plan, the museum developed new exhibits, reconfigured its space, and redesigned core exhibits with a grant of $3 million.[30]

- **Green|spaces:** A nonprofit organization funded in 2008 by the River City Company with grants from the Benwood and Lyndhurst Foundations, green|spaces assists builders and contractors in green building "to catch up with other kinds of sustainable development in the city." Their website says, "We don't need a sharp dividing line between urban park space (eco-beneficial) and buildings (eco-harmful). We want to change the way that we look at construction in Chattanooga. We want buildings that are green|spaces." Between

2008 and 2011, their goal is to complete 20 LEED-certified build-
ings. The green|spaces resource center is meant to model this kind
of green development. One of the first projects is retrofitting a 100-
year-old building owned by Fidelity Trust. The new BlueCross
BlueShield headquarters is the state's largest LEED-certified
commercial building.[31]

- **Take Root:** A five-year urban tree-planting project designed to
  bring 1,500 trees to downtown Chattanooga, Take Root aims to
  raise $1 million. The first trees put in the ground in November
  2008 were Kentucky coffee trees, a species chosen to survive urban
  air and expected climate changes. Urban beautification, carbon
  sequestration, and cooling the urban heat island justify this project.

- **Tennessee Blueway:** Conceived by the Tennessee Valley Authority in
  the 1930's, the Tennessee River Blueway was designated as a river trail
  by the National Park Service in 2002. Flowing through Chattanooga
  and the Tennessee River Gorge for 50 miles, it offers canoeing,
  kayaking, and overnight camping in designated marinas, parks,
  and primitive campsites. As a collaborative effort of federal, state,
  and local governments, including the city of Chattanooga, its stewardship is coordinated by a self-sustaining citizen organization.[32]

The Creeks

The contrast between North Chickamauga Creek and Chattanooga
Creek exposes socioeconomic rifts long a part of Chattanooga's urban
geography. Across the Tennessee River, North Chickamauga Creek
winds its way southward through rural areas, strip malls, and suburbs
and enters the river just below the Chickamauga Dam. Though pristine
in parts of its watershed, its headwaters and upper reaches carry a load
of acid from defunct coal mines. A lengthy citizens' campaign to preserve
and restore the creek has been spearheaded by the North Chickamauga
Creek Conservancy (NCCC), described to us as hard-core, middle-
class, community-minded volunteers with the highest per capita giving
to the arts and other good causes in the city. In response to their
campaigns, the State of Tennessee designated almost 4,000 acres of the
watershed as the North Chickamauga State Natural Area. To attend to
acid mine drainage, NCCC is overseeing a multiyear project to install
passive treatment systems. If successful, as in Monday Creek in Ohio

(Chapter 3), this will lower pH levels and reduce dissolved metals to levels that will support restoration of a warm water fishery and possibly reestablish the endangered Ohio River muskellunge.[33]

Chattanooga Creek, the antithesis of North Chickamauga, flows northward through present and former industrial tracts and the low-income Alton Park-Piney Woods (AP/PW) neighborhoods — economically the county's most distressed area. It enters the Tennessee River at Moccasin Bend. As early as 1994, the US Environmental Protection Agency placed the 2.5-mile segment of the creek flowing through AP/PW on its national priority list because of coal tar residues and other contamination.[34] Since then, cleaning up Chattanooga Creek has been anything but easy. Several neighborhood associations and STOP (Stop Toxic Pollution), led by activist Milton Jackson, have long advocated cleanup in response to what they see as environmental racism. By hammering home the contrast between this polluted African American neighborhood and Chattanooga's oft-touted environmental image, they have pressured city officials to take action and engage the federal government. After more than a decade of struggle, two EPA-funded phases of the cleanup began in the late 1990s. Costing $24 million, they removed tons of toxic waste (including 25 tons of tires), closed and capped a 20-acre landfill, removed coal and coal residues from the creek bed, and lined it with a temporary protectant as there are still heavy metals in bottom sediments. Phase 2 was slated to be completed in mid-2006, but then an oily substance, alleged to be creosote from an active wood treatment factory, troubled the waters again. By late 2008, stop-gap measures had not been able to stem this new pollutant and litigation between the federal government and the company, Southern Wood Piedmont, which denies culpability, continued.[35]

Though Chattanooga Creek is not clean enough to support a full range of aquatic life and its floodplain still presents too many health risks for a once-proposed greenway, citizen activism here spawned diverse collaborative community and conservation projects that many see as models of successful collective action.[36] The savvy activism of the AP/PW community pushed the city to fund a four-day planning and visioning event in 2004 to specify neighborhood redevelopment priorities. From there, ongoing Community Development Block Grants for the Bethlehem Community Development Credit Union, construction of the South Chattanooga Parks & Recreation Center, a Hope VI US Department of Housing and Urban Development housing project, and creation of a Safewalk that connects residences and schools all exemplify the breadth of collaboration in this neighborhood with a clear identity and a strong desire to bounce back.

In leading STOP, Milton Jackson, a sixty-something resident of AP/PW and long-time worker in local industries and the city fire department, has become a trusted collaborative personality well beyond his neighborhood. When we met him in the mid-1990s, he was fighting to raise awareness of the health risks to his neighborhood. He still sees himself as a tough activist who often feels like David against Goliath. And so he's found himself in the mayor's office, at city council meetings, and even in the halls of Congress and the Centers for Disease Control in Atlanta. "Outsiders and foreigners ask, 'How do government and I manage to work together?' I might be poor and black, but you can't bribe me," Jackson explained. "No one can put a figure on the costs of asthma and birth defects around here." Despite personal setbacks and the community's legacy of bitterness, Jackson is hopeful: "I never wanted to close companies. I wanted to clean up. Both sides can win if we listen to one another."[37] Such listening has lifted Alton Park-Piney Woods in many small ways, but there's still a long way to go. A University of Tennessee study concludes that "attainment of neighborhood conditions that are environmentally, economically, and socially just is far from over."[38] John Tucker of the University of Tennessee-Chattanooga, who has worked in the neighborhood on two EPA environmental justice grants, says people are still fearful of living there. "They are distrustful because of the history of illness and toxicity."[39]

Magnets

Hamilton County School District, which includes all of Chattanooga and has been increasing rather than cutting school support, is recognized as a national leader in developing and implementing local standards. It is also cited as having one the country's most successful systems of magnet schools, three of which were launched in the 1990s, when we wrote that the city's renaissance was changing the landscape of learning for Chattanooga children. Now, of the 79 schools in the district 15 are magnets.[40] They offer concentrations in math, science, fine and creative arts, museums, and classic literature, and even environment in a new magnet in South Chattanooga.

Four magnet schools are in workplace zones, reserving seats for students whose parents work downtown. Battle Academy and Normal Park Museum Magnet were 2005 national winners of the Magnet School of America School of Excellence Award.[41] On an urban jog one morning in September 2008, I circumnavigated the block on which Battle Academy has been built. It was before 7 o'clock. Teachers were in their rooms preparing for the day; a mix of black and white parents were dropping off their kids; an activity was underway in the gym; the cafeteria was up and ready for breakfasts — all this in an immaculately kept facility. Beyond the magnets, under a $5 million multiyear grant from the Benwood Foundation Chattanooga is also trying to improve literacy, bump up test scores, and improve teacher preparedness, especially in lower-echelon schools.[42]

On the downside, magnet schools designed to help desegregation have not significantly changed the racial mix of most schools, reinforcing African American impressions that magnets perpetuate segregation. (The award-winning Chattanooga School for the Arts and Sciences, the oldest magnet school, disproves this impression. By 2004 it had achieved a racial makeup that mimics the city's while consistently meeting the city's academic performance goals.) Also, there's the fuel consumption-carbon load argument against magnets, which by their nature end up busing students all over the county. Many believe this is unsustainable.

Neighborhoods and the Economy

As we reported it, sustainability in the 1990s embraced new programs to encourage the revitalization and recycling of neighborhoods. In *The Ecology of Hope* this was given voice by collaborative leaders like Lee Ferguson, director of Chattanooga Neighborhood Enterprises (CNE), Bessie Smith, who fought for 60 years on behalf of Lincoln Park, her neighborhood, and Geri Spring, coordinator of the Chattanooga Neighborhood Network (CNN). Lee Ferguson, like David Crockett, has moved on. Bessie Smith passed away in 2001. And Geri Spring, a teacher, says she's a different version of her activist self of the 1990s, working on watershed organizing across the southeast instead of just in Chattanooga. CNN, her organization of the 1990s, faded from the scene about 1999.

Chattanooga Neighborhood Enterprises, the nonprofit formed in 1986 to help Chattanooga citizens of modest means own homes, is still alive, and in itself that is hopeful. But CNE has gone through a very rough patch in the second half of this decade in both the real estate and fund-raising markets, losing its funding base from the Lyndhurst Foundation, facing legal challenges about its role in the real estate market, going through a succession of directors, and having to cut its staff from 56 to 19. With a much reduced mission, it now focuses on helping low- to moderate-income people secure second mortgages and loans for renovation and on educating homeowners about financing, maintenance, and foreclosure prevention. Despite all this, in the past 15 years, CNE has helped 3,400 people buy homes and participated in the renovation of 2,800 additional homes.[43] According to James Frierson, director of the Advanced Transportation and Technology Institute at the University of Tennessee-Chattanooga, despite its current depleted state CNE needs to be appreciated for its pioneering work.[44] Whether it will thrive again is another matter.

Lincoln Park, the successful urban renewal project we highlighted in *The Ecology of Hope*, lost its driving spirit, Bessie Smith. Many homes in this downtown neighborhood are still privately owned and maintained, according to Vanice Hughley, Smith's successor as president of the Lincoln Park Association, but:

> The spirit of community is gone. People here are getting older; younger people don't care. To the mayors, I say: "You forgot us." Everything in downtown and along the river is refurbished and revitalized; there are fancy condos, but who can afford them? I'm on my knees. There's lots of drug trafficking, which is what happens when people don't own their homes. Chattanooga is just a showplace.[45]

Across town, the Eastside Task Force, formed out of crisis in 2005, is led by James Mooreland, another African American, who's achieved fame as a tough advocate for his neighborhood. His "multicolored" task force combines five low-income, high-crime communities in projects that aim at heading off crime, working with the police, stemming the drug trade, healing addiction, sex education, and "trying to prevent this area from slipping further toward becoming a slum." Reflecting on the hopelessness and insecurity of Eastside neighborhoods, Mooreland remembers what spurred him to action:

> I had hoped to finish my work and retire. But something changed. This neighborhood is in trouble. I just couldn't sit on the porch any more. People here cannot afford to move out. They have become prisoners. They are afraid. That touches you. One person can't do it all. But this is something I can do. I can do this.[46]

In helping make these neighborhoods more secure, the Task Force has had success in slowing down crime but not in revitalizing businesses, stemming the hemorrhage of capital, or attracting sufficient investment in affordable housing. Mooreland admits, "We need many more resources than we have had so people will want to live here or come back."

Meanwhile, in the suburbs the automobile culture thrives and drives suburban sprawl with all its unseemly and unsustainable qualities. The median household income among white households in these neighborhoods in 2007 was $46,419, while in neighborhoods like the Eastside, Lincoln Park, and Alton Park-Piney Woods, for African American-headed households, it was $28,411.[47] A 2008 Brookings Institute study of urban poverty in the Southeast found the share of low-income workers clustered in high-poverty neighborhoods in Chattanooga was six times higher than in Nashville and Knoxville. All the areas of concentrated poverty in Chattanooga were in neighborhoods with high concentrations of minority residents.[48] Poverty levels among school-aged children, particularly in black neighborhoods, are also on the rise, increasing by 30 percent in the first half of this decade.[49] Gaps between the rich (comprising about 3 percent of Chattanooga) and the poor (more than 25 percent) have also been widening.[50]

The curious thing about these statistics is that the city's economy has grown throughout the past decade-plus. Managers and professionals have done well, but those in the middle- and low-income brackets have not, and growth's goodies have therefore rippled disproportionately across the city. The structure of the city's economy has drastically changed. Manufacturing jobs have been replaced by jobs in the service sector (mainly in tourism) that pay less, usually provide no or partial benefits, and frequently offer only part-time employment. Though Chattanooga's unemployment rate was at or better than the state average just before the 2007-2009 recession (about 5.2 percent), the city offered very different work than in the 1990s. Back then, in the foundries, workers averaged $45,000 with benefits; now they are making $25,000 or less. "If you are a middle-aged, working-class person, you'll probably be in a restaurant or hotel with no benefits."[51] This means more hours to survive, less security, and more people at or near the poverty line. In this sense, things have not improved since the 1990s.

New Green?

Perhaps some current leaders in Chattanooga believe that the arrival of the city on the list of cool outdoor adventure destinations in the Southeast keeps its reputation as an environmental city alive. While it's true that many forms of outdoor recreation are classified as ecotourism and some may genuinely be seeking sustainabililty, Chattanooga, "the outdoor city" of today, is not the same as Chattanooga, "the city seeking sustainability," of Crockett's time. On the other hand, Ron Littlefield's signing of the US Mayors Climate Protection Agreement in 2006 does keep Chattanooga somewhere in the mix of American cities attempting to tackle the planet's most serious environmental threat.[52] Joining 235 mayors from across the country, Littlefield pledged to reduce carbon dioxide emissions to Chattanooga's air to 7 percent below 1990 levels by 2012.[53] To achieve this target, the mayor appointed a Green Committee, which then staged a public forum similar to Vision 2000 to brainstorm ways to reduce Chattanooga's footprint by making it greener.[54] Almost 500 citizens attended.

John Tucker, the professor of environmental science at the University of Tennessee-Chattanooga and a committee member, was cautiously optimistic about the committee's work, which at this writing was slated to appear in a draft report to the mayor in late 2008. In an e-mail, Tucker wrote:

> *I do think the Green Committee is helping push sustainability back to the forefront .... While the Green Committee's focus is sustainability in general, the Committee was created to specifically provide guidance to the mayor on how Chattanooga should meet its obligations under the US Mayors Climate Protection Agreement. The true test of this local initiative is whether the Green Committee recommendations will be translated into policy changes.*[55]

Chattanooga Times coverage of a Green Committee meeting in July 2008 referred to the erosion of the city's reputation in the 1990s, when other cities moved "beyond Chattanooga's pioneering vision." However, the story concludes that "Chattanooga is thinking green again,"[56] but the mayor's signature on the US Mayors Climate Protection Agreement carries no obligation. The agreement has no teeth and surely begs for a broader buy-in.

PIECEMEAL PROGRESS?

Thinking green again and pursuing sustainability in the coherent visionary way of the 1980s and 1990s are two different matters. When sustainability dropped off the radar screen in the late 1990s, it was replaced by a pragmatism some of our informants described as implementation of the dreams of the earlier era. One measure of this is that, of the over $2 billion of new capital that has flowed into Chattanooga since 1990, roughly half has funded projects in this decade. Others believe that the passing of the air pollution crisis, the exit of visionaries, and the absence of a coherent city-wide collaborative forum are evidence that Chattanooga has lost its way. "What we have here is piecemeal change in response to business pulses and grant opportunities," one critic said.[57]

This impression is reinforced by Cheryl Horn's quantitative analysis of sustainability that concludes that what has happened recently is little more than pale green economic development. Social sustainability — the equity part of the equation — has not been consistently and effectively pursued. In an interview in 2006, Horn said that most of the city's downtown development is wonderful but not what she would term sustainable because it doesn't address gaps between rich and poor, doesn't lead to well-paying jobs, and doesn't attend to homelessness, which is rampant here as in many American cities. (On the morning jog I mentioned above, I witnessed homeless people sleeping on cardboard on park benches downtown.) Horn noted how quickly Chattanooga moved to attract the new Volkswagen of America assembly plant (which will open in 2011) while it took decades to get Chattanooga Creek declared a Superfund site. These contradictions are embedded in the city's race and class structures, she believes.[58]

African American community leaders we interviewed in 2006 and 2008 agree that the city's track record in improving their lives has been mixed.[59] Sandra Jones, director of the African American Museum, remembers a Visitor's Bureau video of 2001 with virtually no blacks. When asked about it, the filmmakers and the Chamber said, "It's all about money."[60] This has changed for the better, but she said, "We still are real backwards on dealing with white-black relations." In the minds of many in Chattanooga's black minority, any conversation about sustainable development in Chattanooga that fails to take equity into account means that progress toward real sustainability in Chattanooga is an illusion.[61] "Yeah, we're still the underclass mostly," a city worker told me in 2008.[62]

However, Chattanooga continues to celebrate and reinvent itself, to attract gobs of new capital, to land greener industries like VW and TMIO, and to project a positive image. It may have lost its champions and shed some of its idealism, which some believe was naively born, but looking back over the past decade or so, there's no doubt that Chattanooga has put projects on the ground. Chattanooga's sense of place and implementation of cutting-edge design downtown and along the river still make it one of America's most compelling experiments in urban renaissance. As you stroll along the waterfront and think about the hundreds of "sustainability initiatives" across this metro area — community gardens and farmers' markets, slow food, LEED buildings, riverwalks and blueways — you wonder if what the city needs to take it to a new level is another David Crockett.

Crockett, for his part, isn't hopeful. "There was blowback from our initiatives, and sustainability, as we knew it, is dead," he says. Crockett now stays in the background, and though diplomatic and careful in his reflections, he comes across as crestfallen. Mike McGauley of the Trust for Public Land is more upbeat. He says that "interest in high-quality life remains. We may have stopped using the word 'sustainable,' but we still focus on the long term, on quality, and on doing things right at the front end."[63] Missy Crutchfield, Mayor Littlefield's administrator for the Department of Education, Arts, and Culture and a member of an old Chattanooga family, thinks sustainability has been so co-opted that it has lost its meaning. "The mayor is a brilliant, practical guy who knows that if you can't bring business on board, you cannot get anywhere. So sustainability as a word is not always helpful or necessary."[64]

I am left wondering whether Chattanooga's return to the river is the real deal[65] — a sustainable path worth following, a path sufficiently inspiring to take the vision into the decaying and crime-ridden neighborhoods, out to Hamilton Place Mall (Tennessee's version of the Mall of the Americas), and up onto the ridges and mountains where SUVs and McMansions reign. Or whether "return to the river" is just a nifty brand to market a vibrant city for visitors, a place with a world-class music festival, electric buses, fountains, and lovely green spaces, but sadly a city lacking compassion for the least of its residents, a city whose vision got diverted by so-called green development, a city that now "finds itself in the middle of the pack."[66] When I posed this possibility to two vivacious 30-something Chattanooga leaders over coffee downtown, they agreed that the city needs to be less car-focused and must continue to redevelop poor neighborhoods, but they reminded me that these are goals you never really achieve. "It's a journey, not a destination," they said.[67] "There is a lot of positive energy in this city and there are many programs and initiatives bringing these great ideas to fruition. [Our] goal is inspiring positive and sustainable choices. This city wants to be on the cutting edge."[68]

If this is true, then sustainability needs to rise again not as simply one among many choices, or a marketing thing, but rather as a philosophy that underlies urban leadership and planning, putting aside "pale green" efforts that at best are weak and at worst unsustainable. David Crockett's "sustainability blowback," though sometimes subtle, seems real to me. To return to the cutting edge, Chattanooga will need to bring the deeper meaning of sustainability back into the conversation.

11

An Improbable Wilderness:
Sustaining People and Nature in Chicago

> *If it is the path*
> *that makes the garden,*
> *and the garden that*
> *civilizes the wild,*
> *we are disengardening now,*
> *turning on our past*
> *and our pioneering ways*
> *to make amends for the*
> *scythe that went too far,*
> *to say a thank you*
> *audaciously*
> *for the future.[1]*
>
> ~ Cindy Goulder

WHEN WE WENT TO CHICAGO IN THE MID-1990S, WE COLLECTED almost two decades worth of stories about a small army of volunteers "disengardening" by restoring historic ecosystems along the North Branch of the Chicago River. Putting their backs to the slow work of pulling invasive species, conducting controlled burns, opening up the landscape, and seeking native plants and seeds far and wide, these volunteers began to see "a miracle under the oaks."[2] Before their eyes, as they experimented and adjusted their techniques, tall grass prairies and savannas and various shades of open oak woodland took shape and flourished. In time, these sites attracted species of birds, butterflies, amphibians, and insects not widely seen in the Corn Belt for at least a century. Building on decades of ecological restoration science and welcoming new volunteers with an inclusive collaborative spirit, their projects attracted national and international acclaim, both for their ecological success and for the way they hooked residents into what may previously have seemed a bizarre way to spend a Sunday. As dozens of stewardship groups formed, each developed a distinctive identity and each found itself wrapped up in the wider community. They wrote newsletters, cleaned up streams, collaborated in community events, helped start community gardens, and worked to find common ground on divisive issues such as deer control.

By the time *The Ecology of Hope* went to press, what had begun as 13 volunteers just cutting a bit of brush and scattering some seeds on one small tract in the late 1970s had exploded into a stewardship network of 5,000 ordinary citizens working on weekends to restore some 20,000 acres of prairies, savannas, woodlands, and wetlands at 150 sites around Chicago and its suburbs. The principal visionaries in this story — Steve Packard, a charismatic naturalist who inspired and worked along with residents in the North Branch Prairie Project, Laurel Ross, an understated organizer of a growing legion of community volunteers, and Robert Betz, a biologist at Northeastern Illinois University — had become celebrities and Chicago's restoration horizons seemed unlimited. Packard, the most renowned of the three, was once described as a guy willing to play in two rough arenas at once: the science of ecology and Chicago politics.[3]

When we interviewed him in 1995, Steve Packard was reaping more than 15 years of "building congregations" for each site. "They're just like cathedrals over the centuries," he told us. "They need a congregation that can last forever. Individual people will die but the congregation will go on forever." Packard as "pastor" also realized he needed to protect the "creativity and good-heartedness" of his flock from conservation bureaucrats, scientists, and government agencies. As he remembered it: "I absorbed a lot of flak, took endless hits, threw my body in the path to protect this wonderful thing taking hold. I believed that the major threat to this effort was that creative, good-hearted, smart people would be driven off and the leadership would go to defensive, crabby, confrontational or passive, cynical people."[4]

His protective instincts paid off. The good-hearted, smart people he hoped would lead *did* lead. They became a vital cadre of stewards at each site. People like John and Jane Balaban were the "very models of the citizen-scientist who both learns from the ecosystem and turns that knowledge toward its restoration."⁵ The Balabans and hundreds of others with little or no previous knowledge of or experience in the restoration of native habitat became local experts in grasses, wildflowers, snakes, and butterflies. They learned fire science, sprouted seeds in their kitchens, and turned their backyards into native nurseries. And in return they discovered that ecological restoration was as much about renewal of the human spirit and its native connection to the Earth as it was about prairies and savannas. Larry Hodak, another of that original cadre of citizen leaders we met, said, "I can't imagine what my life would be without this. I don't know how I'd define myself environmentally, politically, any other way, even religiously, without my fifteen years on the North Branch."⁶ How could we not arrive at the conclusion that this vast and growing citizen workforce whose main purpose was healing portions of their own environs was on the very cusp of the third wave?

If the North Branch story proved to be compelling and farsighted, one could almost cast it as backstory to a more epic biodiversity narrative taking hold across Chicagoland just as we departed. The success of the Volunteer Stewardship Network propelled The Nature Conservancy and its partners toward a vastly grander vision of restoration that would include tens of thousands more acres in a biosphere reserve to embrace forest preserves, corporate campuses, lakefront parks, greenways, and other undeveloped tracts. Packard called this string of pearls stretching from the Indiana Dunes south of Chicago to the lakes and prairie wetlands of southeast Wisconsin "Chicago Wilderness," and he said, "It's either the beginning of a trend or a fad that will go away."⁷

Chicago Wilderness is anything but a fad. Today it promotes a stunning vision of how city and nature can coexist to sustain both humans and natural biodiversity in perpetuity. After Barack Obama, it is the 21st century Chicago story. But first, a reality check.

BACKLASH

Setbacks and delays could be the storyline for the North Branch and its spinoffs, for they certainly stopped things awhile. What came to be called "the Chicago restoration controversy" of 1997-1998 seemed to undercut what a generation of restorationists had taken as gospel: that their hard work toward restoration of the prairies and savannas of pre-settlement times would be seen by others as unalloyed altruism. By the late 1990s, Chicago had the most vibrant restoration culture in North America, and it had inspired many other places.[8] So the volunteers and their visionaries and leaders simply assumed everybody would be on board. After all, wouldn't a greatly enriched and biodiverse landscape be appreciated by all? Wouldn't endangered ecosystems gloriously return and become resounding symbols of Chicago's rich natural heritage, its wet, grassy, and wooded soul?[9] Wouldn't all neighborhoods understand the payoffs of more birds, dragonflies, butterflies, and wildflowers? Apparently not.

Comprising a small but vocal minority, people with gripes against the forest preserve district in two politically influential neighborhoods (Edgebrook and Sauganash in northwest Chicago), together with deer rights activists there and elsewhere, mounted an effort to stop restoration in its tracks. The notion that restoration is a high calling to engage in ongoing dialogue with nature as given, as self-organizing, and as unpredictable was being turned on its head as too much domestication and obstructing nature from doing its own thing. That the moral and ecological grounds of restoration were not shared by certain conservationists let alone many neighbors was a shock. The great guru of restoration ecology in America, William R. Jordan III, a man swept up by and influenced by Chicago's success, said this controversy amounted to "a loss of innocence."[10]

The roots of this loss lie deep in Chicago's psyche. Chicago's colossal 19th century growth and industrial history as "hog butcher for the world/tool maker/stacker of wheat/player with railroads and the nation's freight handler"[11] led Eugene Debs to observe in 1908 that, "like other great commercial centers, Chicago is unfit for human habitation."[12] On the other hand, at the turn of the 20th century Chicago managed to set aside more green space than any other American city its size. Its present system of forest preserves was first outlined by a commission stirred by Teddy Roosevelt's Progressivism. It then appeared on maps in Daniel Hudson Burham's 1909 *The Plan of Chicago,* a foresighted urban design that conceived of Chicago as "Paris on the Prairie," with a ribbon of contiguous forests in and around the growing metropolis. The system took hold with an enabling 1913 Illinois law and acquisition of 40,000 forested acres. Always envisaged as something more than just city parkland, over the next six decades the forest preserve system became hallowed ground, a place of wild lands and natural areas where people could find solace in a world sullied by smog and soot. Just as our book came out, this very system had become the bone of contention in a reverberating controversy that challenged both the theory and the practice of restoration.[13]

The controversy began to take shape in spring 1996, when a *Chicago Sun Times* columnist reported on a conflict between residents of DuPage County west of Chicago and the DuPage forest preserve district over a plan to restore 7,000 acres of its holdings to oak savanna and tallgrass prairie. A citizens group called ATLANTIC (Alliance to Let Nature Take Its Course) vehemently argued that instead of planting trees and protecting the forest from fire, as had been their tradition, the district intended to cut trees and set fires. The forest preserve board heard the complaints and quickly responded by declaring a temporary moratorium on restoration projects. Like wildfire (so to speak), the controversy spread into Cook County, and after a series of highly emotional hearings, the president of the Cook County board also declared a halt to restoration. In the ensuing months, conferences, hearings, websites, newsletters, and a steady stream of media coverage kept the controversy front and center. The Nature Conservancy (TNC), the organization with the greatest stake in restoration, sponsor of the Volunteer Stewardship Network and promoter of Chicago Wilderness, was criticized (some would say "swift-boated") by the same columnist. As on the Virginia Shore (Chapter 5) and in the Malpai (Chapter 7), TNC was not portrayed as the organization with the white hats. Both Steve Packard and Laurel Ross, "who had given so much of their personal and professional lives to the cause of restoration in Chicago," took hits from this barrage while garnering widespread academic support for their efforts.[14]

The moratorium for most sites was short-lived, especially in DuPage County, which depended less on volunteers. By early 1997, the forest preserve boards of both counties lifted it with the stipulation that volunteers continue restoration projects only after board approval and, for a brief period, only under supervision of district personnel. New guidelines were issued. By fall 1998, restoration activities had been resumed on virtually all sites.

For some months during the moratorium, invasives surged as volunteers sat at home and responded to challenges about the science behind restoration and about whether it constituted a "social good." They found a wedge between themselves and their opponents, many of whom were neighbors. "Those were tough times," said John and Jane Balaban. "The moratorium at Bunker Hill, which restricted some restoration work over a span of 12 months, probably set us back five or six years."[15] But through it all, they continued to defend the ecological fidelity of their work, the promise of more biodiversity and species recovery, and the noble purpose of stemming environmental degradation that restoration is meant to cure.

> Far from sitting at home, we worked hard to counter the great deal of misinformation circulating about restoration. We wrote letters to the newspapers, wrote informative publications, and — importantly — communicated with our elected officials, including the forest preserve board of commissioners. We quickly learned that one of the most significant obstacles to sound land management was a lack of familiarity with basic ecology and natural processes on the part of the public and elected officials.[16]

Their opponents raised doubts about whether prairies and savannas were really "aboriginal habitat" or merely an arbitrary stopping point, abetted by Indian fires, along a much longer continuum of change. They also argued that restoration can harm or kill animals and plants that, like themselves, had become native in the past 100 years, that techniques (like prescribed fire, deer removal, and herbicide application) are hazardous, and that restoration overall is nothing if not disruptive. Nature should be able to take its own course, they concluded.[17]

Despite the furor caused essentially by one *Sun-Times* writer, a survey found little wholesale opposition to restoration. People were troubled by specific restoration practices but most were aware of some of the benefits of restoration.[18] On the other hand, the Chicago restoration controversy raised broader questions about restoration science. Social scientists rushed in to frame the dispute as a values conflict over differing social constructions of nature,[19] or as a question of power dynamics,[20] or as a matter of history — which conferred upon the preserves the aura of hallowed ground — or simply as the outcome of scarce green space in a metro area of eight million.[21] These viewpoints were aired largely in academic circles and typically they have not been resolved. There's still twitter in the deeper intellectual space surrounding restoration.[22]

If the story ended here, we might be writing about the death of the North Branch Restoration Project, the dissolution of the stewardship network, and the demise of Chicago Wilderness. But it doesn't end here. Though setbacks and detours are part of the Chicago story, a far more significant line is the persistence of two key notions about restoration as a part of community sustainability. The first notion is that restoration transforms the landscape "indirectly through the education and transformation of the human beings who inhabit and shape it,"[23] and the second is that the "place-based knowledge" that flows from restoration is an essential element in the relationship between people and their neighborhoods, even in complex and largely "unnatural" urban spaces.[24] Despite the media-generated controversy, the volunteers, staff, and scientists refused to be denied. And so they came to epitomize what planner Rutherford Platt calls an ecological tapestry of decentralized, community-based projects to restore and protect unbuilt urban space. "These initiatives," he's convinced, "help bridge the socioeconomic divides of the contemporary metropolis, [which] itself is beginning to be recognized as the ultimate nature refuge."[25]

The North Branch

The North Branch Restoration Project (NBRP) describes itself as a collaborative that works to restore conditions that will allow forests and prairies to flourish as a permanent part of the North Branch of the Chicago River (Figure 11-1). As measured by the number of acres under management, the number of people who are or have been involved, or the number of school groups who visit and include restoration in their curricula, the NBRP is thriving.[26] Restoration acreage exceeds 2,500 at 16 sites with a mix of prairie, savanna, oak woodland, swamp white oak, and pin oak flatwoods communities, but volunteers could not say by how much, partly because, according to Steve Packard, quality rather than quantity has been the focus of the

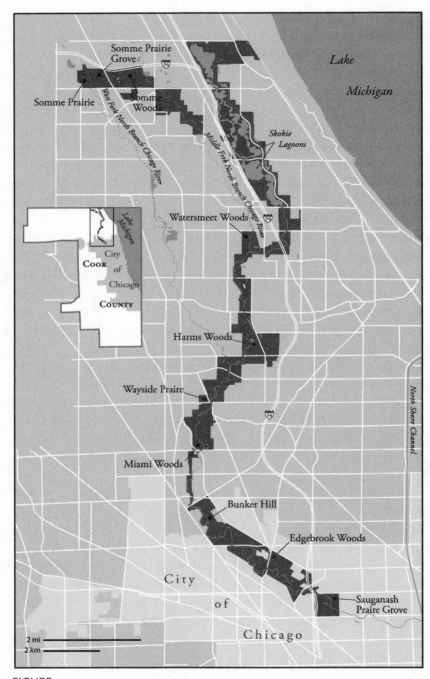

FIGURE 11-1

North Branch of the Chicago River

past decade-plus. "Enhancements in the quality and health of areas that have been worked for 30 years in some cases have been our cause," he said.[27] John Balaban, on duty since 1980, thinks these qualitative changes are breathtaking:

> I remember walking out into Somme Prairie Grove at full summer bloom, so visually struck by the rich biodiversity and the interconnectedness of the plants and animals there that it took my breath away. I literally couldn't get enough oxygen![28]

This is the transformative power of restoration. John and Jane Balaban, like many volunteers, arrived on the scene more than 25 years ago as a white-collar couple — he a high school teacher and she a pharmacist — with a keen interest in plants but no experience in restoration. They have stuck with it in good times and bad. As stewards of Harms Woods, where they contribute the vast proportion of their time, and Bunker Hill Savanna, they help plan restoration projects, lead tours, teach classes, and coordinate workdays and still pull weeds, clear brush, assist with burns, and sow seeds. In 1998 they received one of only three national Nature Conservancy President's Stewardship Awards. The Balabans continue to see the long-term implications of what they do.

> Our work is to change dark, bare soil areas into rich, diverse plant communities with large numbers of species competing, as they have done for hundreds of centuries, for sun, soil, nutrients and water. The rich interconnected communities formed in this way will provide food and shelter for myriad species of insects, and the amphibians, reptiles, birds, and mammals that feed upon them. Will it come out looking like 1830? We doubt it, but we actually won't know since we really don't know what that looked like. But we will have rich assemblages of native species competing and thriving, generating food through photosynthesis and finding ways to eat that food, self-replicating and adapting as they have done here for thousands of years.[29]

Their enthusiasm is infectious. Bird enthusiasts, college students, and watershed volunteers have joined restoration crews. Fencerows are being cleared to attract grassland and shrubland birds, and studies of native remnant-dependent insects guide new management objectives and practices. "It's an amazing time for nature," John Balaban enthused. But like many of his generation whom we befriended in the 1990s, he says it's time to hand over to a new generation. "We need to find the settled 40-somethings to take over the work of stewardship from us gray-haired old-timers."[30]

Equally significant is the diffusion of the North Branch model to other areas in the Chicago region. With the help of Audubon-Chicago Region, the North Branch concept has spread to a vastly expanded system, including Bartel Grassland in Matteson — 1,125 acres (375 of which are restored prairie), Orland Grassland in Tinley Park — 960 acres of prairie and savanna that in 2008 landed a $5 million restoration grant from the US Army Corps of Engineers, and the 3,910-acre Spring Creek project in Barrington that includes prairie, wetland, savanna, and oak woodland.[31]

Volunteer Stewardship Network

The Volunteer Stewardship Network (VSN) is now supported not only by The Nature Conservancy but by other agencies as well. A steering committee, with members from TNC, forest preserve districts, and the Illinois Nature Preserves Commission, supports the VSN with supplies, educational opportunities, and funding for such functions as project newsletters and volunteer recruitment days. In Chicago, Audubon-Chicago Region, whose director is Steve Packard, picked up the network for Chicago Wilderness. In the ten years Packard has been with Audubon, it has embraced the decentralized collaborative structure of the former VSN as its long-term model. Six staff support volunteer restoration activities in the Chicago region and beyond. They train and support stewards, monitors, and advocates and educate the wider populace. Every other year about 1,000 volunteers and professionals come to the regional Wild Things conference on restoration work. This conference gets lots of press and draws bigger audiences each time. Audubon also works closely with public agencies to organize and facilitate collaborative projects among volunteers, staff, contractors, and interns. This work of Chicago Wilderness and its many partners has attracted some $20 million in the past 10 years.[32]

CHICAGO WILDERNESS: OXYMORON OR OXYGENATION?

> Chicago Wilderness is ... a place for people to explore, relax, learn, and appreciate the wonders of the natural world. Our woodlands, wetlands, and prairies are as much a part of our region's identity as our art, music and architecture. They help make the Chicago region a great place to live and work, and they provide solace and inspiration, much needed in our busy lives.
>
> Chicago Wilderness Website
> www.chicagowilderness.org

Urbanist Rutherford Platt was struck by "Chicago Wilderness," the incompatible words Steve Packard strung together 15 years ago. Platt wrote that Chicago's innovative spirit is manifest in this unflinching use of a "remarkable oxymoron."[33] "Chicago Wilderness," at once absurd and profound, has stuck like Velcro and now powerfully drives a historic urban greening. When John Balaban, one of Packard's most stalwart acolytes, wrote of being breathless in the summer bloom of Somme Prairie Grove, he encapsulated the rich dividends that restoration can yield. William Jordan notes that drawing on human curiosity, aesthetics, community, and ambition, environmental restoration creates not only "a new prairie but a deeper understanding of the prairie, and a greater caring for it."[34]

Chicago Wilderness starts from a fact that itself may seem absurd: the greater Chicago metropolitan area harbors more globally significant natural communities than any comparable area in the rural Midwest, which is mostly, in Packard's words, "a corn and soybean desert." In other words, there are more native and endangered species populations among Chicago's towns and businesses than there are among the crop fields that dominate Illinois. Chicago Wilderness embraces sites in the North Branch and those in the recently expanded restoration projects all around Chicago. Here on a late spring stroll you can wander through colorful woodlands and savannas, or in midsummer in prairie wetlands see birds no one would associate with Chicago, or picnic in the presence of sandhill cranes at the edges of vast wetlands, or in fall drink up the colors and fragrances of open oak woodlands.

Taking these as separate jewel-like sites that neighborhoods cherish is one thing; stringing them together as a native necklace is quite another. Imagining the entire Chicago region as a wilderness requires a future eye. It begs you to think of connecting the dots, plotting out corridors, imagining how unprotected areas in the "middle landscape," neither intensely developed nor fully protected (for example, corporate campuses with ponds for migrating waterfowl), figure into building natural community health in this complex urban space. It is, in short, third-wave thinking on a grand scale.

Chicago Wilderness was formally launched in 1996. Its deep roots go back to the earliest volunteer work in the forest preserves in the 1970s, but more pertinently to the early 1990s, when Chicago area conservation organizations began to discuss ways they could collaborate toward fending off the messy urban sprawl despoiling and fragmenting the region's biodiversity.[35] While participants could see the benefits of collaboration, they decided that retaining their autonomy and separate identity would better serve their mission. They agreed on such goals as improved education and public awareness of biodiversity conservation, collaborative fund raising, and better communication and information sharing among scientists and land managers.[36] After much discussion, they crafted and signed a memorandum of understanding, put together an organizational structure, gathered seed funding from the US Forest Service, and publically launched the project with 34 founding members.

Chicago Wilderness is a mammoth concept that begins with the neighborhood but quickly ratchets up the scale to the far horizons. The system now comprises 360,000 acres tied together by a consortium of 233 organizations covering a region of more than 6 million acres. It stretches from northwestern Indiana and southwestern Michigan, across northeastern Illinois, and into southeastern Wisconsin, an area where, to say the least, urbanization has despoiled natural landscapes. Illinois has lost 90 percent of its wetlands and 99.9 percent of its tallgrass prairies, but if you look at maps of existing natural areas in Illinois, you see they are clustered mostly in Chicago's forest preserves. This is also where you'll find most of the threatened and endangered species and many of the remaining remnant community patches.[37] On the other hand, most of Chicagoland's rivers have been hugely disrupted. More than 40 percent of stream and river miles in northeast Illinois have been channelized and virtually all have been destinations for waste disposal. Virtually no river supports diverse and healthy fish communities.[38] As Steve Packard likes to say, when it comes to biodiversity Chicago's rivers are toast.[39]

Consortium partners intend to protect, restore, study, and manage the natural ecosystems of the Chicago region toward the conservation of biodiversity and the enrichment of local residents' quality of life. The partners include park districts, faith-based organizations, regional planning commissions, municipalities, museums, zoos, homeowner associations, a retirement community, federal agencies, and forest preserve districts. More than 25 corporations comprise the Chicago Wilderness Corporate Council. The consortium also partners with dozens of other organizations whose work parallels that of Chicago Wilderness. If you are an average resident somewhere in this vast and highly differentiated urban realm and you want to volunteer, Chicago Wilderness has thousands of opportunities to monitor, steward, and advocate for "wilderness." Since at least a third of its membership is comprised of community-based organizations or coalitions of these, grassroots engagement is the underpinning of all its programs.

From the outset, community outreach and involvement were envisaged as key to the success of Chicago Wilderness. Using Northwestern University's asset-based community development model, in 2001 a subset of Chicago Wilderness members gathered to increase the number of communities touched by the project, to foster neighborhood programs aimed at environmental and biodiversity enhancement, to build a diverse group of ambassadors for biodiversity, and to improve ways conservation agencies and organizations could better support community-based biodiversity projects.[40] One component of this community work is the Habitat Project.

As I write, a person can click on the Volunteer page of the Chicago Wilderness website and, for example, pencil the annual Habitat Hootenanny at the Chicago Botanic Garden on her calendar, and then sign up to help out in one of dozens of projects within a short drive of her home. There is also a Chicago Wilderness Grassroots Task Force,

> ## Chicago Wilderness
> ## – The Habitat Project –
> ### Serving the conservation community
> ### of Chicago Wilderness
>
> Life — for endangered species and rare ancient prairies, for woodlands and wetlands and the wildlife that live in them — depends on people! Though the challenges are great, and the resources rather slim, the choice is ours. By accepting this challenge we not only can make a difference in nature's future, but we can learn about and enjoy all that nature offers us.
>
> The Habitat Project is a network of thousands of volunteers and staff — scientists, monitors, land managers and advocates — who work side by side to assure the holistic and effective conservation of Chicago Wilderness, a regional nature reserve.
>
> www.habitatproject.org

which promotes hands-on habitat restoration and opportunities to work on conservation projects, youth outreach, and mobilization of more volunteers. Then there are the Butterfly Monitoring Network; the Chicagoland Environmental Network; the Volunteer Stewardship Network; various citizen science research and monitoring programs; and the campaign to "leave no child inside," based on the now widely accepted premise that direct contact with nature is critically important for childhood development.[41]

Symbolic of the bottom-up ethic, as a consortium of partners rather than a separately incorporated entity Chicago Wilderness facilitates collaboration among member organizations in areas of common interest where they would not normally compete. A small staff works under the direction of an executive council selected from so-called "executive members" (as opposed to "general members") of the consortium. Executive members donate substantial resources and time to Chicago Wilderness and have a vote on the council; general members, whose commitment is less, do not. For longer-range planning, there are a steering committee (a subcommittee of the executive council) and separate teams to plan and coordinate science, natural resource management, education and communication, and sustainability.[42] At the tenth anniversary celebration in 2006, keynote speaker Rutherford Platt told consortium members that the model they had created begged to be replicated in other North American cities.[43]

In 13 years, Chicago Wilderness has attracted millions of dollars for more than 250 projects, among the most far-reaching of which include:

- **Biodiversity Recovery Plan:** Sparked by the Chicago Wilderness Atlas of Biodiversity, the Biodiversity Recovery Plan, a blueprint for the consortium's goals, was completed in 2000 after three years of discussions. As one of the only regional biodiversity plans in the US, Chicago Wilderness provides a model for successful collaboration. Given the large group of participants, their diverse missions and approaches, and the dispersed organizational structure of the coalition itself, it is remarkable that the plan has successfully guided projects for almost a decade. It has also sparked second- and third-order outcomes that include a strategic plan for 2005 to 2020, a project pipeline spreadsheet, research reports, research papers in the Chicago Wilderness Journal, articles in the Chicago Wilderness magazine, and a raft of educational tools. Despite all this, the first biodiversity plan progress report in 2006 concluded that "overall, the region's natural communities and animal assemblages remain in a declining or threatened state of health."[44] The exceptions are in specific sites that are being actively managed by staffs or volunteers.[45]

The consortium also has produced a Green Infrastructure Vision of 2004 — a map of protected forest preserves, restoration sites, streams, wetlands, prairies, and woodlands, as well as opportunities for expansion and connection. The Green Infrastructure project was coordinated by three staff from the Northeastern Illinois Planning Commission with the input of 80 ecologists, land managers, and planners representing organizations throughout the Chicago Wilderness region. Green Infrastructure Vision aspires to bring life to the Biodiversity Recovery Plan and will be embedded in the 2040 plan of the Chicago Metropolitan Agency for Planning for Chicago. It builds on the over 360,000 acres of natural land in the three-state Chicago Wilderness Region by identifying an additional 1.8 million acres in numerous large "resource protection areas." The Vision recommends continuing acquisition of natural areas and, indeed, the region's voters have approved over $1 billion for local conservation land purchases in the last 10 years. The Vision recognizes that the bulk of land protection must occur through creative approaches, including conservation easements on private lands, farmland protection, and "conservation development," which can preserve an interconnected network of natural areas among clustered residential areas.[46]

- **Sustainability:** Initiatives by the sustainability team include the formation of a Sustainable Watershed Action Team to provide technical, conservation-oriented input for planning and design projects in biologically sensitive areas. With help from the Chicago Metropolitan Agency for Planning, the sustainability team also offers outreach and technical assistance to local governments. This means educating local officials about the significance and benefits of biodiversity protection, energizing them, and helping them find mechanisms for collaborating with one another and with conservation organizations.

- **Education:** Efforts to infuse the region with biodiversity literacy include teacher training hubs, which are clusters of Chicago Wilderness organizations that work to enhance the quantity and quality of biodiversity training opportunities for teachers within specific parts of Chicago. Hubs now exist in five locations. Another highly successful program is Mighty Acorns, which combines classroom instruction with hands-on stewardship to introduce students to nature. In 2006, 20 conservation agencies were helping 8,000 fourth to sixth grade students get involved in stewardship at Chicago Wilderness sites.

CHICAGO AND THE SOFT RESTORATION REVOLUTION

In *The Ecology of Hope* we argued that the stories we told of communities taking conservation into their own hands constituted a third wave of the environmental movement — neither utilitarian nor preservationist, neither anarchic nor regulatory. Our argument drew deeply on Aldo Leopold's enduring tenet that our best hope for a better future is the emergence of a land ethic that inseparably locks humans and nature in community. Leopold understood that human resource use, however wise, has its limits and that wild nature, for many reasons, inherently possesses worth. He also understood that drawing sharp lines between these two concepts would lead nowhere.[47] Success requires not only that we change the ways we view and use land but also that we ourselves become transformed.[48]

William R. Jordan III believes that restoration will be the shepherd that leads the flock toward Leopold's land ethic. Restoration provides the way around the impasse that led to the Chicago controversy. Conflicting beliefs about wild nature (as people imagined the forest preserves to be) and the human-impacted landscapes everywhere else briefly stopped community-based conservation. What is needed is people who can perceive nature with new eyes, based on the fact that the dichotomy of "wild" and "nonwild" is false and unhelpful. Human history cannot be peeled away from any of Chicago's landscapes. Yet trying to restore the biodiversity and natural function of an earlier time is a worthy though surely a highwire act, imbued with variability and unpredictability. "Restoration will emerge," Jordan writes, "as the dominant paradigm for the conservation of natural and historic landscapes, not replacing preservation but properly construing it as an objective and as the link between human cultures and the rest of nature, *the middle landscape* in which we negotiate the relationship between nature and culture."[49]

The middle landscape is where we will find and enhance the fragments of earlier landscapes. Here we will enjoy the rituals that have long sustained the Balabans and thousands of other Chicago restorationists — the work protocols, etiquette, divisions of labor, celebrations of small successes, and appreciation of seasonal rhythms. Engagement at this intensity is what could legitimately be called "performance art."[50] Here we will see a transformation of the human spirit that will become a "self-sustaining force for environmental renewal"[51] such that millions will be able to resonate with Larry Hodak's observation that "I can't imagine what my life would be without this." Restoration of the middle landscape will become as popular an outdoor activity as the destructive things we now do outdoors on ATVs and personal watercraft. It will draw legions of new folk to the environmental movement. This constituency will be "thicker, broader, and tougher than the constituency built on preservationism," Jordan predicts.[52] And in time it will help humanity think of humans and nature as one. Decisions about both nature and society will be undergirded by a land ethic. The dichotomy between the preserved landscape and the working landscape will vaporize and we will "achieve goals that would otherwise be totally unrealistic in a democratic society."[53] Leopold's dream will come to pass. This is William Jordan's sense of the future.

The story of how just a few increasingly savvy neighbors in the 1970s came to be enthusiastically and successfully engaged in the work of restoring wetlands and prairies and open oak woodlands is a story of leaders with a passion for protecting and enhancing natural diversity and function in a large metro area. The forward momentum of Steve Packard and Laurel Ross, both of whom have left The Nature Conservancy, was barely impeded. In 1998, Packard went on to head Audubon-Chicago Region to promote, under its aegis, an expanding stewardship network and to help bring Chicago Wilderness to life. Laurel Ross, a conservation educator with the Field Museum since 2004, has been a primary mover in the Chicago Wilderness coalition. She is the vice-chair of the Chicago Wilderness Executive Council and oversees a growing stewardship effort for the Field Museum in the Calumet region. She continues to be a volunteer steward for a site in Northbrook.

This is also a story of volunteers. Although they may have taken their knocks and had their wings clipped briefly, volunteer stewards like the Balabans and Larry Hodak saw setbacks as opportunities. Instead of wallowing in regret and becoming less flexible, they kept their focus, brought in new collaborators, remained adaptable, and imagined better ways of telling people about their work and enhancing the historic remnants in their urban backyards. They never lost that transformative and optimistic spirit that comes to almost all who do this work. That this work also birthed Chicago Wilderness, the most expansive, creative, and promising urban biodiversity proposal anywhere in North America, speaks volumes about restoration's transformative power and audaciously says, "Thank you for the future."

PART III

Hope

12

Retracing the Path

Everything we see hides another thing.
We always want to see
what is hidden by what we see.[1]

~ Rene Magritte

Whither is fled the visionary gleam?
Where is it now, the glory and the dream?[2]

~ William Wordsworth

THE ROAD TO COMMUNITY SUSTAINABILITY OVER THE PAST DOZEN YEARS has been anything but smooth. The macropolitical economy and global climate change have thrown up almost insurmountable hurdles and forced delays and detours. Cracks have appeared within what seemed cohesive, almost transcendent, partnerships and have side-tracked projects and set back what people saw as progress. We wrote in 1997 that the road most taken usually isn't the way; it alone cannot bear the truth. The most promising discoveries are often found off the path.[3] Now in 2010, this has proven to be fact. Striving toward the goals of an ecological worldview and sustainability is indeed work that takes place off the beaten track and is more challenging than community-based groups expected in their heady early days. Fatigue has set in. Partners have come and gone. Progenitors have aged. Yet none of the stories we collected in the 1990s has written its last chapter.

As I journeyed from community to community, people repeatedly asked, "What do you make of your field work?" One of my more dodgy answers was that it depends on which lens I use — through rose-colored glasses or through a glass darkly. In the four years of this project, I've wafted between the two, normally rosy at the local scale and sometimes dark about what's happening beyond. Father Thomas Berry, the Passionist theologian, believes that the old story of how we are meant to live is bankrupt and that "we are between stories."[4] No matter the lens, if I look at these stories collectively I see that they are neither the old story of human domination of the planet nor fully the new story of humans deeply understanding they are but part of the ecological whole. These stories are "between stories." That much is clear.

As I wrote in the introduction, rather than imposing an unyielding template to frame the narratives, I chose to allow the uniqueness of each place to carry its story. Though I relate the stories as they were told to me, my own biases have surely tinted the telling. Surrealist painter Rene Magritte was absolutely right that what we see usually hides something we don't see. As in his paintings, what we really want to see in these stories is what has been hidden in our telling. That's the challenge now as we try to make sense of this journey back to these communities.

To work our way toward a synthesis, let's first revisit the benchmarks that launched the original project. Using these, we find that some questions about the resilience of collaborative community-based initiatives are answered, but not all. Those that ask about dynamics beg further examination. To get at these, I reframe our narratives so we can see them as human-ecological systems. Looking at each of five human and five ecological benchmarks of sustainability, I seek a clearer view of how these initiatives have changed over time and whether they have the resilience to deal with surprises ahead (see Table 12-4). Finally, in Chapter 13, with the myriad images and experiences of this second journey in mind, I try to answer the ultimate questions egging me on. Can these communities bring forth the new consciousness — in Father Berry's words, become "new stories" — that will be pivotal in surviving the still harder years ahead? Is there cause for hope?

BENCHMARKS

> ... the final exam of my dreams is not one I could pass.
> What will I do when I can? Raise the bar all over again.[5]
>
> ~ John Hobbins

First, are the benchmarks that tied these stories together twelve years ago still germane? The short answer is yes. Disparate though the stories are, the combination of elements that launched them still informs my own understanding of what has happened. The same seems true of the folk on the ground: they kept coming back to these few nuggets. Yet the place where we figuratively set the bar in the 1990s is not where I would put it now. As Hobbins writes in the epigraph above, it needs to be raised again and again to respond to the sadly degenerating conditions we see all about.

The original progression of benchmarks went something like this (Table 12-1): a visionary leadership brought the community to a shared vision; a precipitating crisis pumped urgency and focus into their work; initial small successes propelled projects forward and fostered a spirit of collaboration that was inclusive of personalities who became committed to this form of democracy; alternative forums bypassed bureaucracies but did not exclude bureaucrats; decisions were reached consensually; celebrations of place bubbled up, helping people persist in their work (tenacity), be hopeful, and raise capital. Twelve years later, these benchmarks, which are largely about launching collaborative initiatives, still have diagnostic value. Let's look briefly at each.

Visionaries and Shared Visions

None of these stories would be worth telling had there not been a visionary at the onset with a clear view of an alternative future. The visionaries' gifts went deep, for they could translate their image of the future into words their neighbors could understand and take to heart. They had the capacity "to see tomorrow and make it work"[6] and tell a story that could compellingly "topple the counterstories" gutting our

TABLE 12-1
Finding the Path

Benchmarks for *The Ecology of Hope* Community-Based Initiatives

Visionaries fashion shared vision	New Forums
A Precipitating Crisis	Consensus
Small Successes	Place Celebrations
Collaborative Leaders	Tenacity and Hope
Collaborative Operators	New Capital

Source: Ted Bernard and Jora Young. *The Ecology of Hope.* New Society Publishers. 1997, 194-209.

places.[7] Their communities gathered round their vision. When Mary Stoertz told her Monday Creek colleagues to "step out boldly" she might have been speaking for this group of extraordinary people.

Yet visionaries often also have to step aside. Of the original set, a relative few (Steve Packard in Chicago, Freeman House and David Simpson in the Mattole, Michael Jackson in Plumas, Verna Fowler in Menominee) are still actively embedded in the stories you've just read. Among the others, some left home, some died, a few sit in the background and probably wonder "whither is fled the visionary gleam?" In the most vibrant cases, a new generation of visionaries has moved onto center stage (Bill McDonald in the Malpai, Chris Larson and Jeremy Wheeler in the Mattole, Jim Wilcox and Lorena Gorbet in Plumas, Michelle Decker in southeastern Ohio, and Lisa Waukau in Menominee are examples), while in at least two (Virginia's Eastern Shore and Chattanooga), without the energy and inspiration of the embryonic visionary and vision the story has stalled. As always, "vested interests, dated attitudes, entrenched bureaucracies and ... lack of public support" throw up barriers to the future that visionaries imagine and communities embrace.[8]

Crisis

At the genesis of each story is crisis. In each, it led to almost instant community, brought adversaries to the table, cast new light on dispiriting politics and bad resource management, and helped ordinary citizens become extraordinary activists inspired by their visionaries and leaders. Seeing hidden opportunities in crisis, "when the good news in the bad news becomes apparent," these communities were able to write the first chapters of their journeys toward sustainability.[9] But what happens when the intensity and stress of the initial crisis abate? How do the partnerships sustain their energies, creativity, and direction over the longer term?

Writing about the Applegate Partnership, a community-based forest collaborative in Oregon, Cassandra Moseley observed, "If the partnership continues, it must shift from a group fueled by crisis to one that can maintain itself for the long term, while keeping the innovation and creativity that marked the early years."[10] The quality of leadership will determine how well this works. Strong leaders with energy and vision can keep the group together and on task.[11] Such has been the challenge of the collaboratives in each of our stories. With the Menominee

and on Monhegan, the crisis cycle has repeated itself across many generations. In Menominee in 2009, unfavorable markets and a court ruling
on their new casino are contemporary crises that challenge the people;
on Monhegan, affordable housing and uncertain lobster yields are the
crises of the moment. On the other hand, in Chattanooga and on the
Eastern Shore the resolution of crises — air pollution and land speculation, respectively — seems to have taken the starch out of the
partnerships that formed in the most critical period.

In other stories, long-festering and apparently intractable crises
that never seem to abate threaten to become background noise rather
than something to mobilize the community. Examples of this abound:
intergenerational human poverty, for example, in Menominee, Monday
Creek, and Chattanooga and on the Eastern Shore of Virginia; threatening invasive plants and pathogens (everywhere); acid mine drainage
(Chattanooga and Monday Creek); the pressures of too much tourism
(Eastern Shore and Monhegan); a catastrophic forest fire (Plumas and
Mattole); and fragmentation of ecologically coherent landscapes
(Malpai, Plumas, Mattole, Eastern Shore, and Chicago). Perceiving
new ways out of these "poverty traps" that diminish progress on other
fronts will be important to sustaining the sustainability journey.[12]

Then there is climate change. Thinking about this, Freeman House
of the Mattole grimly observed, "The world beyond us offers frighten-
ing prospects."[13] And so it was that in almost every story (and here is
where our informants seemed to see through a glass darkly) global
climate change is viewed as throwing up unprecedented threats to local
ways of life. Whether it's warming oceans possibly changing lobster
migrations off the coast of Monhegan or overheating spawning waters
for Pacific Northwest salmon, these are enough to discourage the most
hopeful. "All this work, all this expanding consciousness, including all
the work with the ranchers and timber, all that could just be blown to
bits by climate change," worried David Simpson in the Mattole.[14]

But then I think of the Menominee, who have been through many
crises, including climate change at the end of the ice age. Elder poet-
photographer-philosopher Larry Waukau told me, "I don't lose hope;
the forest will take care of itself. But our leaders must again rise to new
challenges."[15] In other words, the bar must be raised. Writing about the
global environmental crisis, William Jordan is "not willing to accept the

idea that the prospect of a crisis is our best, most effective motive for action." He suggests instead a positive vision: "learning to live graciously on this planet."[16] The most stunning outcomes I witnessed confirm this view. And so the challenge of moving beyond crisis management and response continues.

Successes

Back in the 1990s, Leah Wills, watershed activist and collaborative leader in the California Sierras, told us that after nine years of experience "the only thing that has sex appeal and lasts is success," and John Sheehan, also from Plumas, said, "Resist at all costs the temptation to do big fancy things. Go for success first."[17] Success still breeds success. It prompts creativity and innovation and reels in skeptics and others discouraged by the barriers listed above. "Successful collaborative partnerships ... instill hope by working on smaller, more manageable issues first to demonstrate that progress is possible."[18]

In each story, even those treading water or losing sight of their vision, there have been eye-popping successes. Remember, for example, the two wee communities which, after many obstacles, compelled legislatures to pass new laws to reinforce their chosen paths (Monhegan and Plumas). Remember Monday Creek, "dead as a bag of hammers," miraculously coming back to life, step by step, because of hard-working people in a cohesive partnership. Remember a sparkling riverfront in a city that had been despondent and despicably polluted (Chattanooga). New concepts, such as "working wilderness" and "middle landscape," usher in impressive conservation outcomes in virtually every case.

The more I think about it, the more I want to accentuate how the people of the Mattole for more than 30 years have worked toward deeply reinhabiting their watershed by building on successes as small as trapping one spawning salmon, replacing a rusted culvert, installing a water storage tank, and planting trees. Living by a river like the Mattole is a powerful binding force, hydrologist Tasha McKee reminded us. Finally, by many more generations and surely against history's odds, the Menominee demonstrate, forest plot by forest plot, what long-term success means. It could not have happened without countless preceding small successes in managing their forest to ensure "the visionary gleam" of their chiefs would not be extinguished.

Forums, Collaboration, and Consensus

Collaborative community-based initiatives are part of the quickening of local democracy that may lead to a new kind of sovereignty.[19] The quasi-autonomous forums and networks we encountered in these stories bypass institutions with a history of throwing up barriers. They invite stakeholders to peaceably and effectively resolve divisive community squabbles. By arriving at consensus, these forums engage and empower ordinary people with hands-on work like pulling invasives, collecting and saving seeds, nurturing salmon fry, cleaning up creeks, monitoring forest and range, and helping with prescribed burns. Ultimately, citizens can participate in decisions that a federal or state agency might once have made alone. Consensus also endows these partnerships with "a kind of authority to act on behalf of the landscape they share."[20]

This devolved, inclusive, and more intimate form of democracy enriches community and bolsters conservation work. In turn, it makes partnerships more robust. To be successful, it draws on a variety of talents: science from staffers like Ben Brown and Peter Warren in the Malpai; Ray Lingel, Tracy Katelman, and Tasha McKee in the Mattole; and Mike Dockry and Marshall Pecore in Menominee; collaborative leaders like Mitch Farley and Mike Steinmaus (Monday Creek), Mary McDonald and Wendy Glenn (Malpai), Sterling McWhorter and Johanna Rondoni (Mattole), Kathy Ianicelli (Monhegan), Missy Crutchfield and John Tucker (Chattanooga), John Schramel and John Sheehan (Plumas), and Laurel Ross and John and Jane Balaban (Chicago); and a wide swath of facilitators, innovators, operators, and followers.[21] And though successful collaboration requires hard work, here, as in collaboratives across the country, participants themselves invariably find it personally transforming and fun.[22]

When Mitch Farley, a career geologist with the Ohio Department of Natural Resources, said that the Monday Creek partnership had rejuvenated him, I became aware that the outcomes of this new kind of engagement flow both ways. "For all the perceived rigors of collaborative resource management, I haven't seen a better process,"[23] concludes Jim Wilcox, the Feather River CRM manager in California, whom one county supervisor referred to as "one of my minor gods."

About three quarters of the partnerships, councils, groups, visioning forums, and alliances we encountered 12 years ago are still on the ground and many new ones have formed. They still offer safe, alternative places for ideas to flow and power to be relinquished. Most still make decisions using consensus, which by many accounts, though clunky, is an important element. In Monday Creek, Gary Willison of Wayne National Forest admitted: "Collaboration and consensus slow the process, but it's important to stick to the idea of consensus on all decisions. Everybody's better off for it."[24] Decision making by consensus helps equalize the power equation and when it works there are no losers.[25]

Place

If a sense of place is seminal to resilient communities and resilient communities are the building blocks for the bottom-up society we urgently need, then celebrations that reinforce and build pride in place are key markers. They define home as unique. They sustain communitarians and collaborators and draw together and inspire others. They put people and art on the streets. They bring joy.

Nothing pumps me with so much hope as the array of place celebrations I find across the entire set of stories. On Monhegan, on "trap day" in late autumn the island's lobster fishers and year-round residents turn out to launch the new fishing season. In Virginia, the Eastern Shore Birding and Wildlife Festival attracts thousands of visitors and reengages the community year after year. In the vicinity of Monday Creek, Little Cities of Black Diamonds ties together the towns of the Hocking Valley Coalfield to sustain their history and traditions, commemorate the significance of the labor movement, and "enrich the future quality of life in the region." Celebrations include the Appalachian spring festival at the Eclipse Company Town, a "tour de forest" cycle event, a labor conference, and many smaller celebrations and activities.[26] In Chattanooga, the Riverbend Festival, surely the grandest of community celebrations in this set of stories, not only brings art to the streets and riverfront but also generates jobs, income, more than half a million visitors, and pride to the city.

In Chicago, the inclusion of two faith-based groups in the Chicago Wilderness partnership opens the way for a new dimension of their celebration of nature in the city:

> *Faith in Place creates welcoming spaces for people of*
> *all faiths to fulfill two great common responsibilities:*

loving one another and caring for creation.
Recognizing that many people avoid getting involved
in the environment because it is perceived as a hopeless
predicament, Faith in Place reaches out to people in
the places they go to gather strength and hope — their
houses of worship — and seeks to foster environmental
conversations and consciousness.[27]

On the Menominee Reservation, the annual midsummer pow-wow, one of several staged in cooperation with the Great Lakes Intertribal Council, attracts hundreds each year, including Menominee from all over the country, other Native peoples, and tourists. As an ancient place-based celebration, a pow-wow is:

... a social occasion, an opportunity for good times. It's
a chance to renew friendships and make new ones. It's
a chance to affirm the joy of life and the dignity of a
living culture. It's an exhibition of virtuoso dancing
with opportunities to participate. It's a chance to get
back in touch with the heartbeat of Mother Earth.[28]

Getting back in touch with Mother Earth's heartbeat may not be how other communities see their celebrations, but in essence this is the sense of place they seek.

In the Malpai, the science conference brings ranchers together with academic researchers and government scientists for an annual update on many facets of research on their region. Thanks to the hospitality of the Glenn family, the annual meeting of the Malpai Borderlands Group is about partnership business but it also celebrates the ranching life this group means to sustain. In the Mattole, a simple potluck promoting sustainability is a celebration of the valley's history of agriculture and a way to think about gaps in the Mattole food system. The annual fall release of salmonid fry that have been nurtured by school children has long reinforced the importance of salmon to this small California valley. "We don't want the children to forget that spawning salmon swim upstream and their offspring the opposite," said Freeman House.[29]

Tenacity and Hope

Despite setbacks and disillusionments, what surely distinguishes our narratives is the pervasive sense that hope is kindled by hard work, by confronting demons and obstacles, and by being nimble enough to change as new evidence rolls in. This applies to the newest of experiments as well as to stories that go back generations. "There is light at the end of the tunnel," Dee Cobb, the irrepressible Menominee college student and community organizer, confidently told me. "I don't listen to negativism."[30]

These storytellers draw strength from their grounded hopes. Years of organizing and work leave little time for despair. Such persistence bespeaks another of the benchmarks we found in abundance in the 1990s: tenacity. Back then we wrote that most of the communities still needed to learn the real meaning of tenacity. What is stunning now is that not one of these stories can be written off; not one has finished its work. Though leadership may have changed, though collaborators may have come and gone and coalitions may have shifted, these communities have hung tough for the long haul. "We're not there yet," admitted Michelle Decker. "Things [in Appalachian Ohio] just don't happen easily. Forces that have been in play for 70 years are not going to be turned around immediately. But I am confident that ... we will continue to be an organization that responds to change and lifts up this region."[31] She understands fully that some of the most difficult things have already been done — organizing, making decisions to act, accomplishing small successes over many years. Now tenacity must carry the day.

Capital

John Sheehan of the Plumas Corporation in California assured us in the 1990s that "A good solution is the hardest thing to find. Good people to implement the solution, second hardest. And money, the easiest."[32] This seemed so in all the stories we collected in the 1990s and in fact for community-based collaboratives all over the western US.[33] It is still the case. People like Sheehan, very much the optimists, enablers, and resource mobilizers, continue to make people believers. People who know how to seek and secure wherewithal for good ideas, be it actual funds or expertise, labor, space, or equipment, have been essential to the ongoing life of these collaboratives and what they have accomplished.

From very small beginnings — no office or working space, for example, no paid staff, and little cash — targeted grant writing and networking with foundations and various levels of government have

TABLE 12-2

Funding Levels for Selected Projects

Community (Chapter)	Project	Time Frame	Estimated Amount	Sources/Notes
Monday Creek (3)	Monday Creek Project	1994-2012	$26 million	USACE, US/Ohio EPA, WRDA, Rural Action, and others ($21m of this is for projects from 2008-2012).
Eastern Shore (5)	Southern Tip Partners	20 years	N/A	James Taylor concert in 2008 raised $200,000
	Eastern Shore Corp.	3 years	$3.5m	Cobb Island restoration
	STIP	20 years	$9m	Sustainable Technologies Industrial Park
	Seaside Heritage Program	20 years	$1m	Virginia Department of Environmental Quality; NOAA
Menominee (6)	Various	10 years	$105m	Casino revenues to MITW and enrolled members
Malpai (7)	Malpai Borderlands Group	1994-present	At least $2m	Operating income only from various foundation and state and federal sources
Mattole (8)	Salmon Group	2007	$350,000	Annual operating budget; various state and federal sources
	Restoration Council	2007	$3.5m	Annual operating budget; various state, federal, foundation, and fee-for-service revenues
Plumas (9)	Watershed Forum	2003-2006	$8m	From water contractors as result of Monterey Agreement
	Maidu	10 years	At least $250,000	USNFS forest stewardship grant
	FRCRM	20 years	$7m	State, federal, and private sector grants and contracts for Feather River restoration projects
	QLG	1993-present	At least $10m	HFQLG Pilot Projects in Plumas, Lassen, and Tahoe Forests

Community (Chapter)	Project	Time Frame	Estimated Amount	Sources/ Notes
Chattanooga (10)	Chattanooga Venture	10 years	$845m	Various federal, state, foundation, and private sector sources
	Waterfront Plan	3 years	$200m	Various, especially foundation and private sector sources
	School Improvement	10 years	$21m	Foundations, state, and private sector sources
	Chattanooga Creek	5+ years	$24m	USEPA
Chicago (11)	Chicago Wilderness	10 years	>$20m	Private sector, federal, state, and foundation sources

Sources of data are cited in Chapters 3-11.

leveraged funds for projects and enabled budgets to grow and partnerships to flourish. On the other hand, in no case is a particular source of funding secure. "It can be gone with the stroke of a pen," observed Mary Stoertz in Ohio.[34] But such uncertainty also infuses partnerships with creativity and resilience. For example, the loss after over a dozen years of funding from AmeriCorps in 2009 presents Rural Action and Monday Creek "with new opportunities ... [that] will require innovative solutions."[35]

Table 12-2 (on facing page and left) should make it clear that community-based collaborations have been exceedingly successful in raising capital. But nobody I interviewed believes their funding to be sustainable. Instead, almost all the partnerships have begun to think creatively about how to overcome the inevitable resource constraints and "mission creep" that weaken them and threaten their own institutional sustainability. Solutions include fee-for-service projects at several sites, diversification of emphases, further engagement of the private sector, carbon sequestration, payment for ecological services, building endowments, and convincing society to pay for externalities. One of the most intriguing examples of the latter comes from Plumas, where the Feather River CRM partnership seeks to oblige southern California, the end-user of Feather River water, to perpetually pay fees for watershed restoration and protection. "Water is the resource of the future,"

forecasts Plumas Corporation's John Sheehan, "and it will pour thousands of dollars back into our economy for restoration and upkeep of
these watersheds."[36]

Here are some other examples: higher fees for waste disposal on
Monhegan with hopes for behavioral change in reuse and recycling;
land trusts yielding ecological services on the Eastern Shore and on
ranches in the Sierras; habitat conservation planning in the Malpai and
the Mattole and forest harvest plans in the Mattole that pay service fees
and reap long-term ecological benefits; diversification of products and
cogeneration from the MTE mill in Menominee; firesafe planning and
implementation in Plumas and the Mattole; and forest stewardship using
indigenous knowledge and practices in Plumas and Menominee. All
signify thinking that goes well beyond raising start-up capital.

A HUMAN-ECOLOGICAL PERSPECTIVE

> *If we are to balance and direct our remarkable technological
> muscle power, we need to regain some ancient virtues: the
> humility to acknowledge how much we have yet to learn, the
> respect that will allow us to protect and restore nature, and
> the love that can lift our eyes to distant horizons, far beyond
> the next election, paycheque, or stock dividend. Above all, we
> need to reclaim our faith in ourselves as creatures of the
> Earth, living in harmony with all other forms of life.*[37]
> ~ David Suzuki

As I have relayed each story, I have stealthily assumed that these
communities are "human-nature systems" and that sustainability is
mostly about building resilience in these systems. These communities
are, in many senses, exemplary, but when all is said and done they are
comprised of imperfect beings imprisoned by events they cannot fully
influence and institutions and rules they didn't invent. If we could, in
David Suzuki's words, "reclaim our faith in ourselves as creatures of the
Earth," we would be on our way,[38] but in fact no one yet fully understands what it means to live "in harmony with all other forms of life,"
nor to roll resiliently with nature's punches.

There is much to learn. Meanwhile, these communities face enormous real-time challenges with uncertain outcomes — forest fires;
urban, suburban and rural sprawl; big gaps between rich and poor;

TABLE 12-3

What Would Success Look Like?

Elements of Sustainable Resource Management in *The Ecology of Hope*

Communities would have:
• a good working knowledge of the ecosystem
• a commitment to ecosystem health
• a commitment to learning
• a respect for all parts
• a sense of place
• an acceptance of change
• a long-term investment horizon
• an ability to set limits

Source: Ted Bernard and Jora Young. *The Ecology of Hope.*
New Society Publishers, 1997, 182-193.

rivers drying up; species threatened; terribly polluted bays; and rising and warming oceans, to name a few. Yet for all these problems, optimism reigns. Pride of place and "can-do" engagement have inarguably been transformative. Folks in these stories have taken baby steps toward seeing their communities and themselves as part of the living Earth.

In a final chapter, *The Ecology of Hope* posed this question: What would a community need to achieve a longer-term, dynamic relationship with its ecological setting? We wondered just what an environmentally sustainable community might look like. Because most of the stories were newly born, we could do no more than fix distant points on a horizon toward which communities could sail (Table 12-3).

To update this set of traits, I want to take advantage of the advances in the past 13 years in our understanding of complex adaptive systems (Table 12-4). In taking the pulse of these experiments with resilience as our focus, we must recall Walker and Salt's caution in Chapter 2 that, if resilience is the focus for community sustainability, we are far from the finish line.[39] This is surely true of all our stories. Though the dichotomy between human and ecological markers in the summary that follows is obviously artificial and overlapping, it shifts our focus from static to dynamic assessment of the future of our communities.

TABLE 12-4

What Would a Resilient Community Look Like?

Marker	Description
Human/Social	
Organizational Resilience	Organizations that can multi-task, retain social memory,* accumulate social capital;† adapt to change without loss of coherence or direction, and transfer leadership and organizational acumen to new generations are resilient organizations.
Reorganization & Renewal	Crises foster creative responses and periods of innovation, reorganization, and renewal and they open the door for new leadership. Catagenesis — reorganization through breakdown — is often the silver lining in otherwise dark clouds.
Adaptive Management & Governance	Organization focuses on learning. All actions taken are opportunities to learn. Programs and projects on the ground test hypotheses. Management and governance respond adaptively to information from these experiments.
Local Knowledge & Indigenous Knowledge	People cherish their common spaces, architecture, and cultural landscapes. They deeply understand their physical geography and natural assets and cycles. They celebrate the triumphs and struggles of their place and the wisdom such history conveys. Such knowledge is the foundation of resilience.
Equity & Environmental Function	Fair, just, healthy, and equitable societies are resilient societies. Trust, a key lubricant for good collaboration, builds in such societies.
Ecological	
Maintaining Ecosystem Function	Nature functions "naturally" with as little disruption of material and energy cycling as possible. Feedback loops operate as in nature. A full array of functional groups are present: plants that can fix nitrogen, root deeply, use water efficiently, contribute litter to soils; animals at all trophic levels, with a diversity of masses and foraging behaviors; and microorganisms to decompose matter.

Marker	Description
Maintaining Eco-system Services	Complex sets of interactions that control carbon assimilation, transpiration, water retention and extraction in soils, nutrient cycling, herbivory, and predation are protected to provide pollination, purification of air and water, and regulation of nutrients. Biodiversity adds texture, beauty, childhood lessons, intellectual challenge, and wonder to life and underwrites human/ecological existence.
Resilience Thinking	The ability of the community to absorb disturbance without shifting to another regime is the bottom line. The community identifies and understands thresholds that control their human/ecological system. They learn how to manage critical variables to avoid tipping points.
Learning, Monitoring, & Experimentation	There is commitment to a culture of environmental learning from toddlerhood to the golden years. The community keeps abreast and remains humble, for it can never uncover all nature's secrets. Learning about natural systems builds on carefully crafted experiments and long-term monitoring. Constantly expanding and evolving knowledge fosters flexibility, openness, and creativity.
Setting Limits	Informed understanding of human-ecological tolerances leads to long-term thinking about how to live within means, how to have a life of sufficiency, and how to set limits. Setting and maintaining limits is a significant marker of progress toward sustainability.

*Social memory: Knowledge about past successes and failures in adapting to change

†Social capital: Interactions between people that rely on trust, mutual understanding, and shared values

Sources: Lance H. Gunderson and C.S. Hollings, eds. *Panarchy: Understanding Transformations in Human and Natural Systems.* Island Press, 2002.; Brian Walker and David Salt. *Resilience Thinking: Sustaining Ecosystems and People in a Changing World.* Island Press, 2006; Fikret Birkes and Carl Folke, eds. *Linking Social and Ecological Systems: Management Practices and Social Mechanisms for Building Resilience.* Cambridge University Press, 1998; Thomas Princen. *The Logic of Sufficiency.* MIT Press, 2005.

HOW THE STORIES STACK UP AS RESILIENT HUMAN-ECOLOGICAL SYSTEMS

If we apply the criteria in Table 12-4 to each of the nine communities, we ought to be able to qualitatively assess the resilience of each and make some educated guesses about whether a researcher looking at sustainability in these places a dozen years hence would have something to write about. It might be possible to perform this assessment quantitatively by assigning scores community by community, trait by trait, but the numbers, no matter how they are derived, would grant unjustified precision both to the methods employed and, to be perfectly honest, to our ability to fathom how these communities really tick as human-ecological systems.

By my reckoning, the communities cluster in three distinct groups: one that seems highly resilient for many reasons, a second that has one or more reasons to appear a bit less resilient, and a third with enough uncertainty to wonder about its future.

Top Cluster: Menominee, Mattole, Malpai

Each of these three communities nurtures partnerships or organizations that in the past decade have responded resiliently to significant disturbances: in the Mattole, the collapse of the Watershed Alliance, drought, and upper river desiccation; in Menominee, a tornado and market swings for wood products; in the Malpai, market swings for livestock, long struggles crafting fire and endangered species plans, and the need to deal with increased border activity and landscape fragmentation.

Innovative reorganization led to renewed social capital in all three stories and added to the social memory built over decades (generations in Menominee). For example, ongoing desiccation of the upper Mattole River offered opportunities for reinvention and brought several groups to higher levels of collaboration aimed at water conservation to save salmon. In the Malpai, by working through their US congresswoman the Malpai Borderlands Group brokered collaboration with the Border Patrol to limit construction of new roads across their ranches. And it's hard not to admire Menominee Timber Enterprises for reinventing itself in its hundredth year.

Exemplary leadership has fostered a collaborative spirit that gathers partners at "the radical center." The radical center is neither a place of more regulation nor a place of rugged individualism. "Rather than splitting the difference between two extremes, the radical center aim[s] to discard the polar oppositions that defined the spectrum in the first place."[40] On the Menominee reservation this happens through formal institutions such as the Menominee tribal legislature and Menominee Timber Enterprises; Jeremy Wheeler guides the Mattole Restoration Council and Bill McDonald the Malpai Borderlands Group to that mystical place of new thinking and consensus. Wheeler is still astounded by how inclusive the radical center can become: "We have never accomplished more and never collaborated with so broad a cross-section of the community."[41] For the Borderlands, McDonald wrote: "In a political climate where the traditional position on this issue of land use is usually to be at one end of the spectrum or the other, we find ourselves in the 'radical center.' We invite you join us right there."[42]

In each case, resilience has been improved by the accomplishment of conservation objectives that aim to restore or maintain ecosystem function. Examples include enhancing biodiversity in the Menominee forest; protection of old-growth redwoods in the upper Mattole; and maintaining the diverse habitats and species of the Malpai. Restoring and enhancing biodiversity and hence ecosystem services is similarly at the core of collaborative work. Think back to the stellar work (with still uncertain outcomes) of restoring chinook and coho salmon and steelheads to the Mattole, of the Menominee history of protecting a full range of aquatic life, birds, and mammals along the Wolf River and in the surrounding forest, and of reintroducing aplomado falcon and bighorn sheep in the Malpai. If jaguars set up housekeeping someplace in southern Arizona or New Mexico, one predator long missing from Malpai foodwebs will have rightfully come home.

A commitment to experimental science and monitoring means all three communities adapt their management decisions to what they learn in the field. As participants in the most successful of the community initiatives in this book, leaders and collaborators of the Menominee, in the Mattole, and across the Malpai nourish a vibrant culture of learning with an eye toward ecological time. These paragons of best practice spent hours explaining how science informs their decisions. Marshall Pecore and Jeff Grignon in Menominee, Ben Brown in the Malpai, and

Tasha McKee in the Mattole have convinced their partners that their very future rests on good science. Pecore told me that even climate change can be dealt with: "We must work with change, not be a victim of it."[43] Yet in every case, experiments, data collection, and monitoring only scratch the surface of full understanding of the thresholds and feedback loops in the human-ecological systems these collaboratives seek to sustain.

As a consequence, each community exercises caution, establishes limits. In Menominee, limits are built into the forest management system that comprises more than 90 percent of the reservation and allows no more than 20 million board-feet to be cut each year. In the Mattole, limits are expressed in plans to selectively harvest Douglas fir, to prohibit salmon fishing, to limit further road development, to "put to bed" particularly troublesome and erosive roads, and to foster summer water conservation to improve salmonid habitat. In the Malpai, Jim Corbett's "viable land ethic" translates into managing not only for livestock but also for other members of the ecological community that enhance the wild beauty, stability, and integrity of the high desert. It also means setting and carefully monitoring fire across the Borderlands. As I think about this, I see that collaborative operators and scientists in each of these stories have uncommon awareness of what Jonathan Adams calls conservation of the middle landscape, a science not only of wild preserves but also of the places where people live and work.[44] How can one not find hope here?

As for the equity part of the equation, the Menominee, cooped up on an iota of their original territory, have suffered heaps of environmental injustice since the 19th century. The harsh and misguided termination in the mid-20th century opened the gate for poverty and other social ills the tribe still fights. Dee Cobb's Bridges Out of Poverty program aims to uplift Menominee at the low end of a low spectrum with education, job skills training, and life coaching. In the Mattole, land prices and the potent marijuana economy increasingly marginalize struggling ranchers and other residents. Through pooling capital, cohousing, and diversification of the ranching economy, the rising generation may be able to afford to live here and carry forward the three-decade history of restoring this beautiful California valley.

Middle Cluster: Monhegan, Plumas, Chicago, Monday Creek

Many of the human and ecological markers that enable Menominee, Mattole, and Malpai to stand out prevail in Monhegan, Plumas, Chicago, and Monday Creek as well. Collaboratives in all four communities have been called upon to respond to surprises in the past ten years or so.

Monhegan dealt with a challenge to their lobstering regime and rededicated themselves to a sustainable fishery and to extending conversations about limits to other sectors of island life. This rededication rippled upward to the Maine legislature and ultimately into statutes protecting Monhegan's fishing territory and seasonality. Later, based on experiments by lobster biologists, Monhegan fishers agreed to reduce their trap limits.

In Plumas, the Feather River CRM and the Quincy Library Group not only survived but also found ways to respond successfully to wildly shifting federal and state funding environments. In light of unprecedented numbers of forest fires in California, community collaborators and the private sector joined forces to make the landscape more fire resilient. New collaboratives have arisen to tackle new problems. "Every time you swing a cat, you hit another collaborative," joked Mike Jackson in Plumas.[45] The Maidu meanwhile quietly ponder how old ways may apply to national forest stewardship.

Chicago restorationists rode out a tempest over the worth of two decades of prairie and savanna restoration. Though temporarily stopped in their work, their leadership and group cohesion proved highly resilient and returned anew to restoration based on a combination of deep place-based knowledge and conservation populism. They also helped launch the Chicago Wilderness initiative.

Forced to regroup after the sudden death of Mary Stoertz, one of its founders and leaders, the Monday Creek partnership surged forward to continue their fruitful blend of technical cleanup and environmental education, and they rededicated themselves to engaging watershed communities more fully. Their work significantly advanced the practice of stream restoration in the Eastern Coal Lands.

As I think about these robust responses to change, in each case I observe learning organizations that were forced to renew themselves in challenging situations. I see projects and work plans focused on ecosystems as dynamic entities requiring restoration of both function and diversity. This is best encapsulated in the words of Jim Wilcox, Plumas watershed restorationist extraordinaire, who after seeing success in upland meadow restoration said:

> ... when a project is going through its first runoff, its first spring, it's just so enlightening to watch the landscape burst to life. It's been sleeping for decades and suddenly, boom! We've helped raise it from the dead.[46]

In Plumas, Monhegan, Monday Creek, and Chicago, I surely see sound science and attention to adaptive management based on scientifically backed local knowledge. I see limit setting and a long tradition of self-organization in Monhegan. In the Maidu approach to forestry in Plumas, I see ecological wisdom almost none of us possesses.

Why then are these four cases "slightly south" of the previous cluster? The answer is that each possesses less favorable outcomes in one or more of the human and ecological markers. For Monhegan, the threshold to sustain a year-round population involves real estate prices, land for affordable housing, the well-being of the lobster fishery and the tourism sector, and diversification of income opportunities for permanent residents. The adequacy of responses to these challenges is uncertain, though Monhegan Associates (long a resilient organization) and the plantation government work to face them. Will Monhegan close down in winter and become a shallower, less resilient domain? I doubt it. But I cannot say for certain whether the current downturn in lobstering, the lack of affordable housing, the excessive numbers of day tourists, and the demography of the resident population, separately or in combination, are enough to undermine seven generations of resilience.

Plumas presents a different prospect. The Feather River CRM has two decades of successful, inclusive, and ecologically impressive accomplishments. The Feather River system is less toxic and ecologically healthier. It is increasingly able to withstand environmental pulses like rapid snowmelt. It provides enhanced ecological services such as flowing water in summer, a diverse array of fish and other aquatic species, and wildlife and waterfowl habitat. The Feather River CRM is a model of how experimental thinking and monitoring lead to learning and adaptation. "These people go out and kick the dirt, weigh the stream, look at willows, check out the fish, come to an agreement, then try a project experimentally," journalist Jane Braxton Little told me. "If it works, they go forward; if not, they make changes."[47]

Firesafe councils and resource advisory committees in Plumas are new examples of resilience thinking. They are finding innovative and cost-effective ways to buffer communities against catastrophic fire, invest in ecological services, and rebuild community. The Maidu stewardship project invites the Forest Service and Sierra residents to consider embracing, in small measure, indigenous pathways. The Maidu, themselves a tragically forgotten and marginalized people, bear the brunt of environmental injustices stretching over decades with little hope of full restitution. Unsustainable income and lifestyle gaps between golf resort dwellers and local folk like the Maidu and unemployed mill workers undermine what, in 1997, was a community-wide proposal for "community stability."

The Quincy Library Group (QLG) meanwhile plugs away on ecological and economic stabilization. While ecological and economic resilience are the essence of its work, ironically the QLG as an organization has itself been less inclusive and adaptable than in the 1990s. "This is my biggest concern," said QLG member Mike DeLasaux; "The QLG is a bunch of old growth with no regeneration."[48] Facing contentious court battles over their plans to manage forests and keep logs flowing to the mills, they are constantly behind schedule. For this reason and others, the jury is still out on their famous experiment. Continued legal battles and controversy over budgets and shuttering the sawmill in Quincy further challenge QLG's pilot project.[49] Real estate speculation, expanding golf resorts, and threats to the ranching economy make me wonder whether it's possible for Plumas and adjacent counties to set limits to California's notorious rate of exurbanization. This had not occurred at mid-decade, but the burst of the housing bubble may temporarily attend to it.

In Chicago, despite the impressive cohesion of restoration groups and the path-breaking Chicago Wilderness initiative, sprawl, pollution, traffic, invasives, a spate of other urban ills, and the economic recession conspire to threaten ecological gains and undercut the organizational and ecological resilience of restoration projects. Where are the thresholds in the forest preserve system? Can folks who use the preserves and those who dream of Chicago Wilderness come to grips with setting limits? Will resistance to what restorationists see as crucial to their work — cutting trees, setting fires, pulling invasives, and controlling deer — become obstacles again? Can the impressive restoration science base be conveyed to wider audiences in the interest of making Chicago a center of urban resilience thinking?

For Monday Creek residents, decades of living in a degraded regime have led to a declining population, a depleted sense of place, and low levels of social capital. This is the outcome of environmental injustices that a mere 15 years of technical restoration and environmental education cannot overcome. Until the residents come fully on board and embrace the ecological verities of their watershed, the resilience of this project and others like it cannot be ensured. Sustaining technical solutions long enough for the creek to return to natural function and to restore its ecological components and feedbacks is yet another uncertainty dependent ironically on various agencies of government that have long turned a blind eye to water pollution from mining. Job creation and backlinks to the local economy have been so modest as to be unnoticed by most watershed residents.

On the other hand, Monday Creek is one of a suite of restoration projects looked after by Rural Action, an organization with almost three decades of experience and a national reputation for the successful pursuit of sustainability in Appalachian Ohio. It has shown an acute awareness of the social markers that form this analysis — sustaining organizational resilience and learning, a history of reorganization and renewal in changing times, nimble adaptive management, and rock-solid dedication to equity and environmental justice.

Lower Cluster: Eastern Shore of Virginia, Chattanooga

Virginia's Eastern Shore and Chattanooga both display an array of somewhat disparate pockets of activity aiming toward sustainability, but the collaborative forums and organizations that gave such cohesion and creative energy to projects in the 1990s have vaporized and, with them, some of the social memory. Thus, it is impossible at this point to find organizations dedicated primarily to sustainability. When I visited these places, I discovered one institution in each (the Eastern Shore Regional Partnership and the Mayor's Green Committee in Chattanooga) that could become a new focus for the reorganization and renewal of sustainability initiatives. I am not confident that these organizations have either the breadth of participation or the allegiance to put resilience of their respective ecosystems at the forefront of their economic agendas. Further, as I search the evidence of what's happened since the 1990s, there are other weaknesses in the organizations carrying forward what are now called "green" or "environmental" initiatives. There is no indication, for example, that they are primarily learning organizations committed to adaptive management that draws on pools of local and systematically collected scientific knowledge. Nor is there sufficient awareness of the threat of conventional forms of development to the ecological functions and services that undergird their respective economies.

Perhaps coincidentally, both communities were focal points of Clinton-era sustainable development, which itself was not sustainable enough to survive the political shift of 2001. Some of the loss of direction on the Eastern Shore and in Chattanooga might be attributed to this shift. If so, might one conclude that these communities both failed to reinvent themselves after loss of federal funding? Not quite. As it turns out, local centrifugal forces, including political tensions and the loss of visionary leadership, were equally significant. An apparent low degree of organizational resilience ultimately also doomed both Virginia's Sustainable Development Action Strategy and Chattanooga Venture. So now, without cohesive collaborative organizations in these communities, one cannot speak confidently of either coordinated social or ecological responses to shocks coming down the pike.

However, it would be incorrect to conclude that nothing of value survives to maintain ecosystem functions and services, to enhance local knowledge of place, and to right social and income inequities. Neither of these stories has written its last chapter. On the Shore, The Nature Conservancy continues as a principal player in protecting the barrier islands, beaches, and other lands, promoting partnerships toward protecting and enhancing biodiversity, and conducting research and monitoring toward a fuller understanding of barrier island ecosystems. TNC also works with the aquaculture industry to enhance the ecological and economic viability of clam and oyster production and to lessen the environmental impacts of the industry. And it continues to play a role in promoting affordable housing for low-income residents. Short of overwhelming sea-level rises, the resilience and scientific worth of the Virginia Coast Reserve, TNC's turf on the Eastern Shore, seems assured. What is uncertain is TNC's role in building resilience in the enveloping human-ecological system, especially as threats of inappropriate development encroach from two directions and gaps between well-off and poor increase.

Chattanooga's best hope for rebounding from the demise of Chattanooga Venture and the loss of their exemplary leader, David Crockett, is a Green Committee arising in 2007 and 2008 out of the mayor's signing of the US Mayors Climate Protection Agreement. This committee may provide the stimulus to revive conversations about sustainability. Although Chattanooga's highly touted downtown rebirth is impressive, the ecosystem functions and services on which the city depends (especially green space and clean air and water) are once again at risk. Moreover, poverty, crime, and other social ills and inequities that James Mooreland, Milton Jackson, and other African Americans work to overcome cannot persist if the city really seeks sustainability. And Chattanooga's failure to limit sprawl, strip development, and automobile dependence augers poorly for the kinds of deep changes the mayor's $CO2$ target implies. In these respects, Chattanooga seems no different from most American cities, which is not what we expected in the 1990s, when their dream was to become "America's environmental city."[50]

13

The Sacred Hoop and the Genius That Invents the Future

In this thick night of darkness that may be felt ...
Never heed the tempests or the storms[1]

~ George Fox

... today's challenges require a rapid evolution to a new
consciousness .... today's problems cannot be solved
with today's mind.[2]

~ James Gustave Speth

You have noticed everything an Indian does is in a circle,
and that is because the Power of the World always works
in circles, and everything tries to be round. In the old days
when we were a strong and happy people, all our power
came to us from the sacred hoop of the nation and so
long as the hoop was unbroken the people flourished.[3]

~ Black Elk

The challenge ... is to transform human laws to match
natural laws, not vice versa. In order to do that, we
must close the circle.[4]

~ Winona LaDuke

Indigenous prophecy now meets scientific prediction.
What we have known and believed, you also now
know: The Earth is out of balance. The plants are dis-
appearing, the animals are dying, and the very
weather — rain, wind, fire itself — reacts against the
actions of the human being. For the future of the chil-
dren, for the health of our Mother Earth, Father Sky,
and the rest of Creation, we call upon the people of the
world to hold your leaders accountable.[5]

~ Albuquerque Declaration

THE SACRED HOOP

Driving back from my last field session in late 2008, quietly, across the miles, my headlights piercing the darkness, I tried to get clear about where along the gradient of hope I should place the good work of these communities, knowing that the facts just summarized — the details of collaboration, the good and bad organizational behavior, even the conservation techniques and outcomes — will not alone get these communities, nor the rest of us, through "this thick night of darkness." As Speth rightly suggests above, the deep changes in lifeways we require must rest on even deeper transformations of the spirit. And so, at the close of my journey, I wonder: Can these exemplary communities bring forth the new consciousness demanded by the still harder years ahead?

Were I fully forthright, I would admit that the kind of wisdom needed to get there is, at best, subliminally understood by even the most avid players in our stories. On the other hand, the expanding consciousness Speth speaks about is right before our eyes and as old as the human occupation of this continent. We can tap into it by recalling our Native American storytellers. Maidu elder Lorena Gorbet tells us that

> ... we're not doing what we were put here to do: to take care of the land. How do we take care of the land? We talk to our relatives — the plants and animals, fishes and birds — and sing to them, listening for what they require, and then we tend them with care. Already they are beginning to respond .... It's like they are saying, 'Welcome back. Where have you been?'[6]

Her fellow Maidu, Farrell Cunningham, advises:

> We need to complete the circle of life. We would all become place based and love the landscape and this landscape would form the basis for this circle .... We would take care of it and love it and seek to understand these other plant people, tree people, wind people and what they are trying to tell us about the land we live in, so that finally we might evolve into [a] civilization that would actually be able to survive another thousand years.[7]

"Like ecology, we're ever evolving,"[8] a Menominee forester observes. His tribal chair reminds us that "we have sustained ourselves for 10,000 years and 10,000 years from now, we'll still be here."[9] "We learned how to live at peace with our own people, with neighbors, and with this beautiful forest," relates another Menominee elder.[10] A third says, "I keep my mind open and clear and I listen to the forest. I ask what I can do. How can I leave it better than I found it? Some of what I look for is spiritual. I have no fear. What I have is hope."[11] And along the border of the United States and Mexico, life on the land, a gringo admits, is a blend of his practical knowledge with an enduring, Native "more romantic, older non-mechanistic view of how men should live."[12]

Traditional knowledge and practice offer some of the tools for tapping into this new consciousness.[13] From the Everglades to the Arctic, indigenous peoples are calling for a return to their ancient ways of knowing. Even NASA is listening. In 1998, a group of their scientists met with elders from across the western hemisphere to listen to their wisdom on global warming.[14] In the report of this historic meeting, the Native American cochairs wrote:

> Native peoples carry sharpened skills of observation, special knowledge and time-tested ecological wisdom embedded within various aspects of our cultures, but also the awesome responsibility to speak from the broader base of human experience sadly lacking in those concerned with the commodification of this planet, its nature and climate.[15]

Native peoples are trying to "close the circle," to reverse the commodification of the planet so that future generations may prosper. "There is no easy fix, no technological miracle," writes Winona LaDuke, a member of the Mississippi Band of Anishinaabeg.[16] No big thunderclap will right this wounded world, she says. Lasting change must come from within. As it is with these Native teachers, so also is this true for the rest of us, this mandate of new consciousness. At the heart of it lies Aldo Leopold's simple truth that, like Native peoples, we see ourselves and the land as one, a circle. "Who is the land?" Leopold asked. "We are, but no less the meanest flower that blows. Land ecology discards the fallacious notion that the wild community is one thing, the human community another."[17]

Writers and thinkers across the spectrum embrace this view, though many are doubtful we can make the transformation quickly enough.[18] As in the days before Euro-American society slashed the circle that enabled the Menominee and the Maidu to live on the land in perpetuity, we must again become part of the sacred hoop. This means, among other tasks, that we must "transform human laws to match natural laws," undoing the orgy of consumption and materialism, closing the circle on wastes, rededicating ourselves to the enlargement of the human spirit, making war obsolete, hunkering down locally, and, yes, bringing back the elders.[19] The journey toward this new consciousness begins in the human heart and with listening to nature.[20] From there, we can talk about prescriptions.

THE GENIUS THAT INVENTS THE FUTURE

[Hope] is the singular gift
we cannot destroy in ourselves,
the argument that refutes death,
the genius that invents the future ....[21]

~ Lisel Mueller

To cherish what remains of the Earth and to foster its
renewal is our only legitimate hope of survival.[22]

~ Wendell Berry

...there has never been anything false about hope.[23]

~ Barack Obama

The very least you can do in your life is
to figure out what you hope for. The most you
can do is live inside that hope ....[24]

~ Barbara Kingsolver

Hope for poet Lisel Mueller is "the genius that invents the future."[25] "Hope is the thing with feathers that perches in the soul ... and never stops at all," Emily Dickinson famously wrote.[26] For Barack Obama, hoping bears no false witness.[27] For writer Barbara Kingsolver, while holding hope you must "tiptoe past the dogs of the apocalypse that are sleeping in the shade of your future" and always you must try to "live inside [your] hope."[28] For Wendell Berry, our "only legitimate hope of survival" is to cherish and restore this planet.

In the best of times, hope may be a mysterious notion, a thing that perches in your soul, a gift that greets the new day. In the worst of times, hope may have to be packed up or passed on "like a bad check" while you "fly by the seat of your pants" without it.[29] Studs Terkel, the late American oral historian, believed that hope in the absence of activism yields little.[30] "He was, after all, a man who knew that anyone can hope in good times but that in bad times, to feel hopeful you have to act, you have to take a step, even on an unknown path."[31] Hope, in other words, implies not just wishful thinking but diving in to resolve difficult challenges no matter the uncertainty. It also means keeping the faith in spite of all the evidence and never flinching when the evidence changes.[32] Through disappointment and dreams deferred, you come to understand hope's obstinacy. The thing with feathers reasserts itself. You trust intuition, you dare, you defy convention. And in the end, despite pain, guilt, and despondency, you say "yes" to life and move on with what Viktor Frankl called "tragic optimism."[33]

The collaborators in each of our stories realize these things about hope, for though often discouraged in the past decade, they remain positive and committed to their communities. They understand that to embody "tragic optimism" you must pour your heart into the place you love most. "It's so tragic to see the fish die, but we are also really hopeful now that we know how to prevent this from happening," Tasha McKee told me after showing off water-saving systems that will help sustain summer flows in the upper Mattole River.[34] Like Tasha, all our collaborators understand Studs Terkel's advice that taking action, even on unknown paths, empowers and uplifts. "You see a tremendous degree of hope for the future of this tribe," said Verna Fowler of College of Menominee Nation. "This is all about hope."[35] "I have hope for the future of the Mattole," ventured Sterling McWhorter, a rancher in a place where ranches must struggle to make ends meet.[36] "Our hope is that the healthy, diverse ecosystems we are building will withstand big changes in the future," John Balaban wrote of the savannas and open oak systems being restored in his Chicago neighborhood.[37] "We will find our niche in the great transition. We are all about giving the people here more hope," Michelle Decker told me as she looked to the future of Appalachian Ohio.[38]

In each wave of conservation, despite evidence to the contrary, hopeful visionaries pulled us from the brink. Muir's passionate defense of the Sierras and Leopold's land ethic still inspirit advocates of wild lands. Carson's advocacy of kinship with other forms of life is the ecological intention we seek in environmental laws and enforcement. Ehrenfeld's dream of nature as a source of joy and a measure of our best and worst acts reassures us that a resilient society may be in reach. None spoke of wishful thinking or fond illusions, which are different from hope.[39] All were active and expectant. For them hope still hovered "in dark corners before the lights are turned on."[40]

What kind of values will lift us from this season of despair? The answer lies not in technological miracles, as our Native advisors know well, nor in tweaking markets, nor in better access to information, nor in fear. What is needed, according to farmer and poet Wendell Berry, our best hope, is cherishing the Earth and working toward its restoration, promoting local self-sufficiency and peaceful living, and learning anew about thrift and conservation instead of excess and waste. In other words, "the great transition" portends a peaceable economy, a return to the sacred hoop.[41]

If I understand the platforms from which the thinkers and doers in this book launch their daily work — people like Lorena Gorbet, Larry Waukau, Bill and Mary and Sarah McDonald, Dee Cobb, Jim Wilcox, Laurel Ross, Jeremy Wheeler, Steve Parker, Freeman House, Michelle Decker and many others — if I comprehend their narratives, I see the seeds of a new consciousness. I see Berry's vision, Leopold's land ethic, and Mueller's genius. I see small but replicable examples on the ground. I want to embrace these visionaries and workers and tell them that what they offer us is imbued with practical wisdom and, if only we would listen, evocative of a sustainable future. Their struggles and successes reveal to me "a radical hope ... that a better world is possible and that we can build it."[42]

America needs such radical hope as it strives to emerge from a time of great lamentation, an "epoch of incredulity,"[43] a heap of trouble. And lo, miraculously, in these hardest of times we acted audaciously. We elected a government than ran on hope. Evoking our better angels, our president now exhorts us to rededicate ourselves to community, to work toward the well-being of the whole, to trust science, to listen to one another, and to engage in planetary healing. If there is downshifting to the landscape and the village, if there is more equity in this new era, then we shall have cause to celebrate. Our quest for "the genius that invents the future" will be fruitful.

Notes

Introduction

1. Bob Eichenberg. Interview (6 February 2009).
2. E-mail communication (17 February 2009).
3. Interview (3 February 2009).
4. Timothy Beatley. *Native to Nowhere: Sustaining Home and Community in a Global Age.* Island Press, 2004, 1-24.
5. Bill McKibbon. *Deep Economy: The Wealth of Communities and the Durable Future.* Holt, 2008.
6. Wes Jackson. "It's the W(holes), not the Donuts, that Count" in Ted Bernard and Jora Young. *The Ecology of Hope: Communities Collaborate for Sustainability.* New Society Publishers, 1997, 5.
7. Paul Hawken. *Blessed Unrest: How the Largest Movement in the World Came into Being and Why No One Saw It Coming.* Viking, 2008, 183.
8. David Harvey. *Explanation in Geography.* St. Martins Press, 1970, 352-353.
9. Lance H. Gunderson and C.S. Hollings, eds. *Panarchy: Understanding Transformations in Human and Natural Systems.* Island Press, 2002.
10. Richard Heinberg. *Peak Everything: Waking Up to the Century of Declines.* New Society Publishers, 2008, 23.
11. Bill Moyers. Quoted in James Gustave Speth. *The Bridge at the Edge of the World: Capitalism, the Environment, and Crossing from Crisis to Sustainability.* Yale University Press, 2008, 213.
12. Speth. *The Bridge at the Edge of the World.* 5; Heinberg. *Peak Everything;* David Korten. *The Great Turning: From Empire to Earth Community.* Berrett-Koehler, 2006; Paul D. Raskin. *The Great Transition Today: A Report from the Future.* Tellus Institute, 2006.
13. Quoted in Speth. *The Bridge at the Edge of the World.* 5-6; Martin Rees. *Our Final Hour: A Scientist's Warning.* Basic Books, 2003.
14. Hawken. *Blessed Unrest.*172.
15. Al Gore. "The Moment of Truth." *Vanity Fair,* May 2006. vanityfair.com/politics/features/2006/05/gore200605 (10 February 2009).
16. brainyquote.com/quotes/authors/p/pearl_s_buck.html (10 January 2009).
17. Aldo Leopold. *Round River.* Oxford University Press, 1972, 165.
18. Curt D. Meine. "The Oldest Task in Human History" in Richard L. Knight and Sarah E. Bates, eds. *A New Century for Natural Resources Management.* Island Press, 1995, 26.
19. Aldo Leopold. "The Land Ethic." *A Sand County Almanac.* Oxford University Press, 1949, 224-225.
20. Speth. *The Bridge at the Edge of the World.* 237.
21. Leopold. "The Land Ethic." 204.
22. Leopold. "The Land Ethic." 224.
23. David W. Orr. "Four Challenges of Sustainability" in *The Last Refuge: Patriotism, Politics, and the Environment in an Age of Terror.* Island Press, 2004, 58-59.
24. David W. Orr. *Ecological Literacy: Education and the Transition to a Postmodern World.* State University of New York Press, 1992; Mitchell Thomashow. *Ecological Identity: Becoming a Reflective Environmentalist.* MIT Press, 1995; Richard Louv. *Last Child in the Woods: Saving Our Children from Nature Deficit Disorder.* Algonquin Books, 2005.
25. William Vitek. "These Revolutionary Times." *Prairie Writers Circle.* The Land Institute, 2008. landinstitute.org (9 January 2009). Click on Publications: Prairie Writers.

Chapter 1. Hard Times

1. Charles Dickens. *A Tale of Two Cities.* Signet Classics, 2007, 1.
2. Woody Allen. quotationspage.com/quotes/Woody_Allen (31 December 2008).
3. William Vitek. "These Revolutionary Times." *Prairie Writers Circle.* The Land Institute, 2008. landinstitute.org (10 January 2009). Click on Publications: Prairie Writers.
4. Wendell Berry. *What Are People For?* North Point Press, 1990, 200.
5. With thanks to Erin Sykes, who assembled the chronology from news stories in the *Athens News* by Jim Phillips and in

the *Columbus Dispatch* primarily by Mike Lafferty and Spencer Hunt, and interviews with principals.

6. Longwall mining takes place along the edge of a coal seam. The coal is mined in a single slice by heavy equipment underground. After mining, equipment is removed and supports are withdrawn along the former longwall. The land is allowed to subside. Typically, 80 percent or more of the coal is removed, compared to about 60 percent in room and pillar mining.

7. In an agreement, Ohio Valley Coal Company promised to help the university study the effects of mining under the woods by constructing three monitoring wells, worth about $15,000. ODNR also pledged $10,000 in grant funding for the study.

8. Kevin Knobloch. Union of Concerned Scientists. Blogpost (8 December 2008). energy.nationaljournal.com/2008/12/coal-plants.php (9 December 2008).

9. E-mail communication (21 July 2008).

10. "Utilization" emerged as the "wise use" doctrine of the Progressive era of President Theodore Roosevelt.

11. Chad Kister. *Arctic Quest: Odyssey Through a Threatened Wilderness.* Common Courage Press, 2003.

12. Quoted in John McPhee. *Encounters with the Archdruid.* Farrar, Straus, and Giroux, 1971, 85.

13. David W. Orr. *The Last Refuge: Patriotism, Politics, and the Environment in an Age of Terror.* Island Press, 2004, 21.

14. James Gustave Speth. *The Bridge at the Edge of the World: Capitalism, the Environment, and Crossing from Crisis to Sustainability.* Yale University Press, 2008, 1-4.

15. Garrett Hardin. "The Tragedy of the Commons." *Science,* 162 (1968): 1243-1248.

16. Richard Layard. *Happiness: Lessons from a New Science.* Penguin, 2005.

17. William Greider. *The Soul of Capitalism: Opening Paths to a Moral Economy.* Simon and Schuster, 2003.

18. American Coalition for Clean Coal Electricity. cleancoalusa.org (3 December 2008).

19. Jeff Goodell. *Big Coal: The Dirty Secret Behind America's Future.* Mariner Books, 2007.

20. Goodell doubts that the supply is this big because all the high quality and easily mined coal has already been taken in the 150-year history of coal mining in the US.

21. abandonedmines.gov/ep/htm (3 March 2009).

22. Patrick M. Hunkler. "Lands Unsuitable for Surface Coal Mining: Legal Pursuit to Preserve and Protect the Resources of Barnesville, Ohio." Master's thesis, Ohio University, 1989.

23. Julia Roberts Goad. "Coal CEO Calls Environmentalists Crazy." *Williamson Daily News,* 22 November 2008, 1.

24. Renee Schoof and Bill Estep. "EPA to Gut Mountaintop Mining Rule that Protects Streams." *McClatchy Newspapers,* 2 December 2008. mcclatchydc.com/homepage/ story/56921.html (4 December 2008).

25. ILoveMountains.org (13 May 2009).

26. John G. Mitchell. "When Mountains Move." *National Geographic,* March 2006. ngm.nationalgeographic.com/2006/ 03/mountain-mining/mitchell-text (4 December 2008).

27. Mitchell. "When Mountains Move."

28. Shoof and Estep. "EPA to Gut Mountaintop Mining Rule"; Eric Reece. *Lost Mountain: A Year in the Vanishing Wilderness.* Riverhead, 2006.

29. Patricia Hynes. *The Recurring Silent Spring.* Pergamon Press, 1989, 163 (my emphasis).

30. David Ehrenfeld. *Beginning Again: People and Nature in the New Millennium.* Oxford University Press, 1995, 137.

31. Hazel Henderson. "A Guide to Riding the Tiger of Change: The Three Zones of Transition" in William Irwin Thompson, ed. *Gaia, A Way of Knowing: Political Implications of the New Biology.* Lindisfarne Press, 1987, 144-166.

32. Data extracted from Lisa Mastny. "State of the World: A Year in Review, October 2006-September 2007" in *State of the World: Innovations for a Sustainable Economy.* Worldwatch Institute, 2008, xiii-xvii. Jonathan S. Adam's *The Future of the Wild: Radical Conservation for a Crowded World* (Beacon Press, 2006) aptly encapsulates the outcome of too much information about the biodiversity crisis. The public becomes weary and tunes out, he says.

33. Orr. *The Last Refuge.* 17.

34. Graydon Carter. *What We've Lost: How the Bush Administration Has Curtailed Our Freedoms, Mortgaged Our Economy, Ravaged Our Environment, and Damaged Our Standing in the World*. Farrar, Straus, and Giroux, 2004, 25.

35. Kate Sheppard. "A Voice in the Wilderness: James Hansen's testimony on climate change has made him a celebrity but it sadly hasn't done much to influence Congress." *The Guardian UK*, 23 June 2008. guardian.co.uk/commentisfree/2008/jun/23/climatechange.carbonemissions2 (29 November 2008). Safe levels are in the range of 350 ppm of CO2. At this writing there are 387 ppm of CO$_2$ in the planet's atmosphere. 350.org (14 January 2009).

Chapter 2. Striving for Home: Community, Collaboration, and Sustainability

1. Scott Russell Sanders. *Staying Put: Making a Home in a Restless World*. Beacon Press, 1993, 150.

2. W.S. Merwin. Interview with Terry Gross on "Fresh Air," National Public Radio, 16 December 2008. npr.org/rss/podcast/podcast_detail.php?siteId=7060034 (18 December 2008).

3. Carl M. Moore. "What is Community?" in Philip Brick *et al.*, eds. *Across the Great Divide: Explorations in Collaborative Conservation and the American West*. Island Press, 2001, 73.

4. Donald Snow. "Coming Home: An Introduction to Collaborative Conservation" in Brick *et al.*, eds. *Across the Great Divide*. 1.

5. Brian Walker and David Salt. *Resilience Thinking: Sustaining Ecosystems and People in a Changing World*. Island Press, 2006, 9.

6. Sanders. *Staying Put*. xv.

7. Quoted in Sanders. *Staying Put*. 109.

8. For example: David W. Orr. "A World That Takes Its Environment Seriously" in *Earth in Mind: On Education, Environment, and the Human Prospect*. Island Press, 1994, 154-171; Wes Jackson. *Becoming Native to This Place*. University Press of Kentucky, 1994; Robert L. Thayer, Jr. *LifePlace: Bioregional Thought and Practice*. University of California Press, 2003; William Vitek and Wes Jackson. *Rooted in the Land: Essays on Community and Place*. Yale University Press, 1996.

9. Gary Snyder. *The Real Work*. New Directions, 1980, 81.

10. Thayer. *LifePlace*. 1.

11. James Howard Kuntsler. *Home from Nowhere: Remaking Our Everyday World for the Twenty-First Century*. Simon and Schuster, 1998, 17.

12. Orr. *Earth in Mind*. 135.

13. Orr. *Earth in Mind*. 135.

14. Daniel B. Botkin. *Discordant Harmonies: A New Ecology for the Twenty-First Century*. Oxford University Press, 1990.

15. Thomas Homer-Dixon. *The Ingenuity Gap*. Alfred Knopf, 2000, 9.

16. Homer-Dixon. *Ingenuity Gap*; and Thomas Homer-Dixon. *The Upside of Down: Catastrophe, Creativity, and the Renewal of Civilization*. Island Press, 2006.

17. Carl Folke *et al.* "Adaptive Governance of Social-Ecological Systems." *Annual Review of Environment and Resources*, 30 (2005): 441-473; Walker and Salt. *Resilience Thinking*.

18. Daniel Kemmis. *Community and the Politics of Place*. University of Oklahoma, 1990.

19. William Shutkin. *The Land That Could Be: Environmentalism and Democracy in the Twenty-First Century*. MIT Press, 2000.

20. Moore. "What is Community?" 73-74.

21. Wes Jackson. *Becoming Native to this Place*. University of Kentucky, 1994, 77.

22. Robinson Jeffers. "The Answer." *Selected Poems*. Vintage Books, 1965, 56.

23. Kuntsler. *Home from Nowhere*. 22.

24. Multiple Member Online Role Playing Games.

25. Melvin Webber. "Order in Diversity: Community without Propinquity" in J. Lowdon Wingo, ed. *Cities and Space: The Future Use of Urban Land*. Johns Hopkins Press, 1963, 23-54.

26. Herman E. Daly and John B. Cobb, Jr. *For the Common Good: Redirecting the Economy Toward Community, the Environment, and a Sustainable Future*. Beacon Press, 1989.

27. Wendell Berry. *In the Presence of Fear*. Orion Society, 2001, 8.

28. Quoted in Edward Goldsmith. *The Way: An Ecological Worldview*. Shambhala, 1993, 325. The recently coined term "locavore," which promotes a diet drawing from a foodshed of not more than

100 miles distant from the consumer, is swadeshi in our time. Alisa Smith and James MacKinnon. *Plenty: Eating Locally on the 100-Mile Diet.* Three Rivers Press, 2008.

29. Ted Bernard and Jora Young. *The Ecology of Hope: Communities Collaborate for Sustainability.* New Society Publishers, 1997, 209.

30. Jonathan S. Adams. *The Future of the Wild: Radical Conservation in a Crowded World.* Beacon Press, 2006, 230.

31. For examples of collaborative conservation websites, see: rlch.org; warnercnr.colostate.edu; partnershipresourcecenter.org; cooperativeconservationamerica.org; smartgrowth.org/about/principles/resources.asp?resource=10&type=8; cbcrc.org; cpn.org (all 8 June 2009).

32. Snow. "Coming Home." 2.

33. Snow. "Coming Home." 1.

34. Barb Cestero. *Beyond the Hundredth Meeting: A Field Guide to Collaborative Conservation on the West's Public Lands.* Sonoran Institute, 1999; Consortium for Research and Assessment of Community-Based Collaboratives, Udall Center for Studies in Public Policy, University of Arizona. www.udallcenter.arizona.edu (19 December 2008); Brick *et al.*, eds. *Across the Great Divide.* 251-264; Government Accountability Office. *Natural Resource Management: Opportunities Exist to Enhance Federal Participation in Collaborative Efforts to Reduce Conflicts and Improve Natural Resource Conditions.* Report to the Chairman, Subcommittee on Public Lands and Forest, Committee on Energy and Natural Resources, US Senate, February 2008, 120-132; Julia M. Wondolleck and Steven L. Yaffee. *Making Collaboration Work: Lessons from Innovation in Natural Resource Management.* Island Press, 2000; Ronald D Brunner *et al. Finding Common Ground: Governance and Natural Resources in the American West.* Yale University Press, 2002; Paul A. Sabatier *et al. Swimming Upstream: Collaborative Approaches to Watershed Management.* MIT Press, 2005; Tomas M. Koontz *et al. Collaborative Environmental Management: What Roles for Government?* Resources for the Future Press, 2004.

35. George Coggins. "Regulating Federal Natural Resources: A Summary Case Against Devolved Collaboration." *Ecology Law Quarterly,* 25, 4 (1998): 602-610. For other critique, see Alex Conley's bibliography, "Appendix: Selected Resources in Collaborative Conservation" in Brick *et al.*, eds. *Across the Great Divide.* 263.

36. Matthew McKinney and William Harmon. *The Western Confluence: A Guide to Governing Natural Resources.* Island Press, 2004, 221.

37. Government Accountability Office. *Natural Resource Management.* 6.

38. Interview (27 March 2008).

39. Hazel Henderson. "A Guide to Riding the Tiger of Change: The Three Zones of Transition" in William Irwin Thompson, ed. *Gaia, A Way of Knowing: Political Implications of the New Biology.* Lindisfarne Press, 1987, 156.

40. Paul Hawken. *Blessed Unrest: How the Largest Movement in the World Came into Being and Why No One Saw It Coming.* Viking Press, 2007, 13. See also Tom Mertes *et al.*, eds. *A Movement of Movements: Is Another World Really Possible?* New Left Books, 2004.

41. WiserEarth.org (13 May 2009).

42. For America, Paul Loeb conveyed some of the same notions a decade earlier in *Soul of a Citizen: Living with Conviction in a Cynical Time.* St. Martins, 1999.

43. Hawken. *Blessed Unrest.*26.

44. Thomas Princen. *The Logic of Sufficiency.* MIT Press, 2005, 30; Adrian Parr. *Hijacking Sustainability.* MIT Press, 2009.

45. Bob Doppelt. *Leading Change Toward Sustainability: A Change-Management Guide for Business, Government and Civil Society.* Greenleaf, 2003, 40 (emphasis in the original).

46. ecocitycleveland.org (5 March 2009).

47. Walker and Salt.*Resilience Thinking.* 9.

48. Aldo Leopold. "The Land Ethic" in *A Sand County Almanac.* Oxford University Press, 1949, 214.

49. For example see Chevron's expansion plans for its Richmond, California, refinery. umich.edu/~snre492/sherman.html (18 December 2008).

50. Andres R. Edwards. *The Sustainability Revolution: Portrait of a Paradigm Shift.* New Society Publishers, 2005, 49.

51. Paul Hawken. *The Ecology of Commerce.* Harper Collins Publishers, 1993; Paul Hawken *et al. Natural Capitalism: Creating the Next Industrial Revolution.* Little Brown, 1999; Bob Doppelt and Lawrence Watson. *It's Just Plain Good Business: The Economic and Environmental Benefits of Sustainability as Exemplified by 160 Case Examples.* Portland State University Center for Watershed and Community Health, 2000.

52. James Gustave Speth, quoting a 1996 United Nations Development Commission report on human development, lists all these kinds of despicable growth in *The Bridge at the Edge of the World: Capitalism, the Environment, and Crossing from Crisis to Sustainability.* Yale University Press, 2008, 109.

53. Speth. *The Bridge at the Edge of the World.* Chapters 2, 5, and 6.

54. John McNeil. *Something New Under the Sun: An Environmental History of the Twentieth-Century World.* W.W. Norton, 2000.

55. J. Russell Whitaker and Edward A. Ackerman. *American Resources: Their Management and Conservation.* Harcourt, Brace and Company, 1972, 457.

Chapter 3. Step Out Boldly: Monday Creek, Ohio

1. Rachel Cook and I collaborated on the field work and she wrote a paper on which this chapter is partly based.

2. Mitch Farley. Remarks to Rural Action fund-raising breakfast (7 November 2008).

3. Mary Stoertz. Interview (30 June 2005).

4. Scott Miller. "Random Thoughts on the Monday Creek Restoration Project." *Up the Creek,* Winter 2004, 9.

5. Gary Willison. Interview (12 May 2005).

6. Mitch Farley. Remarks (7 November 2008).

7. Michelle Decker. Interview (27 August 2008).

8. US Army Corps of Engineers. *Hocking River Basin, Ohio, Monday Creek Subbasin Ecosystem Restoration Project: Final Feasibility Report and Environmental Assessment.* USACE, 2005, 3.

9. "Importance of AML in Ohio." Eastern Coal Regional Roundtable. eastern-coal.org (14 July 2005).

10. ILGARD and Rural Action. *A Comprehensive Plan for the Monday Creek Watershed: A Collaboration of the Partners of the Monday Creek Restoration Project and the Residents of the Monday Creek Watershed.* 1999, 51.

11. Ohio unemployment in September 2008 averaged 6.9%; in Hocking County, 7.5%; Athens County, 7.7%; Perry County, 8.3%. Civilian Labor Force Estimates, September 2008, Ohio Department of Job and Family Services. lmi.state.oh.us/ LAUS/ ColorRateMap.pdf (19 November 2008). Poverty rates in southeast Ohio averaged 19%, compared to 13.3% for the entire state in May 2008 — the highest level recorded statewide since the War on Poverty in the mid-1960s. communityresearchpartners.org/uploads/publicat ions//Executive%20Summary%20with %20Cover%20no%20TOC%206-6-08.pdf (19 November 2008).

12. Erin Martin. "Monday Creek: Restoration Spills Over Stream Banks." *Environmental Justice Quarterly.* 2002.

13. In 2000, 16% of residents were over the age of 65.

14. Harry M. Caudill. *Night Comes to the Cumberlands: A Biography of a Depressed Area.* Jessie Stuart Foundation, 2001, iv.

15. Cameron Blosser. Interview (29 June 2005).

16. Interview (27 August 2008).

17. In 2007, the Monday Creek Restoration Project was one of more than 2,600 single-basin watershed groups world-wide. Paul Hawken. *Blessed Unrest: How the Largest Movement in the World Came into Being and Why No One Saw it Coming.* Viking, 2007, 297.

18. Robert L. Thayer, Jr. *LifePlace: Bioregional Thought and Practice.* University of California Press, 2003, 191.

19. Interview (27 August 2008).

20. Thanks to Scott Miller of Ohio University's Voinovich School of Leadership and Public Affairs for helping recall these early days. Interviews (25 February 2005, 9 March 2005, and 28 June 2005).

21. Scott D. Wood. *Hope and Hard Work: Making a Difference in the Eastern Coal Region.* US Environmental Protection Agency, 2001.

22. Interview (30 June 2005).

23. Harry Payne. Interview (30 June 2005).

24. Ted Bernard and Jora Young. *The Ecology of Hope: Communities Collaborate for Sustainability.* New Society Publishers, 1997, 173.

25. Section 319 of the Clean Water Act, as amended in 1987, is directed toward nonpoint sources of water pollution. Ohio EPA administers the program for the state via watershed groups and others who implement locally developed watershed management plans to restore surface waters impaired by nonpoint source pollution.

26. US Army Corps of Engineers. "Draft Feasibility Study." 2005, 11-14.

27. Rebecca Black. Interview (10 August 2005). Between 1996 and 2005, EPA grants for Monday Creek projects totaled $3.3 million. Dan Imhoff. E-mail communication (1 August 2005).

28. Rebecca Black. Interview (10 August 2005); USACE. "Draft Feasibility Study." 2005, 14-15.

29. Rebecca Black. Interview (10 August 2005).

30. Monday Creek Restoration Project, pH logs, accessed in July 2005.

31. Monday Creek Restoration Project, pH and bioassay logs, accessed in July 2005.

32. Matt Miller. "Congress Agrees to Fund US Army Corps for Cleanup of Monday Creek." *Up the Creek,* Summer 2008, 1.

33. Mike Steinmaus. "From the Coordinator's Desk." *Up the Creek,* Summer 2008, 2.

34. Rural Action. *Annual Report 2007.* 1.

35. Interview (27 August 2008).

36. Scott Miller. Interview (28 June 2005).

37. Scott Miller. Interview (28 June 2005).

38. Interviews with residents. (9 March and 29 June 2005).

39. Ron Eaton. Interview (9 March 2005).

40. Mike Steinmaus. Interview (9 March 2005).

41. Betsy Gosnell. "Volunteering with Monday Creek." *Up the Creek,* Summer 2005, 3.

42. Mike Steinmaus. Interviews (9 March and 29 June 2005).

43. Gail Doyle. Phone interview (14 March 2005); Scott Miller. Interview (28 June 2005); Gosnell, "Volunteering with Monday Creek." 1.

44. Conversations with a dozen or so residents from New Straitsville and Murray City in 2005 uncovered a general lack of awareness of the Monday Creek Project.

Those who knew about it took little ownership of its accomplishments and had no time for participation. "People are not involved because their main priority is feeding their families and keeping jobs," said Rebecca Black, MCRP water quality specialist. Interview (2 March 2005).

45. Scott Miller. Interview (28 June 2005).

46. Mike Steinmaus. Interviews (9 March and 28 June 2005).

47. Mitch Farley. Phone interview (30 June 2005); M Kessinger. Phone interview (27 June 2005); Harry Payne. Phone interview (30 June 2005). The "proving ground" notion in the epigraph at the head of this chapter is that of Scott Miller of the Voinovich School of Ohio University.

48. Interview (12 May 2005).

49. Mitch Farley. Phone interview (30 June 2005).

50. Michelle Decker. Interview (27 August 2008).

51. Mary Stoertz. Interview (30 June 2005).

52. Ron Eaton. Interview (9 March 2005).

53. Mike Steinmaus. Interview (12 February 2005).

54. Mary Stoertz. Interview (30 June 2005).

55. Interview (31 July 2005).

56. Interview (29 June 2005).

57. Lynda Andrews. "Monday Creek Wetland Gains New Recreation Site." *Up the Creek,* Summer 2008, 5.

58. Dan Imhoff. Phone interview (14 July 2005).

59. The phrase "destination rather than devastation" I owe to Gary Willison of the US Forest Service.

60. Douglas S. Kenney. "Are Community Based Watershed Groups Really Effective? Confronting the Thorny Issue of Measuring Success" in Philip Brick *et al.,* eds. *Across the Great Divide: Explorations in Collaborative Conservation and the American West.* Island Press, 2001, 188-193.

61. Interview (27 August 2008).

Chapter 4. Into the Eighth Generation: Monhegan Island, Maine

1. Paul Croce conducted field work on Monhegan in 2007, contributed his notes and observations, and offered helpful critique of an earlier draft of this chapter.

2. Richard Nelson. *The Island Within.* North Point Press, 1989, xiii.

3. D.J. Mabberley. "Pachycaul Plants and Islands" in David Bramwell, ed. *Plants and Islands*. Academic Press, 1979, 259-277. Quoted in Robert J. Whitaker. *Island Biogeography: Ecology, Evolution, and Conservation.* Oxford University Press, 1998, 7.

4. Philip W. Conkling. "Toward an Island Ethic." *The New Monhegan Press*, III, 3 (May 1991), 3.

5. Thomas Princen. *The Logic of Sufficiency.* MIT Press, 2005, 287.

6. http://islands.unep.ch (23 July 2008).

7. http://islands.unep.ch/#united%20 nations%20documents (22 July 2008).

8. Brian Walker and David Salt. *Resilience Thinking: Sustaining Ecosystems and People in a Changing World.* Island Press, 2006.

9. Craig Idlebrook. "Island high-speed internet? Well, sometimes ...." *The Working Waterfront, Incorporating the Inter-Island News*, July 2008. workingwaterfront.com/articles/Island-high-speed-Internet-Well-sometimes/12443/ (29 July 2008).

10. maine.gov/spo/economics/economic/towndata.htm (22 June 2009).

11. Philip W. Conkling. *Islands in Time.* Down East Books, 1999, 51. Interview (1 June 2007).

12. Conkling. *Islands in Time.* 35.

13. maine.gov/spo/economics/economic/towndata.htm (22 June 2009)..

14. Interview (31 May 2007).

15. Sally McVane. Quoted in Princen. *The Logic of Sufficiency.* 248.

16. Michelle Mason Webber (Compiler). *Compilation of Shellfish Laws and Regulations.*Maine Department of Marine Resources, 2008. maine.gov/dmr/rm/public_health/shellfishlaws&regs12-08.pdf (08 February 2009).

17. Monhegan Associates. Certificate of Organization, State of Maine, Chapter 50 of the Revised Statutes and Amendments, 2(a).

18. Ted Bernard and Jora Young. *The Ecology of Hope: Communities Collaborate for Sustainability.* New Society Publishers, 1997, 54. Political self-rule is partly a myth as Monhegan has had to battle the state to keep its school, to deal with solid and liquid waste, and to conduct its lobster fishery.

19. Princen. *The Logic of Sufficiency.* 275.

20. *Monhegan Island Plantation: An Inventory and Analysis.* Maine Land Use Regulatory Commission, 1991, 3-2.

21. Quote from Peter Boehmer. Personal communication (23 January 1996).

22. Williard J. Boynton and Jacqueline Boegel. Letter to Marine Resources Committee, January 25, 1998, quoted in Princen. *The Logic of Sufficiency.* 286.

23. Phyllis Austin. "Pollution, Tourism, and the Future of Monhegan Island." *Maine Environmental News,* 12 July 2002. www.meepi.org (31 July 2008).

24. Austin. "Pollution, Tourism, and the Future."

25. Austin. "Pollution, Tourism, and the Future."

26. According to the *Portland Press Herald,* as the summer of 2008 got underway gas prices were depressing overall tourist numbers in Maine. pressherald.com (25 May 2008). On Monhegan, according to two permanent residents I called in July 2008, "numbers were steady," meaning as good as the previous year.

27. On offer in 2008 were six daily round-trip excursions from the mainland, dropping visitors off in the morning and midday and collecting them several hours later.

28. Ralf Buckley and Narelle King. "Visitor-Impact Data in a Land Management Context" in R. Buckley *et al.,* eds. *Nature-Based Tourism in Environment and Land Management.* CABI, 2008, 89-100.

29. Quoted in Bernard and Young. *The Ecology of Hope.* 57.

30. Austin. "Pollution, Tourism, and the Future."

31. Barry Timson. "The Monhegan 'Meadow' Aquifer: Preliminary Hydrology and Management Considerations." James Haskell and Associates, 1989; Holden Nelson. Personal communication (19 January 2008); Richard Farrell. Personal communication (11 October 2007).

32. Douglas A. Stark and Vladek Kolman. "Report to Monhegan Associates and Offices of the Plantation of Monhegan on the Status of Woodlands on Monhegan Island." Unpublished document, Maine Forest Service, 1987.

33. Bernard and Young. *The Ecology of Hope.* 56.

34. Mark Miller. "Monhegan Forest Stewardship Management Plan." Unpublished document, Monhegan Associates, 2005.

35. Lester C. Kenway. "Monhegan Island Trail Assessment." Unpublished document, Maine Conservation Corps, 2005.

36. Quoted in Austin. *Pollution, Tourism, and the Future.*

37. "Report to the Trustees of Monhegan Associates on Values, Issues, and Plans." Unpublished document, 2005-06, 1-2.

38. Princen. *The Logic of Sufficiency.* 223-289.

39. Princen. *The Logic of Sufficiency.* 276.

40. Princen. *The Logic of Sufficiency.* 273; Paul Croce. E-mail communication (29 September 2008).

41. Data in this paragraph are from Steve Mistler. "Lobster fishing 'on the edge of disaster'?" *The Forecaster,* 28 February 2008, 3. theforecaster.net/story.php? storyid=13979 (26 July 2008).

42. On climate change, the Island Institute has initiated a survey of fishers' "indigenous wisdom." Island Institute News and Press Release. "Climate Change Online Survey Available: Island Institute asks lobstermen for observations on climate change," 23 July 2008. islandinstitute.org (1 August 2008).

43. Mistler. "Lobster fishing 'on the edge of disaster'?" 2.

44. James A. Wilson. "A Test of the Tragedy of the Commons" in Garrett Hardin and John Baden, eds. *Managing the Commons.* W.H. Freeman, 1977, 96-111.

45. Carl Wilson. Interviews by Paul Croce (8 February and 27 February 2008).

46. Terence P. Hughes *et al.* "New paradigms for supporting the resilience of marine ecosystems." *Trends in Ecology and Evolution,* 20, 7 (2005): 380-386.

47. Susan Curran and Jeremy Gabrielson. *Island Indicators: A Report by the Island Institute.* The Island Institute, 2007.

48. maine.gov/spo/economics/projections/index.htm (24 July 2008).

49. Dissolution letter from Susan McDonough, Monhegan Emergency Rescue Service director. midcoast.com/~wisp/MERS3.html (29 March 2007).

50. "'Relevant, Meaningful, Reliable, Accessible': Institute assembles a set of island indicators." *Island Journal,* 23(2007): 92-93. islandinstitute.org (28

July 2008). I wrote this chapter just before the burst of the housing bubble in 2008. This point and the paragraph that follows may be moot by the time the book goes to press.

51. Richard Farrell. Personal communication (7 July 2007).

52. misca.info (27 July 2008).

53. In this case, the fisher wished to remain anonymous.

54. monheganhouse.com (4 August 2008).

55. Kristen Lindquist. "Who needs Arizona When We've Got Monhegan?" *Down East,* March 2009. downeast.com/node/6545 (8 June 2009).

56. Conkling. Interview (1 June 2007).

57. "Report to the Trustees of Monhegan Associates on Values, Issues, and Plans."

58. Mabberley. "Pachycaul Plants." See quote in chapter epigraph.

59. Nelson. *The Island Within.* xiii. See quote in chapter epigraph.

60. Sherman Stanley. Interview (6 May 1994).

Chapter 5. Ever Vulnerable: The Eastern Shore of Virginia

1. Paul Croce generously provided his notes and other documents from a field session on the Eastern Shore in March 2007. Citations for interviews in that month are those conducted by Paul. These are supplemented with further research and interviews in fall 2008.

2. Alice Coles. Interview (7 March 2007).

3. quickfacts.census.gov/qfd/states/51000.html (16 October 2008). Ethnically, the Eastern Shore is 50% white, 42% black, and 8% Hispanic, the latter almost all in Accomack.

4. Curtis J. Badger. "Eastern Shore Gold." *The Nature Conservancy Magazine,* July/August 1990, 10-11.

5. Mike Potter *et al. Community Economic Development for the Eastern Shore: Summit Report.* Office of Economic Development, Outreach and International Affairs, Virginia Tech, 2007, 27-31.

6. cbes.org (15 October 2008).

7. Potter *et al. Community Economic Development for the Eastern Shore.* 30; Scott Harper. "Water quality protection plan introduced." *The Virginian-Pilot,* 30 July 2008, B3.

8. "Your Passport to Virginia's Eastern Shore." Eastern Shore Chamber of Commerce brochure, 2007.

9. In 2008, just before the financial crisis

broke, unemployment was 5.2%. esvachamber.org/ecoprofile.html (20 August 2008).

10. Statistics are from Potter *et al. Community Economic Development for the Eastern Shore.* 27-31.

11. quickfacts.census.gov/qfd/states/51/51001.html (16 October 2008).

12. *Federal Register*, 73, 15 (23 January 2008): 3971-3972.

13. quickfacts.census.gov/qfd/states/51/51001.html (16 October 2008).

14. Quoted in John E. Bright and Marc Sagan. *Beaches, Islands, Marshes, and Woodlands: Outdoor Recreation Plan on Virginia's Eastern Shore.* National Park Service, 1987, 6.

15. Badger. "Eastern Shore Gold." 9.

16. Tom Harris. Personal communication (9 November 2008).

17. Jane Cabarrus. Personal communication (15 June 1994); bls.gov/data/#unemployment (2 October 2008).

18. Though not an integral part of this particular strategy, in practical terms because of webs of connections between the two counties that included TNC holdings and actions, Accomack could not be excluded.

19. Quoted in Ted Bernard and Jora Young. *The Ecology of Hope: Communities Collaborate for Sustainability.* New Society Publishers, 1997, 88.

20. Quoted in Bernard and Young. *The Ecology of Hope.* 90.

21. Quoted in Bernard and Young. *The Ecology of Hope.* 91.

22. Citizens for a Better Eastern Shore. Focus group (7 March 2007). The group also explicitly blamed the then county director for sustainable development.

23. STIP stimulated the birth of the Eco-Industrial Development Council, an international group of practitioners who advocate for and study eco-parks. Its founding meeting took place on the Eastern Shore in 1994. The Eco-Industrial Development Council is now part of the International Society for Industrial Ecology.

24. Christopher Dinsmore. "Green Dreams Go Bust — Once Promising Industrial Development in Cape Charles is up for Sale." *The Virginian-Pilot*, 6 August 2004. infoweb.newsbank.com (August 22 2008); Katherine Nunez, Northampton

County administrator. Interview (8 March 2007).

25. Sara Nosanchuk. "Analyzing the Successes and Failures of Northampton County, Virigina's Eco-Industrial Park." Unpublished seminar paper, University of Michigan, Natural Resource and Environmental Conflict Management Program, December 2003.

26. Tom Harris. E-mail communication (15 November 2008).

27. David B. Ottaway and Joe Stephens. "On Eastern Shore, For-Profit 'Flagship' Hits Shoals." *Washington Post*, 5 May 2003, A11.

28. Dinsmore. "Green Dreams Go Bust."

29. Telephone interview with Paul Croce (21 February 2007).

30. This critic (who is no longer on the Shore) wished to remain anonymous but expressed a category of critique we frequently heard from African American residents.

31. E-mail communication (8 November 2008).

32. Interview (8 March 2007).

33. "US Fish and Wildlife Service and The Nature Conservancy complete multi-year, $6 million effort to expand Eastern Shore of Virginia National Wildlife Refuge." The Nature Conservancy press release, 14 March 2008. nature.org/wherewework/northamerica/states/virginia/press/press3404.html (21 October 2008).

34. Interview (4 September 2008).

35. Scott Harper. "Environmental Group Sets New Goals for Eastern Shore: Nature Conservancy Focuses on Bay Property." *The Virginian-Pilot*, 20 January 2003, A1.

36. Steve Parker. Interview (4 September 2008).

37. Quoted in Badger. "Eastern Shore Gold." 12-13.

38. *The Virginia Coast Reserve.* The Nature Conservancy, March 2005, 3.

39. Ottaway and Stephens. "For-Profit 'Flagship' Hits Shoals." A11. The real estate was sold to a private company in 2007 with a conservation easement on 32 surrounding acres. nature.org/wherewework/northamerica/states/virginia/press/press3064.html) (22 August 2008).

40. Ottaway and Stephens. "For Profit 'Flagship' Hits Shoals." A11.

41. Michael Lipford. Interview (4 September 2008).
42. Scott Harper. "Push on to Restore VA Barrier Islands." *The Virginian-Pilot,* 20 September 2002, B3. infoweb.newsbank.com (29 August 2008); Laura McKay. "Paddling the Seaside." *Virginia Coastal Zone Management,* Spring/Summer 2006, 12-13; Steve Parker. Interview (4 September 2008).
43. Michael Lipford. Interview (4 September 2008).
44. Steve Parker. E-mail communication (8 May 2009),
45. Thomas E. Harris. Letter to the Editor in *ShoreLine,* June 2001, 7-8.
46. E-mail communication (8 November 2008).
47. Tim Hayes. E-mail communication (9 November 2008).
48. Jeff Johnson. "Eco-Development Tested on Virginia's Eastern Shore." *Environmental Science and Technology,* 25 (1995): 221-229.
49. Roy Otten and Lance Metzler. Quoted in Dinsmore. "Green Dreams Go Bust." D1.
50. Robert Burke. "Second homes are growing in Eastern Shore's fields." *Virginia Business,* June 2005, 12-14.
51. Scott Harper. "It's crunch time: Eastern Shore shellfish, Eastern Shore building." *The Virginian-Pilot,* 17 October 2007, A1.
52. "Creek Closures Threaten Major Industry." *ShoreLine,* August 2007, 6.
53. Carol Vaughn. "Virginia speaker faces crab sanctuary criticism." *The Daily Times* (Salisbury, MD), April 5, 2008, A2.
54. Scott Harper. "Water quality protection plan introduced." *The Virginian-Pilot,* 30 July 2008, B3.
55. Northampton-Accomack Regional Planning Commission. *Regional Update: A Monthly Report of Activities on the Eastern Shore.* March-April 2008, 1.
56. http://factfinder.census.gov (October 23 2008).
57. Kessler Burnett. "Finally Getting Over." *Chesapeake Life,* November-December 2003. chesapeake-lifemag.com/index.php/cl/features_article/fe_bayview_ nd03/ (13 November 2008).
58. Steve Miner. Interview (6 March 2007).
59. Mary Miller. "The Community Housing Plan: A Comprehensive Strategy for Northampton County." *ShoreLine,* January 2008, 4-5.
60. Interview (8 March 2007). On moral economy see J.C. Scott. *Weapons of the Weak: Everyday Forms of Peasant Resistance.* Yale University Press, 1985.
61. Another resident, who also wished to remain anonymous, said, "They are undoing all the good of the last 15 years, foisting an elitist concept on us."
62. Eastern Shore Regional Partnership. *Eastern Shore of Virginia Comprehensive Economic Development Strategy.* 2007, 8-9.
63. Steve Miner. Interview (6 March 2007).
64. Interview (8 March 2007).
65. The heading is borrowed from Bill Lohman's travel piece, "Sweet Life on the Shore: Unspoiled barrier islands are rare gems of East Coast wilderness." *Richmond Times-Dispatch,* 18 November 2007, B7.
66. Robert L.Thayer, Jr.*LifePlace: Bioregional Thought and Practice.* University of California Press, 2003.

Chapter 6. Millennia of Resilience: The Menominee Indians of Wisconsin

1. David W. Orr. *Ecological Literacy: Education and the Transition to a Postmodern World.* State University of New York Press, 1992, 34.
2. Verna Fowler. Interview (10 July 2007).
3. On the Enhanced Fujita (EF) scale, the severest storm is 5. This storm was judged to be EF-3, sustaining winds of 140-160 mph. crh.noaa.gov/images/grb/events/070607/NEWI_map.jpg (14 May 2009).
4. Paul M. Klocko. "When Tornado Meets Timber!" *Great Lakes Timber Professionals Association Magazine,* September 2007, 43.
5. Mike Waukau. Interview (12 July 2007).
6. Marshall Pecore. Interview (13 July 2007); Klocko. "When Tornado Meets Timber!" 2007, 43.
7. Adrian Miller. Interview (9 July 2007).
8. Patrick L. Delabrue. "Tornado Inflicts Heavy Damage on Menominee Forest." *Menominee Nation News,* 25 June 2007, 9-10.
9. Delabrue. "Tornado Inflicts Heavy Damage." 10.
10. Klocko. "When Tornado Meets Timber!" 44.
11. Bill Schmidt. Telephone interview (21 March 2008).

12. Ted Bernard and Jora Young. *The Ecology of Hope: Communities Collaborate for Sustainability.* New Society Publishers, 1997, 96.
13. Pecore. Interview (13 July 2007).
14. Pecore. Interview (13 July 2007).
15. Interview (13 July 2007).
16. Brian Walker *et al.* "Resilience Management in Social-Ecological Systems: a Working Hypothesis for a Participatory Approach." *Ecology and Society,* 6, 1 (2002). consecol.org/vol6/iss1/art14 (9 June 2009); Orr is quoted in the epigraph at the beginning of the chapter.
17. Nicholas Peroff. *Menominee Drums: Tribal Termination and Restoration, 1954-1974.* University of Oklahoma Press, 1982, 89.
18. Patricia Ourada. *The Menominee.* University of Oklahoma Press, 1979, 204.
19. A full recounting of this period is in Bernard and Young. *The Ecology of Hope.* 103-107; see also David J.Grignon. *Menominee Tribal History Guide: Commemorating Wisconsin Sesquicentennial 1848-1998.* Menominee Indian Tribe of Wisconsin, 1998.
20. Interview (10 July 2007).
21. Interview (9 July 2007).
22. Interview (10 July 2007).
23. Quoted in Bernard and Young. *The Ecology of Hope.* 109.
24. Eric Epstein. Quoted in Bernard and Young. *The Ecology of Hope.* 94.
25. Miller. Interview (9 July 2007); "2003 Forest Stewardship Award." *Hardwood Matters,* October-November 2003, 4; Larry Waukau. Interview (10 July 2007).
26. In addition to the 1996 Presidential Award for Sustainable Development, mentioned in Bernard and Young's. *The Ecology of Hope,* MTE won the National Hardwood Lumber Association Forest Stewardship Award in 2003.
27. Larry Waukau. Interview (10 July 2007).
28. Pecore. Interview (13 July 2007).
29. Jeff Grignon. Interview (12 July 2007).
30. Pecore. Interview (13 July 2007).
31. Grignon. Interview (12 July 2007).
32. Pecore. Interview (13 July 2007).
33. Grignon. Interview (12 July 2007).
34. gameoflogging.com (14 May 2009).
35. Eric Epstein. Quoted in Bernard and Young. *The Ecology of Hope.* 94.
36. Melissa Cook. Interview (9 July 2007).
37. Grignon. Interview (12 July 2007).
38. James Kaquatosh. Interview (12 July 2007).
39. Bill Schmidt. Interview (11 July 2007).
40. scscertified.com (14 May 2009). Adrian Miller. "Menominee Tribal Enterprises Celebrates 100 Years of Sustainable Forest Management." *Hardwood Matters,* October 2008, 48-49.
41. Interview (11 July 2009).
42. Interview (9 July 2007).
43. Interview (10 July 2008).
44. mtewood.com/RFP%20renewable%20energy.pdf (14 May 2009).
45. warmsprings.com (14 May 2009); Michael Dockry. Interview (10 July 2007).
46. Interview (12 July 2007).
47. Interview (12 July 2007).
48. Interview (10 July 2007).
49. Interview (9 July 2007).
50. Fowler. Interview (11 July 2007).
51. aashe.org/resources/profiles/cat1_109.php (9 June 2009).
52. National Center for Educational Statistics, http://nces.ed.gov/pubs2008/native trends/tables/table_6_2.asp, and College of Menominee Nation, menominee.edu (both 2 June 2009).
53. Interview (10 July 2007).
54. Jacquelyn Askins. "Menominee Nation signs new transfer agreement." *The Badger Herald,* 30 October 2007. badger-herald.com/news/2007/10/30/menomine e_nation_ sig.php (14 May 2009).
55. Interview (9 July 2007).
56. Interview (9 July 2007).
57. Michael J. Dockry and Holly YoungBear-Tibbetts. "Indigenous/Native Tribes: Owners and Rights, USA" in *Forest Ownership, Tenure and Social Systems.* 2007. Go to http://encyclopediaofforestry.org/index.php/Main_Page and click on Forest Ownership, Tenure, and Social Systems (14 May 2009).
58. Communities of interest are others who manage and harvest Indian forestlands and use forest products from these lands.
59. Michael Dockry. Interview (10 July 2007).
60. Dockry. Interview (10 July 2007).
61. US Bureau of Labor Statistics.

"Wisconsin Economy at a Glance." stats.bls.gov./ eag/eag.WI.htm (9 February 2009). Menominee officials claim that Bureau of Labor statistics mask the chronic unemployment on the reservation, where after job-seeking for many months, years even, people give up and are no longer considered "actively seeking work." Unemployment may be twice the official rate.

62. Interview (10 July 2007).
63. Interview (13 July 2007).
64. College of Menominee Nation Institutional Research and Assessment, 2006; William VanLopik. Interview (9 July 2007).
65. Interview (10 July 2007).
66. Interview (13 July 2007).
67. Interview (11 July 2007).
68. americangam-ing.org/Industry/factsheets/statistics_detail.cfv?id=7 (14 May 2009).
69. James Reiter. Interview (10 July 2007). Sixty percent of casino employees are Menominee, including the general manager.
70. Interview (10 July 2007).
71. kenoshacasino.com/info (23 January 2008).
72. Lisa Waukau. "Menominee Will Fight It Tooth and Nail." *Building the Future,* website of Kenosha Casino, 9 January 2009. kenoshacasino.com/ (9 February 2009).
73. Interview (11 July 2007).
74. Interview (12 July 2007).
75. Cora Merritt, as quoted by CMN president Verna Fowler. Interview (10 July 2007).
76. Interview (10 July 2007).
77. Interview (9 July 2007).
78. Alex Medina. "Blackowl achieves goal with PEOPLE program." *Native Beat: Pre-College Enrichment Opportunity Program for Learning Excellence.* 2 July 2007, 1.
79. "Seven Fires." Quoted in Winona LaDuke. *All Our Relations: Native Struggles for Land and Life.* South End Press, 1999, 198.
80. Interview (11 July 2007).

Chapter 7. Gathering the Borderlands: The Sky Islands of the Southwest

1. Drum Hadley. "Old Earth." *Voice of the Borderlands.* Rio Nuevo, 2005, 16. I anchor the Malpai story to Hadley's fertile borderlands voice. Read on for more.
2. Jonathan S. Adams. "The Native Home of Hope" in *The Future of the Wild.* Beacon, 2006, 118.
3. Words of Wendy Glenn and Bill McDonald respectively (26 March and 27 March 2008).
4. Hadley. "A Mystery." *Voice of the Borderlands.* 31.
5. Douglas had about 16,700 citizens in 2004 and Agua Prieta at least 110,000. douglasaz.gov/Administration/Administration.htm (10 July 2008).
6. Gerry Gonzales. Interview (25 March 2008).
7. Jim Hightower. "Fencing Around Privilege." *The Progressive,* 72, 7 (July 2008): 46.
8. Alan Weisman. *La Frontera: The United States Border with Mexico.* University of Arizona, 1986, 122.
9. Peter Warren. Interview (27 March 2008).
10. Quoted in Weisman. *La Frontera.* 121.
11. Nathan Sayre. *Working Wilderness: The Malpai Borderlands Group and the Future of the Western Range.* Rio Nuevo, 2006, 33.
12. "Geronimo, the last of the Apache warrior chieftains," succumbed to the US Army in the Malpai region on September 6, 1886, "forever ending Indian warfare in the United States" (from the text of a monument near Skeleton Canyon on Arizona Highway 80, erected by the City of Douglas).
13. Sayre. *Working Wilderness.* 162.
14. Adams. "Native Home." 132.
15. Diamond A species count thanks to Seth Hadley. Interview (20 August 2009); Dan Dagget. *Beyond the Rangeland Conflict: Toward a West that Works.* Good Stewards, 2000, 15.
16. People in the MBG refer to this area as either "our planning area" or "our working area."
17. Adams. "Native Home." 118.
18. Adams. "Native Home." 118.
19. Hadley. "Businessmen Overheard in the Palm Court Restaurant, Plaza Hotel, New York City, America." *Voice of the Borderlands.* 278.
20. William Reibsame. "Geographies of the New West" in Philip Brick *et al.,* eds. *Across the Great Divide: Explorations in*

Collaborative Conservation and the American West. Island Press, 2000, 45-51.

21. Interview (25 March 2008).
22. This sign was within sight of a large commercial grader at the entry to the subdivision on 29 March 2008.
23. Interview (28 March 2008).
24. Mari N. Jensen. "Can Cows and Conservation Mix?" *Bioscience,* 51, 2 (February 2001): 85-94.
25. Wendy Glenn. Letter in *Malpai Borderlands Group Newsletter,* October 2007, 1.
26. Sayre. *Working Wilderness; Jay Dusard.* "Afterword" in Dagget. *Beyond the Rangeland Conflict.* 103.
27. Malpai Borderlands Group mission statement. malpaiborderlandsgroup.org (14 May 2009).
28. Courtney White. *Revolution on the Range: The Rise of a New Ranch in the American West.* Island Press, 2008. White terms this phenomenon "new ranch."
29. Ray Turner. *The Changing Mile.* University of Arizona, 1967.
30. Gerry Gottfried. Presentation to MBG (27 March 2008); Dagget. *Beyond the Rangeland Conflict.* 20
31. Warner Glenn. *Eyes of Fire: Encounter with a Borderlands Jaguar.* Printing Corner Press, 1996; Wendy Glenn. Interview (26 March 2008). There has been no breeding population of jaguars in the US since 1910 (Sayre. *Working Wilderness.* 112).
32. Wendy Glenn. "Jaguar Update." *Malpai Borderlands Group Newsletter,* October 2007, 7.
33. Bill McDonald. Interview (26 March 2008).
34. Nathan F. Sayre. *Ranching, Endangered Species, and Urbanization in the Southwest: Species of Capital.* University of Arizona, 2002, 218-233.
35. Glenn. "Jaguar Update." 7. The jaguar has been listed as an endangered species in the US.
36. Dagget. *Beyond the Rangeland Conflict.* 7.
37. Malpai ranchers were incensed that TNC in the early 1980s turned over the San Bernardino Ranch Spanish Land Grant to the US Fish and Wildlife Service for a national wildlife refuge.
38. Dagget. *Beyond the Rangeland Conflict.* 16.
39. Dagget. *Beyond the Rangeland Conflict.* 16.
40. Dagget. *Beyond the Rangeland Conflict.* 16.
41. Sayre. *Working Wilderness.* 60-61.
42. Hadley. "The Borderlands." *Voice of the Borderlands.* 328.
43. Peter Warren. Interview (27 March 2008); see also White. *Revolution on the Range.*
44. Sarah McDonald and Bill McDonald. Interview (26 March 2008).
45. Adams. "Native Home." 129-130.
46. Quoted in Dagget. *Beyond the Rangeland Conflict.* 21.
47. Bill McDonald. Interview (26 March 2008).
48. Interview (27 March 2008).
49. Bill McDonald. Interview (26 March 2008).
50. John Cook. Interview (27 March 2008).
51. malpaiborderlandsgroup.org (22 June 2009).
52. Don Decker. Interview (25 March 2008).
53. Sayre. *Working Wilderness.* 47.
54. Bill McDonald. Interview (26 March 2008).
55. NRCS, once called the Soil Conservation Service, is a branch of the US Department of Agriculture.
56. Reese Woodling. Interview (27 March 2008).
57. Hadley. "Preamble." *Voice of the Borderlands.* 15.
58. Peter Warren. Interview (27 March 2008).
59. Sayre. *Working Wilderness.* 127; Mary McDonald. Interview (26 March 2008).
60. Sayre. *Working Wilderness.* 130-131.
61. Adams. "Native Home." 131.
62. Mary McDonald. Interview (26 March 2008). The estimated cost of land protection to ensure the ecological integrity of the Borderlands in early 2008 was an additional $15 million. See stories at Red Lodge Clearing House: rlch.org (3 June 2009).
63. Interview (27 March 2008).
64. Interview (25 March 2008).
65. Hadley. "Preamble." *Voice of the Borderlands.* 107.
66. Ted Bernard and Jora Young. *The Ecology of Hope: Communities Collaborate for Sustainability.* New Society Publishers, 1997, 124.
67. Interview (25 March 2008).

68. John Cook. Interviews (26 March and 27 March 2008).
69. Bill McDonald. Interview (26 March 2008).
70. In 1998 McDonald received a genius grant from the MacArthur Foundation for his leadership of MBG. cbsnews.com/stories/1998/06/01/national/main10732. shtml (23 August 2008).
71. Peter Warren. Interview (27 March 2008).
72. Bill McDonald. Interview (26 March 2008).
73. Van Clothier. "Galloping Gullies, Batman!" *Malpai Borderlands Newsletter,* September 2003, 3.
74. Bill Edwards. Interview (28 March 2008); Sayre. *Working Wilderness.* 99; Dan Dagget. *Gardeners of Eden: Rediscovering Our Importance to Nature.* Thatcher Charitable Trust, 2005, 52-55.
75. Sayre. *Working Wilderness.* 107.
76. Warner Glenn. Quoted in Adams. "Native Home." 117.
77. Glenn. *Eyes of Fire.* 21 and Comments (26 March 2008).
78. fws.gov/laws/lawsdigest/ESACT.html (17 March 2009).
79. Sayre. *Working Wilderness.* 113.
80. Wendy Glenn. "Jaguar Update." 7.
81. Don Decker. "Natural Resources Conservation Service Coordinator Report." *Malpai Borderlands Group Newsletter,* October 2007, 4; Interview (25 March 2008).
82. Bill McDonald. Interview (26 March 2008).
83. Adams. "Native Home." 118-119.
84. Information and quotes in the paragraph are from Sam Smith. "Fire History on the Diamond A Ranch." *Malpai Borderlands Group Newsletter,* October 2007, 2-3 and from Seth Hadley. Interview (20 August 2008).
85. Smith. "Fire History on the Diamond A." 3.
86. Interview (28 March 2008).
87. Ray Turner Interview (27 March 2008).
88. Interview (27 March 2008).
89. Bernard and Young. *The Ecology of Hope.* 124.
90. John Cook. Interview (26 March 2008).
91. Ray Turner. Interview (27 March 2008).
92. Alan Savory. *Holistic Resource Management.* Island Press, 1988; White. *Revolution on the Range.* 10-11, 33-40.
93. Bill McDonald. Letter in *Malpai · Borderlands Group Newsletter,* 11 (November 2004): 1.
94. Bill McDonald. Letter in *Malpai Borderlands Group Newsletter,* 11 (November 2004): 1.
95. Interview (27 March 2008).
96. Larry Allen. Interview (27 March 2008).
97. Interview (27 March 2008).
98. Ben Brown Interview (27 March 2008). Preliminary attempts to link McKinney Flats data across scales to satellite imagery fail to show statistically valid patterns.
99. Quoted in Sayre. *Working Wilderness.* 42.
100. Hadley. "The First Summer Rains." *Voice of the Borderlands.* 314.
101. Interview (27 March 2008).
102. Interview (28 March 2008).
103. Interview (27 March 2008).
104. Wallace Stegner. *The Sound of Mountain Water.* Penguin, 1997, 38.
105. Ed Pilkington. "US south-west warned of dire climate challenges." *The Guardian,* 28 May 2008. guardian.co.uk/world/2008/may/28/usa.climatechange (14 May 2009).
106. Interview (27 March 2008).
107. Mary McDonald and Wendy Glenn. Interview (26 March 2008).
108. Sarah McDonald. Interview (26 March 2008) and Sarah McDonald. "The Next Generation." *Malpai Borderlands Group Newsletter,* October 2007, 2. I witnessed active involvement of the "next" generation in my brief time in the Malpai region in 2008 — from the Glenns' 12-year-old granddaughter Mackenzie Kimbro and her mom Kelly Glenn-Kimbro helping make the annual meeting successful to the service on the Malpai board of second-generation members Seth Hadley and Rich Winkler.
109. Interview (27 March 2007).
110. Interview (27 March 2008).

Chapter 8. Healing Relationships, Healing Landscapes: The Mattole Valley, California

1. Jeremy Wheeler. E-mail communication (4 April 2007).
2. Freeman House. *Totem Salmon: Life Lessons from Another Species.* Beacon Press, 1999, 213.
3. Interview (7 August 2006).
4. Sterling McWhorter. "A passion for ranching." *Times-Standard,* 14 March 2006, 4.

5. Johanna Rondoni. Interview (7 August 2006). buckeyeconservancy.org (14 May 2009).

6. http://rlch.org (14 May 2009). Click on Story Index and then on Mattole Restoration Council.

7. Bob Doran. "If you rebuild it, will they come back?" *North Coast Journal,* 2 March 2000, 1.

8. Freeman House. *Totem Salmon.* 176.

9. Peter Berg and Raymond Dasman. "Reinhabiting California" in Van Andruss *et al.,* eds. *Home! A Bioregional Reader.* New Society Publishers, 1990, 35; Freeman House. "Cultivation of the Wild 1000-1850" in Ray Raphael and Freeman House. *Two Peoples One Place.* Humboldt County Historical Society, 2007, 15-37.

10. House. *Totem Salmon.* 177.

11. Freeman House. "Dreaming Indigenous: One Hundred Years from Now in a Northern California Valley." *Restoration and Management Notes,* 10, 1 (Winter 1992): 60.

12. Quoted in Ted Bernard and Jora Young. *The Ecology of Hope: Communities Collaborate for Sustainability.* New Society Publishers, 1997, 131.

13. Interview (7 August 2006).

14. Mattole Restoration Council. "Distribution of Old-Growth Coniferous Forests in the Mattole River Watershed" (map). MRC, 1988.

15. Quoted in Bernard and Young. *The Ecology of Hope.* 131.

16. Mattole Restoration Council. *Elements of Recovery: An Inventory of Upslope Sources of Sedimentation in the Mattole River Watershed.* MRC, 1989, 11.

17. House. "Dreaming Indigenous." 61.

18. Sanford E. Lowry. Personal communication (1 May 1996).

19. House. *Totem Salmon.*

20. House. *Totem Salmon.* 206.

21. Ray Lingel. E-mail communication (7 April 2007).

22. Interview (3 August 2006).

23. David Simpson. Interview (3 August 2006).

24. Interview (3 August 2006).

25. By 2009, both the coho and the chinook salmon had been listed by the US Fish and Wildlife Service as threatened. Kate Cenci. "Ladies and Gentlemen, We are Now in the Red." *Mattole Restoration News,* Winter/Spring 2009, 16.

26. David Simpson. Interview (3 August 2006).

27. Amy Baler. "Mattole Salmon Group News: State of the Salmon." *Mattole Restoration Newsletter,* 25 (Winter/Spring 2006), 16.

28. David Simpson. Interview (3 August 2006).

29. Ray Lingel. "The Mattole Salmon Group Digs In." *Mattole Restoration Newsletter,* 21 (Winter/Spring 2003-04), 16.

30. Lingel. "The Mattole Salmon Group Digs In." 16.

31. Ray Lingel. E-mail communication (7 April 2007).

32. Ray Lingel. "Mattole Salmon Group News: Fish on a Roller Coaster." *Mattole Restoration Newsletter,* 22 (Summer/Fall 2004), 16.

33. Baler. "State of the Salmon." 16; Eric Goldsmith. "Mattole Flow Program Takes Off." *Mattole Restoration Newsletter,* 28 (Summer/Fall 2007): 12; quote from Cenci."Ladies and Gentlemen, We Are Now in the Red." 16.

34. *The Mattole Watershed Plan.* Mattole Restoration Council, Mattole Salmon Group, Sanctuary Forest, Bureau of Land Management, and the State Coastal Conservancy, 2005, 24.

35. House. *Totem Salmon.* 217.

36. Freeman House. "To Learn the Things We Need to Know: Engaging the Particulars of the Planet's Recovery" in Andruss *et al.,* eds. *Home! A Bioregional Reader.* 112.

37. House. "To Learn the Things." 7.

38. Interview (7 August 2006).

39. *Thinking Like a Watershed.* Johan Carlisle, director. The Video Project, 1998 (film). videoproject.org (14 May 2009).

40. mattole.org (18 February 2009).

41. Bernard and Young. *The Ecology of Hope.* 143.

42. Bernard and Young. *The Ecology of Hope.* 143.

43. Interview (3 August 2006).

44. *Mattole Restoration Newsletter,* 10 (Winter 1995-1996): 2.

45. Clair Trower. Interview (3 August 2006); http://rlch.org (14 May 2009). Click on Story Index and then on Mattole Restoration Council.

46. Chris Larson. Interview (12 April 2007).

47. mattole.org (18 April 2007).

48. Chris Larson. Interview (12 April 2007).

49. Interview (4 August 2006).
50. Chris Larson. "From the Executive Director." *Mattole Restoration Newsletter,* 26 (Summer/Fall 2006): 2.
51. Interview (3 August 2006).
52. Chris Larson. Interview (12 April 2007).
53. Larson. "From the Executive Director." 2. For more detail on the MRC, see their excellent website: mattole.org (14 May 2009).
54. Interview (12 April 2007).
55. Interview (7 August 2006).
56. Interview (12 April 2007).
57. David Simpson. Interview (3 August 2006).
58. Buckeye Conservancy. "Forest Stewards Face Painful Choices." *California Forests in Danger.* Buckeye Forest Project, 2006, 2.
59. Interview (5 August 2006).
60. Mattole Restoration Council. *Elements of Recovery.* 11.
61. C. Moss. "Ecological Education: Variety, the Spice of Life." *Mattole Restoration Newsletter,* 23 (Winter/Spring 2005): 8.
62. "Good Roads, Clear Creeks on Wilder Ridge." *Mattole Restoration Newsletter,* 25 (Winter/Spring 2006): 3.
63. Available at mattole.org (14 May 2009).
64. C. Moss. "Ruminations on Despair and Hope." *Mattole Restoration Newsletter,* 25 (Winter/Spring 2006): 12.
65. Tasha McKee. "Whitethorn Community Takes Action to Keep the River Flowing." *Mattole Restoration Newsletter,* 20 (Summer/Fall 2003): 1, 8.
66. Tasha McKee. Interview (4 August 2007); data at sanctuaryforest.org/stewardship. Click on "Options and Obstacles — Low Flows in the Mattole River" (8 June 2009).
67. Goldsmith. "Mattole Flow Program Takes Off." 12.
68. Goldsmith. "Mattole Flow Program Takes Off." 12.
69. Tasha McKee. Interview (4 August 2006).
70. Interview (4 August 2006).
71. Laura Walker, ed. *Mattolia: Visions of our Grandchildren's World by Residents of the Mattole Valley.* Mattole Historical Society, 1993.
72. Ali Freedlund. "The Importance of Community" in *Mattolia.* 201-205; House. "Dreaming Indigenous" in *Mattolia.* 142-147.
73. Interview (2 August 2006).
74. Jim Merkle. *Radical Simplicity: Small Footprints on a Finite Earth.* New Society Publishers, 2003.
75. C. Moss. "Ruminations on Despair and Hope." 12.
76. Freeman House. Interview (6 August 2006); Seth Zuckerman. "Rethinking Restoration While the Climate Changes Around Us." *Mattole Restoration Newsletter,* 28 (Summer/Fall 2007): 1, 7; Freeman House. "Watershed Work in a Changing World: Lessons Not Yet Learned." *Mattole Restoration Newsletter,* 28 (Summer/Fall 2007): 8-9, 13.
77. Ali Freedlund. "Pacific Lumber Co. Watershed Analysis Update." *Mattole Restoration Newsletter,* 26 (Summer/Fall 2006): 6-7.
78. Johanna Rondoni. Interview (8 August 2006).
79. Tracy Katelman. Interview (8 August 2006).
80. Ken Young. Interview (2 August 2006).
81. "Thoughts from a Back Country Pot Grower." Posted 21 May 2001 at mattole.org/html/publications_article_6 8.html (21 October 2007); The phrase "pot smoke mixes with fragrance of greenbacks" derives from this post.
82. Laura Cooskey. Interview (2 August 2006).
83. "Thoughts from a Back Country Pot Grower."
84. Interview (6 August 2006).
85. Chris Larson. Interview (12 April 2007).

Chapter 9. The Eyes of the World Are Upon Us: Plumas County, California

1. Gary Snyder. "Foreword" in William Shipley, ed. and translator. *The Maidu Indian Myths and Stories of Hanc'ibyjim.* Heyday Books, 1991, vii.
2. Interview (17 May 2005).
3. Interview (25 July 2005).
4. Plumas National Forest Supervisor. *Forest Statistics: 1991-1994.* Plumas National Forest, 1994.
5. Christine H. Colburn. "Forest Policy and the Quincy Library Group" in Ronald D. Brunner *et al.,* eds. *Finding Common Ground: Governance and Natural Resources in the American West.* Yale University Press, 2002, 163.
6. Jane Braxton Little. "The Quincy Library Group." *American Forests,* 101 (1995): 22-24, 56.
7. Little. "The Quincy Library Group." 23.

8. Quincy Library Group. "Community Stability Proposal." Unpublished document, 1993.

9. The bill, still in force, is called the Herger-Feinstein Quincy Library Group Forest Recovery Act.

10. This was the conclusion of the editor of *High Country News,* Ed Marston. "The Quincy Library Group: A Divisive Attempt at Peace" in Philip Brick *et al.,* eds. *Across the Great Divide: Explorations in Collaborative Conservation and the American West.* Island Press, 2001, 79-90.

11. Quoted in Ted Bernard and Jora Young. *The Ecology of Hope: Communities Collaborate for Sustainability.* New Society Publishers, 1997, 156, 165.

12. Plumas County's population in 2007 was 20,615. quickfacts.census.gov/qfd/states/06/06063.html (21 March 2009).

13. Aldo Leopold. "Marshland Elegy." *A Sand County Almanac.* Oxford University Press, 1949, 95-96.

14. Sam Wilbanks, Sierraville District Ranger, US National Forest Service. Interview (26 July 2005).

15. Leopold. "Conservation Esthetic." *A Sand County Almanac.* 177.

16. Plumas County's population declined by about 1% between 2000 and 2007, with 18% under age 18 (compared to over 25% for the state) and 19% over 65 (compared to 11% statewide). quickfacts.census.gov/qfd/states/06/06063.html (23 February 2009). The unemployment rate was for February 2009. qlg.org (15 March 2009).

17. quickfacts.census.gov/qfd/states/06/06063.html (23 February 2009).

18. Interview (18 May 2005).

19. plumascounty.org/Outdoor%20Recreation/golf.htm (15 March 2009).

20. Interview (28 July 2005).

21. plumascorporation.org/pdf/2008ecoinds.pdf (19 March 2009).

22. As elsewhere, Plumas real estate values have seriously deflated. Home prices in northern California plunged 46% between February 2008 and February 2009. Associated Press. "California's Median Home Price Down 40%." *Los Angeles Times,* March 20, 2009. latimes.com/business (20 March 2009).

23. John Sheehan. Interview (18 May 2005).

24. Bill Powers. Interview (26 July 2005).

25. Leopold. "The Land Ethic." *A Sand County Almanac.* 214.

26. D.S. Kenney. "Historical and Sociopolitical Context of the Western Watersheds Movement." *Journal of the American Water Resources Association,* 35, 3 (1999): 497.

27. Donna S. Lindquist and Jim Wilcox. "New Concepts for Meadow Restoration in the Northern Sierra Nevada." Unpublished paper, 2000, 2.

28. montereyamendments.water.ca.gov/docs/JointStmt-20030227.pdf (10 June 2007).

29. countyofplumas.com/publicworks/watershed/Watershed%20Forum (19 March 2009).

30. Jim Wilcox. Interview (19 May 2005).

31. J. London and J. Kusel. "Applied Ecosystem Management: Coordinated Resource Management in the Feather River Watershed" in *Sierra Nevada Ecosystem Project: Final Report to Congress.* University of California, Davis, Centers for Water and Wildland Resources, 3 (1996).

32. Feather River Coordinated Resource Management. *Report to Signatory Agencies.* Plumas Corporation, 2005. www.feather-river-crm.org/publications/AnnualRep/2008AnualReport.html (19 March 2009).

33. Interview (27 July 2005).

34. Interview (27 July 2005).

35. Ivan Sohrakoff. *The Benefits of Watershed Management: Water Quality and Supply.* Planning and Conservation League Foundation, 1999, 36-40.

36. Interview (19 May 2005).

37. Jim Wilcox. Interview (19 May 2005).

38. Interview (19 May 2005).

39. Interview (19 May 2005).

40. The QLG has been the subject of a number of in-depth case studies, including: Liz Claibourne-Art Ortenberg Foundation. "The Quincy Library Group." *Workshop on Collaborative Resource Management in the Interior West.* 2001; Pat Terhune and George Terhune. "QLG Case Study." Unpublished paper prepared for the Workshop on Engaging, Empowering, and Negotiating Community, West Virginia University, 1998; Charles Davis and M. Dawn King. "The Quincy Library Group and Collaborative

Planning Within US National Forests." Unpublished paper, 1999, glg.org/pub/Perspectives/daviskingcasestudy.htm (21 July 2005); Colburn. "Forest Policy and the QLG"; Marston. "A Divisive Attempt"; Barb Cistero. *Beyond the Hundredth Meeting: A Field Guide to Collaborative Conservation on the West's Public Lands.* Sonoran Institute, 1999; Mark Sagoff. "The View from Quincy Library: Civic Engagement in Environmental Problem Solving" in R.K Fullinwider, ed. *Civil Society, Democracy, and Civic Renewal.* Rowman and Littlefield, 1999, 151-183; Douglas S. Kenney *et al.*, eds. "Quincy Library Group" in *The New Watershed Source Book.* Natural Resources Law Center, University of Colorado School of Law, 2000, 347-349.

41. Colburn. "Forest Policy and the QLG." 197.

42. The vote in the House of Representatives was 429-1.

43. Jane Braxton Little. "A Year Later, Quincy Forest Plan Leaves Saws Mostly Silent." *Sacramento Bee,* 21 August 2000, A1.

44. Frank Stewart. Quoted in Lynn Walters. "Despite setbacks, QLG comes out swinging." *Feather River Bulletin,* 25 January 2007. pcn.com (21 July 2007).

45. Linda Blum. "Coming Together to Sustain Forests." *California Forests,* 13, 1 (Winter 2009): 12-13.

46. Bernard and Young. *The Ecology of Hope.* 152, 159.

47. Quincy Library Group. *Community Stability Proposal.* 1993, 2.

48. Jane Braxton Little. "Court Fight over Plumas Logging Plan: Lawsuit Challenges US Project to Prevent Fires by Thinning Forests." *Sacramento Bee,* 2 December 2004. sierraconservation.org/plumas%20Harvest%20Lawsuit.htm (20 June 2009).

49. fs.fed.us/r5/hfqlg/news/2008 (19 March 2009).

50. P. and G. Terhune. "QLG Case Study"; Davis and King. "Quincy Library Group and Collaborative Planning"; Claibourne/Ortenberg, "Quincy Library Group"; Colburn. "Forest Policy and the QLG"; Marston. "A Divisive Attempt"; Cistero. *Beyond the Hundredth Meeting;* Sagoff. "The View from Quincy Library."

51. Arlene Hetherington and Lou Piotrowski. "Democracy in the Woods."

Yes! Magazine, Winter 2004/2005, 22-23; Bernard and Young. *The Ecology of Hope.* 148-165.

52. According to the QLG website, in early 2009 21 thinning projects totaling about 100,000 acres were tied up in legal proceedings. These projects might have yielded 320 million board-feet for milling. qlg.org (15 March 2009).

53. "Pre-settlement" is a conventional usage as well as a conceit. It means "pre-industrial" or "pre-European" settlement, i.e., pre-gold rush.

54. Little. "The Quincy Library Group."

55. Quincy Library Group. "The QLG Fuelbreak Strategy." Unpublished paper, 1997. qlg.org (15 July 2005).

56. R.D. Olson. "Appraising a Forest Fuel Treatment: The DFPZ Concept." Unpublished manuscript, Lassen National Forest, 1997.

57. "Large" is defined at 30 inches (diameter at breast height) or bigger. This is a controversial threshold. Forest activists argue it should be 20 inches (Preschutti. Interview [18 May 2005]). In March 2009, Craig Thomas of Sierra Forest Legacy, one of the main environmental litigators, told ClimateWire that negotiations with the Obama administration were closing in on a compromise and that one of main points still in contention is this definition of "large." climatewire.org (9 March 2009).

58. Quincy Library Group. "The QLG Fuelbreak Strategy."

59. Interview (27 July 2005).

60. In summer 2008, the Canyon Complex and Rich Bar fires burned 44,000 acres of Plumas National Forest. According to the QLG website, the Rich Bar fire was significantly slowed by the DFPZs into which it spread. qlg.org (15 March 2009).

61. Little. "Court fight over Plumas logging plan."

62. John Preschutti. Letter to the Editor. June 2004. earthjustice.org/news (22 July 2005).

63. G. Phillip Weatherspoon and Carl N. Skinner. "Landscape-Level Strategies for Forest Fuel Management" in *Sierra Nevada Ecosystem Project: Final Report to Congress.* University of California, Davis, Centers for Water and Wildland Resources, 2 (1996): 1471-1492; Carl N. Skinner and C. Chang. "Fire Regimes,

Past and Present" in *Sierra Nevada Ecosystem Project,* 2: 878-897.

64. Weatherspoon and Skinner. "Landscape-Level Strategies for Forest Fuel Management." 1471.

65. Jane Braxton Little, a journalist who has covered the QLG from its onset, told us this: "Some scientists believe that the QLG approach will actually increase fire danger in the long term by opening the canopy, increasing grasses and flashy fuels, and prescribing no maintenance for the DFPZs and group selection areas. Without maintenance you create a far worse fire risk than now." Interview (27 July 2005).

66. Colburn. "Forest Policy and the QLG." 175.

67. Jane Braxton Little. "Judge clears way for Plumas logging." *Sacramento Bee,* 10 May 2005, B5.

68. fs.fed.us/r5/hfqlg/news/2008/HFQLG%20Fact%20Sheet%202008.pdf (19 March 2009).

69. Mike Yost. Interview (25 July 2005).

70. Interview (18 May 2005).

71. Interview (18 May 2005).

72. Interview (19 May 2005).

73. Rose Comstock. Interview (19 May 2005).

74. Joshua Sebold. "Supervisors Hear QLG Update, Prognosis." *Plumas County News,* 21 January 2009. plumas-news.com (25 March 2009).

75. Interview (25 July 2005).

76. Interview (27 July 2005).

77. Jessica Leber. "Logger Withdraws from California Fire Reduction Effort." *New York Times* online, 5 March 2009. nytimes.com (6 March 2009).

78. Linda Blum. Interview (27 July 2005).

79. Interview (17 May 2005).

80. Kenney. "Historical and Sociopolitical Context." 502.

81. Interview (19 May 2005).

82. Blum."Coming Together to Sustain Forests." 22.

83. westinstenv.org (20 March 2009).

84. Harold Biswell. "Forest Fire in Perspective." *Proceedings of the Seventh Annual Tall Timbers Fire Ecology Conference.* Tall Timbers Research Station, US Forest Service, 1967, 43-63.

85. Quoted by Jane Braxton Little. "Maidu Stewardship Project: Restoring the Understory." *Forest Magazine,* Summer 2002. fseee.org/forestmag/02Summer MaiduLittle.shtml (14 May 2009).

86. Lorena Gorbet. Interview (25 July 2005).

87. B.M. Kilgore. "The Ecological Role of Fire in Sierran Conifer Forests: Its Application to National Park Management." *Quaternary Research,* 3 (1973): 496-513, cited in Weatherspoon and Skinner. "Landscape-Level Strategies." 1472; Skinner and Chang. "Fire Regimes, Past and Present"; C.P. Weatherspoon *et al.* "Fire and Fuels Management in Relation to Owl Habitat in Forests of the Sierra Nevada and Southern California" in *The California Spotted Owl: A Technical Assessment of Its Current Status.* US Forest Service, Pacific Southwest Research Station, 1992, 247-260.

88. Shipley. *The Maidu Indian Myths and Stories of Hanc'ibyjim.*

89. Lorena Gorbet. Interview (25 July 2005).

90. quickfacts.census.gov/qfd/states/06/06063.html (21 March 2009).

91. Farrell Cunningham. "Take Care of the Land and the Land Will Take Care of You: Traditional Ecology in Native California." *News from Native California,* Summer 2005, 24-34.

92. Lorena Gorbet. Interview (25 July 2005).

93. Ross W. Gorte. *Stewardship Contracting for the National Forests.* Congressional Research Service, 2001, 1-6. csa.com/discoveryguides/ern/04jan/RS20985.php (9 June 2009).

94. Jane Braxton. Little. "Saving Maidu culture, one seedling at a time." *High Country News,* 4 April 2005. hcn.org/issues/295/15407 (9 June 2009).

95. Jane Braxton Little. "Maidu Stewardship Project." Red Lodge Clearing House. http://rlch.org/content/view/221/36 (18 May 2009). The other organizations are: the United Maidu Nation, Maidu Elders Council, Roundhouse Council, Indian American Legion, Forest Community Research, Greenville Rancheria, Plumas County Indians, Inc., and Indian Head Logging, Inc.

96. Cunningham. "Take Care of the Land." 25-26.

97. Little. "Maidu Stewardship Project."

98. Interview (25 July 2005).

99. By contrast, Lorena Gorbet said, "When the Forest Service burns, it burns everything. It's a hot fire. You look at the hills where they've done prescribed burns and you see brown trees." Interview (25 July 2005).

100. Little. "Maidu Stewardship Project."
101. Lorena Gorbet. Interview (25 July 2005).
102. Interview (27 July 2005). In 2005, a tribal relations officer was posted to Plumas National Forest. His job is "to help us Europeans understand traditional ways."
103. Ferrell Cunningham and Katie Bagby. "The Maidu Stewardship Project: Blending of two knowledge systems in forest management." Unpublished paper, Pacific West Community Forestry Center, 2004, 5.
104. Lorena Gorbet. rlch.org (20 March 2009).
105. Cunningham. "Take Care of the Land." 24.
106. Lorena Gorbet. rlch.org (20 March 2009).
107. University of California Forestry Extension agent Mike DeLasaux thinks this is a training and capacity-building role the university might consider embracing. Interview (17 May 2005).
108. H.K. Steen. *The US Forest Service: A History.* University of Washington, 2005.

Chapter 10. Blowback on Sustainability?: Chattanooga, Tennessee

1. Paul Croce and Jora Young conducted field work in Chattanooga in July 2006. I have greatly benefited from their interview transcripts, other documents, and commentary. In August 2008, Erin Sykes conducted phone and e-mail interviews. I returned to Chattanooga to wrap up field work in September 2008.
2. Bruz Clark. Interview (26 July 2006).
3. Melissa Turner. E-mail communication (20 August 2008).
4. Ron Littlefield. Interview (24 July 2006).
5. "Chattanooga: Population Profile." city-data.com/us-cities/The-South/Chattanooga-Population-Profile.html (29 September 2008). Based on Census of 2000.
6. James Franklin. Interview (25 September 2008).
7. Kim Cross. "Splashy River Town." *Southern Living Magazine,* 42, 7 (July 2007): 25.
8. Interview (14 December 1994).
9. See also Mary E. Rogge *et al.* "Leveraging Environmental, Social, and Economic Justice at Chattanooga Creek: A Case Study." *Journal of Community Practice,* 13, 3 (2005): 33-53.
10. Interview (28 July 2006).
11. Interview (25 August 2008).
12. Interview (27 July 2006).
13. Missy Crutchfield. Interview (24 September 2008).
14. Ann Coulter. "Recycling a Downtown: A Ten-Year Retrospective on Chattanooga's Rebirth." *EnviroLink Handbook Southeast,* 2002. environlinkhandbook.com (22 August 2008).
15. William F. Hull. *Chattanooga: Then and Now.* Arcadia Publishing, 2007, ix.
16. "TVA plans to repurchase its downtown buildings." *Chattanooga Times Free Press,* 10 February 2008. timesfreepress.com/news/2008/feb/10/tva-repurchase-downtown-buildings-chattanooga (26 September 2008).
17. Rogge *et al.* "Leveraging Environmental, Social, and Economic Justice."
18. David Crockett. Interview (14 December 1994); *A History of Air Pollution Control in Chattanooga and Hamilton County.* Air Pollution Control Bureau, 1999.
19. James Gustave Speth. *The Bridge at the End of the World: Capitalism, the Environment, and Crossing from Crisis to Sustainability.*Yale University Press, 2008, 202-203.
20. James Catanzaro. Interview (25 August 2008).
21. Interviews with John Tucker and Missy Crutchfield (23 September and 24 September 2008).
22. Interview (15 December 1994).
23. Hugh Bartling and Don Ferris. "Chattanooga: Is this Sustainable?" 1997. uky.edu/classes/PS/776/Projects/chattanooga/chattnga.html (21 August 2008); Cheryl Horn. "Sustainable Development or Just Plain Development? An Analysis of Sustainability Indicators for Chattanooga Tennessee." Master of Science in Environmental Science thesis, University of Tennessee-Chattanooga, 2006.
24. Timothy Beatley. *Native to Nowhere: Sustaining Home and Community in a Global Age.* Island Press, 2004.
25. Beatley. *Native to Nowhere.* 5.
26. Much of this information came from an interview with Jed Marston, vice president of marketing and communications for the Chattanooga Area Chamber of Commerce on 27 June 2006, from its website: chatanoogachamber.com (9 June 2009), and from Jed Marston, ed.

"The Scenic City Returns to the River." *Urban Land*, 63, 6 (2004): 38-41.

27. tnaqua.com (26 September 2008).

28. chattanooga.gov/30_108.htm (29 September 2008).

29. carta-bus.org/routes/elec_shuttle.asp (29 September 2008).

30. cdmfun.org/page/about (30 August 2008).

31. greenspaceschattanooga.com (30 August 2008).

32. environlinkhandbook.com (22 August 2008).

33. Larry Cook, executive director of North Chickamauga Creek Conservancy. E-mail communication (6 August 2008).

34. Rogge *et al.* "Leveraging Environmental, Social, and Economic Justice." 42-43.

35. "Extra Cleanup Suggested for Chattanooga Creek." *Chattanooga Times Free Press*, 5 May 2008. http://timesfreepress.com/news/2008/may/05/extra-cleanup-suggested- chattanooga-creek/?mobile (9 June 2009).

36. Rogge *et al.* "Leveraging Environmental, Social, and Economic Justice"; John Tucker. Interview (23 September 2008).

37. Interview (26 July 2006).

38. Rogge *et al.* "Leveraging Environmental, Social, and Economic Justice." 50.

39. Interview (23 September 2008).

40. Beverly A. Carroll. "Three County High Schools Awarded $6 Million Magnet Schools Grant." *Chattanooga Times Free Press*, 5 August 2004, B1; Hamilton county has received $20 million in federal magnet school grants since 1998.

41. buildingchoice.org (5 August 2008).

42. hcde.org/media/pdf/items/HCDE_Student_Achievement_initiatives.pdf (5 August 2008).

43. Jason M. Reynolds. "CNE Seeks Director to Help Refocus Mission." *Chattanooga Times Free Press*, 16 May 2008, 10.

44. Interview (24 July 2006).

45. Vanice Hughley. Interview (24 July 2006).

46. Interview (26 July 2006).

47. Rogge *et al.* "Leveraging Environmental, Social, and Economic Justice." 44.

48. Dave Flessner. "Chattanooga: Poverty concentrations St. Elmo, Downtown, East Lake draw poorer workers." *Chattanooga Times Free Press*, 13 August 2008. timesfreep-ress.com/news/2008/aug/13/chattanoog

a-poverty-concentrations-st-elmo-downtow/ (29 September 2008).

49. Dave Flessner. "Poverty Grows as Does Economy." *Chattanooga Times Free Press*, 10 January 2008. timesfreep-ress.com/news/jan/10 (15 August 2008).

50. Horn. "Sustainable Development or Just Plain Development?" 144.

51. James Catanzaro. Interview (27 August 2008).

52. Pam Sohn. "Green Report Calls for Transit Options." *Chattanooga Times Free Press*, 11 July 2008, B1.

53. Richard Beeland. E-mail communica-tion (30 September 2008). By 2008, the number of participating cities had reached 800.

54. Melissa Turner. E-mail communication (19 August 2008).

55. John Tucker. E-mail communication (8 August 2008).

56. Sohn, "Green Report," B1.

57. James Frierson. Interview (26 July 2006).

58. Horn. "Sustainable Development or Just Plain Development?"; Interview (24 July 2006).

59. Interviews with Sandra Jones, Vanice Hughey, Milton Jackson, and James Mooreland (July 2006) and Rita Brown, James Franklin, and M.T. Haynes (September 2008).

60. Interview (27 July 2006).

61. Paraphrase of comments by Jones. See also Hugh Bartling and Don Ferris. "Chattanooga: Is this Sustainable?"

62. M. T. Haynes. Interview (23 September 2008).

63. Interview (24 July 2006).

64. Interview (24 September 2008).

65. Marston. "The Scenic City Returns to the River."

66. James Catanzaro. Interview (25 August 2008).

67. Missy Crutchfield and Melissa Turner. Interview (24 September 2008). Words are Melissa Turner's.

68. Melissa Turner. E-mail communication (19 August 2008) and Interview (24 September 2008).

Chapter 11. An Improbable Wilderness: Sustaining People and Nature in Chicago

1. Cindy Goulder. "Volunteer Revegetation Saturday." *Restoration and Management Notes*, 14, 1 (1996): 62.

2. The full story may be found in William K. Stevens. *Miracle Under the Oaks: The*

Revival of Nature in America. Pocket Books, 1995.

3. Russ Van Herrick. Quoted in Stevens. *Miracle Under the Oaks.* 292.

4. Ted Bernard and Jora Young. *The Ecology of Hope: Communities Collaborate for Sustainability.* New Society Publishers, 1997, 177.

5. Stevens. *Miracle Under the Oaks.* 280.

6. Stevens. *Miracle Under the Oaks.* 281.

7. Stevens. *Miracle Under the Oaks.* 296.

8. Peter Friederici. "Engagement and Hope: An Interview with William R. Jordan III." *Chicago Wilderness,* Spring 2004. chicagowildernessmag.org/issues/spring 2004/jordan.html (16 Sept. 2008).

9. Ray Wiggers. "North Branch Prairies: Along the North Branch of the Chicago River, Illinois." *Chicago Wilderness,* Summer 2000, 13.

10. Paul H. Gobster. "Introduction: Human Actions, Interactions, and Reactions" in Paul H. Gobster and R. Bruce Hull, eds. *Restoring Nature: Perspectives from the Social Sciences and Humanities.* Island Press, 1997, 1.

11. Carl Sandburg. "Chicago." *The Complete Poems of Carl Sandburg.* Harcourt, 2003, 213.

12. J. Robert Constantine, ed. *Letters of Eugene V. Debs, Volume 1, 1874-1912.* University of Illinois Press, 1990, 145.

13. Margarita Alaria. "Urban and Ecological Planning in Chicago: Science, Policy and Dissent." *Journal of Environmental Planning and Management,* 42, 4 (2000): 489-504.

14. The chronology of the controversy and the quote are from Gobster. "Introduction." 1-19.

15. Chris Larson. "Jane and John Balaban: A Natural Partnership." *Chicago Wilderness,* Spring 1998. chicagowildernessmag.org/issues/spring 1998/toc.html (3 September 2008).

16. Jane and John Balaban. E-mail communication (28 October 2008).

17. Alaria. "Urban and Ecological Planning in Chicago." 500.

18. Paul H. Gobster. "The Chicago Wilderness and its Critics. III. The Other Side: A Survey of the Arguments." *Restoration and Management Notes,* 15,1 (Summer 1997): 32-37.

19. Gobster. "Introduction." 1.

20. Reid M. Helford. "Constructing Nature as Constructing Science: Expertise, Activist Science, and Public Conflict in the Chicago Wilderness" in Gobster and Hull. *Restoring Nature.* 119-131.

21. Alaria. "Urban and Ecological Planning in Chicago."

22. See especially Gobster and Hull. *Restoring Nature.* and William R. Jordan III. *The Sunflower Forest: Ecological Restoration and the New Communion with Nature.* University of California Press, 2003.

23. William R. Jordan III. "Restoration: Shaping the Land, Transforming the Human Spirit" in Richard Nilsen, ed. *Helping Nature Heal: An Introduction to Environmental Restoration.* Ten Speed Press, 1991, 5.

24. Suzanne Bott *et al.* "Place and the Promise of Conservation Psychology." *Research in Human Ecology,* 10, 2 (2003): 100-112.

25. Rutherford Platt. "Regreening the Metropolis: Pathways to More Ecological Cities." *Annals, New York Academy of Sciences,* 1023 (2004), 60.

26. John Balaban. E-mail communication (30 July 2008).

27. Steve Packard. E-mail communication (3 August 2008).

28. E-mail communication (30 July 2008).

29. E-mail communication (28 October 2008).

30. E-mail communication (30 July 2008).

31. Steve Packard. E-mail communication (3 August 2008).

32. Steve Packard. E-mail communication (3 August 2008).

33. Platt. "Regreening the Metropolis." 56.

34. Jordan. *The Sunflower Forest.* 204.

35. Laurel Ross. "The Chicago Wilderness: A Coalition for Urban Conservation." *Restoration and Management Notes,* 15, 1 (1997): 17-24.

36. Lucy Hutcherson. "Chicago Wilderness: A Collaborative Model for Urban Conservaton" in Ted Trzyna, ed. *The Urban Imperative.* California Institute of Public Affairs and International Union for the Conservation of Nature and Natural Resources, 2005, 135-139.

37. Laurel Ross. E-mail communication (28 October 2008).

38. Dennis Dreher *et al. Chicago Wilderness Green Infrastructure Vision Final Report.* Chicago Wilderness Consortium, 2004, 9.

39. E-mail communication (30 August 2008).

40. Peggy Stewart. "Natural Partners: Chicago Wilderness and Asset-Based Community Development." *Chicago Wilderness Journal*, 1 (2003): 6-11.

41. Richard Louv. *Last Child in the Woods: Saving Our Children from Nature Deficit Disorder*. Algonquin Books, 2006.

42. Hutcherson. "Chicago Wilderness."

43. Rutherford Platt. "Chicago Wilderness: Flagship of the Urban Biodiversity Movement." *Chicago Wilderness Journal*, 4, 3 (2006): 2-10.

44. Chicago Wilderness Consortium. *The State of Our Chicago Wilderness: A Report Card on the Ecological Health of the Region*. CWC, 2006, 10.

45. Rebecca Coleen Retzlaff. "Planning for Broad-based Environmental Protection: A Look Back at the Chicago Wilderness Biodiversity Recovery Plan." *Urban Ecosystems*, 11 (2008): 45-63. Progress Report quote also appears in this article on page 59.

46. Dreher *et al*. *Chicago Wilderness Green Infrastructure Vision Final Report*.; Dennis Dreher. E-mail communication (28 October 2008) via Jane and John Balaban.

47. Aldo Leopold. *A Sand County Almanac*. Oxford, 1949.

48. Curt D. Meine. "The Oldest Task in Human History" in Richard L. Knight and Sarah Bates, eds. *A New Century for Natural Resources Management*. Island Press, 1995, 7-35; Leopold quote in Susan Flader and J.B. Callicott, eds. *The River of the Mother of God and Other Essays by Aldo Leopold*. University of Wisconsin Press, 1991, 254.

49. Jordan. *The Sunflower Forest*. 197 (emphasis mine).

50. Jordan. *The Sunflower Forest*. 200.

51. Jordan. *The Sunflower Forest*. 202.

52. Jordan. *The Sunflower Forest*. 201.

53. Jordan. *The Sunflower Forest*. 202.

Chapter 12. Retracing the Path

1. Rene Magritte (1898-1967), Belgian artist. http://thinkexist.com/quotes/rene_ magritte (10 January 2009).

2. William Wordsworth. "Intimations of Immortality from Recollections of Early Childhood" in Arthur Quiller-Couch, ed. *The Oxford Book of English Verse*. Oxford University Press, 1919, 536.

3. Ted Bernard and Jora Young. *The Ecology of Hope: Communities Collaborate for Sustainability*. New Society Publishers, 1997, 194.

4. Thomas Berry. *The Dream of the Earth*. Sierra Club, 1988, 123.

5. John Hobbins. "Setting the Bar High in the Study of Ancient Hebrew." *Ancient Hebrew Poetry*. http://ancienthebrewpoetry.typepad.com (4 March 2009).

6. Attributed to David Sarnoff, founder of NBC. Eugene Lyons. *David Sarnoff: A Biography*. Harper and Row, 1966, 28.

7. Howard Gardner. *Changing Minds: The Art and Science of Changing Our Own and Other People's Minds*. Harvard Business School Press, 2006, 69.

8. Richard Slaughter. *The Foresight Principle: Cultural Recovery in the 21st Century*. Praeger, 1995, 53.

9. Hazel Henderson. "A Guide to Riding the Tiger of Change: The Three Zones of Transition" in William Irwin Thompson, ed. *Gaia, A Way of Knowing: Political Implications of the New Biology*. Lindisfarne Press, 1987, 156-157.

10. Cassandra Moseley. "The Applegate Partnership: Innovation in Crisis" in Philip Brick *et al.*, eds. *Across the Great Divide: Explorations in Collaborative Conservation and the American West*. Island Press, 2001, 111.

11. Steve Selin and Deborah Chavez. "Developing a Collaborative Model for Environmental Planning and Management." *Environmental Management*, 19, 2 (1995): 189-195.

12. Poverty traps are impoverished social and ecological situations from which there is no easy exit. C.S. Holling *et al.* "Sustainability and Panarchies" in L.H. Gunderson and C.S. Holling, eds. *Panarchy: Understanding Transformations in Human and Natural Systems*. Island Press, 2002, 95-96.

13. Interview (6 August 2006).

14. Interview (3 August 2006).

15. Interview (10 July 2007).

16. William R. Jordan III. *The Sunflower Forest: Ecological Restoration and the New Communion with Nature*. University of California Press, 2003, 6.

17. Both quoted in Bernard and Young. *The Ecology of Hope*. 197.

18. Julia M. Wondolleck and Steven L. Yaffee. *Making Collaboration Work: Lessons from Innovation in Natural Resource Management*. Island Press, 2000, 169.

19. Daniel Kemmis. *This Sovereign Land: A New Vision for Governing the West.* Island Press, 2001, 153ff. See also David Chrislip. *The Collaborative Leadership Handbook: A Guide for Citizens and Leaders.* Jossey-Bass, 2002, 7-19.

20. Nathan Sayre. *Working Wilderness: The Malpai Borderlands Group and the Future of the Western Range.* Rio Nuevo, 2005, 47.

21. Wondolleck and Yaffee. *Making Collaboration Work.* 176-180.

22. Wondolleck and Yaffee. *Making Collaboration Work.* 252; Chrislip. *Collaborative Leadership.* 32-33.

23. Interview (19 May 2005).

24. Interview (12 May 2005).

25. Wondolleck and Yaffee. *Making Collaboration Work.* 252; Donald Snow. "What Are We Talking About?" *Chronicle of Community,* 3, 3 (1999): 33-37; P.W. Mattessich and B.R. Monsey. *Collaboration: What Makes It Work.* Amherst H. Wilder Foundation, 1992; Chrislip. *Collaborative Leadership.* 47.

26. littlecitiesofblackdiamonds.org (17 January 2009).

27. Michelle Uting. "Chicago Wilderness Welcomes One City and Two Faith-Based Groups." *Chicago Wilderness Magazine,* Winter 2006. chicagowildernessmag.org/ issues/winter2006 (17 January 2009).

28. glitc.org/events/pow-wows (17 January 2009).

29. Interview (5 August 2007).

30. Interview (13 July 2007).

31. Interview (29 August 2008).

32. Bernard and Young. *The Ecology of Hope.* 208.

33. For information on dozens of others, see rlch.org.

34. Interview (30 June 2005).

35. Michelle Decker. Quoted in Clay Flaherty. "Vista Program to End in November 2009." *Rural Report,* 20, 1 (2008): 7.

36. Interview (18 May 2005).

37. David Suzuki. *The Sacred Balance: Rediscovering Our Place in Nature.* Greystone Books, 1999, 207-208.

38. Fikret Birkes and Carl Folke, eds. *Linking Social and Ecological Systems: Management Practices and Social Mechanisms for Building Resilience.* Cambridge University Press, 1998;

Edward Goldsmith. "There is no fundamental barrier separating man and other living things" in *The Way: An Ecological World-View.* Shambhala, 1993, 193-196.

39. Brian Walker and David Salt. *Resilience Thinking: Sustaining Ecosystems and People in a Changing World.* Island Press, 2006, 9.

40. Nathan Sayre. *Working Wilderness.* 91.

41. "On Maturing." *Mattole Restoration Newsletter,* 29 (Winter/Spring 2008): 2.

42. Quoted in Sayre. *Working Wilderness.* 103.

43. Interview (13 July 2007).

44. Jonathan S. Adams. *The Future of the Wild.* Beacon Press, 2006, 229-233; Jordan. *The Sunflower Forest.*

45. Interview (13 May 2005).

46. Interview (19 May 2005).

47. Interview (27 July 2005).

48. Interview (17 May 2005).

49. Joshua Sebold. "Supervisors hear QLG update, prognosis." *Plumas County News,* 21 January 2009. plumas-news.com/news_story.edi?sid=7145 (25 March 2009); Lyn Walters. "Critics, Quincy Library Group, Meet with Senator." *Plumas County News,* 5 September 2007. plumas-news.com/news_story.edi?sid=5404 (23 January 2008); Jessica Leber. "Logger Withdraws from California Fire Reduction Effort." *New York Times,* 5 March 2009. nytimes.com/cwire (9 March 2009).

50. Bernard and Young. *The Ecology of Hope.* 69.

Chapter 13. The Sacred Hoop and the Genius That Invents the Future

1. Based on words of George Fox. "Sing and Rejoice," music and lyrics by William Guthe in Peter Blood and Annie Patterson, eds. *Rise Up Singing.* Sing Out! Publications, 1992, 47.

2. James Gustave Speth. *The Bridge at the Edge of the World: Capitalism, the Environment, and Crossing from Crisis to Sustainability.* Yale University Press, 2008, 204.

3. Black Elk. Quoted in John Neihadt. *Black Elk Speaks.* University of Nebraska Press, 1932, 194.

4. Winona LaDuke. *All Our Relations: Native Struggles for Land and Life.* South End Press, 1999, 198.

5. "The Albuquerque Declaration."

Submitted to the Fourth Conference of the Parties to the United Nations Framework Convention on Climate Change, Buenos Aires, Argentina, November 1998. nativevil-lage.org/Inspiration-/Albuquerque%20 Convention.htm (7 January 2009).

6. Interview (25 July 2005).
7. "Culturally Important Properties." *Feather River Land Trust Newsletter,* 2004, 3-4.
8. Marshall Pecore. Interview (10 July 2005).
9. Lisa Waukau. Interview (11 July 2007).
10. Verna Fowler. Interview (10 July 2007).
11. Larry Waukau. Interview (12 July 1994).
12. Drum Hadley. Quoted in Alan Weisman. *La Frontera: The United States Border with Mexico.* University of Arizona Press, 1986, 121.
13. Fikret Berkes *et al.* "Rediscovery of Traditional Ecological Knowledge as Adaptive Management." *Ecological Applications,* 10, 5 (2000): 1251-1262.
14. Nancy C. Maynard, ed. *Native Peoples — Native Homelands Climate Change Workshop Final Report.* NASA Goddard Space Flight Center, 2002.
15. Robert Gough and Patrick Spears. "Foreword" in Maynard. *Native Peoples — Native Homelands.* ii.
16. LaDuke. *All Our Relations.* 200.
17. Aldo Leopold. "The Role of Wildlife in a Liberal Education" in Susan L. Flader and J. Baird Callicott, eds. *The River of the Mother of God and Other Essays by Aldo Leopold.* University of Wisconsin Press, 1991, 303.
18. Speth summarizes this literature in an excellent chapter on "new conscious-ness" in *Bridge at the Edge of the World.* 199-216.
19. Fikret Berkes and Carl Folke. "Back to the Future: Ecosystem Dynamics and Local Knowledge" in Lance H. Gunderson and C.S. Holling, eds. *Panarchy: Understanding Transformations in Human and Natural Systems.* Island Press, 2002, 121-146.
20. Peter M. Senge *et al. Presence: An Exploration of Profound Change in People, Organizations, and Society.* Doubleday, 2005.

21. Lisel Mueller. "Hope." *Alive Together: New and Selected Poems.* Louisiana State University Press, 1996, 103.
22. Wendell Berry. *The Gift of Good Land.* North Point Press, 1981, 270.
23. Barack Obama. "Yes, We Can." Campaign speech, Nashua, NH, 8 January 2008. youtube.com/watch?v=Fe751kMBwms (11 March 2009).
24. Barbara Kingsolver. "How to be Hopeful." Commencement address, Duke University, 11 May 2008. duke.edu/officeofnewsandcommunicatio n (23 November 2008).
25. Mueller. "Hope."
26. Dickinson. "Hope." *Collected Poems.* Dover Thrift, 1990, 56.
27. Obama. "Yes, We Can."
28. Kingsolver. "How to be Hopeful."
29. Kingsolver. "Hope: An Owner's Manual." Poem in "How to be Hopeful."
30. Terkel's last book, written at age 92, was an oral history of hope: *Hope Dies Last: Keeping the Faith in Troubled Times.* New Press, 2004.
31. Tom Engelhardt. "Hard Times Without Studs." *The Nation,* 29 December 2008, 9.
32. Paul Loeb, ed. *The Impossible Will Take A Little While: A Citizen's Guide to Hope in a Time of Fear.* Basic Books, 2004.
33. Viktor E. Frankl. *Man's Search for Meaning: An Introduction to Logotherapy.* Simon and Schuster, 1984, 139-154.
34. Interview (4 August 2007).
35. Interview (10 July 2007).
36. Interview (6 August 2006).
37. E-mail communication (30 July 2008).
38. Interview (27 August 2008).
39. David W. Orr. "Hope in Hard Times." *Conservation Biology,* 18, 2 (2004): 297.
40. Mueller. "Hope."
41. Wendell Berry. *In the Presence of Fear.* Orion Society, 2001.
42. Speth. *The Bridge at the Edge of the World.* 237.
43. Charles Dickens. *A Tale of Two Cities.* Signet Classics, 2007, 1. See epigraph to Chapter One for entire quote.

Index

Page numbers in **bold** indicate information found in tables.

About the Author

T ED BERNARD is a professor of geography and environmental studies at Ohio University. He has studied community-based conservation in Africa and North America for more than three decades. With Jora Young, he co-authored *The Ecology of Hope*. He lives ten miles upstream from the Ohio River in the Shade River watershed. On a ridge-top farm he and his wife, Donna Lofgren, their two Maine Coon cats, and an array of wild critters participate daily in the rapid rebirth of an oak-hickory forest ecosystem that only two generations ago was barren pasturelands and corn fields.